THE LIBRARY OF HOLOCAUST TESTIMONIES

A Little House on Mount Carmel

A Little House on Mount Carmel

ALEXANDRE BLUMSTEIN

VALLENTINE MITCHELL
LONDON • PORTLAND, OR

First Published in 2002 in Great Britain by
VALLENTINE MITCHELL
Crown House, 47 Chase Side
Southgate, London N14 5BP

and in the United States of America by
VALLENTINE MITCHELL
c/o ISBS, 5804 N. E. Hassalo Street
Portland, Oregon 97213-3644

Website: http://www.vmbooks.com

British Library Cataloguing in Publication Data
Blumstein, Alexandre
    A Little House on Mount Carmel. – (The library of Holocaust
    testimonies)
    1. Blumstein, Alexandre – Childhood and Youth. 2. Jews – Poland
    3. Holocaust, Jewish (1939–1945) – Personal narratives, Polish
    I . Title
    940.5'318'09438'092

ISBN 0-8530-34230
ISSN 1363-3759

Library of Congress Cataloging-in-Publication Data

A catalog record for this book is available from the Library of
Congress

Typeset in 11/13pt Palatino by FiSH Books, London WC1.
Printed in Great Britain by MPG Books Ltd, Victoria Square,
Bodmin, Cornwall.

To the memory of my parents, Chaim Mordechai Blumstein and Estera Bouchin-Blumstein. To the memory of my brother Nataniel.

'I am a Jew who does not go to temple on Saturdays, who does not know Hebrew, who does not observe any religious practice, but I call myself a Jew because the monotheistic conscience is indestructible in me, because every, even disguised, form of idolatry repels me, because I regard with Jewish severity the duties of our life on earth and with Jewish serenity the mystery beyond the tomb – because I love all men as in Israel it was commanded and have therefore that social conception which descends from our best tradition.'

Nello Roselli,
Zionist, Italian Republican and Anti-fascist,
Livorno, November 1924

Contents

List of Illustrations

The Library of Holocaust Testimonies

It is greatly to the credit of Frank Cass that this series of survivors' testimonies is being published in Britain. The need for such a series has long been apparent here, where many survivors made their homes.

Since the end of the war in 1945 the terrible events of the Nazi destruction of European Jewry have cast a pall over our time. Six million Jews were murdered within a short period; the few survivors have had to carry in their memories whatever remains of the knowledge of Jewish life in more than a dozen countries, in several thousand towns, in tens of thousands of villages and in innumerable families. The precious gift of recollection has been the sole memorial for millions of people whose lives were suddenly and brutally cut off.

For many years, individual survivors have published their testimonies. But many more have been reluctant to do so, often because they could not believe that they would find a publisher for their efforts.

In my own work over the past two decades, I have been approached by many survivors who had set down their memories in writing, but who did not know how to have them published. I realized what a considerable emotional strain the writing down of such hellish memories had been. I also realized, as I read many dozens of such accounts, how important each account was, in its own way, in recounting aspects of the story that had not been told before, and adding to our understanding of the wide range of human suffering, struggle and aspiration.

With so many people and so many places involved, including many hundreds of camps, it was inevitable that the historians and students of the Holocaust should find it difficult at times to grasp the scale and range of the events.

The publication of memoirs is therefore an indispensable part of the extension of knowledge, and of public awareness of the crimes that had been committed against a whole people.

Sir Martin Gilbert
Merton College, Oxford

Preface

> And I alone am left to tell the tale.
> Job, 1, 19

Packed with detail, this moving and deeply felt memoir describes the survival of a single Polish-Jewish family, the Blumsteins. It should be stressed how unusual a phenomenon this was. The overwhelming majority of Polish Jewry (which numbered nearly three and a half million people on the eve of the Second World War) perished in the Holocaust. According to the records of the Central Committee of Jews in Poland (*Centralny Komitet Żydów w Polsce* – *CKŻP*) the principal Jewish body in post-war Poland, 74,000 people had registered by June 1945. Of these, 5,500 had returned from concentration camps in Germany, 13,000 had served in the pro-Communist Polish Army, established in the USSR after the withdrawal of the Anders Army, about 30,000 had made their way back from the Soviet Union and 10,000 had been freed from concentration camps in Poland. This suggests that 20,000 had survived on the 'Aryan' side. This figure is certainly too low, since it does not include those who did not register with the *CKŻP*, whether because they wished merely to stay away from Jewish organizations or because they were assimilated or baptized. But even if we double the figure, we still do not have more than 40,000 Jews who survived in hiding. In the next two years 137,000 Jews returned from the USSR, mostly people who had been deported or evacuated to the interior of the country.[1] In 1956, several more thousand returned to Poland, while between 100,000 and 150,000 remained in the Soviet Union. Thus, more than 90 per cent of Polish Jewry perished

---

[1] Józef Adelson, 'W Polsce zwanej Ludowà', in Jerzy Tomaszewski (ed.), *Najnowsze Dzieje Żydów w Polsce*, Warsaw, 1995, 388–9.

in the Holocaust. Only in the Baltic states was the percentage of Jewish casualties higher.

Alex Blumstein's account of the survival of his parents, his elder brother Nataniel (Tolya) and himself is, above all, as he points out 'a description of my life...the life of a Jewish boy caught at the crossroads of the ethnic hatreds and political turbulence of Eastern Poland in the years 1939–1947'. This is based partly on his wartime diaries, lost when he moved from Poland to France in 1947, which provide a vivid picture of his life and that of his family. The central figure is that of his father, Chaim Mordechai. Born in Plock in 1886, he was expelled from his Polish secondary school during the stormy years of the revolution of 1905–7 for Polish patriotic agitation. Barred from access to the universities in the Tsarist Empire, he qualified in Germany as a doctor and served as a medical officer in the Tsarist Army during the First World War. He succeeded in escaping from a German prisoner-of-war camp and on his return to active service was awarded a high Russian decoration and honorary nobility. It was during his military service that he met his wife Estera (Tatyana) in Ekaterinoslav (now Dnepropetrovsk), who came from a Russified Jewish family settled in Poltava. A strong Russian patriot, she was also a strong opponent of Bolshevism and felt unwilling to remain in the new Soviet Russia. The couple therefore settled in Grodno, where Chaim Mordechai established a successful medical and surgical practice, and also set up a sanatorium in the spa town of Druskieniki. The family was prosperous and lived well, with servants and trips abroad. Young Alexandre, who was born in 1930, had a German governess and attended an elite Polish school. However, Chaim's Polish patriotism was severely undermined by the growing anti-Semitism, particularly after 1935, and he became a Zionist, hoping to settle in a 'little house on Mount Carmel'. It was his foresight and determination that, above all, determined the family's survival and his death of a heart attack, which by a tragic coincidence occurred on 4 July 1946, the day of the Kielce pogrom, the worst outbreak of anti-Jewish violence in post-war Poland, finally precipitated his son's decision to leave Poland. His father's funeral is the occasion for one of the most moving passages in the autobiography, which sums up the tragedy of a generation of acculturated Polish Jews:

> This was the end of your journey, father. You were spared nothing. You fought for a just Poland against the Tsar, you were arrested and banned from schools in Russia only to see an anti-Semitic Poland emerge and persecute your people. You went to study in Germany, where a German student, an anti-Semite, insulted you in Leipzig. You challenged him to a duel and you chose pistols: but the German did not show up for the duel, he lost his nerve. As a young lieutenant, surgeon of the Russian Imperial Army in the First World War you saw the misery of defeat and slaughter at the killing fields of Tannenberg. You spent two years in a German prisoner-of-war camp and escaping to England you made your way back to St Petersburg in 1916. You were decorated with one of the highest honours that could be bestowed on a Jew in Tsarist Russia: personal knighthood. You got the distinction only to see the empire disintegrate in 1917 while you were fighting the Turks at Erzerum in Armenia. There you were overcome by typhoid fever and almost died. You saw the revolution, misery and pogroms in Ukraine and you found your own father assaulted by the Ukrainian hoodlums of Petlyura. You were spared nothing.
>
> You went back to the country you were convinced was yours by right of birth and heart only to realize the depth of hatred and intolerance pervading the new Poland. If you were not wanted, you would not stay. You became a Zionist and a partisan of armed struggle with the enemies of our people. You dreamt of the little house on Mount Carmel. You were trapped by the Germans in the Grodno ghetto and displayed inordinate courage, standing tall even at the Gestapo. '*Der Jude war frech!*' ['The Jew was arrogant!']: this phrase by the SD killer Wiese gave one measure of the man you were. You led us out of the ghetto and you saved us, but at what cost to yourself when you were forced to abandon your old and helpless mother. You were spared nothing. You were ready to cut your veins when your friend and saviour Dr Docha insisted on us converting to Catholicism. You were spared nothing. In the aftermath of the Holocaust

it was not a 'Medal of the Ghetto' that awaited you, but new
humiliations of a menial job in a small dispensary, because
you refused to 'Catholicize' your name to Matevsz
Kwiatkowski. You always proudly wore the name of Chaim
Mordechai Blumstein and never would dream of changing
it for expediency or profit. You were spared nothing. When
illness struck, you knew exactly that the end was near, you
never lost your composure and never let us know what you
knew so well. Your thoughts were for your family; your
wife, whom you knew could not remain alone – and your
sons whom you wanted more than anything to set on their
way to life. You looked beyond the surface into the future.
You were spared nothing. (pp. 405–6).

There are well-drawn portraits of other members of the
family, his mother, an accomplished cook and manager, who
was the life and soul of the hotel the family ran in Druskieniki
where she would entertain the guests with Russian, Polish
and Yiddish songs; his senile grandmother, traumatized by
the battles of the First World War around her native
Ciechanów and responding to every situation with the ritual
formula, 'Straszne to słowo wojna' ['The word "war" is a
terrible thing']; and his dashing elder brother, nine years
older than Alexandre, who ultimately failed to fulfil his
father's hope he would follow him into the medical
profession. There are also his father's sister and her vigorous
and enterprising husband, who came from a shtetl
background and, although lacking in formal education, was
one of the first to perceive the murderous and genocidal
character of Nazi policy towards the Jews, and who survived
the war first hidden in the forests between Grodno and Vilna
and then as part of a communist guerrilla group. The family
was very close to Nadia, the Belarussian manager of the
Druskieniki hotel, whose Communist sympathies were
eroded by the reality of Bolshevik rule after 1939 and who
died in the battle for Grodno in 1941. Finally, as in Ida Fink's
stories, there are the dogs, who often seem to behave better
than human beings: the family pet, Asio, who pined away and
died when he had to be given to an acquaintance when Jews
in the ghetto were forbidden to keep dogs; and Tsatus, the dog

of the farming couple with whom the Blumsteins hid, who, after he had overcome his initial suspicions, provided invaluable warning about the approach of strangers.

It was the closeness of these family ties, together with their connections with the outside world, which enabled the family to survive first the horrors of the Grodno ghetto, established after the Nazi invasion of the Soviet Union in the autumn of 1941 and then for over a year in hiding with a village family found by a medical associate of Chaim's. After the war, the family moved first to Łódź, the largest concentration of Jews in Poland, and then, following the death of Chaim (worn out by his exertions to save his family), and uneasy about the persistence of anti-Semitism and hostile to the communism of the new Poland, they moved to France; from where Alexandre emigrated in 1960 to the United States.

The skilfully drawn portrait of the maturing of young Alexandre and the ordeals of his family are placed against the larger historical context. Grodno was located in the ethnically mixed area between the ethnic core of the Polish lands and Russia and is today a part of Belarus. In the interwar period, the town itself had a population of nearly 50,000, of whom just under half were Jews (42 per cent according to the census of 1931). The surrounding countryside was divided both religiously between Roman Catholics and Orthodox, and ethnically between those who considered themselves Poles and those among whom a Belarussian national consciousness was slowly developing. The area had been an integral part of the Tsarist Empire and had been subjected to severe Russification after the Polish uprising of 1863. This, the Polish Government attempted to reverse after 1921, bringing in settlers from the remainder of the country and retaking churches that had been transferred in Tsarist times to the Orthodox community. Their methods were often heavy-handed and provoked considerable anger among the Belarussians, among whom sympathy for communism was widespread. The book provides vivid descriptions of the deterioration of Polish–Jewish relations in the last years before the war, seen through the eyes of the young Alexandre, who was frequently humiliated by anti-Semitic teachers and pupils.

In August 1939, the area was assigned to the Soviet Union in the Nazi–Soviet pact and between September of that year and the outbreak of the Nazi–Soviet War in June 1941, it was subjected to a policy of enforced Sovietization, described by Jan Gross as 'revolution from abroad'. After the nightmare of three years of Nazi rule it was liberated by the Red Army and today is part of the nominally independent state of Belarus.

We have relatively few memoirs of the Jewish experience of the Holocaust in this ethnically mixed area, described in Polish as the *kresy* or borderlands. Yet, it was precisely in this area that the anti-Jewish genocide began. Its initiation was part of the radicalization of Nazi policy which accompanied Operation Barbarossa, with the notorious *Komissarbefehl*, which ordered that Soviet officials and adult Jews be shot during the invasion of the Soviet Union to prevent the development of guerrilla resistance. Its final adoption accompanied the euphoria of victory in September and October 1941. At this time, mobile killing squads, the *Einsatzgruppen*, advanced behind the *Wehrmacht* killing Soviet officials and Jewish adult men and then, after a period, also Jewish women and children.

During the first phase of the genocide, the SS – the body entrusted with carrying out policy towards the Jews – was not sure how to proceed. They had had a number of failures, most notably the scheme for a Jewish reservation around Nisko, near Lublin, and the attempt to send Jews to Madagascar, to which a great deal of effort had been devoted. They were eager to exploit anti-Jewish resentment among the local population – which had been greatly exacerbated by the alleged Jewish support for the Soviet invasion and communization of the area – and to see whether these could be harnessed to their purposes. Thus Reinhard Heydrich, a key figure in the SS instructed his subordinates in the Commanders of the *Einsatzgruppen* after the invasion of the Soviet Union to:

trigger pogroms by the local population against Communists and Jews...intensify them if necessary and channel them properly...without leaving any trace...and without giving the perpetrators any opportunity to plead later that they were following our instructions.[2]

There has been extensive debate on a number of issues; particularly in the wake of the debate about Jan Gross's book *Neighbors*,[3] which describes in detail, on the basis of evidence produced for a trial in 1949, an incident in the town of Jedwabne in the north-east of today's Poland (in the same general area as Grodno). Here, with some German incitement but little actual assistance, the local population brutally murdered the overwhelming majority of their Jewish neighbours. The debate concerns how far the growing anti-Semitism in Poland before the war created two separate societies on the eve of the war, and what was the nature of the Jewish 'collaboration' with the Soviets in northeastern Poland in 1939 and later? This memoir adds significantly to our understanding of these problems. The worsening relationship between Poles and Jews (Grodno had been the scene of outbreaks of anti-Jewish violence in 1935 and 1937) is documented through the growing alienation of Chaim and Alexandre's frequent humiliation at his Polish school at the hands of anti-Semitic teachers and fellow pupils.

There is relatively little on Jewish responses to the establishment of Soviet rule in the area, perhaps because Alexandre was only nine at the time. However, there is a reference to the outbreak of anti-Jewish violence which marked the end of Polish rule, when a pro-Soviet uprising in Grodno – in which the principal role was taken by local Jewish and Belarussian Communists – was put down by force and a number of innocent people perished. As one would have expected, the Blumsteins were strongly opposed to communism and expected to be deported. Yet, like most Jews, they welcomed the establishment of Soviet rule, seeing it as a far

---

[2] Heydrich's operation orders of 29 June, 1 July and 2 July; Bundesarchiv R 70 SU/32, quoted in Christian Streit, '*Wehrmacht, Einsatzgruppen* and anti-Bolshevism', in David Cesarani (ed.), *The Final Solution: Origins and Implementation* (London, 1994), p. 104.

[3] *Sàsiedzi: Historia zaglady Żydowskiego miasteczka* ('Neighbours, The History of the Destruction of a Jewish Shtetl') (Kraków, 2000), which was published in English as *Neighbors: The Destruction of the Jewish Community in Jedwabne* (Princeton University Press, 2001).

less dangerous alternative than the Nazis and as bringing an end to anarchy. The initially mixed character of the Communist authority in Grodno comes out clearly in the narrative and has been confirmed by other Polish memoirs. According to one, 'after the seizure of Grodno began the governments of Jews, Belarussians, Communists, criminals and the outcasts of Polish society.'[4] As Soviet authority was consolidated, power came to rest firmly in the hands of the Communist Party of the Soviet Union. The key role in both the Gorispolkom (*Gorodskoi Ispolñitelnyi Komitet* – the main municipal authority) and the NKVD was held by *vostochniki* (Soviet officials brought in from the East).

There is more on the collapse of Bolshevik rule in the summer of 1941 when, as Alexandre relates, there was widespread expectation of an outbreak of anti-Jewish violence (as had occurred in many towns in the area). In the event this did not take place, and the most strongly anti-Semitic views expressed were those of a Belarussian woman living in the same building as the Blumsteins, who hoped by collaborating with the Germans to expunge the memory of her support for the Bolsheviks.

The account of life in the Grodno ghetto contains much that is new and confirms the unwillingness of the majority of Jews to accept that the Nazis were intent on murdering all Jews. The prevalence of hope, another widespread phenomenon in the ghettos, is also well documented. The Blumsteins were able to survive the war because they were able to escape from the ghetto with the aid of Christian associates and hide on the 'Aryan' side for over a year. The question of who rescued Jews in the Polish lands is a complex one and this memoir provides important details on this subject. Those involved in the survival of the Blumsteins came from all sections of the local population. Their escape was organized by a medical acquaintance of Dr Blumstein's, Antoni Docha, a devout Catholic who clearly felt a religious obligation to 'love his neighbour as himself'. This did not prevent him on several occasions from putting strong pressure on the Blumsteins to

---

[4] Quoted in Marek Wierzbicki, *Polacy i Żydzi w Zaborze Sowieckim* (Warsaw, 2001), p. 98.

convert to Catholicism, and thus ensure their salvation, given that they might be killed at any moment, something which caused Chaim Blumstein considerable anguish. They were transported to the countryside by Mikhalko, a Belarussian in the service of Dr Docha and they were hidden in the village cottage of Edward and Aniela Staniewski. The picture of the Staniewski family is most clearly drawn and illustrates some illuminating paradoxes about the area. Barely literate, the family considered themselves to be of noble descent (they were members of the *szlachta zagrodowa*), and although their way of life did not differentiate them in any significant way (apart from their Catholic faith) from the largely Belarussian peasantry – like Mikhalko – they clearly looked down on the latter as a *'chlop'* [peasant]. Edward, dying from osteo-TB, was dependent on Dr Blumstein for medical care, but often resented the large group of Jews quartered in his house, particularly as their supply of money dried up. He was not above expressing strongly anti-Jewish views and was also strongly anti-Communist and anti-Soviet, unlike the Blumsteins whose dislike for communism was greatly diminished by the successes of the Red Army. His wife Aniela is a much more sympathetic character. Although she could also express resentment at the 'incompetent urban women, only interested in make up' who made up part of her involuntary guests, she did not balk when the number of Jews was increased first by three and then by an additional fugitive. Deeply attached to her native soil, she did not move to Poland, as did the Dochas, after the Second World War.

One valuable feature of the memoir is the picture it draws of post-war Poland and life in Łódź. Far from being a society which was dominated by 'Jew-Communists', it was one which demanded that Dr Blumstein change his too-Jewish name before he is offered a hospital post, and one in which Jews trying to start up businesses were subjected to constant harassment from zealous Communist officials (some of whom were also Jews). In these circumstances, the decision to leave came naturally to the surviving Blumsteins.

Although the bulk of Polish Jewry did not survive the war, nearly 300,000 did survive to see liberation. The failure to create a viable post-war community was the result of a number of factors: the difficulty of living on a cemetery where the Nazis had murdered the overwhelming majority of the pre-war community; the persistence of anti-Semitism and anti-Jewish violence; and the character of the post-war communist regime, which was clearly distasteful to the majority of Jewish survivors. It may be that this failure was inevitable given all the difficulties the community faced. Nevertheless, the fact that there was no place in post-war Poland for the Blumsteins and people like them provides a sad epilogue to the tragic Jewish fate during the war and constitutes a posthumous victory for Hitler.

Alexandre and his brother moved to France, to where his mother and her new husband followed. He flourished in the peaceful, tolerant and democratic atmosphere of his new country and qualified as an engineer. He also met his wife, Rita, a survivor from Kraków. In 1960, they left for the United States, where they had two daughters and settled in the Boston area. Their story, and that of the Blumstein family as a whole, is a testimony to the resilience of the human spirit.

Introduction

This memoir was written for my family – to leave behind a description of the most momentous period of my life. As a Holocaust survivor I feel I have an additional duty to remember, and bear witness to a tragedy unprecedented in the annals of inhumanity. To do this I wanted to recreate as faithfully as possible the atmosphere surrounding my life, the life of a Jewish boy caught at the crossroads of the ethnic hatreds and political turbulence of Eastern Poland in the years 1936–47. I tried to describe my childhood and early adolescence swept away in a whirlwind; my whole world – my family, friends, playmates and acquaintances sucked into the extermination universe of Nazi Germany. This memoir is also my tribute of love for them and respect for their memory. Finally, the process of writing helped me to come to terms with myself and with a period of my own life which had left me bewildered and deeply scarred.

The fact that I had lost my diaries, written in 1943–44 while hiding from the Germans, weighed on me for many years. I feared that time would dim my memory; I was acutely aware of the passing of those whose recollections I could check against mine. But I was wrong. When I sat down in 1970, more than 25 years later, to give a factual frame to the book which I intended to complete at a later date, I still remembered most of the events as clearly and as vividly as if they had happened yesterday.

It was only recently, however, that I had the time to reopen my writing and give it a final form. No matter how good my memory, I realized that some details of dates, names and even events were fading. The story of my brother's eventful trip from Lvov to Grodno, as well as the stories of survival of my Uncle Izak and my Aunt Ada are based on personal interviews and tape recordings. As for the rest, I tried to render honestly and accurately the atmosphere surrounding my life, my perceptions and my inner feelings at that time; yet here and there I may have still incorrectly assigned the chronology of events or forgotten the names of some of the protagonists. I hope that the reader will forgive me such mistakes.

Each story of a survivor, each testimony is a precious and very special document because it describes the Holocaust from a unique perspective. Such perspectives assembled together may enable future generations to reconstruct the past and minimize the distortions and myths that inevitably arise with the passage of time. They could even help us to fathom the unfathomable. My hope is that this memoir will in small measure add to this endeavour.

I dedicate this book to the memory of my father and my mother. The price they had to pay to live through the Holocaust as parents was dreadful. I dedicate it to my children and grandchildren. May they never know the agony that my generation of parents and children experienced in Europe during the war.

My thanks go to all those who helped me in my effort. First and foremost, I would like to thank my wife Rita who spent countless days editing the manuscript. Without her labour of love and her encouragement this work could not have been completed. I thank my daughters Sylvie and Tanya and my son-in-law Uri. Their comments and input were invaluable to me.

Special thanks are due to my childhood friend and fellow survivor from Grodno, Dr Felix Zandman, for his help and for his comments which contributed to correct some inaccuracies in my recollections.

I would like to thank my friends Sidney and Francine Friedland for their invaluable help and encouragement. Thanks are also due to my friends Linda and Jim Kistler and Susan Julian Gates and Professor Melissa Pennell of the University of Massachusetts Lowell, for reading the manuscript and for their valuable input. I am grateful to my editor at Vallentine Mitchell, Georgina Clark-Mazo, for her invaluable help and all that she contributed. Last but not least, I would like to thank Yad Vashem for permission to use some photographs and a map from *Lost Jewish Worlds*.

I have occasionally cross-checked my own recollections and the chronology of events using the following books and documents: *Lost Jewish Worlds*, S. Spector, ed., B. Freundlich, co-ed., (Yad Vashem, Jerusalem, 1996); *Documents Concerning The Destruction of the Jews of Grodno*, 1941–1944, S. Klarsfeld, ed. (Beate Klarsfeld Foundation, Grodner Association of Israel, Ramat-Gan, 52443 Israel); and *On the Edge of Destruction: Jews of Poland between the Two World Wars*, Celia S. Heller (Wayne State University Press, Detroit, 1994).

Finally, I should like to add a few words of explanation concerning the names, titles and diminutives of the protagonists in my story. One and the same person may have several names, Hebrew, Yiddish, Polish or Russian. Titles and polite forms of address may also vary, as do diminutives and terms of endearment. Thus, my father's first name was Chaim Mordechai in Hebrew and Matviei in Russian, while the familiar diminutive was Motek (or Musik). My mother's Hebrew name was Estera, or its diminutive Esterka; however, her Russian name was Tatyana or its diminutive Tanya. My brother Nataniel was called Tolo in Polish or Tolya in Russian. As for me, the diminutive of Alexandre is Alik or Aliczek in Polish, and Sasha or Shura (sometimes Shurik) in Russian. Though I was called Sasha by my Russian friends, my friend Alexander Lampert was addressed as Shura or Shurik. To add to the confusion, male and female diminutive names can be interchangeable in Russian and boys' names often end with an 'a' - as in Lolya, Danya (Danyusha) or Sala.

The formal way of addressing someone in Russian is to attach a patronymic to his or her first name. My mother would thus be called Tatyana Pavlovna, and my father Matviei Natanitch. In Polish, on the other hand, one uses either *Pan* or *Pani* (Mr or Mrs) followed by the surname or a title referring to the person's occupation, such as '*Pan* Doktor' or '*Pani* Doktorowa' (the latter referring to the wife of a doctor). In a similar vein, our landlords in the village of Staniewicze, Aniela Staniewska and Edward Staniewski, are also referred to as *Gosposia* and *Gospodarz*, that is 'landlady' and 'landlord'.

A child never addresses an adult by his or her first name,

except in terms of endearment such as *Tante* Thea ('Auntie' Thea in German) or *Diadia* Grisha ('little Uncle' Grisha in Russian) which signify a loving, but not necessarily a family, relationship.

1 The Family

Though she did not know it, Mother was doomed to be separated from her family when in her native Ukraine she married a handsome young surgeon from Warsaw, a captain in the Imperial Russian Army. The year was 1917 and Warsaw was still the capital of the Western Region of the Russian Empire. Soon the Tsar would be deposed, Warsaw would become the capital of independent Poland, and the young couple would be faced with choosing between life in the Soviet Union and life in Poland. But let me go back to the beginning.

Father was born in 1886 in the town of Plock near Warsaw, in the Russian part of dismembered Poland. A few years later the Blumsteins moved to the nearby town of Ciechanow where my grandfather, Nussen Mendel, worked as a teacher in a Jewish primary school. A young idealist, Father joined the Polish revolutionaries in 1905, the year the foundations of the Tsarist Russian empire shook. Father's dream was of an independent Poland where Jew and Gentile would enjoy the same privileges and share the same duties. Together with a large group of Ciechanow high-school students he organized a strike in solidarity with other Polish patriots protesting against the Russification of Poland. The Tsar's police moved swiftly throughout the country. Many strike leaders were arrested and sent to Siberia; high-school students were blacklisted and thrown out of school with a *Voltchii Bilet* (a 'wolf's identity card'), which in tsarist Russia was tantamount to a juvenile criminal record. Father was barred from ever entering a Russian institution of higher learning. Were it not for my grandfather Nussen Mendel and my grandmother Fryda, who would literally not eat to save some money for their children's education, it would have been impossible for him to study medicine abroad.

Actually, Father's longing was not for medicine; he dreamt

1

of becoming an astronomer. But what kind of a profession was that for a Jewish boy? How would he make a living and help his family as an astronomer? He opted for medicine and began his studies at the Faculté de Médecine in Geneva. Father loved Switzerland – the hiking and mountain climbing – but it was too expensive for the son of a modest schoolteacher from Ciechanow and after a year he moved to Leipzig in Germany. He put himself through medical school in Leipzig by giving private lessons in high-school mathematics, his favourite subject, to avoid starving on the minuscule allowance scraped together by his parents. In 1910 he presented his dissertation *Zur Kasuistik der Pneumonia Kruposa*. He graduated in 1911 with the title of *Doctoris Medicinae Chirurgiae Artisque Obstetriciae Jura et Ornamenta*. After his graduation from Leipzig, Father spent a year at the medical school of the Imperial University of Kiev, where he had to undergo rigorous examinations in order to be allowed to practise as a surgeon in Russia. The tests were made especially difficult for Chaim Mordechai Blumstein, a blacklisted Jew, but he passed in 1912 and moved to Warsaw to practise surgery.

My parents met for the first time in 1913 in Warsaw where Mother was visiting a friend. She had an attack of appendicitis and father operated on her. Mother often joked that she 'fell for his beard *à la* Nicholas II'. Mother returned to her home in Ukraine, a thousand kilometres to the east, and was studying in Ekaterynoslav when the First World War broke out in 1914. Father was mobilized and joined the Imperial Russian Army as a surgeon, with the rank of Lieutenant. He was attached to the Samsonov Army Corps and sent into East Prussia in August 1914. He was a witness to the Russian debacle at Tannenberg and was made prisoner by the Germans. He spent almost two years in a German POW camp from which he made a daring escape in the spring of 1916. After many adventures he found his way through Germany into neutral Holland and, in the summer of 1916, returned to St Petersburg, where he was decorated with the 'Order of Alexander of the Third Grade', conferring on him 'personal nobility' by the tsar – quite an achievement for a blacklisted Jew from Ciechanow. He was promoted to Surgeon-Captain of the Imperial Army.

By that time the Blumsteins were refugees in Ekaterynoslav, having fled the big German offensive into Poland. And this is how my parents met for the second time, while Father was on leave from the front. They dated and fell in love. Mother was 23 and Father 31 when they married in 1917 just before Father was sent to Erzerum on the Turkish front, where he contracted typhoid fever and nearly died. After the Russian Army disintegrated in 1918, Father, making his way through the Caucasus, joined his young wife and his family in Ekaterynoslav. The Blumsteins were now trapped in Russia, first by the Revolution and the ensuing civil war, then by the war between newly independent Poland and the victorious Bolsheviks.

In March 1921 came the Polish–Soviet peace treaty and, shortly thereafter, the treaty of Riga, establishing the eastern borders of Poland. The Blumsteins could at last move back to Poland, though Grandfather Nussen Mendel was seriously ill after being savagely beaten in a Ukrainian pogrom. He died shortly afterwards.

As my brother Tolo was born in July 1921, Father left first, to explore the possibility of establishing a practice in Poland, while his young wife and Tolo remained with Mother's family in Poltava, in the Ukraine. After a long time, when the first letter finally reached Mother, she was happy to learn that her husband was working as a surgeon in a hospital in Grodno, a scenic, historical city on the river Niemen, close to the Lithuanian border of Poland. But it was bitter-sweet news. She knew that she would have to leave her beloved family and Russia. Mother was Russian, Russian to the core, and would never fully accept the ways of foreigners. This was the tragedy of her life.

When she married, Mother did not expect to live outside Russia. After the 1917 February Revolution, with Kerensky in power, there was real hope that a new Russia, liberal and progressive, free of the tsar and his corrupt aristocracy, would provide a better life for the population and its minorities, Jews included. That was wishful thinking. The October Bolshevik Revolution brought with it counter-revolution and foreign interventions. The exhausted, impoverished and hungry country was plundered by the Germans and, after their withdrawal in 1918, was ravaged by a savage fratricidal war between the Reds and the Whites.

This war was taking a staggering toll on the Ukraine, where German occupation had rekindled the old ultra-nationalist fervour and propensity for violence. Bands of armed, disgruntled Ukrainians – army deserters, hungry peasants, adventurers and common criminals – roamed the countryside under the banner of nationalism, spreading terror and death. Millions were dying of starvation, of typhoid fever, dysentery, and even cholera. Especially cruel was the fate of Jews in the Ukrainian pale of settlements; they were singled out for punishment by the Ukrainian nationalists. Not since the seventeenth-century pogroms of Boghdan Chmielnitzki had the Ukrainian soil been drenched in as much Jewish blood as during those dark years of civil war.

It is against this background that Father decided to return to his native Poland, where a newly reborn, independent state had emerged. Mother was not enthusiastic; she always repeated *'Polsha sesonnoie gosudarstwo'* [Poland is a seasonal state]. 'Her existence will depend on the goodwill of her two powerful neighbours.' She loathed the idea of leaving her family. Father saw things differently. A born optimist, he expected the independent and democratic Poland to be an island of sanity and a haven for all its citizens, including the Jews.

When Mother left her home to join Father in the cold early spring of 1923, she travelled through a war-devastated land with an 18-month toddler, my brother Tolo. She feared that she might never see her family again, but she was young, pretty, and full of energy, eager to take care of her new family and looking forward to her new life.

Estera (Tatyana/Tanya) Bouchin, my mother, had a very strong attachment to her family in Russia. She used to tell me stories with tears in her eyes about her parents and her 'baby' brother in her native Poltava, about her childhood and adolescence. Apparently, Grandmother Bouchin, whom we called *babusya*, was allowed to visit us when I was born in 1930, but this was the last time she could come; the border between the Soviet Union and Poland was closed shortly after 1930, under Stalin. Grandfather Bouchin, *diedushka*, was a self-made man, a construction foreman. Due to their rather humble background, the Bouchins were not mistreated by the Bolsheviks; however,

4

in the atmosphere of terror under Stalin, *diedushka* had been harassed by the NKVD (Soviet secret police) because of a daughter living abroad. I saw letters from *babusya* and *diedushka* with photographs of a handsome elderly man with a short, stately beard and a moustache, a small lady, a slender young man and a young woman holding a baby girl, my cousin Tamara. The photographs were displayed on my mother's dresser in the bedroom. Especially sad was the news in 1938 when *diedushka* died. Every time a letter arrived, Mother would sit me on her knees to read in Russian the lines written for me or my brother Tolo.

And now in 1941, after the annexation of our part of Poland by the Soviet Union, Mother finally succeeded in wresting from the authorities in Grodno the permit to visit her family deep inside the Ukraine. Being granted a permit to travel was an extraordinary achievement in the atmosphere of suspicion prevailing under Soviet rule, but Mother had a way with the authorities; she had the energy to run through the bureaucratic maze of party councils, never taking 'no' for an answer. Her flawless Russian and, above all, her two recitals of *starinnyie romansy* [old love songs] at the Grodno theatre earned her the admiration of many in high places. She was also a good interpreter of gypsy love songs, considered decadent by the Communists, but immensely popular with the older generation.

Mother received permission for a visit to the city of Kharkov in the Ukraine and the nearby small town of Zugress in the coal-mining Don-Bass region, where her family now lived and where Uncle Lolya worked as a surgeon. She left in January 1941, loaded with gifts, and came back six weeks later with many interesting stories and a magnificent stamp collection, a present for me from Uncle Lolya. The house was again alive with the excitement and effervescence which only she could provide and I was happy to see her back after so long an absence.

After she returned, Mother kept trying to convince Father to apply for a permit to move from Grodno to Kharkov, a big city, so much more exciting than Grodno and close to her home. In Grodno everybody was fearful of being only 60 kilometres from the German border at Augustowo as war was expected. Father hesitated. He believed that the Western powers, in whose ultimate victory he never doubted, would never accept the dismemberment of Poland. His youthful attachment to Poland was all but gone by now, eroded by the relentless Polish anti-Semitism, yet he was not eager to bury himself in the vast prison that was the Soviet Union. He was a Zionist and his ultimate goal was to settle in Palestine – 'a little house on Mount Carmel' was now his dream.

It took a lot to convert Father from a Polish patriot to a Zionist, but in the end he could no longer swallow the sordid anti-Semitism of this new country in which Jews were blamed for every misdeed under the sun. From the very beginning, following the Polish–Soviet War of 1919–20, Jews were accused of helping the Bolsheviks. Several bloody pogroms followed. Ironically, no Pole seemed to remember that pogroms were also staged by the retreating Soviet cavalry under Budennyi, the Bolsheviks accusing the Jews of siding with the Poles.

The Treaty of Versailles, which had granted Poland its independence, also committed the newly independent country to grant equal status to its ethnic minorities but Poland between the two world wars did not live up to its obligations. There was an ever-increasing oppression of Jews in all walks of life: an official economic boycott, a minuscule Jewish quota (*numerus clausus*) at state institutions of learning, heavy taxation on Jewish cultural institutions; official anti-Semitism in the judiciary, government and army; a rabidly anti-Semitic press and a government dominated by the powerful nationalistic and anti-Semitic National Democratic Party, the *Endecja*; and jeering and beatings of Jews in Polish schools. There were sermons about the 'Christ-killers' in the churches of Poland, where prominent priests like Father Jozef Kruszynski, Father Stanislaw Trzeciak, and others, authored various renditions of *The Protocols of the Elders of Zion*, the tsarist canard about a Jewish conspiracy to dominate the world. Even the primate of Poland, Cardinal Hlond, openly joined the anti-Semitic chorus.

I was barely six when Tolo and his handful of Jewish classmates came home from their Polish state high school bloodied and beaten up by a gang of older students. There was nothing Father could do to punish these hooligans, even though their names were known to him and some belonged to prominent families in town. The director, himself not an anti-Semite, told Father: 'I understand you, Dr Blumstein, but my advice to you is to forget it; if you lodge a complaint it will only harm you.'

It was an ugly time. Shops were looted and synagogues desecrated. At universities, especially in Warsaw, Cracow and Lvov, the handful of Jewish students who were 'lucky' to be admitted were attacked by thugs from the *Endecja* with sticks and razor blades. 'Bench ghettos' were now widespread at Polish universities: Jewish students were compelled to sit on segregated benches. Shops in our town proclaimed their status of 'Christian shop' [*Sklep Chrzescjanski*]; even cab and taxi drivers decorated the rims of their caps with the logo 'Christian cab' or 'Christian taxi' written in large black letters on a white ribbon. Posters called for the boycott of Jewish goods and shops and for the expulsion of Jews: '*Precz z Zydami*' [Out with the Jews], or '*Zydzi do Palestyny*' [Jews to Palestine]. The powerful right wing of the *Endecja*, inspired by the Nazis in Germany, openly expressed their overall objective of depriving the Jews of Polish citizenship, and expropriating and expelling them.

The head of the state, the hero of the war against the Soviets, Marshal Jozef Pilsudski, was himself not an anti-Semite. In fact, he tried hard to control the tide of anti-Semitism, but this was a difficult task. Jozef Pilsudski died in 1935 and I vaguely remember fear and gloom sweeping over us at that time. Pogroms and anti-Jewish incidents followed. One month after Pilsudski's death a crowd of about 1,000 Poles armed with iron bars, knives and clubs attacked Jews and looted shops in Grodno's Jewish quarter. Many Jews were wounded; some, like the son of the synagogue's choirmaster Izzy Berezovski, died of their wounds. In 1936 over 20 pogroms and hundreds of serious anti-Semitic incidents took place in the Bialystok region alone.

In pre-war Poland I had been enrolled into the public *cwiczeniowka* [grammar school] named after a famous Polish writer from Grodno, Eliza Orzeszkowa. My first day in school will stay in my memory for ever. I was six. I wore a shiny new black smock with a white collar and a red tie. I was so proud of my uniform of a first grader! It was a magnificent

September day and the class went for an outing to the municipal garden nearby. At recess time the boys divided into two camps to play a handball game called 'between two fires', while the girls went about their own games. Two bigger boys, the captains, were selecting their teams. When I gave my name my team captain growled with contempt, imitating a Jewish accent in Polish: 'Blumshteeein? I do not want the kike.' The only Jewish boy in a class of 25 children, I did not play ball with my schoolmates that sunny day. Ashamed, offended and crying, I returned home to ask my parents, 'What is a kike?'

My acceptance into this school, supposedly of the 'highest educational standard', and from which one graduated directly into the Polish state high-school system, was a favour to my father for his services as one of Grodno's handful of civilian surgeons. In turn, graduation from a Polish state high school [*Gimnazjum Panstwowe*], which also had a quota on Jews, considerably increased one's chances of being admitted to a Polish university. By enrolling me into the *cwiczeniowka* my parents hoped to increase my chances of being accepted into a Polish university, but my three years at that school were a bitter experience, one I shall never forget. I was called *zydek* or 'little kike', treated as someone impure, and had almost no one to play with. There were also three Jewish girls, Sarcia, Irenka and Helcia, and I envied them because they at least could play together, while I was an outcast.

One very notable exception was my Polish friend Zdzich Kuksewicz who, despite the frequent jeering, played with me as if nothing was amiss. I liked Zdzisio very much and we often visited each other's homes, played hide-and-seek, 'lead soldiers' and other exciting games. His father was a prosecutor in the Grodno District Court and the Kuksewiczes made no difference between me and Polish friends of Zdzich. I felt welcome in their home. But there was only one Zdzich in a class of 25.

Another event, which happened when I was eight, deeply marked my memories of the *cwiczeniowka*. It was a beautiful, sunny day in 1938, one of those days of the 'golden Polish autumn'. The air was crisp and the whole municipal park of Grodno was ablaze with gold and purple. A few boys from the *cwiczeniowka* were crossing the park on their way home, walking along the embankment of a brook running through the park, the Chorodniczanka. The boys were speaking with pride about the profession of their fathers. Overhearing, I could not resist the temptation of saying that my father was a doctor and a very good one at that. 'No,' one of the boys interjected, 'your father is a dirty Jew!' It was as if somebody had scalded me with boiling water. I threw myself on him and pushed him down the embankment into the Chorodniczanka. The boy slipped and fell. When he got up, he was wet and covered in mud. He cried and summoned others for help. Bigger boys fell on me. I tried to escape but they were faster. When I came home, I was a bloody mess.

My *Tante* Thea – my German governess – was beside herself: her *Buebchen*, her little boy, coming from school covered with blood and crying! 'How can one distress a small child to such an extent? Why don't you go to the school director, Herr Doktor, and make a scandal?' she fumed. Father went to the principal of the *cwiczeniowka*, a handsome elderly lady, and complained, but there was little anyone could do in the prevailing atmosphere of the post-Pilsudski era.

Particularly unpleasant for me was the beginning of classes when all the children were reciting a Catholic prayer and I was standing up, my arms hanging at my side, not moving my lips, eyes fixed on the floor, attracting the derisive stares of my classmates; or when I had to leave the classroom during the lesson of religion while my classmates giggled and whispered, looking at the *zydek* and the three *zydoweczki* walking out before the priest and the cross. The daily reminder that I was different from others and an object of contempt was hard to bear. Once a week, Sarcia, Helcia, Irenka and myself had lessons with a rabbi, but the only thing I remember is that they were boring.

Father often took me onto his knee and tried to explain what it means to be Jewish. His explanations dwelt on the rich historical and, above all, moral heritage of the Jewish people. He repeated to me that there were three great peoples which gave the Western world the basis of their civilization: the Greeks, who excelled in art and philosophy; the Romans, who codified the Civil Law; and the Jews, who established the moral and ethical code of behaviour as expressed in the Torah.

'We are the people of the Book,' he would say, and read me stories about King David, King Solomon and Judah Maccabee and about Jewish wars against the Romans. 'We were a proud people fighting for what we knew was right, against powerful tyrants.' These stories lifted my spirit, helped me meet the next day with my head held high in my all-Polish school. I fought back when insulted, remembering Father saying, 'Only those are respected who fight back when insulted.'

The pre-war years were a time of great distress for the Jewish community of Grodno. Our seamstress, Nechama, decided to emigrate to Argentina with her husband and her two children. Our clinic's certified paramedic, Sarah Kagan, was waiting for a permit to leave for Palestine with her family. Our friend Sasha Slucki left for Palestine. It was at that time, during the summer of 1935, that our dear friend Dr Grisha Altfeld (*tata* Grisha, as I lovingly called him) died suddenly of a heart attack at our hotel in Druskieniki. His wife, *mama* Edzia, and their daughter Musia decided to leave for Palestine. Edzia was a very close friend of Mother's from Poltava; they both married Polish doctors who both settled in Grodno but, unlike my Mother, Edzia did not have any nostalgia for Russia. She knew that life in Palestine would not be easy but she was happy to receive an affidavit and leave Poland. Naturally, Mother became more amenable to thinking about leaving, but Father wanted first to specialize in Paris in cosmetic surgery. I overheard him saying: 'We will meet with Edzia in our little house on Mount Carmel, but our road first leads through Paris.'

The war cut short all this wishful thinking and dreams. As Poland's army collapsed, lawless bands of Polish hooligans roamed the streets of Grodno, looting Jewish shops and murdering Jews. Twenty-five Jews were killed and scores were wounded and only the arrival of the Red Army stopped the pogrom. We were relieved to find ourselves in the part of Poland annexed by the Soviets, escaping the German occupation. The refugees from the German-occupied part of Poland, who filled our city to overflowing during the autumn of 1939 and the winter of 1940, proclaimed the incredible might of this invincible German army. Father was not impressed. I remember his daily discussions with Lenka, my cousin from Warsaw and her husband Rysio, who took refuge with us. Rysio tried to convince Father that the Germans were invincible. This was also the opinion of other refugees, many former guests at our hotel in Druskieniki and now frequent visitors at our home. (My parents had built this hotel in the early 1930s. It had 32 rooms and was called Dr Blumstein's Sanatorium. Although there was a resident physician, the guests were generally in good health and came to 'take the waters' for which the spa town of Druskieniki was famous.) Father remained unmoved. He was an admirer of the French army of 1914–18, of the *Poilus* with whom he had shared a common enemy and a common fate in the German POW camps in 1914–15. Father also admired the British and their navy and could not think for a moment that two great Western democracies could be defeated by a ranting and raving German tyrant. He waited with impatience for the Allied offensive that never came. Any news about some renewed fighting he greeted with a cheerful, 'They have started, they have started, they march on Berlin!' But it was only some local skirmish and soon he was again anxiously listening to the evening BBC news, trying to make sense of the communiqué drowned in the static from German and Soviet interference stations.

He was not impressed by the Red Army when we learned from the BBC about the extent of its defeat at the hands of the Finns. We admired brave little Finland battling so gallantly against the Russian bear. We knew that Uncle Lolya, a surgeon-major in the Soviet Army, was somewhere on the Finnish front but we did not know that he almost died from hunger, pneumonia and the horrible conditions under which the Soviet Army fought in Finland.

My poor Father! All his forecasts and hopes were suddenly dashed when the Germans defeated France in a mere six weeks. It was a sad day for all of us when in June 1940 they marched into Paris. I had never seen Father so crushed. It took a long time for him to recover, but from then on, slowly and reluctantly, he yielded to Mother's urging about leaving for Kharkov.

2   The Refugees

Several hundred thousand refugees from the German occupied zone flooded the Soviet part of Poland in September 1939. Mother kept our house always open to the many needy refugees in Grodno. My cousin Lenka from Warsaw came to live with us. She was only 18, a soft-spoken, slim blonde with the light blue eyes of the Blumstein family. Her fiancé, Rysio Gherman, came three weeks later, dirty, hungry, a real picture of distress with his broken glasses. He was of average size, with dark hair and thick horn-rimmed glasses, without which he was as blind as a bat. Lenka's parents, my uncle Eliasz and his wife Sonya, had refused to leave Warsaw despite Lenka and Rysio's urging.

Ten years younger than my father, Uncle Eliasz was an upbeat, blue-eyed, blond giant with a huge belly that made me ashamed before my friends to be with him on the beach when he and Lenka came to visit us at our hotel in the spa town of Druskieniki. A brilliant mathematician, he had displayed his skills while still in high school in Poland under the tsar. In 1913, he was accepted to the Mathematical Institute at Kharkov University from which he graduated in 1917 summa cum laude, with a gold medal. Because of his size, he briefly served in the Hussars in the tsar's army just before it collapsed. After the Revolution, the Reds offered him a faculty position at Kharkov University, but Eliasz did not like the Bolsheviks and chose to return to his native land, hoping to become a professor of mathematics at a university in Poland. He married Sonya, a bacteriology student whom he met at the Kharkov University, and left for Warsaw. His expectations of a university appointment were not realistic in the anti-Semitic atmosphere of pre-war Poland. He became a teacher of mathematics for upper levels of high school and, in time, director of a Polish-Jewish high school in Warsaw called *Zjednoczenie*

Nauczycieli [The Association of Teachers]. Sonya opened a medical testing laboratory.

Lenka and Rysio were married at a *Zaks* (Soviet Office for Civil Marriages) in Grodno two weeks after Rysio's arrival. They smooched all the time, and I was very amused and enjoyed the show. Beside his smooching with Lenka, I enjoyed watching Rysio devour his favourite dishes, including *schab z kapusta*, pork roast with cabbage on rye, which he washed down with strong, sweet tea. I observed with fascination as his Adam's apple moved with a faint gulping sound after each swallow. I got along splendidly with Rysio, who was 12 years my senior. We played chess, 'naval battle', dominoes and even 'lead soldiers', of which I had a magnificent collection. We both enjoyed displaying them in impeccable, orderly, shining columns. My collection of more than 1,000 soldiers had been built up over the years. Everyone knew that a box of French Zouaves, Polish Uhlans or Austrian Hussars would make me happy for many days. Before the war, Father used to bring a box of soldiers whenever he joined us for weekends in Druskieniki. Every Friday afternoon at four o'clock I waited with great anticipation at the entrance on Lesna Street for the car with my father to appear, or rather for my box of 25 beautiful, new, lead soldiers.

Rysio also read me stories when I was sick and cheered me up with the magic tricks that he knew by the dozen. He often went to parent–teacher meetings in place of my busy parents. I would hide behind Father's big black armchair or pull the covers over my head when, back from the interview, he would exclaim in a teasing voice: 'Your grades are all bad Alexander! Where is he hiding this *leniuch* [lazy-bones]?'

Unlike many of Father's friends, Rysio was always losing to him in chess and this made him the perfect adversary. I sometimes watched them locked in combat, Father smoking his eternal pipe and Rysio drumming his fingers. They sat like this for hours, staring at the chessboard and each other. I knew that Rysio's inevitable debacle was around the corner. The approach of this moment of triumph for my father was announced by his off-key humming of a tune from *Cavaleria Rusticana* – this was my father's way of saying that Rysio was on the ropes. It then took only a few minutes for the *coup de grâce* of checkmate which put Father in the best of moods for the rest of the evening.

Since my brother Tolo was mostly away at the medical school in Lvov, it was exciting for me to have Rysio and Lenka with us. There were other young adults who also played with me. One was Marek Chorazycki, the son of our friends from Warsaw. He was tall and handsome but not in the best of health. He used to gallop through the apartment with me riding on his back. His two sisters, Stefa and Mila, were both very pretty. Stefa was with her husband Nitek, a slim and sickly engineer, gloomily predicting a German victory. Mila was in a state of shock after witnessing the murder of her husband by a band of marauding Ukrainians during their flight across the River Bug in September 1939, and I felt sorry for her.

There was also Lusia Alapin-Menes, the daughter of our dear friends Nika and Herman Alapin from Warsaw. She was with her husband Jozio Menes, a talented artist who now made his living painting not so subtle propaganda posters for the Soviets. I regarded him with admiration, as a great painter and a genius. Then there was Julian Schiff, a middle-aged bachelor from Lodz, who liked a glass or two; his cheeks and the tip of his nose were tinged with a reddish blue, betraying this weakness. There were many others whose names I do not remember but who found shelter, food and moral support in our house. Some stayed with us for a few days or weeks, then moved on after finding a job and housing. Lenka and Rysio lived with us permanently.

Our old German Shepherd dog, Asio, was also displaced by the war from his usual living place guarding our hotel in Druskieniki. Asio came to us as a puppy six months before my birth. He used to stand guard by my pushchair when *Tante* Thea took me to the municipal park. With Asio beside us, *Tante* could safely leave me for a short time. Nobody could approach me without Asio giving an impressive growl and curling back his lips to reveal his impressive teeth. However, when Asio attacked the postman, ripping off his trousers and biting him, Father had many problems and had to pay a huge indemnity. My parents then decided to move Asio to our property at the health resort of Druskieniki, in the custody of our maintenance man, Leiba, who trained him and taught him many tricks such as fetching a newspaper or any other object upon command. Leiba had only to say, 'Asio take off this gentleman's hat', and Asio was already jumping on the petrified fellow, gently taking his hat into his muzzle and bringing it to Leiba. In the autumn of 1939, Leiba brought Asio back home to Grodno for there was no more property to keep after the Soviets had confiscated our hotel. By then Asio was old; he slept curled up near our big ceramic stove and rarely ventured further than the kitchen. His growl when someone inadvertently approached his bowl remained frightening but, with most of his teeth gone, it was much worse than his bite.

In November 1939, all permanent residents of the Soviet part of Poland were made Soviet citizens and thus my family and I became citizens of the Byelorussian Soviet Socialist Republic. The refugees from German-occupied Poland were given what appeared to be a choice between accepting Soviet citizenship and remaining Polish. The discussions in our house were interminable; everyone was afraid of reprisals against refugees who rejected Soviet citizenship. Shortly thereafter, as relations with Germany deteriorated, the NKVD intensified arrests of those considered *nieblagonadiezhnyie* [untrustworthy]. Many prominent Poles were arrested, as well as many Jews – Zionists, Bundists and refugees from German-occupied Poland. Blacklists of *nieblagonadiezhnyie* were established in the *Gorispolkoms* (party-run town halls). These lists included not only refugees who had refused Soviet citizenship but also locals – liberals, clergy, former business or property owners and others considered as *byvshyi burzoui* [former bourgeois]. By the summer and autumn of 1940, thousands of refugees had been deported to the Urals and Central Asia. Many of our close friends were arrested as early as June 1940, including Nitek, Stefa and Mila Chorazycki. Marek, who took Soviet citizenship, was spared for the time being. He worked at the railway station and visited us often. Many months later, we received from Nitek and Stefa an anguished letter from Central Asia. Nitek was getting very sick as his stomach ulcer worsened.

Following our advice, Lenka and Rysio took Soviet citizenship and avoided deportation. For how long, nobody could say. It was a difficult time and we all lived in fear for our friends and even for ourselves, since we were considered *nieblagonadiezhnyie* as former owners of a hotel in Druskieniki and a clinic in Grodno. To make matters worse, Father was a prominent Zionist and an outspoken pro-Western liberal. Everybody in town knew that. As chief surgeon of the 7th City Hospital (one of the largest in Grodno), he was unhappy with the 'new order', with the omnipotent party bureaucracy patched together from unskilled elements of the health-care profession and party hacks. These people were ruining the hospital through incompetence and arrogance. They insulted senior medical staff and abused their power. They gave full meaning to these lines of the Soviet Anthem: '*Kto byl nichem tot staniet vsyem*' [He who was nothing will become everything].

While many senior medical staff resigned themselves to this situation, Father did not, and one day the inevitable happened. He spoke sternly to a young nurse, a Communist and a party member, who repeatedly and pointedly referred to him as *ty* and *on* (a disrespectful 'you' and 'him' in Russian). 'I remind you,' father thundered, 'that I did not keep pigs with you in your village. For you, I am not *ty* or *on* but "Dr Blumstein".' A few weeks after this incident we were informed confidentially that Dr Blumstein, the former Zionist and *burzoui*, and his family had been placed by the authorities on a blacklist.

When arrests resumed in the spring of 1941, we were as uneasy about being deported as our refugee friends. We knew that the town could not spare one of its three surgeons, the only one performing non-routine surgery, but we also knew that political considerations always took precedence over the interests of the population. This worry was weighing on Father's mind when he finally yielded to Mother's insistence that we move to Kharkov and possibly avoid deportation. In the meantime, we expected to be deported. We listened carefully to the noises of the street at night. It usually happened at around two o'clock in the morning – the rumbling of a lorry, the screeching of brakes, heavy steps, a knock on the door, blue, red-rimmed caps of NKVD soldiers with rifles and a man in a leather coat announcing that the entire family was under arrest and granting them one hour to pack.

There was no appeal, no arguing; everyone stumbled out of bed, packed as quickly as possible and left their home in a daze to climb into a canvas-covered lorry. Then there was the bumpy ride through the dark, sleepy streets; the railway station with many lorries discharging their cargo of stunned, frightened, sometimes half-naked people, dragging their suit-cases and hastily thrown together bundles. At the station, a long train of cattle trucks waited at the platform and was filled to the loud *'Davai, davai poskoree!'* [Move, move faster!] of NKVD soldiers. At dawn, the doors were locked and the fully loaded train slowly left the station – sometimes to be sent on its way, sometimes directed to wait for hours on end on an auxiliary track before proceeding into the vastness of Russia.

A railway crossroads located a mere 60 kilometres from the German border at Augustowo, Grodno was strategically important to the Soviets, who brought in a sizeable garrison. As 1941 began, the political situation deteriorated. Stepan Grigoryevitch Mourashov, a major in the Air Force, our next-door neighbour, was of the opinion that war with Fascist Germany was inevitable. Like many other Soviet personnel, he felt very uncomfortable about the non-aggression pact with Nazi Germany, a sworn enemy of the Soviet Union. The Mourashovs were good neighbours; Varvara Petrovna Mourashov was friendly with my mother, and Kolya, their 11-year-old son, was my classmate and friend. Major Murashov and Varvara Petrovna sometimes came over for a cup of tea, while Kolya and I played with my lead soldiers. While the children were allowed in the dining room to get some cake, I overheard Stepan Grigoryevitch trying to explain to my father why 'we' (the Soviets) were not yet at war with Germany. It all boiled down to mistrust of the French and the British who, according to Mourashov, were bent on destroying the Soviet Union and gave ample proof of their intentions when they sent troops to intervene on the side of the Whites during the October Revolution. 'They have nurtured Hitler from 1933 on', Stepan Grigoryevitch Mourashov contended, 'in order to destroy us. Now, Matviei Natan'ich', he addressed Father, 'we have turned the tables on them; let them get a taste of their own medicine.'

Father could not tell Murashov what he really thought of

Hitler and Stalin alike and only expressed to family and close friends: *'Sie schtinken alle beide* – They both stink.' Father recognized that Stepan Grigoryevitch was no fool and the two men were on friendly terms, although suspicious of each other. Father, a Westerner, a former 'bourgeois' with a wife who had left her native Russia after the revolution, could not possibly be what was designated in the Soviet jargon as a 'trustworthy element' and I, their son, was not even enrolled into the Young Pioneers.

None of this seemed to bother the Murashovs on the surface, but Kolya asked me once, 'Sasha, why aren't you enrolled in the Pioneers?' Conscious of danger, I answered, 'You know Kolya, my father has a weak heart; he wants me to enrol so badly that I am hesitating because if I tell him, "Dad, I just have enrolled and have taken the Pioneers' oath" he will be so overwhelmed with joy that, I fear, he will have a heart attack.' Guileless Kolya Murashov believed me and I was off the hook with him but not with our teacher, who stubbornly nagged me to enrol so that our class be closer to having 100 per cent of Young Pioneers. I promised her that I would enrol after the summer vacation, when I would be promoted to the fifth grade.

In retrospect one can be impressed with Murashov's courage in befriending a 'Western' family with 'a bourgeois background' at a time when the Red Army had just undergone a gigantic purge, in which thousands of officers like Murashov were shot by the NKVD for being 'enemies of the nation'. I remember that, owing to a shortage of new books at the beginning of the school year 1940–41, we were given a 1937 edition of the textbook *Soviet History for Fourth Graders*. In this book, some photographs were covered with black paper and some paragraphs were painted over with black ink. The teacher told us: 'These pages and photographs relate to *vragi naroda* – enemies of the nation. You should never look at these traitors, their names should never be mentioned.' My Soviet classmates avoided these forbidden pages as if they were contaminated. I was itching to peek at them, but afraid to show it. On one page only did I succeed, with my heart racing, to unglue some of the paper. Here, before me, was a photograph of the recently executed commander of the Soviet

Far Eastern Army, General Blukher, in full military regalia. I was afraid to touch the other photographs but they were doubtless those of Marshal Toukhachevskii, the brilliant commander of the Red Army, Boukharin and other old Bolsheviks also executed in 1938 on Stalin's orders.

Many of my Russian schoolmates were children of military personnel who kept much to themselves and did not mix with the natives, *zapadniki* [Westerners], as we were called. They lived in the *Voyennyi Gorodok* [military compound] – blocks of houses out of the city, separated from civilian dwellings. A few, such as the Mourashovs, lived in the centre. An Air Force lieutenant lived with his young wife and baby in a house adjacent to our yard. The Rybak family lived right above us; their 12-year-old daughter Galya was one year ahead of me in school. She played the piano very well and I was secretly 'in love' as I listened with admiration to her interminable arpeggios, which drove all adults crazy. I was too shy to address her but waited anxiously for Mother to invite the Rybaks into our home. This never happened. Unlike the Murashovs, Mother criticized the Rybaks, especially Galya's mother.

Mother's attitude toward Mrs Rybak was typical of our 'Western' women, who felt somehow superior to those *Sovietki* [Soviet women] who knew nothing of fashion and our 'Western finesse', in their clumsy *valenki* [felt boots], poor-quality, unfashionable dresses, their red berets and cheap furs. People laughed at Soviet women who bought silk nightgowns only to parade in them at local theatre galas.

During the winter of 1941, Mourashov kept repeating that there would shortly be war with Germany. He did not elaborate, but we knew from peasants treated by my father – who still kept an occasional private practice – of formidable Soviet military formations on the move towards the German border. Tanks rumbled at night through the streets of Grodno. Hundreds of planes were massed on airfields nearby. Something was in the air and BBC broadcasts, which my father tried to catch faithfully at night, spoke of an imminent German invasion of the Soviet Union. Then, in April, came news of a German move to extricate their clumsy Italian allies from certain defeat at the hands of the Greeks. Glued to the BBC, we learned that German divisions were diverted from   east to south and moving towards Greece and Yugoslavia. Father, who remembered the Balkan battles of the First World War, had a healthy respect for the military prowess of Serbian soldiers and joyfully repeated that this operation would not be easy for the Germans. He was convinced that the Germans would now postpone their planned drive into Russia by an entire year in order to give themselves enough time before the *raspoutitsa* [rainy season] made the Russian roads impassable.

As Father and Mother continued their discussions about our move to Kharkov, the wave of NKVD arrests continued into April and Marek Chorazycki was arrested. News spread that the train with the arrestees had been standing for several days on a side-track in the direction of Slobotka. One could only imagine the awful conditions under which the detainees were living in their cattle trucks. Mother managed to send Marek a package of food and necessities through someone who worked on the railway, but I wanted to go and see him myself.

It was a beautiful day of early spring, a Saturday. Mother and Nadia Lomashevitch, our housekeeper before the war, were both busily engaged in spring cleaning. The windows in the house were wide open and gusts of cool, crisp air entered the apartment from the garden. I had just come back from my Saturday morning classes and was planning to go after lunch with my best friend, Shurik Lampert, to watch a practice game for next day's soccer match, the first of three between the two most ferocious soccer adversaries in Grodno: the *Vielosipiednyi Zavod* [The Bicycle Factory] and the *Dom Krasnoi Armii* [The Red Army House]. My friends and I were on the side of the Bicycle Factory because most of its players were former members of the pre-1939 Maccabi Club. This made the Bicycle Factory *our* soccer club and we looked forward with anticipation to *our* victory. But, anxious to see my good friend Marek, I decided in a flash to sacrifice my Saturday soccer show, without telling my mother.

The transport stood in the western outskirts of the city in a small valley limited by two steep embankments. It had to be approached from the Vorstadt section of the city, over the Niemen Bridge. It was a good hour's walk from home. It took me some time to get close enough to see the train and people

who looked like toy figurines. Coming closer, I could distinguish people going in and out of the railway wagons. When I
was still closer, I could see that a few were carrying what
looked like pails of water from a nearby tap. I started my
descent to the railway track, slowly, trying not to attract attention and hoping that the soldiers would let me pass through
to the train and find Marek. But, just as I was almost down at
the level of the track, I heard a loud '*Stoi!*' [freeze!]. Two
soldiers were running towards me, waving their hands and
shouting. I saw the blue, red-rimmed caps of the NKVD. I
stopped and tried to look innocent. They approached me
shouting, 'What have you come here for, you little rascal? This
is a military zone, get back at once!' They did not look very
ferocious but they gave me a mighty scare. I turned around
and climbed the steep embankment on all fours. When I
reached the top, I ran as fast as I could without looking back.

On my way home, I thought about all the people packed into
cattle trucks without any comfort for a journey of many weeks.
How many to a cattle truck? Where was Marek? He, like Nitek,
was not in the best of health. How would he survive the
journey? I walked and thought that in a few weeks, days
perhaps, our family too would be packed into such trains and
thrown from our comfortable life into the unknown.

Back home I met an angry Mother, who had been looking
for me everywhere. Mother was living under severe
emotional stress. She was trapped between the desire to join
her family in Russia and the menace of deportation which
hung over our heads. I sensed also that something was badly
amiss between Father and her. On top of it all, Mother was
preparing for a new recital of old Russian songs, the third
since the arrival of the Soviets. This was supposed to be for a
private party and was planned as an informal evening at the
Murashovs. Murashov's boss, Colonel Nikitin and his wife,
were expected. Word spread among the air-force officers of a
performance of old Russian and gypsy songs and the number
of those interested got out of hand. Murashov's apartment
was much too small and the party was moved to the villa of
Nikitin at the military compound. All this made Mother very
nervous: *Tsiganshchina* [old gypsy love songs] were considered romantic, nihilistic and, from the communist

perspective, rotten. Singers indulging in such 'rotten bourgeois' tastes were sometimes accused of counter-revolution.
Not only those who sang but also the listeners could get into
trouble. In short, one could sing oneself into a gulag. This was,
however, far from a consistent pattern because Russians, like
the Italians, love to sing. Singing, and above all romantic
singing, is a part of the Russian soul. No tsar or commisar was
ever successful in stemming the turbulent river of Russian
music. *Tsiganshchina* were sung in private despite official
prohibition. Even staunch communists would sometimes
attend and very few would inform about this 'counterrevolu-
tionary activity'. The Murashovs had been consistently
begging Tatiana Pavlovna, as they called Mother, to sing some
Tsiganshchina and she had finally, reluctantly agreed.

She had a powerful and pure mezzo-soprano voice and
before the revolution had taken singing lessons at the
Kharkov Conservatory, at great expense to her struggling
parents. In the 1930s she gave recitals at our hotel in
Druskieniki, or at charity events for Jewish welfare organizations in Grodno. Audiences loved her. Her Yiddish renditions
of *Eili-Eili, Indele und Mendele, Oif dem Pripetchek*, her repertoire
of classic Russian songs and romances, as well as her Tsigane
love songs brought enthusiastic worshippers of her voice to a
frenzy. Flowers kept arriving after each recital, making our
apartment look like a florist's shop, and the telephone did not
stop ringing. Even old Pastor Plamsch of the Lutheran congregation, to which my *Tante* Thea Boehm belonged, would send
flowers and cases of his home-made apple wine. Cases of soft
drinks were sent by Sasha, Leicia and Havcia Slucki, brother
and sisters, the owners of the Slucki soft-drink factory. There
was little doubt, had she stayed in Russia, that Mother could
have had a brilliant career as a concert singer.

All this commotion did not impress my father, who had
little by way of musical, melodramatic or artistic inclination.
Father loved philosophy, sciences, his armchair, his pipe and
his books. He did not relish the idea of Mother being a concert
singer. Hence, mother gave up any hope of becoming a prima
donna. Her energy was devoted to the management of our
'sanatorium' at Druskieniki where, at the unanimous request
of her guests, Mother often sang at the Saturday afternoon

dances which were called the 'Five O'clock'. I was allowed with my *Tante* Thea into the vast dining room. Our neatly dressed, pretty waitresses ran to and fro, their trays laden with puddings, cakes and desserts of the week, such as Mother's famous crème brulée, always studded with candied fruit and roasted nuts, or the unique English vanilla pudding laced with thick, black-cherry syrup and 'drunk' with rum. The band played the latest dancing hits, or *schlagers* – some Yiddish, some Polish. I remember *By Mir Bist Du Shein, Das Stetele Belz and Indele und Mendele* which Mother sang first in Yiddish and then in a Polish translation.

Indele ma piekne oczy,	Indele has beautiful eyes,
Oczy jak iskry dwie.	Eyes like two sparks.
Mendele chce je calowac;	Mendele wants to kiss them;
Indele mowi nie.	Indele says 'no'.
Indele ma pelne usta,	Indele has full lips,
Usta jak wisnie dwie.	Lips like two cherries.
Mendele chce je calowac;	Mendele wants to kiss them;
Indele mowi nie.	But Indele says 'no'.

The songs were interlaced with Argentinian tangos, slow foxtrots, charlestons, and, occasionally, the slow waltzes that were called English waltzes in Poland. Recent Polish *schlager* tunes were mixed in. I remember *Ostatnia Niedziela, Jutro sie Rozstajemy* [Our Last Sunday, Tomorrow We Part], *Bo Zakochany Zlodziej Promienie Slonca Kradl* [The Thief in Love Was Stealing the Sunshine] and *Gdy Odejdziesz* [When You Leave Me].

Gdy odejdziesz, mnie zostawisz	When you leave me
Ja nie powiem wcale ze mi serce krwawisz,	I won't tell you how you have broken my heart,
Bo gdy samo zycie cos potarga,	Because when life destroys something in us,
Nie pomoze zadna skarga,	No complaint will help,
Nie pomoze nigdy nic.	Nothing will help.

It was all very romantic and couples shuffled and swirled about our dance floor. Father and Mother danced together.

Never again did I see them dance after those 'Five O'clock's' in pre-war Druskieniki.

The evening at the Nikitins' villa was a total success. Mother sang her best repertoire of *Tsiganshchina*. Among the most appreciated were songs such as *Stoiala Notch*:

Stoiala Notch,	The night was still,
Lunoi byl polon sad.	The orchard full of moonlight.
Sidieli my s toboi,	We were together,
V gostinnoi bez ogniei.	Enveloped by the night.
Royal byl vies otkryt,	The piano was open,
I struny v niem drozhali	Its strings quivering
Kak i serdtsa ou nas...	Like our hearts...

These *dousheshtchipatelnyie* ['soul-pinching'] languid tunes were perfectly expressed by Mother's warm soprano and she was given a standing ovation.

Father did not attend the concert. In fact, things were not all that good between my parents. Father longed for peace and quiet; Mother was always in motion. After her return from Russia, things had got worse and I often saw Mother crying and confiding in Nadia, our Byelorussian housekeeper.

3   *Nadia and* Tante *Thea*

Nadiezhda Mikhailovna Lomashevitch – Nadia, our Byelorussian housekeeper – was a lonely soul. Tall and plain, her angular features had a rather masculine appearance. Now in her mid-forties she was still single. Very concerned with problems of social justice and an ardent communist, she was elated when the Red Army entered Grodno. She always found ways of explaining the Soviets' misdeeds: arrests, deportations, the blacklisting of prominent citizens, the high price of essential goods. She would argue with my sceptical parents that the Bolsheviks were committed to social justice and that the loss of our property in Druskieniki and Grodno, although unfortunate – she knew so well how much sweat and toil my parents had poured into it – was necessary in the large scheme of things. However, disappointed with the reality of Soviet life, Nadia progressively lost her zest for defending the Soviet rule. She was troubled by the unjust and harsh treatment of blacklisted people and by the long jail sentences meted out for trivial offences, such as being five minutes late for work. She was appalled by the conditions under which people were sent on transports to Russia. She tried to get some food to Marek and came back profoundly shaken. But, above all, she was distressed by the lack of news from her sister Mania, who lived in Moscow.

Nadia's life had been difficult. She was born in Poland to a rather poor but proud Byelorussian family. Her father, a school teacher in pre-war Poland, tried hard to give his two daughters an education. The older daughter, Mania, became an architect, while Nadia graduated from high school, a rather rare occurrence in those days. The family, like so many Byelorussians, did not sympathize with the semi-Fascist rule of Polish colonels, which oppressed Poland's minorities. Nadia and Mania became communist sympathizers and dreamt of social justice; they ardently believed in the communist experience just across the border. Both sisters were in trouble when Mother met Nadia: Mania was in jail (for communist activities) at the penal camp of Bereza Kartuska and Nadia was under police surveillance. Nadia's father had just died and she was having to support her ailing mother. Her personal life was also at a low point as she had recently broken up with the man she intended to marry.

Mother recognized Nadia for the energetic and intelligent woman that she was and hired her as supervisor of personnel at our hotel in Druskieniki. Nadia worked there during the three months of the summer season. An expert in the art of embroidery and decoration, she designed tablecloths, bed linen and curtains for the sanatorium during the winter. Mother helped her in this task and soon became almost as skilled as Nadia. There were different designs of tablecloths used for different occasions and countless hours were spent on embroideries that featured floral and other colourful themes from Russian and Ukrainian folklore.

Mother paid Nadia very well and was generous with her, as with the rest of the staff. A warm friendship developed between the two women, a tie so strong that Nadia became almost a member of our family. She worshipped my mother and this somehow bothered me: I thought that she pushed their relationship a bit too far. When my nanny *Tante* Thea, a German citizen, was arrested and expelled from Poland in December 1938, Mother decided that Nadia would take care of me. But I could not allow anybody to replace my beloved *Tante* and resented Nadia. I called her *bolszewiczka* [the Bolshevik] and teased her, saying 'Why don't you go to Minsk?' Yet, for all our quarrels, I eventually learned to like and respect Nadiezhda Mikhailovna.

Nadia was happy when the Red Army came to Grodno in 1939; she called them 'liberators'. Under the bigoted rule of the Polish colonels she had suffered both as a Communist and as a Byelorussian, and she had also suffered for the Jews, for us, her 'adopted family'. Her sister Mania, after being released by the Poles from Bereza Kartuska in 1935, had illegally crossed the border into the Soviet Union. From occasional letters, Nadia knew that Mania had married Kostya, an architect like herself. The couple lived and worked in Moscow. In 1936 Mania gave birth to a boy, Misha, but in 1938 Mania and her family suddenly disappeared and Nadia's letters were returned postmarked 'addressee unknown'.

Now that they were both under Soviet authority, Nadia hoped to be able to find her sister. However, in the spring of 1941 she received from one of Mania's friends in Moscow the address of the now five-year-old Misha – a children's home somewhere in the Don–Bass region. Nadia tried desperately to learn what had happened to Mania. She finally discovered that Mania's husband had been arrested in 1937 as an 'enemy of the nation' and Mania had disappeared six months later. Misha had been placed in a children's home and, told almost nothing about his origin and his parents, was raised as an orphan by the Soviet state. Nadia was discouraged from communicating with him. She was heartbroken and sank into a deep melancholy.

We were all sitting around the big round table in our dining room, Father, Mother, Lenka, Rysio, Nadia and myself, that evening in May 1941 after Mother's triumphal recital. I was sitting next to Nadia. The apartment was awash with the scents and colours of lilac, tulips and narcissi. The sun cast its last golden-red glow through the open window. Carried on the crisp evening air were the noises of the town: voices from the street, the rumble of cart wheels on cobble stones, a church bell announcing an evening service, and Galya's evening piano practise which had already begun. Our meal was simple as usual: an omelette, various breads with butter and cheese and steaming, strong tea. Our old German Shepherd dog, Asio, was curled up and fast asleep. After dinner the men tuned in to the BBC, behind closed doors. Listening to foreign broadcasts was forbidden; there were no radios for sale except for a Soviet model which could be tuned only to a few Soviet stations. Tampering with a radio was a crime. Fortunately, our 'Western' Telefunken could easily catch on short waves any station around the world. The men were discussing the situation in Greece and in the Balkans and the massive German bombardment of Malta and Crete. The big question was whether the Germans would attack the Soviet Union that summer, as some BBC analysts suggested, or whether it was an English ploy to bring the Soviet Union into an unwanted conflict with Germany, as Soviet analysts intimated.

There were rumours – which Tass denounced as unfriendly towards the Soviet Union – of German divisions on the move towards the Soviet border. Father did not believe in a German attack at this late date; there were barely five months left before the onslaught of the autumn rains – the *raspoutitsa* – which would transform Russia into a vast quagmire, and barely six months before the onset of winter. Besides, Father argued, at this late date the summer crops could be easily destroyed by the retreating armies and the harvest lost for the Germans. Rysio held a different view; he thought a German attack was imminent.

Now, when I think of this time in May 1941, only five weeks before the German attack on the Soviet Union, I am amazed by the composure of the adults weighing the prospect of a German invasion. Everybody expected the Germans to break rapidly through the Russian defences. My father was fond of calling Russia 'a colossus on legs of clay', especially after the disastrous performance of the Red Army in Finland. And in Grodno, barely 60 kilometres from the German border, nobody was thinking of escaping a possible German occupation. We were caught between the terror of the NKVD and of Nazi racism. Being sent to Siberia or Kazakhstan in cattle trucks seemed equally distasteful as an alternative to Nazi rule.

And then came the day when my little universe was shaken. Everything was forgotten; the international situation, the possible war, even the NKVD arrests and deportations, all became irrelevant. Father had an affair! The woman was a nurse at the hospital. Mother found out and it was horrible. She refused to let Father into the bedroom; there was not a moment of respite as Mother cried and lamented. She was talking of divorce. How I wished that my older brother Tolo were home to explain to me what was going on, to talk some sense into both of them! But Tolo was far away in Lvov and I was utterly alone and helpless. I tried to talk to Father but he brushed me aside; he said that I was too young to understand and, although I worshipped my father, I sided with Mother. I prayed to God every night: 'Let it be war! Let the Germans attack! Maybe this will bring my parents together.' And then came the climax: Mother swallowed a tube of Veronal sleeping pills, had her stomach pumped and was very, very sick. The shock of Mother's attempted suicide brought Father back home, attending to her every evening as her fever soared. In the first week of June, Mother felt better and I thought that the crisis was over.

This was one of the most acutely traumatic episodes of my childhood, second only to the loss of my *Tante* Thea. *Tante* had been with me for as long as I could remember. She had always worked as a governess for Jewish families, most recently in London. My parents hired her in 1929 to help take care of the expected new addition – me. *Tante* held me when I was an infant, she taught me to walk and later to read; she tucked me in every night, reading from Grimm and Andersen fairy tales or from the stories of the two little pranksters *Max und Morritz*. She was with me when, a sickly child, I would run a high fever; she held my hand every time I had my eardrums pierced to relieve my frequent ear infections and would scream with pain. She was by my side when my infected tonsils were removed. She gave me little sweets (*Pflasterchen*) to comfort me. She was there with me when, wearing a kipah or a hat, I would light the Hanukkah candles; she played *draidle* with me. Every year at Christmas she decorated a small Christmas tree for me – which we called a Hanukkah bush – and she put presents into a sock in the chimney, so that her *Buebchen* would not feel deprived. It was a sort of a Jewish-Christian mish-mash, but it felt good.

She could also be very strict. I had to behave, eat my cream of wheat, cauliflower and spinach, drink milk with honey and a health concoction composed of egg yolks, sugar and butter called *goguel-moguel*, all of which I hated. I had to get up early in the morning, do my assigned chores and my homework. Only then was I allowed to play. When I misbehaved, which was quite often, *Tante* called me Alexânder instead of *Buebchen*, and I hated that too! When I was really impossible *Tante* meted out corporal punishment, three to ten lashes on my naked buttocks with a bunch of twigs called *die Rute*. She kept this instrument out of my reach on the top of the cupboard. Most of the time such extremes were avoided as *Tante* only had to remind me, with a deep, grave note in her voice: 'Alexânder, where is *die Rute*?' But, on occasion, I had to take down my trousers and lie on the table where the punishment was executed.

Some whipping occasions I still vividly remember. I was about six years old when Mother travelled to Vienna to take a course at the famous Pupp's School of Cooking to improve on her menus at our hotel. She came back in high spirits, with a lot of presents for everybody. For me she brought a magnificent Tyrolean outfit: green leather shorts and a traditional Tyrolean jacket, a tie and a green hat. I was undoubtedly the only child in Grodno with such an outfit. Words cannot express my hatred of this garment which attracted the attention of passersby and children. Especially vexing to me was to see Mother's friends and acquaintances displaying admiration and envy: 'How beautiful, how interesting; what a magnificent outfit; isn't he splendid in it!' Children stared at me and laughed. Every time I had to put on my Tyrolean costume I felt like a little circus monkey at a show and would refuse to wear it. Mother could not understand my stubbornness. 'All the way from Vienna I brought this brat such a beautiful outfit and he won't wear it!' I would then be whipped and forced to submit. Thank goodness I soon outgrew this horrible ensemble.

Another battle was frequently over the enemas I was given when my stomach was upset. Often Mother and *Tante* together could hardly manage as I screamed, twitched, squirmed and jerked to defend myself before the administration of the pint of warm, soapy water. Sometimes Nadia and our cook had to be called in to help before I could be overpowered. The punishment for such an ungodly upheaval was five or six lashes with *die Rute*.

Despite these little upsets it was good to be with *Tante*. She was there to protect and to love me; I was her *Buebchen*, her little boy, and I saw my universe through her. I planned to marry her as soon as I grew up. At the *Pastorat*, the rectory of the small Lutheran community of Grodno where *Tante* would occasionally take me on Sundays, everybody would tease me: *Buebchen* cannot marry *Tante* Thea because she is already *verlobt* [betrothed] to *Der Dume Bernie* [stupid Bernie], a retarded man who lived and worked at the estate of Pastor

Plamsch. 'No, *Tante* will marry me, not Bernie!', I cried, jealous and miserable.

Pastor Plamsch, the head of the Lutheran congregation of Grodno, was a handsome 80-year-old gentleman with a flowing white mane of hair and a thick, curled-up white moustache. He was full of life and had a spring in his step in spite of his age. His wife, *die Frau Pastorin*, was from Baltic Curland nobility. She appeared much older than he and had to be wheeled around the *Pastorat*. On many a Sunday, I was left to play in the beautiful garden of the *Pastorat* while *Tante* went to the services in the church. The garden was full of flowers arranged in beds around a big veranda attached to the building, where *Herr Pastor* and *Frau Pastorin* enjoyed the breeze during the summer. Further away was the orchard, brimming with apple, pear and cherry trees. Quiet, shady alleys of old chestnut and oak trees interspersed with thick flowering bushes provided an ideal ground for various games. I walked these alleys listening to the twitter of birds and playing with Kaeth and Fritzl, the grandchildren of *Tante* Kazin, a friend of *Tante* Thea. In winter I stayed inside the *Pastorat*, which was full of wonders: big rooms with spiral staircases, walls covered with paintings of men with moustaches and traditionally dressed women. They all stared sternly at me and sometimes frightened me. Grandfather clocks ticked and there were caged birds throughout the house, filling the air with their cooing and fluttering. Some German-speaking parakeets were the main attraction, but the house was also full of other exotic birds – canaries, swallows, owls, and some beautiful specimens which Pastor Plamsch had brought from Africa.

Tante used to join me after services and we would move to the dining room for *Kuchen und Kaffee*. A marvellous aroma of coffee pervaded the Pastorat and the cake, the famous *Sandkuchen*, was out of this world! *Tante* Thea often hummed *'Garnichts schmeckt so gut wie Kuchen mit Kaffee'* [Nothing tastes as good as cake with coffee]. I sat next to her at a long oak table covered with a snow-white tablecloth. The silverware glistened; dishes and cups with the rich designs of Meissen china looked beautiful and solemn. Around the table sat the guests of the Plamsches, some with their progeny, some single: *Tante* Kazin, *Tante* Uli, *Tante* Johanna, the Muellers with their pretty 11-year-old daughter Katharina, with whom I was secretly 'in love' but who did not even grace me, the *Buebchen*, with as much as a glance – and others whose names I do not remember. *Herr Pastor* sat at one end of the table while *Frau Pastorin*, at the opposite end, was in her wheelchair. There was also their retarded son Poussie, who lived at the *Pastorat*, and spoke in a high-pitched voice. Their second son, Fritz, was never there; he lived in Koenigsberg. He was a Nazi, an enthusiastic supporter of Hitler, and an embarrassment to Pastor *Plamsch* and *Frau Pastorin*.[1]

Der Dume Bernie brought in the steaming coffee and whipped cream. Several cakes were on the table and the guests were soon into the latest gossip of the Grodno Lutheran community. After coffee Pastor Plamsch often took me to his study where he kept his famous collection of stamps of Middle Lithuania, arranged in tightly packed rows of albums. Each of the thousands of stamps was categorized, dated and priced. It was one of the best collections of Lithuanian stamps in the world and he had received awards at various international exhibitions. The medals were displayed on shelves. Pastor would give me stamps for my starter collection and show me the countries of their origin on a world map. I could spend a long time looking at the stamps and maps without getting bored. I learned the geography of tiny and exotic countries, like Touva or Montenegro, which I could point out on a map without hesitation, to the whispers of admiration from grown-ups.

At the end of our visit, Pastor would go down to his cellar and bring a bottle of his own home-made apple wine or *Mied*, a delicious golden drink made from fermented honey, a favourite beverage of the Polish and Baltic gentry. '*Ein kleines Geschenk fuer meine liebe frau Doktor*' [A small present for my dear Mrs Blumstein], he used to say. He loved Mother's singing and never missed an opportunity to go to her recitals. Beside the world of stamps and geography, Pastor Plamsch introduced me to the world of birds, flowers and plants; he made me love nature. I will always remember him with fondness.

---

[1] I learned later that he became an important person in the Nazi party. Now, with hindsight, I wonder how many Nazi agents operated from the Lutheran congregation of Pastor Plamsch.

One evening in December 1938, two uniformed policemen came to our door and arrested *Tante* Thea. My *Tante* was arrested by the Polish police like a criminal! Eyes red from crying, I went with Father from police station to police station, with a thermos of hot coffee and sandwiches, to look for her. I was desperate. Hanukkah and Christmas came and went, but they meant nothing to me as my *Tante* was not there. Father explained that she had gone back to her family in Koenigsberg. He showed me on the map that Koenigsberg was not that far, only some 250 kilometres away. But this did little to appease my despair. I remained heartsick and inconsolable for a very long time and whenever I thought of *Tante* I would weep.

Those warm Sundays spent in Grodno's *Pastorat* with my beloved *Tante* and Pastor Plamsch were to stay in my memory for a long time. Pastor Plamsch died in 1939 after a short illness. The Lutheran congregation of Grodno disintegrated after most of the congregants with German citizenship were expelled from Poland in December 1938. The remaining Lutherans, those with Polish citizenship, fled in September 1939, across the border to Germany.

4   Before the Storm

Days flew by, warm and sunny days. I was still shaken by the recent upheavals at home but June was here in all its splendour. School holidays were already upon us and I was proud of having passed my tests and graduated into the fifth grade of the Russian *diesiatiletka* [ten-grade school]. I was now preoccupied by the impending departure of my dearest playmate and best friend, Shurik Lampert, as his mother Lena was finally about to join her sister in Moscow. Our friendship went back to our kindergarten years and we were bound 'until death us part' through a blood oath ceremony.

Shurik's parents were divorced. His father had remarried and left for Baghdad, while Shurik and his mother remained in Grodno. They lived in a one-room apartment on Listowskiego Street, just a few blocks from our home. Shurik's father sent him beautiful stamps of Iraq, Kuwait, Bahrain, and his stamp collection was famous for his Arab stamps. Shurik's mother was a chain-smoker who often left him locked in their room while she was out playing cards and he had to take care of himself from a tender age. He was almost two years older than me and one year ahead of me in school, an *otlitchnik* (for straight 'A's student). He was a very intelligent and resourceful boy and I looked up to him. I felt guilty for having so much more than he, and for being so pampered; I had both parents, a wealthy home, a room full of toys, just for me. I even had a big brother who came back from France with a funny little moustache, like Errol Flynn's. I admired and worshipped my big brother.

Before the war, Shurik had attended the Hebrew *Tarbut* school and through him I got to know many *Tarbutniks* who in time became my friends and playmates too. We played soccer and were organized into gangs (we were then all under the influence of a wonderful Hungarian book for boys, *Chlopcy z*

Placu Broni [Boys from the Weapons' Square]). We fought Polish hooligans, the *Shkotzim*, who yelled anti-Semitic obscenities, threw stones at us and tried to beat us up. Shurik and I were enamoured with the same Jewish girl, Basia, who lived only a few blocks away on Brigitska Street. I secretly admired Shurik's ways with girls; had I been a girl, I would have chosen Shurik without hesitation. With Basia I had no chance, but with Galya Rybak I had a small advantage over Shurik – a good ear for songs, which Shurik did not.

Mother had made me take piano lessons for almost two years following my not too successful attempts at playing the violin. My teacher, Mrs Reinhart, did not make those lessons easy. Very nervous and impatient, she was no beauty and reminded me of a dried-out herring. When my scales and arpeggios were not smooth enough she made hand signs and twitched her mouth with obvious disgust. And, when I tried desperately to please her by rolling my fingers over the keyboard, she suddenly shouted in my ear, *Staccato!*, while jerking my wrist upwards. After two years of this I knew that I would not become a concert pianist but I was able to play with one finger some songs from popular films, such as the recent *Istrebitieli* [Fighterplanes]. When I heard that Galya was home (her room was just above my piano), my seduction was simple and direct. I would open the window of our living room and sing while hitting the piano keys with my index finger.

V delekii krai tovarishch ulietaiet, rodnyie vetry v sled za nim letiat.	To a far away country the comrade is flying, carried by friendly winds.
Lioubimyi gorod v siniei dymkie taiet	Beloved city disappears in a blue haze.
Lioubimyi dom, zelenyi sad i niezhnyi vzgliad.	Beloved home, the green orchard and loving eyes.

The effect was often magical, for Galya would appear on the balcony above our living room and extend an invitation to sing together. 'Sasha this is nice, let's sing something together.'

How I loved to be called Sasha! How sweet it was to be equal to others! At my former pre-war, all-Polish school my classmates and teachers had never called me by my first name. Classmates sometimes used a derisive tone of voice with emphasis on the Yiddish drawl, 'Blumshteeein'. While the other children were called Jozio, Zdzisio, Tereska, or Bozenka, my teachers just called me 'Blumstein'. This reminded me that I was different, a stranger. I became very sensitive and would overreact to words that often meant no harm. To be called 'Alik' or 'Sasha' by my Russian classmates and, especially by Galya, had a sweet ring to it. True, I was a *zapadnik* [Westerner], not quite *nash* (ours), but unlike at my Polish *cwiczeniowka*, my belonging to the human race was never questioned by my Russian friends at school.

Shurik did not have this problem because, like most Jewish children, he was enrolled in a Jewish school – the *Tarbut*, with Hebrew as the primary language. With the arrival of the Soviets, all schools became either Russian, Byelorussian or Polish. Hebrew was forbidden; Yiddish was only tolerated. *Tarbut* became a Russian school, and now Shurik and I had Russian as our common school language. We recited Pushkin and Lermontov, borrowed Russian books from each other and sometimes did our homework together. I admired the accomplishments of my senior friend in subjects still unknown to me, such as zoology or botany. And now Shurik was leaving for good. I wrote a farewell poem for him in Polish; a long, overcooked poem inspired by Pushkin, it accurately reflected my sorrow.

But June was so magnificent and balmy that year; no school and so much to enjoy. I forgot all the drama and tension at home as soon as I was in the warm sunshine with my friends. I played with Kolya Murashov and also with Mirek Tropkrynski, a delicate third grader and one year my junior, whose father was a dentist and who lived not far from my house. Mirek treated me with the admiration due to my seniority and I liked that. There was a circle of other kids. We played in the spacious garden which our house shared with the neighbouring obstetric hospital on former Rydza Smiglego Street. The garden was full of blooming lilacs, apple trees and gooseberry bushes. We invited Galya and her friends to sing the latest hits with us. We played 'Whites' and 'Reds' (a sort of Soviet 'Cowboys and Indians') and hide-and-seek, and we also played chess. In the yard adjacent to the garden we played our favourite handball game, 'between two fires', and we played soccer or volleyball. At weekends, we attended soccer games for the championship of BSSR (Byelorus Soviet Socialist Republic). Our favourite team was, of course, the Bicycle Factory. As in the previous year, it was opposed by the Grodno DKA (*Dom Krasnoi Armii*), the Red Army House team. The victor was to proceed to the capital of Byelorus, Minsk, to have a crack at the championship of BSSR. The Bicycle Factory members were local Jewish boys who played a solid soccer game and respected the rules. The DKA players were Red Army military who played a normal game as long as they were winning; when things were going badly they resorted to brutish tactics consisting of kicking the ankles of their opponents – we called this 'shoeing the team'. The umpires, afraid of the Soviets, ignored this foul play while penalizing the Bicyclists for the slightest fault. Our lads would usually do well in the first half but then the entire team would be 'shoed' by the DKA during the second half. 'Our' team would end up losing the game, with the majority of players leaving the field limping. We vented our fury by yelling in Polish, '*Sedzia kalosz!*', which meant, approximately, 'To hell with the umpire!'

The weather was so warm that on occasional Sundays Father would take me, as in the summers past, kayaking on the River Niemen. We let ourselves be carried by the current for five to six kilometres towards the beautiful pine forest of Pyszki. Along the route the river wound its way through the steep sandy banks, peppered with spruce and pine, behind which one could see the gleaming white hills of the Chalk Mountains, an old formation of limestone. At Pyszki, we turned back and worked our way against the current. Actually, Father did the work and I tried not to get in the way. It felt so good to be there with my father, trying to coordinate my movements with the powerful, rhythmic strokes of his double-ended paddle. Slowly the city approached with its bridges and church spires on which the evening sun cast an orange glow.

On a steep hill overlooking the river stood the sixteenth-century castle of the Hungarian king of Poland, Stefan Batory. The castle was beautiful with its ramparts and drawbridges. The mouths of cannons visible from the river reminded one of past battles. Batory had built here an outpost against the

Muscovites and, so ran the story in Polish history books, defeated his enemies and protected Poland from Russian invasions. In our Soviet history books the references to the defeat of the Muscovites were deleted.

Sometimes along our way when the sun was hot we would land on a sandy embankment, pull our kayak ashore and bathe in the cool, brisk waters of the Niemen. Father swam the crawl 'Cossack' style, with his shoulders, neck and head emerging from the water and with an outstretched palm beating the surface at each stroke. I was not much of a swimmer, especially against the swift current of the river, but my father was a patient teacher and I became proficient enough to keep him company for a few minutes on shallow stretches. I was very proud of my newly acquired swimming skills and burned to show them off to my friends, classmates and, of course, Galya.

This I could do at the town beach, where I would find many of my friends on hot days. The beach was always crowded with families. Izak Kobrowski, who had married my aunt Ada, was a frequent visitor. Uncle Izak was unusually strong and he was not modest about it. He exhibited his Herculean talents by lifting huge stones (and the occasional lady!) and I remember him winning contests with other muscular men who were bigger and taller than he.

Izak Kobrowski – Itchke, as he was called in Yiddish – was a man of humble background. His father, a mushroom merchant from the village of Marcinkance located at the edge of a dense Lithuanian forest between Wilno and Grodno, had 11 sons and one daughter. The modest means of the family did not allow for an education but every child was taught a trade. Izak specialized in wood and lumber. Mother told me that one night he was brought to our clinic with acute appendicitis. Father operated on him and he was nursed by Aunt Ada, who lived with us and helped out at the clinic. She fell in love with this 'house of a man', so strong and full of life. It was the second time that appendicitis acquired a romantic ring in our family! Ada did not impress Itchke with her beauty – she was not blessed with that attribute – but he was overcome by her good nature and sweetness. Itchke proposed to Ada after a very short time and asked my father for her hand in marriage. They were married in 1933 and my cousin Aviva was born in 1934.

Izak by nature was a ladies' man but Aunt Ada did not appear to mind and their relationship remained strong. Izak loved Ada and never took his affairs too seriously – he used to call them *seitensprungs* (literally 'jumps to the side'). However, Mother was cross with Itchke for the gossip that was 'spoiling the name of the family'. She also considered that Ada had entered into a misalliance by marrying a man so much below her in social status and education. Mother and Izak, both being hot tempered, were not on the best of terms. Mother found him *luftmench* [unreliable], but Father got on well with him. To me, Izak became a hero when he lifted in his teeth the big oaken table in our dining room (the table was first secured with a rope which he gripped in his teeth). I was proud to have him in the family.

Grandmother Blumstein, who had lived with us until Ada's wedding, moved in with the Kobrowskis, near the Grodno City Theatre in the vicinity of the municipal garden and of President Hoover's Square. Grandmother received a widow's pension from the Polish government because Grandfather had for many years before the First World War worked as a school teacher in Plock and in Ciechanow. I visited her quite often and looked forward to my visits. She always gave me a *zloty*, which could buy a whole week of Tarzan, Gordon the Astronaut or Popeye the Sailor comic strips, or several little halvah bars, or even a box of 'slim' lead soldiers. Once a year, around my birthday, she gave me an entire silver dollar which was worth five *zlotys*. This was a fortune for which I could get a big box of 'fat' soldiers on 'fat' horses. She called me sweet names like *robaczku* [little worm].

Grandmother had been stone-deaf for as long as I could remember, apparently as a result of shell shock during a German bombardment of Ciechanow in 1915. She liked to read but it seemed to me that she read the same book over and over again. She repeated endlessly: '*Straszne to slowo wojna*' [the word 'war' is a terrible thing]. As I was not impressed either by Grandmother's or by Aunt Ada's cooking, *Tante* Thea always brought along my favourite lunch in a small covered dish: hamburger and fried potatoes. Poor Grandmother was slowly losing her grip on reality and I visited her less and less as school and playmates became an increasing part of my life.

And the month of June was rushing by, exceptionally sunny and beautiful. As Tolstoy wrote, 'happy, unforgettable, and irretrievable is the time of childhood'. After a full day of fun and games, I was exhausted and swiftly collapsed into bed after supper without giving a thought to the storm that was gathering ominously on the horizon. I was fast asleep as Father and Rysio played chess late into the night while waiting impatiently for the the latest BBC news. There were reports of massive German military concentrations along the entire Soviet-German border and warnings of an impending German attack; and denials by TASS blaming the 'bourgeois circles' for spreading false rumours 'to poison the friendly relations between the Soviet Union and Germany'. Father, who was perplexed both by the Germans choosing such a late date for the invasion, defying all logic of strategic thinking, and the frantic Soviet denials, just asked: 'Have they all gone mad?'

**PARTITION OF POLAND
September, 1939**

5   Invasion

Sunday, 22 June 1941: a boom reverberated and rolled; the house shook and small pieces of plaster fell to the floor. I opened my eyes out of a deep sleep. What was that? Was it thunder? I pulled the blanket over my head and continued my dream, but the rumbling persisted and again the house shook. Suddenly a loud crashing noise drove me out of bed, my heart pounding. Had we been hit by lightning?

I still remembered the summer of 1939 in Druskieniki just before the outbreak of the war, when the roof of our hotel was hit by lightning. Most of our guests had departed, and I was sitting in the big dining hall with Mother, Nadia and the few remaining guests. The day was stormy, it was pouring with rain and thunder rumbled overhead. I had always been afraid of thunder and was counting the time between the flashes of lightning and the booms of thunder. The lightning was still striking quite far away, maybe on the Lithuanian side of the Niemen. Suddenly a ball of fire appeared at one of the big picture windows, followed immediately by a crashing, deafening blast. The lights went out and the smell of burning permeated the room. We scrambled out in panic. The lightning had hit the antenna, perforating the roof with a big hole. Luckily the heavy rain had protected the wooden structure from the spread of fire and no major harm was done, but this incident gave me a mighty scare and decidedly confirmed my dread of thunderstorms.

Was this another one? I approached the window of my room which overlooked the back yard and the garden. The weak, grey light of dawn was seeping through the curtains. I pulled them wide open and looked at the sky; it was pale blue with a tinge of red, not a trace of clouds. I opened the window. Fragrant gusts of acacia and linden enhanced by the morning dew filled my lungs – the dawn of a hot summer's day. What

41

was this rumble, sometimes near, sometimes coming from afar?

I could already hear Mother and Father talking in their bedroom. Father said, 'It could be war.' Stepan Grigoryevitch Murashov, in his pyjamas, was stepping into the yard, carrying field binoculars. Across the yard, the young air force lieutenant greeted Stepan and pointed at something in the sky. The roll and rumble had now subsided but we were all too excited to go back to bed and went out into the yard. The young lieutenant insisted loudly: 'These are manoeuvres.'

The sun was now rising, its light cast obliquely. A red-orange glow enveloped the side of the yard and garden facing the open street. 'It will be another scorcher,' said Murashov. It was all quiet now. I was sleepy and was just about to crawl back into bed when I heard a rumble and a screech of brakes just below the windows of our living room. A heavy truck was there, engine running. The sound of boots on the stairs, loud voices in Russian and – a roar of the engine, a screech of tyres – the truck was gone.

'They came to take Murashov,' I heard Mother saying. By now we were all wide awake and joined the other people who were already in the yard: Varvara Petrovna and Kolya, Galya's father, the air-force lieutenant, fully dressed, with his wife holding their baby; some nurses and patients from the maternity ward of the Women's Hospital adjacent to our house. Varvara Petrovna said that Stepan had to report to headquarters so hastily that he left in his underwear, putting on his uniform on the way to the airfield. 'I still hope this is not war,' she said. A short while later another truck stopped in front of our gate and two soldiers ran into the yard. 'It must be for me,' the lieutenant said. He kissed his wife, waved good-bye and the truck was off.

A feeble drone from afar grew stronger by the second: planes approaching. A brief wailing of sirens followed and suddenly a burst of crashing noises sent us running in panic back into the house. White puffs of smoke appeared in the still pale sky. 'This is anti-aircraft fire,' said my father. 'The firing battery must be located not far from here.'

The crashing and banging merged into one giant cacophony with the ever-stronger and uneven hum of approaching aircraft. Suddenly, they were over our heads and a frightening whistle and whine tore the air above us, followed by deafening explosions. The ground shook as we took cover, flat on the floor of the dining room. Windows were breaking and glass was flying. The crashing and banging continued for a while, then stopped, and the hum of planes became more and more distant. As the noise subsided, Father ordered us out of the house and into the garden. We rushed outside, dragging our blankets. Even our two lovebirds, Lenka and Rysio, were running. Rysio was brushing aside the lock of dark hair which invariably kept falling over his glasses, a sign of tenseness which I knew so well from his losing chess games. Blankets were comfortably installed amid acacias, linden trees and gooseberry bushes. The sun had risen by now but the garden was still cool. The bushes were full of the still-green fruit. The linden trees were in full bloom and, together with the acacias, filled the whole garden with a delightful scent.

Rysio said excitedly that he had just seen a truck coming from Piaskowa Street to evacuate the Rybaks; the whole family was leaving – Father, Mother, Galya and little Lyonya. 'This is war and the situation must be bad. They have been caught literally with their pants down,' he said.

The planes were gone and we savoured the silence. Nadia brought a big pot of coffee, sugar and milk and we all drank from the same cup. I was filled with excitement: if this is war, then so far it is just a lot of noise and a few broken windows. The family here in the garden, with Varvara Petrovna and Kolya, drinking coffee – a sort of a forced picnic – it could be worse.

'Here, here they are coming again,' said Rysio.

'Matviei, Matviei, where are you?' shouted Mother. 'Come here, they are coming again!' Father was slowly crossing our yard from the street into the garden. Suddenly, the terrifying wailing of sirens resumed, merging with a distant drone of approaching planes. The deafening sound of the anti-aircraft batteries resumed somewhere behind our house. The explosions started again.

'Keep your heads low!' shouted Father as the whining and whistling filled the air. Heaven and earth shook with a thunder of explosions. I started to tremble all over: this must really be war! What is going to happen to us? I was lying flat with my arms around my head, my whole body pressed into the ground, smelling the raw dampness of the earth.

'Here they are again, duck for God's sake!' yelled Rysio, who was losing his composure. And again this dreadful whistling sound, and explosions rocking everything around. The acrid smell of smoke filled the air. 'God, please let us come out of this alive,' I prayed.

A few minutes later the planes were gone. The sky was covered with white puffs that swelled into strange shapes before slowly dissipating. A column of black smoke was rising from the direction of Listowskiego Street. Something must have been hit nearby. Rysio's face was pale, his hair falling over his eyes as he cleaned earth and grass from his glasses. He was trembling. Mother sobbed: 'They will kill us today!' Varvara Petrovna was crying. I was suddenly cold and shivering. Only Nadia, Lenka and Father appeared calm. The pillar of smoke nearby was growing in size; it rose beyond the building of the hospital. We soon learned that a nearby house had been hit by a bomb, and people had been killed and wounded.

A car stopped in front of our house and a policeman came into the garden, summoning Father to the hospital. 'The emergency clinic is already filled with casualties. All medical personnel are mobilized; you are to report immediately,' said the policeman. Father was ready; he ordered us to stay in the garden, promised to be back as soon as possible, kissed us goodbye and was off. We went into our street to watch him leave. It was an eerie sight: the streets looked deserted, the pavements were covered in splintered glass, in the sunshine. From time to time, a truck with police, soldiers or civilians drove by at full speed, horns blaring. Columns of dark smoke rose from the corner of Listowskiego where a three-storey house had been obliterated less than an hour ago.

Father was gone; I felt alone, fearing for him and for us without him. I recalled Stepan Murashov mentioning that a prime bombing target for the Germans in Grodno would be the railway bridge across the Niemen. The Seventh City Hospital, where father worked, was in close proximity to the bridge. I went back as Mother called, 'Alik, Alik where are you, come back at once!'

Again the yowl of sirens. The growing hum of the approaching bombers, flying much lower than previously; the earth shook again, the bombs this time falling further away. People were running from the Women's Hospital across the garden. The neighbouring anti-aircraft battery opened up with a deafening salvo. I pressed my body into the ground. The planes were gone but the drone of engines hung in the air. More planes were coming and, furiously, the anti-aircraft batteries continued their fire. The cloudless sky was now completely covered with white puffs of smoke. Here, here I could see them... one, two, three, five, six: two formations of three planes were rapidly approaching. They were now over our heads, a terrifying sound like wailing and a whine growing in intensity. I pressed my body and face into the ground once more. The earth shook again and again. The dry, crashing sound of anti-aircraft guns pierced my eardrums. This seemed to last for ever as the Stukas hung over our city like evil birds of prey.

'Where are our fighters?' cried Varvara Petrovna in despair. Kolya was silent at her side. We learned later that not a single Soviet fighter plane took off from the military airfield to challenge the invaders: they were either without fuel or destroyed on the ground.

The hum of planes was already receding and the furious *ack-ack* barking of artillery had stopped when a strong voice called out in Russian: 'Varvara Petrovna Murashov, where are you?' A stocky military man stood at the entrance to the garden. Varvara ran towards him with Kolya. She returned a few minutes later to say goodbye. A truck had been sent by her husband to evacuate them to the east. She cried, we all kissed farewell and this is how I saw my friend Kolya Murashov for the last time. All my thoughts, however, were with Father; he had left just when the bombers were coming in low. The explosions came from the direction of the bridges over the Niemen, not far from the Seventh City Hospital where he was heading.

It was almost nine o'clock, the fourth hour of the war. Nadia and Lenka went to the kitchen to prepare breakfast. I admired both women for their coolness, functioning as if nothing much had happened. In contrast, Rysio was ashen and Mother was sobbing and kept repeating, 'How are things in Lvov with Tolo? Is Matviei all right? What will become of us?' As for me, my juvenile excitement evaporated with the bombs falling close and I had no appetite for breakfast.

Here was Nadia coming with a tray – coffee, steaming milk, bread, eggs and cheese. She put down the tray and filled the cups with coffee. Nobody was hungry. 'Eat, Alik,' Nadia urged, 'you have to have strength for the coming day.' We all ate in silence. A few yards away from us, an elderly Polish couple from a neighbouring house, Mr and Mrs Krzyszewski, came into the garden. They spread out thick blankets and pillows and made themselves comfortable next to Rysio.

'Maybe they'll let us catch some sleep before the Ruskis are driven out of here,' said Mr Krzyszewski. 'They say the Germans are bastards,' he continued, 'maybe so, but they are unknown bastards; the Soviet Bolsheviks I know only too well, and good riddance!' According to Mr Krzyszewski the Germans had broken through from Augustowo-Suwalki and from the direction of Brest-Litowsk and were taking our entire area in a pincer movement: they would enter the city within hours.

The sun was already hot but a light breeze made it so pleasant to stretch out, listen to the buzzing of bees and dragonflies, look at the sky and filter the warmth of the sunshine through half-closed lids. I fell asleep. I was awakened by Nadia. 'Here they come,' she gently touched my arm, 'get ready.' There was no siren this time, no one bothered any more. Suddenly I could count the planes; they were not too high, little silver birds glittering in the sun: one, two...five, six...and there were more. The anti-aircraft batteries opened up and all hell broke loose again. I was now stretched on my blanket, face down, heart pounding. Next to me somewhat lower on my left was Nadia and, on my right, Mother. The earth shook from nearby explosions as the air was torn again by the frightening howl of diving bombers and the ear-piercing, crashing noise of *ack-ack* batteries. I burrowed my head deeper into the ground and moved slightly forwards under the gooseberry bush, while praying to God to let us come alive out of this ordeal. The terrifying roar became unbearably intense, a deafening explosion, a blast of hot air.

When I opened my eyes, the sun was black; debris of earth and gravel were raining down on us and a stench of acrid smoke hung in the air. I tried to lift my head, half-dizzy from fear and shock. Mother was moving; I saw her face grey from earth and smoke, the pupils of her eyes dilated in terror; she was feeling me. 'She is alive!' I thought. But once again this terrible howl, and again the earth shook while the furious barking of *ack-ack* guns continued... But what is this? My left thigh and hip were covered in blood! I moved my leg, it moved... The dust was settling. I heard Rysio scream, pointing to blood on his scalp. His face was white, his glasses were gone and he had earth all over his hair. 'I am wounded,' he screamed, removing blood from his scalp with the palms of both hands. Lenka was at his side, shaking off the dirt and sand which covered all of us. I was terrified by the blood on my leg and hip; there was a lot of it. I must be severely wounded, but nothing hurts; how strange, I thought. Mother came to my side. The Krzyszewskis were removing the debris that was covering them. Only Nadiezhda Mikhailovna remained immobile, her face down, blood soaking through the French twist of her dark hair, staining the blanket.

'Nadiezhda, Nadiusha, Nadienka, what happened to you?' Mother was screaming and shaking her arm. Nadia was not moving and not responding.

'On the ground! Here they come again!' somebody yelled. And the terrifying, familiar sounds resumed around us. Now the bombs fell further in the direction of the Niemen bridges and of Father's hospital. The black smoke from fires hung thick over Grodno. Mother was screaming in the direction of the Women's Hospital.

'Help, help here; there are severely wounded here; we need a doctor, a doctor, quick a doctor!' After some interminable time two nurses came out from the hospital. Meanwhile I noticed that I could move my leg freely. On the left side, at hip level, there was a black-rimmed hole in my blood-soaked trousers. I did not feel any pain. Rysio had calmed down, realizing that his bleeding was from a superficial scalp wound probably caused by flying gravel. Lenka also had some superficial bleeding on her leg from gravel and sand.

One of the nurses looked at my hip and took me by the arm.

She helped me to get up and walk towards the hospital. I turned to look at Nadia who now lay on her back; a nurse was taking her pulse. Nadia's face was strangely pale, blue eyes gazing blankly into the sky. My God she is dead, I thought, hearing behind me Mother sobbing: 'Nadiya, Nadyusha, what happened to her?'

I was led into a big maternity ward. There was a smell of camphor and ether mixed with the acrid odour of smoke which hung everywhere. The windows were shattered. Broken glass was on the floor, on empty beds under the windows and in some empty cribs. Infants were crying. Panicked nurses were running in and out of the room. Some were attending to infants hastily assembled in cribs inside windowless rooms, to protect them from flying glass. Others were carrying babies and trying to calm them. Army evacuation trucks were stopping continuously at the entrance, motors running, and taking off with a screech of tyres. Dishevelled young women, many visibly sick and pale, hastily dressed, carrying their bundled infants, were climbing into the waiting trucks. Some were accompanied by soldiers, some in shock, some in panic, some sobbing. '*Poskoree, poskoree, bystro, bystro!*' [Faster, faster, hurry, hurry!] They were all wives of Red Army men, being evacuated from Grodno.

'Come here,' said the nurse, leading me through the ward into a small white-walled room with two baby cribs and an examination couch. Vigorously sweeping a chunk of plaster from the couch, she ordered me to sit on it. With a swift motion of surgical scissors she cut through my blood-soaked trousers and underwear. She cleaned the bleeding wound with a cotton swab soaked in perhydrol. Only then did I realize that a large piece of flesh was torn out of where the hip joins the buttock – a gaping hole.

'No big damage to the bone; the wound is large, but not too deep, it will heal before your wedding,' she joked. 'A bomb fragment tore into your flesh; you are a lucky, very lucky boy,' she said, 'if it had hit your head you would not be here now, but like this poor woman over there.' She made a sign with her head in the direction of the garden.

Nadia was dead! I had suspected it, she was so pale... and those glassy eyes! Nadia, Nadyusha is no more... I could not believe it. The nurse disinfected the wound and applied a dressing over my entire left hip and thigh. I started to feel a strong burning pain and was moaning softly as she bandaged my hip. She left to prepare an anti-tetanus shot. As I waited I looked at the cribs with a newborn in one of them, a strikingly ugly little creature. Suddenly, through the half-opened door leading to the main maternity ward, I heard a blood-curdling cry in Russian: '*Gospodi pomiloui! Gospodi pomiloui! Gospodi pomiloui!* [God have mercy! God have mercy! God have mercy!] It is not my baby! Where is my baby? What have you done to my baby? Give me back my baby!' A young woman followed by a nurse stood at the door. She was trembling; dressed hastily, her long fair hair dishevelled, her pretty face bewildered. She glanced at the infant in the crib. 'No, this is not my baby. For heaven's sake, give me back my child! Where is the director of the hospital? To whom did you give my baby?' Tears were streaming down her face. 'God, what did you do to me?' she cried, '*Gospodi pomiloui!*'

The woman ran out of the room, her heart-breaking lament now merging with the cacophony of crying infants, nurses, patients, the voices of men urging their wives in the wards to hurry, and the uninterrupted sound of truck motors and the screeching of tyres and brakes.

The tragedy played out here reflected the general panic which befell all Soviet military personnel and their families during the first days of the German attack. Here, at the hospital, a number of nurses and doctors simply did not show up; civilian non-medical personnel were gone and those medics and nurses who stayed on were overwhelmed. Wounded patients were constantly brought in from the street, babies were cut by flying glass and falling plaster. Trucks with fleeing Red Army personnel were evacuating wives and babies in frantic haste.

No time now! '*Davai, davai, poskoree, pobystree!* – Come on, come on, faster, move it! You have a better chance of finding your baby among the evacuees. *Davai, davai!*' The heart-breaking '*Gospodi pomiloui!*' of that Soviet military wife – a normally forbidden 'bourgeois' phrase for which one could pay dearly – remains in my memory as a part of that terrifying Sunday of June 1941.

The nurse came back with a sterilized syringe in a metallic box and a capsule of anti-tetanus serum. 'Poor Masha, we switched her baby, this is the second switch today. They are all crazy to flee like this in panic instead of standing fast and fighting the German.' She was angrily muttering as if to herself as she rapidly injected the serum. 'You are all set now, Sasha; let me help you off the table. Take my arm. Here. You can go, your mother is waiting for you.' Trying to avoid putting weight on the wounded leg, I hobbled out of the room. Mother, looking ashen, her eyelids swollen, handed me a pair of Father's pyjama bottoms and a belt. I must have been quite a sight with this huge bandage around my hips and buttocks, dressed in pyjamas. I could feel every move.

'Nadia is dead, she was killed instantly, Nadia, Nadyusha,' Mother sobbed. A chunk of Mother's life, of her energy, of Druskieniki, and maybe even her memories of Russia, had gone in an instant, for ever.

Again the pulsating buzz of approaching planes. A nurse led us into a small entrance hall next to the main staircase. It was windowless and almost totally dark. Someone switched on a torch. The hall was crowded; people were sitting on chairs, they moved in silence to make room for us. Lenka and Rysio were there. Someone moaned 'Jesus, Maria', someone sobbed, and one could hear the commotion of the hospital and cries of infants in the adjacent rooms. As the hum of approaching bombers grew in intensity, the darkness and anticipation combined to increase my dread. We are trapped here in this hall and we will all perish if a bomb hits the building, as it did a few blocks away, I thought. One, two, three, four whistles and the whine of falling bombs merged with the *ack-ack* of the artillery. We rocked back and forth under the impact of explosions, like a ship swayed by a sudden gale. Plaster was falling all around us.

There were voices outside and somebody yelled on the street in Russian: 'They have been hit, we need a doctor, help!' A bright burst of light, the door opened and two civilian men pushed their way through the hall, dragging a soldier in a grey military coat. 'The truck was hit by shrapnel,' one of them breathlessly explained in Russian, 'the driver lost control and slammed into a telephone pole. There are wounded women and children in the truck. *Bystro, bystro!* We need help!'

Soon nurses with stretchers were pushing their way through the hall, out into the street, into the unending noise of artillery and the roar of planes overhead. They came back carrying a child and a woman and helping another to walk. The door closed and we were again in this frightening darkness, feeling the earth shaking from explosions which now seemed further away. Someone said that the Seventh City Hospital was on fire. Father, is it possible that I will never see you again?

The drone of the German planes receded and the furious barking of anti-aircraft guns died down. Doors opened, the darkness dissipated and people went outside again but I remained sitting on my chair, unable to move for the sharp pain in my hip and buttock. I paid little attention to it as my thoughts were jumping from Father to Nadia, who was still lying there in the garden, under the gooseberry bush, her eyes staring blankly into the sky. What a strange twist of fate condemned her and spared me... 'O God,' I prayed, 'may Father come back from the hospital in one piece.'

Lenka, with a composure and coolness so typical of the Blumsteins, decided to check on our apartment. The door had been left wide open, the windows blown in; although few people were out in the streets, rumours were already spreading about gangs of looters 'cleaning out' abandoned apartments. Mother was completely shattered by Nadia's death and Rysio – our cheerful Rysio – was totally despondent. Lenka came back after some time and declared that everything was all right in the apartment; no looters. Nadia's body was taken to the hospital morgue.

Lenka brought with her some sandwiches and a Thermos of hot tea. We all ate in silence. It was already past two o'clock. and the lull in the bombing was unusually long. Maybe the bombing was over. But later in the afternoon the Stukas returned. The dark entrance hall shook and swayed and hell was upon us once again. Hands clutched spasmodically and lips prayed to God for mercy. At times I thought: 'This is it!' A bomb fell a few hundred yards from the hospital; the blast ripped our door to the staircase wide open. The flash of light, the falling plaster, the smoke and dust made me think that the whole building was collapsing and that our last moments were at hand. Why did we continue to stay in this dark little room, heightening our anguish by feeling trapped? I do not know. We were like animals instinctively crawling into the darkest and deepest corner at the approach of death, to escape the world gone mad.

The bombing stopped late in the afternoon. Reluctantly the Stukas left their prey. We decided to return to our apartment. A nurse gave me a walking-stick to keep the weight off my left leg; I was limping, feeling a sharp pain with each step. The streets were eerie, full of broken glass, with no one in sight. A thick cloud of smoke still hung over the destroyed house at the corner of Listowskiego. Smoke rose in the direction of Dominikanska Street and the city centre; it joined the grey shroud sprawling over the western sky in the direction of the Niemen, over the suburb called Vorstadt, on the left bank of the river, and the western part of the city where Father was. At the corner of Piaskowa, an army truck wrecked against a telephone pole stood tilted and abandoned. The deserted city was on fire.

We entered our home. The neighbouring apartments were now empty: the Murashovs, the Rybaks and other neighbours were all gone. The yard was empty. In our apartment, broken window glass littered the floor, unwashed coffee cups and dishes were piled in the kitchen sink, the beds were unmade. Only yesterday this house was alive: we were all sitting in the dining room; Rysio was joking; Nadia and Mother were in the kitchen preparing supper and through the open windows one could hear the talk of passersby, the laughter of young couples and Galya's interminable piano scales. I limped into the yard; the late afternoon sun was now low on the horizon, its orange glow reflected in the broken window of our kitchen. The sky was cloudless, announcing another beautiful day. From far away, in the direction of the setting sun one could clearly hear the crackling of rifle and machine-gun fire. The Germans were very close.

A resounding noise came suddenly from behind our house, a powerful swishing sound, and a short time later the muffled thunder of a distant explosion.

'We are now in the midst of a developing battle,' Rysio said. I limped back into the house and stretched on my bed, engulfed in pain. I could hardly move. I closed my eyes and heard Father's strong voice.

'What happened to *funfer*, where is he?' (*Funfurek* was Father's nickname for me.)

Am I dreaming? Father is back! He is here in one piece! Thanks to the Almighty! I almost sprang up from my bed and, ignoring the pain, hobbled into the dining room. And there he was – without his jacket, his shirt and trousers blackened and torn, his face stained grey with soot and dust, but thank God alive and unharmed. He came towards me with anguish in his eyes which were reddened by smoke. He stretched me on the bed and with the expert hands of a surgeon felt around the wound. He was visibly relieved: it was superficial. Mother was crying and kissing him: 'Oh! What we have been through; Nadia killed, Alik wounded! God, what luck that I see you in one piece!'

Father told us that he had known something was wrong at home – rumours spread fast – but he could not leave the hospital; he was operating non-stop despite the heavy bombing. The whole area around the hospital was burning and the hospital was hit several times, notwithstanding the big canvas sheet with a painted red cross stretched on the roof. It was set on fire in the early afternoon and when it became impossible to operate, Father helped with the evacuation of patients. Three nurses were severely wounded and seven patients burned to death as the planes continued their bombing, hitting the burning building again in their efforts to target the bridge. The Seventh City Hospital was now a heap of smouldering rubble, but the bridge was still standing.

Father had to cross the burning city on his way home. The sight was terrifying: the road towards the east, from across the Niemen and through the city, was littered with destroyed vehicles. There were many civilian casualties. 'It is a slaughter difficult to imagine. The Germans do not observe any rules of warfare or the Geneva Convention,' Father said. He saw Red Army units installing artillery near Batory Square and also quite near us on Piaskowa Street. It looked as though the German infantry was already quite near the Niemen bridges but the Soviet army was trying to make a stand to defend these crossings. 'Unless the Germans have already outflanked them in the south, we may have a night of fun,' concluded Rysio glumly.

Father now insisted that we spend the night in our cellar; he was convinced that an artillery duel was inevitable. He himself, however, would spend the night in his bed, here in the apartment, to keep looters at bay; he had seen some of them already. At night the looting would intensify, he argued, and he would be there to fend off the thieves. Mother pleaded: 'Matviei, forget the belongings, don't get yourself killed because of some junk. I beg you to come!' Aunt Ada and Izak, who came to join us for the night with Grandmother and my cousin Aviva, agreed with Mother. Grandmother lived in a world of her own. She kept repeating, again and again: 'How terrifying is the word "war", my child, how terrifying!'

As dusk fell, we went into our cellar, a concrete structure below ground. It consisted of two rooms accessible through a narrow hallway by two narrow, steep flights of steps; one from our pantry, adjacent to the kitchen, the other leading directly to the yard from under our dining room. Thick steel beams ran across the ceiling. The cellar was used for storage: big blocks of ice for the ice box; *kvas*, soda and beer in big one-litre pressurized bottles, all neatly boxed; vegetables and potatoes in closed containers. Wood for our big ceramic stoves was stacked against the wall.

The cellar was too deep for windows and the two electric bulbs dangling from the ceiling were dead. There was no electricity and no water in town but Nadia had filled several big cooking pots and half of our bathtub with water early that morning. We had candles, an oil lamp and two torches. We brought down bedding, food and even a small alcohol burner. There was a smell of mildew and I would bet that some rats were lurking in the crevices. Flickering candles pierced the darkness of these depressing, damp surroundings. As unpleasant as it was, the cellar felt safer than the apartment.

'Why didn't we use the cellar before? Nadia would still be alive and I would not have this burning hole in my hip! Why did we go into the open?'

'Cellars are ineffectual bomb shelters,' said my father,

'bombs explode deep inside buildings, with the building structure collapsing on top. Artillery shells, on the other hand, explode at shallower levels and are better resisted by underground structures such as cellars.'

With dusk the artillery duel intensified; a furious battle was being waged. Soviet artillery was firing from several points in town – one ominously close to us in the direction of Piaskowa Street. Father was still stubbornly refusing to go down to the cellar and was joined by Izak, who proclaimed that it was a man's duty to fend off looters and protect his home.

'It is improbable that we will be hit during the night,' Father argued. Mother became hysterical, beseeching them to join us in the cellar, but Father, a stubborn Blumstein, still refused.

'Matviei,' she cried, 'I know that something terrible will happen to you if you stay in the apartment! You have no right to leave me and Alik for the sake of some *shmates* (rags)!' Aunt Ada joined Mother in begging Izak to come down. Mother cried and shouted, but to no avail. Finally, she used blackmail: 'If you do not come down at once, we all will come up to sleep in the apartment! At least we will all die together!'

Father reluctantly gave in. This stubborn and rational man sometimes believed in Mother's 'antennae' when she was on the crest of her highly emotional states. Izak followed; in fact, I had the impression that he had agreed with Mother but was too 'macho' to concede it openly.

The battle intensified and we were rocked several times by strong blasts. We cowered on our mattresses, inhaling the mildewed, chilly dampness of the cellar: Mother, Ada, Aviva, Rysio, Lenka and Grandmother – her tarnished blue eyes staring emptily at the moving flame of the candle, her lips whispering in the dark, over and over, 'How dreadful is the word "war", my child, how dreadful.' Father and Izak were in the little corridor at the entrance, listening to the sound of battle, and Asio, curled up in the corner, was getting ready for a snooze. I was very tired and scared. The burning pain in my hip kept me awake; I was also thinking of Nadia, of my first face-to-face experience of death.

The sound of explosions and artillery salvos grew in frequency and intensity, the cellar shook, the candles flickered. I do not remember when I finally dozed off and for how long, but I was brutally awoken by a series of very strong blasts shaking the cellar and peppering us with dust. The candles were blown out and we were now in total darkness. A new inferno was upon us; the thunder and drumbeat of artillery, the howl and whining of shells, the boom and roll of explosions joined in one huge cacophony. The terror of the dark hospital hallway was upon me again.

Another swishing of incoming shells, this one stronger than the others; two powerful bursts in short succession. We all rolled under the impacts, logs from the wood stacks tumbled down on us; Mother was holding her head with both hands; I prayed. The eardrum-tearing whine of a shell was followed by a crashing burst. Cement and dust showered on us. We could hear bricks and pieces of masonry hitting the entrance to the cellar, rolling down the steps, and the crashing noise of collapsing walls. The cellar swam back and forth under the shock. The now familiar, dreaded acrid smell of explosive smoke entered my nostrils. This is the end, I thought, the cellar is collapsing! 'We have been hit, but the cellar is holding out!' shouted my father as new explosions continued to rock us. It was 30 minutes past midnight.

Father, Izak and Rysio tried to move out of the cellar but both exits were blocked by rubble. The rest of the night was spent in anxious listening to the now dying, now renewed artillery salvos. At some point we heard the muffled clatter of tanks moving over the cobblestones of our street. Around 4 a.m., the men went to work feverishly to dig us out from beneath the rubble. They worked with their bare hands. After an interminable time they succeeded in breaking through the stairs leading to the yard; the other end of the cellar was blocked off completely: the wooden stairs leading to the pantry had collapsed under the weight of rubble. Dad and Izak went to check the extent of the damage to the apartment and to the house, although the women argued that they should stay in the cellar, for fear of something unexpected. When they came back, we learned that a shell had impacted the pantry and kitchen, point blank.

Later we crawled out from under the rubble into the weak light of dawn and an unbelievable sight opened before my eyes: the pantry and kitchen were replaced by a huge gaping hole. Part of the dining-room wall and part of the ceiling were gone; gone were our dining table, the chairs and the heavy candelabra, of which only a chain fragment was dangling from the mangled ceiling. One could actually see the Rybaks' apartment through a hole in the ceiling. My room was only a few yards from the impact. It was in complete shambles, with huge holes through the wall into the dining room. The window frames were torn out and only broken pieces remained. The other walls were full of pockmarks and holes of all sizes. Every room was littered with plaster, masonry fragments and grey dust. How providential that Mother had made such a scene!

A hole in the roof of our house was visible from the yard, just above the Rybaks' apartment. Father went up to the attic to investigate. He came down in a few minutes to announce that a big 200-pound shell had broken through the roof into the attic and lay there unexploded, with its detonator tip broken off. How incredibly lucky we were that it did not go off!

The dawn gave a purple tinge to the cloudless sky – another beautiful summer's day. A strange silence had settled on the city. Father went into the street and said that smoke was billowing from all directions; a house was hit just behind ours. The sky was covered with a black haze in the direction of the Vorstadt. The town appeared abandoned by the Russians but no Germans were in sight, at least around our street.

By now we were all out of the cellar. My leg was hurting terribly. I could not walk and staggered into my parents' bedroom, which was still in one piece. Paying no attention to the plaster and brick dust on the bed, I collapsed, staring at the scarred ceiling, appalled by how much one's life can change in just 24 hours. Lenka, my slender cousin, came with tea she had prepared on a kerosene stove and some bread with butter. I had no appetite and I could not drink; I was exhausted and my eyes were open only because of the pain in my hip. Finally I dozed off…Rysio's voice woke me up: 'The Germans, the Germans! They are coming by our street!'

6 The Germans

He seemed excited, almost cheerful. My first reaction was one of curiosity and relief. Curiosity about this army which, from victory to victory, was marching through Europe and relief because this meant an end to the bombing and shelling. I had little fear of the Germans. They could not be all that bad, the people from which came my beloved *Tante* Thea and Pastor Plamsch. I knew them from the *Pastorat*; they were the sons of *Tante* Kazin and *Tante* Johanna and *Tante* Mueller. Even the infamous 'Fritzi' Plamsch, whom I saw only once in my life, did not appear ferocious. The books which *Tante* Thea used to read aloud depicted the German burghers as skilled, hard-working and civilized. Father's account of mistreatment of the Russian POWs by the German Imperial Army during the First World War and his escape through Germany into neutral Holland was no more to me than an interesting adventure story. And all the talk about atrocities towards Jews in the German-occupied part of Poland, their cruelty towards the civilian population, bombardment of open cities, machine-gunning of refugees along the roads, was still an abstraction to me despite the ordeal of the last 24 hours.

And presently I saw a detachment of soldiers in green-grey uniforms and steel helmets pedalling on bicycles towards Listowskiego Street. They all looked very young. Rifles slung across their shoulders, sleeves rolled up, gas masks and bayonets suspended from their belts. One of them wore spectacles with a wire rim. They were relaxed, some laughing as if on their way to a Sunday outing. This was not how I imagined an army entering our town. The streets were deserted. 'This must be the rear guard,' concluded Rysio looking at the Germans, 'the front units must have passed through earlier.'

Father and Mother were trying to find a place to live. A colleague of Father's, Dr Max Heller, invited us to share his apartment some two blocks down the street. Dr Heller lived with his wife, his three-year-old daughter and his widowed father-in-law, Mr Zilberblatt, in a large eight-room apartment on the ground floor. The first floor had been occupied by some highly placed Soviet officer and now stood empty. Soon Mother, Father, Rysio and Lenka were all engaged in the move from the rubble of our apartment. In pain and unable to walk, I stayed behind. I tried to help, emptying drawers, sorting out remnants of broken kitchenware and dishes, books and linen removed from broken furniture. The sun reflected in myriads of pieces of broken glass littering the floor near the windows. Machine-guns clattered in the distance. The furniture and broken window frames quivered from the roar of low-flying German planes.

The whole day passed in feverish activity and by early evening a good proportion of our belongings had been moved to the Hellers'. Loudspeakers on German military vehicles blared out in Polish that a curfew would be in effect from 9 p.m. until 6 a.m.; anyone caught in the street in defiance of the curfew would be executed. Father changed my dressing, which had adhered to the wound and had to be cut and removed piece by piece. The wound was ugly and inflamed, and I moaned with pain.

That night, the grown-ups discussed our situation. We were all afraid of the Poles. Now that the Russians had fled we feared that the Poles, with the blessing of Germans, would take a bloody toll on Jewish lives. The Poles had resented the Russian occupation of Grodno, which they considered a Polish city despite its ethnically mixed population. They were angry at the Soviets for the arrest of many prominent Poles. The Poles often expressed their anger and frustrations through violence directed at their minorities, above all the Jews whom they always blamed for the misfortunes befalling Poland.

Indeed some Jews of Grodno, scarred by Polish anti-Semitism, had greeted the Soviets as liberators. Many, especially the poor, were Communist or Communist sympathizers. After all, Soviet banners proclaimed equality of all races, creeds and nationalities. The Soviets provided these people, for the first time in their life, with hope for a better future for them and their children. Many leaders of the Bolshevik revolution were Jews. Knowledge of Stalin's bloody purges was not yet widespread and his rabid anti-Semitism was still in the future. Some Jews took revenge on Polish nationalists by collaborating with Soviet authorities. And so we feared a Polish retaliation. My father, the eternal optimist, dissented. 'The Germans will not let this happen,' he argued. 'They cannot afford chaos in the vicinity of the front.'

The next day, bad news came by word of mouth. The Minsk highway was littered with trucks and hundreds of abandoned Soviet tanks littered the roads. Many trains were destroyed; Grodno's railway station was burned. Scores of aircraft stood intact on airfields, unable to take off. People spoke about the cruelty of German pilots who machine-gunned anything that moved along the road, deliberately targeting civilians. Some people had witnessed a dogfight between Soviet and German planes. The Russian planes were shot down and some pilots parachuted. The German planes turned around and machine-gunned the suspended, helpless Russians, one by one, until none remained alive.

Father and Dr Max Heller went to the *Feld Kommandantur*, the new site of authority, to get ration cards for our daily staples. They came back visibly shaken. The Germans had blocked off Listowskiego Street, which was crammed with Red Army prisoners. Father and Dr Heller caught a glimpse of these unfortunates as they were beaten and abused by their German guards and stoned by the Polish populace. Many were wounded, but had received no medical attention; many were shot on the way. An uninterrupted staccato of machine-guns came from the direction of the city prison on Listowskiego – we could even hear it from the Hellers', quite a distance away. The Germans were shooting Soviet soldiers in the prison courtyard. Scores of Russian soldiers were shot in the Chalk Mountains. The Wehrmacht was simply not taking prisoners. A good Polish friend, *Pani* Marta, a nurse, witnessed the summary execution of two simple Red Army soldiers who were shot with their arms raised in surrender. More and more unbelievable stories of German atrocities filled the air of the city. Rumours were heard about a gigantic pogrom by the Lithuanians in Kaunas. Thousands of Jews were allegedly killed by the Lithuanian police, as the Niemen ran red with Jewish blood.

Persistent noises about preparations for a big pogrom by the Poles continued to circulate. Before evening the men set out to board up and barricade the windows and doors. I fell asleep to the banging of hammers and axes. Father was still optimistic and kept repeating that these atrocities could not be part of a deliberate policy, but only isolated criminal acts by local authorities. The Germans, he argued, would not systematically violate the rules of warfare and civilized behaviour.

A day passed without a pogrom, and then another and another. We were almost in July. My father got permission from the *Feld Kommandantur* to move into the empty apartment above the Hellers'. We were continuing the move from our bombed-out apartment to our new quarters with the help of a former patient who came with his horse-driven cart to transport our furniture. I left our old apartment – its shattered walls, littered floors, cracked ceilings and hollow windows – with a feeling of loss; it had been a warm and sunny place where I had spent many a happy day. The new apartment was very big, empty and cold. A heavy entrance door led into a long hallway which was lined with eight rooms, including the kitchen, a bathroom and a toilet. Daylight filtered in at each end of the hallway through two large frosted picture windows which somehow survived the bombing. Since the rumours of pogroms persisted, the five of us and Asio all slept in the room that was furthest away from the front door. We barricaded the entrance with a heavy chest of drawers which we pushed behind the door every evening and pulled back every morning.

The killing of Soviet soldiers subsided. Some normality returned to the city and the Germans decided to deal with unexploded bombs and shells left from the invasion. The shell in the attic above Murashov's apartment was to be buried and exploded in the garden. Everybody within a radius of half a mile was ordered to evacuate and we stayed at Aunt Ada's until sirens announced the end of the alert. Izak was very excited: he already knew some Germans at the *Kommandantur*; it was extraordinary how quickly he made contacts and even friendships with the most unlikely people, Poles, Byelorussians, Lithuanians, and now Germans.

During the Soviet rule, Izak had befriended many prominent Party members and local dignitaries; his energy, good-
humoured nature, coupled with an indisputable largesse, his
humble 'proletarian' background – and his readiness to drink
a glass or two – made him very popular with the Soviets. He
worked for some time at a truck depot and could forecast the
forthcoming mass arrests by the NKVD, as these were always
preceded by the requisition of trucks for the transport of
arrestees to the trains. He used this knowledge to warn a
number of former Polish officers and national activists of the
impending arrests. Sometimes he even bought train tickets
for them. His ability with people gave Izak the key to many
deals in the fertile fields of 'wheeling and dealing' provided
by the war. Now, only a few days into the German
occupation, he was already acquainted – through Mrs
Roznatowska, the wife of a former Polish officer whom he
had helped hide during the Soviet rule – with one of the
senior Germans at the *Kommandantur, Hauptmann* [Captain]
Riegel, the right hand of the *Feld Kommandant*, who lived in
Roznatowska's house. The woman was an anti-Semite but
she never forgot what Izak did for her during the Soviet rule
and introduced Izak to Riegel.

Riegel was convinced that the Soviet Army had ceased to
exist as a fighting force and that in three, at most four, weeks
the Germans would enter Moscow. He assured Izak that after
the German victory *der Fuehrer* would take good care of the
peoples he had conquered; the Jews would be sent to
Palestine. He was filled with an abstract hatred of the
Bolsheviks and said the 'Commissars' must be dealt with: 'No
pity for them.' Riegel and Izak soon became friends. They
played chess or just talked at length behind the drawn
curtains in Roznatowska's apartment. Riegel was very keen to
find a beaver coat for his wife and Izak assured him that, with
all his connections among locals and some of his family in
Kaunas, he was the man who could deliver. He and the
captain were to go to Kaunas in two-weeks' time to procure
this fur. Father warned Izak not to get too familiar with the
Germans and not to leave home at such an uncertain time,
with all the rumours of Lithuanian atrocities, but Izak with his
usual boldness, entered right into the lion's den.

The news from the front was terrible. Within a short week, the Germans were deep into the Soviet Union; Minsk was encircled, Riga was taken and the Dvina crossed. In the south, Lvov was still holding out but was encircled and about to fall. German radio was claiming hundreds of thousands of prisoners. It boasted the Soviet Army had ceased to exist. During the day, motorcycles and heavy trucks loaded with Germans in full battle gear – green summer uniforms with rolled-up sleeves – rumbled endlessly through the streets. The soldiers were very young, blond, tanned and dusty; some wore dark sunglasses. They sang defiantly, over and over again: *'Heute gehort uns Deutschland und Morgen die ganze Welt! –* Today, Germany belongs to us, and tomorrow the whole world!' Planes of all sizes, black crosses painted on their fuselage, flew overhead in formations. The German war machine was rolling eastwards.

I asked Father whether *Tante* Thea could now come from Koenigsberg for a visit, but got no answer. He had other things to worry about. As the population was ordered to give up all their private radios, we listened to the BBC news for the last time: heavy fighting was reported around Lvov. Then, in the first week of July we learned from German papers that Lvov had fallen. Was Tolo trapped there? Mother was constantly crying and Father kept repeating, 'Tolo will certainly wait in Lvov until the roads are safe, and join us later. We shall soon see our *syneczek* (sonny) again.' But I felt that he was very worried himself.

Pani Marta came by in tears. Her husband, a lawyer, had been arrested by the Germans that morning along with a great number of Polish and Jewish intelligentsia: lawyers, priests, teachers and public figures, but – interestingly – no physicians. The arrests were unexpected and only a few individuals had thought of hiding beforehand. *Pani* Marta was disconsolate; she feared the worst. A day later Izak learned from an allegedly reliable source that all those arrested were taken out of prison at night, driven in the direction of Pyshki, and executed. Father refused to believe it; he was convinced the men were interned in some labour camp. He was an unabashed optimist, his vision of Germany was of his youth, of Leipzig, of the Kaiser. It was a mixed picture:

anti-Semitism, contempt for foreigners, intolerance and brutality – which he experienced first hand as a Russian POW during the First World War – but also order, respect for work, sensitivity to poetry, music and learning. 'A nation of poets and thinkers', as the Germans liked to call themselves. It did not square with the rumours of senseless murder that were filtering in from all sides.

Rysio and Lenka, who had fled German occupation of Warsaw in 1939, shared Father's opinion and could not imagine a deliberate campaign of murder. They decided to go back to join their families in the Warsaw ghetto. So did a number of other refugees from Warsaw. Permission for their trip by rail was granted by the *Kommandantur*. We cried, kissed good-bye, and wished them all a happy journey. I never saw them again.

To our surprise, we soon discovered that another doctor, a Soviet Byelorussian woman by the name of Kruglik, was assigned by the *Kommandantur* to our new apartment. She was to have two rooms and share the bathroom and kitchen with us. Kruglik was in her late thirties, tall and large – 'a house of a woman'. She was neatly dressed, her long fair hair tied in a big knot behind her head, but her features were coarse. She walked with a heavy step. Crude and arrogant, she barely spoke to us and tried to order us around, especially Mother, implying that as Jews we should be grateful to her for consenting to live in the same apartment. She spoke neither German nor Polish, only Russian, and referred to Jews as *Yudiei* and *Zhidy*, demeaning epithets. I did not like her, and we could foresee trouble ahead.

My wound was not healing well, it was infected with pus, swollen and painful. I dreaded the evenings with their daily change of dressing. As I could barely walk, Shurik and other boys started to congregate at our house for passionate sessions of stamp trading.

On these summer days of 1941, when it was humiliating and dangerous to walk the streets, when one was unsure of tomorrow, it was good to surrender entirely to our passion for stamp trading. I was proud of my collection as I showed my albums to the other boys installed in a half-circle around me. Some boys would in turn bring their collections and show them around. These sessions were ego trips for me, as some sighed with envy looking at many of my rare stamp series. Deals were made, and sometimes a stamp or two would disappear from my collection, 'gone with the wind'.

An incident taught me not to be so trusting and naive: I traded several of my most valuable stamps from Abyssinia for some magnificent Turkish triangular stamps which were neatly glued on to a big piece of cardboard. I was very proud of myself for having concluded such a good deal, and for several days before falling asleep I gazed with pride at these beautiful stamps, now part of my collection. But when I tried to remove these beautiful 'Turkeys' from the cardboard by soaking them in water, I was horrified to discover that they separated into small strips. The cardboard of 'Turkeys' was a masterpiece of patience, a work of art by a dishonest boy. I vainly tried to recover my 'Abyssinias' and was completely crushed for several weeks.

There were also other games, chess championships and, above all, surreptitious reading of sexy stories and mysteries. We read Boccacio's *Decameron*, *The Secrets of Paris* and *Zmory* by Zagadlowicz, *Aloha* by Marczynski, and many others.

Mirek Tropkrynski introduced me to Danya, a Russian boy from Mogilev whose aunt was married to a Soviet officer stationed in Grodno. Danya had arrived a few days before the outbreak of the war to spend his school vacation with his aunt. Danya's uncle was away when the war started and Danya and his aunt were now alone, separated from his family. Danya was a child of remarkable beauty: he was slender and tall for a boy of 11, with a fair, almost translucent complexion. His delicate lips, finely chiselled nose, subtly arched brows and long eyelashes gave to his face the harmony and nobility of a Greek statue. There was something so extraordinarily dignified and graceful in his demeanour that many would turn their heads when he walked by. There was also something girlish and fragile about him which made me afraid to hurt or offend him, and pushed me to protect him.

Life was now very difficult for Danya and his aunt: left without resources, they were like most families of Soviet personnel under special German surveillance. A few Soviets, such as Dr Kruglik, our new room-mate, ingratiated themselves with the Germans by declaring their hatred of the

Bolsheviks and admiration of the Germans. Rumour had it that Kruglik was the former mistress of Ponomarenko, one of the big wheels in the Communist Party of Byelorus. Now she proclaimed her love for the Germans and her 'suffering' under the former 'Judeo-Bolshevik' rule. She was rewarded with two rooms in our apartment and a good job in a local hospital. Most Soviet families, however, preferred to suffer rather than lick the German boot. Kruglik was growing more and more arrogant. It was easy to know when she was home since the corridor resonated under her heavy military step. A big gold cross dangled from her neck and she would address us only in a demeaning, contemptuous way.

Tolo's birthday went by on 10 July with still no news from Lvov. The Germans issued a *Befehl zur Judischer Bevolkerung*, a decree to the Jewish population. We were ordered to wear on the left upper arm an armband with a blue star of David so that a Jew could be recognized from afar. A Jewish Authority, the *Judenrat*, was organized to deal with matters affecting the Jewish community and its relations with the German *Kommandantur*. Some 25,000 people, half of Grodno's population, were Jewish. Dr Brawer, the former Director of the Tarbut high school, became President of our *Judenrat*. A curfew was imposed and the punishment for noncompliance was death.

We were not surprised by the armband decree because we knew from rumours that such badges had been worn by Jews in the German part of Poland, but it was still a shock. Mother was making the badges by embroidering the blue star of David onto white fabric. 'Let us wear this as a badge of honour for us and shame for those who make us wear it,' she said. But this was easy to say! I felt awkward and humiliated by having to wear it. Not that I ever hid my Jewishness, I was proud of it, but I considered this 'branding' as a rape of my identity. It was a depressing experience to walk in the streets of Grodno on Monday with my armband, all clean and pinned to my sleeve. Many passersby did not hide their satisfaction, but some displayed sympathy and uneasiness which could be seen in their eyes.

Although many Poles were happy to see the Jews humiliated, there were also many exceptions, such as Father's friend Dr Antoni Docha. He was a country doctor who lived in

Zukiewicze near Indura, a village located some 30 kilometres south-west of Grodno. Antoni was a very religious man, a devout Catholic and an ardent Polish patriot with deep roots in the soil of Kresy (north-eastern Poland). As a young doctor Docha had practised surgery, sometimes assisting Father, and he continued to visit us after moving to the country. Father and Docha used to disappear for hours into Father's office, discussing the latest surgical techniques and books, which Father brought from his trips to medical meetings in Warsaw and abroad. As a country practitioner, Docha was always extraordinarily busy and had little time to travel. These visits provided him with an opportunity to learn something new and to catch up.

As a Polish patriot, Docha considered that Wilno and Lvov are sacred Polish cities. He may even have thought of Lithuania as a part of Poland; as the Wilno-born great Polish poet Mickiewicz said so eloquently in the opening verse to his epic poem *Pan Tadeusz*:

Oh Lithuania, my homeland
You are like health!
How much you should be valued.
Only the one will ever know
Who has lost thee.

During the Soviet rule, we feared that Docha might be deported for his open nationalistic and religious views but somehow he managed to escape arrest and deportation, possibly a tribute to his immense popularity among peasants.

Docha was an extraordinary man but his appearance was not commanding. He was slender, without a trace of hair on his bony skull; narrow lips were surmounted by a long, pointy nose, slightly split at its end. Spectacles with gold-wire rims framed his small, myopic blue eyes in which burned a strange fire. He was maintaining a home and a dispensary for elderly and disabled poor peasants. He often came to our clinic with cases requiring immediate surgical attention. On other occasions he showed up unannounced, bringing along a retinue of beggars and homeless people. He would then address Mother, 'Excuse us, *Pani Doktorowo*, could you kindly spare some food for these people? They are my friends.' It was said so naturally that one could hardly take offence at this unexpected intrusion. Mother used to tease Father about Docha. 'Matviei,' she would ask, 'when is Docha due to arrive with his "*cour de miracles*"?' When she expected Docha for dinner, extra portions were prepared and the poor ate in the kitchen. I was fascinated watching him cross himself before a meal, lower his eyes and fold his hands in silent prayer. Father and Docha were friends despite Docha's belief that our souls were damned because we had not been baptized.

According to mother, Docha used to be quite spirited but he changed suddenly and became a fervent Catholic. He settled in his ancestral village, married a beautiful and very religious young doctor, Janina, and found peace of mind. His burning faith grew only stronger with time. And presently, after over a year of absence, he unexpectedly appeared at our doorstep. Father and he swiftly disappeared into the office and locked the door. They talked for a long time and only Mother was allowed in and out. He left abruptly and I certainly did not suspect that this man would save my life and the lives of many others.

Following the armband decree, the *Kommandantur* imposed a huge tax on the Jewish community. This money was to be levied in a matter of days. Non-compliance would result in the arrest and execution of 100 prominent members of the community taken as hostages. Hints were dropped that special detachments of the SS and the Lithuanian police were in the vicinity. The *Judenrat* was assigning the specific amounts to be paid by each Jewish family, based on the assessment of wealth. Being relatively wealthy, we had to pay a very large sum. Although there were many complaints of inequities, the required money was raised in record time as everybody understood the seriousness of our situation.

Rumours persisted of massacres of thousands of Jews, men, women and children, carried out in Baranovitche and Lida. The Jews were ordered to dig their own graves. After the news of bloody pogroms in Kaunas, we feared the Lithuanians more than the Germans because Grodno was included in the Baltic *Reichskommissariat* territory, where the Lithuanian and Lettonian police had freedom to carry out pogroms and executions. I tried in vain to distinguish between various German uniforms in the street, looking with a pounding heart for the black uniforms of the SS and the yellow-brown uniforms of Lithuanians. The Polish 'navy-blue' police made its reappearance. They were armed with rifles and pistols and assisted the Germans in the round-ups and arrests but, unlike the Lithuanians, they did not participate in mass executions.

Grodno was awash with German troops moving east. There were air-force troops in their light grey uniforms with silver wings on their collars, and engineering troops in brown uniforms with swastika armbands. Detachments of infantry clad in green-grey marched through the city, their boots resonating on the pavement, singing a strange, meaningless song which echoed and re-echoed through the streets like a devilish laughter.

Hailee, hailoh, hailah,
Hailee, hailoh, hailah,
Hailee, hailah, hailahahahaha!

For the moment, the only black uniforms I saw were the uniforms of the German tank corps. We were still under the jurisdiction of the Wehrmacht but everybody feared the imminent arrival of civilian authorities and the Gestapo.

The news from the front was worse than bad: the entire central front was in a state of collapse. Orsha and Mogilev were taken; the defensive 'Stalin Line' was crossed, the German panzers were already in Estonia and racing towards Leningrad. A huge battle was shaping up around Smolensk, two-thirds of the way to Moscow. In the south the situation was less clear; fighting still continued east of Lvov, and German and Romanian forces were making only modest progress. The fortress of Brest-Litovsk on the Soviet–German border, surrounded by Germans since the first day of the invasion, fell after a heroic stand. The German High Command claimed hundreds of thousands of prisoners and declared that the fighting force of the Red Army was totally spent.

Another humiliating decree was issued in early August: Jews were forbidden to walk in groups. All male Jews had to wear head-gear and take it off when they met a German soldier in the street. Failure to comply was to be severely punished; it was left to the 'offended' party to decide what this punishment should be. That night I heard for the first time Father muttering to himself in Russian, '*Sukiny, pra-sukiny, pra-sukiny syny!*' [Bastards, s.o.b. arch-s.o.bs!]. I can only imagine what it must have cost him to bow in the street to the German soldiery.

To add to our gloom, Aunt Ada came sobbing with bad news: Izak had been caught in a police round-up in Kaunas, to where he had travelled with *Hauptmann* Riegel in search of a fur coat for Riegel's wife. Riegel came back alone and told Ada that Izak had been caught in a street-sweep operation by the Lithuanian police and the SS. He was grabbed with hundreds of others and driven directly to the prison, a fort outside of the city. Riegel tried hard to get Izak out; he intervened with the *Kommandantur* but was told that the Jews were under the exclusive jurisdiction of the Lithuanian police and the SS. He stayed an extra 24 hours in Kaunas, all in vain. He promised to do whatever he could to get Izak out of this predicament. Very embarrassed, he brought Ada chocolate and food from the officers' commissary to show his genuine concern. Ada was now alone with seven-year-old Aviva and Grandmother. Meanwhile, news of the Kaunas sweep spread with lightning speed. Some put the number of those arrested in the thousands, men, women and children. There were rumours of prison executions, of executions in the nearby forest, of a labour camp outside the city. My poor aunt came almost every day with Grandmother and Aviva to spend the afternoons with us. Father, using his inborn optimism, tried hard to cheer her up and dispel the most pessimistic rumours.

It was now less and less fun to play in the yard with my friends. The streets became dangerous; I had constantly to check my armband and my hat. Every time I came across a German soldier in the street I had to uncover my head and bow. One sunny, hot day in August I witnessed a scene which remained etched in my memory and gripped me with fear. Turning the corner on Listowskiego on my way to Shurik's house, I saw on the other side of the road a middle-aged man with a Jewish armband and a tall German in his green uniform. The Jew bowed to the German and lifted his hat. The German shouted, 'Come here Jew!' and started to scream words which I could not understand, except for *Schwein*, which he repeated many times. Then, with one powerful blow of his fist, he swept the man off his feet into the gutter. The brute contemptuously straightened out his uniform, hitched up his belt and marched on as if nothing happened. The poor man slowly got up, wiped the blood off his face with a handkerchief, shook the dirt off his trousers, picked up his hat from the gutter and proceeded on his way. A few Poles gathered on my side of the street, some looking on with satisfaction. One of them addressed me in Polish: 'The good times for you Jews are over now.' No, it was no fun to go out any more.

By the beginning of August the Spanish 'Blue Division' passed through Grodno. We were at first surprised to see so many soldiers with dark hair and skin in German uniform. Noisy and undisciplined, they did not look very martial. On their sleeves they wore insignia which, I later learned, were those of the Phalanga – Fascist Party – and Spanish colours. These were very strange 'Germans', outgoing and sociable, visiting civilian homes, walking casually, laughing. The midsummer days are long and warm in Grodno and one could see these soldiers joking with Polish and Jewish girls, singing Spanish songs, playing the mandolin. Some appeared to be embarrassed by the bowing and the armbands worn by the Jews. Dr Heller told us that on Zamkowa Street, near the old Jewish quarter of Grodno, he saw two Spaniards in German uniform playing cards with some young Jews on the front steps of a house. This must have driven the Germans crazy!

One afternoon, the bell rang in our apartment. I opened the door and saw a big German soldier with a black moustache. I was frightened, but the soldier's face took on a large grin: the fellow had visibly peaceful intentions. He spoke a few German words and I realized that he was Spanish. He feverishly tried to explain something in broken German to Mother, who came behind me. The fellow's face grew pale as he was progressively losing patience with us. Finally, he grabbed his military belt and started to undo the big buckle engraved with *Gott Mit Uns* [God is with us] making desperate gestures of trying to pull down his trousers. Suddenly, we realized that the fellow had an urgent call of nature. We showed him the way to the bathroom. When he reappeared, he tried to excuse himself in a mixture of languages, during which '*grazias*' and '*danke*' were repeated several times. He became very mellow when we offered him some tea which he accepted with alacrity. He showed us a picture of his family, a three-year-old son and a young wife, taken just before he left Toledo, his home town.

Our story was typical. The Spaniards were not used to the heavy German food, about which they complained bitterly, and which made them sick. In towns like Grodno there were practically no public toilets and the Spanish soldiers were driven by desperation into private homes.

My wound was almost healed, but to keep me in pain nature developed a large, ugly cavity in one of my molar teeth. It hurt day and night and required a root canal filling. Our dentists, Izak Gitis and his wife Rosa, were also our close friends. Their daughter Rita, a very gifted girl, was three years' my senior. Until Izak's sudden death of a heart attack the previous winter, theirs was a happy home where Jewish tradition flourished. Since in our home tradition was more culinary than religious, I was thrilled to go to their house for the Passover *Seder*. Dr Gitis ran a very strict *Seder* and, as the youngest at the table, I had to ask the *kashot*, the traditional four questions. I made preparations for this happy evening a long time in advance, learning the *kashot* by heart and trying to guess where the *afikoimen* would be hidden. I liked to hear Dr Gitis read the *Hagadah* in Hebrew even though I did not understand a word of it. Above all, I liked Rosa's traditional cooking. Her chopped liver was the very best. When we were invited for a traditional *shabes* meal, my mouth watered long in advance just thinking of Rosa's *choolent*.

Crushed by her husband's death, Rosa was slowly resuming her dental practice. I was to have another session of drilling. It was sheer torture to sit in that chair with my mouth wide open, looking at Rosa who, pedalling away on her drill, cautiously approached the nerve of my big molar.

From the nearby officer's club in the Hotel Europejski I could hear the sounds of a piano and maudlin voices of inebriated Germans:

Es kommt alles vorueber,	Everything disappears,
Es geht alles vorbei.	Everything passes.
Nach dem Dezember	After December
Kommt wieder der Mai.	Again comes May.

Entering Rosa's office, I was surprised to find there a very young German soldier with Spanish insignia. The fellow was paying for his filling job and was in a very expansive mood, showing everybody photographs of his parents and sisters. He said, 'I am on my way to Moska' – he meant Moscow; and repeated several times: *'Russ kaputt bei Molenk!'* – he meant Smolensk.

The brief presence of Spanish soldiers in Grodno was a refreshing interlude, a change from the passage of disciplined and cold German divisions. After a lay-over of less than a week, the 'gay Spaniards' departed to the misty forests of northern Russia, leaving behind them good impressions and a few broken hearts.

But it did not seem that *'Russ kaputt bei Molenk'*. In fact, we learned from *Der Voelkischer Beobachter* and other German newspapers, that a gigantic battle, a *Kesselschlacht* [cauldron-battle], as the German press called it, was taking place in the Smolensk–Yelnya sector, with literally over a million troops and thousands of tanks engaged on each side. Notwith-standing German claims of surrounding and annihilating two Soviet armies, after two weeks of ferocious battles the German progress was slow. In the west, a number of cities encircled by the German tide had been holding out for many weeks. Odessa, on the Black Sea, was still holding out. On the approaches to Leningrad the German progress also slowed down. In the south, east of Lvov, where the front had not moved much since the invasion, a big German offensive was now in progress but the Soviet resistance stiffened considerably and the going was much rougher than the Germans had expected. Rumours of military trains filled to overflowing with wounded German soldiers passing every night through Grodno gave us hope. Unlike Poland or France, Russia would not be easy to defeat. The Red Army did not appear to be a spent force. In bed at night, before falling asleep, I could now hear Father – who only two weeks ago was certain of total Russian collapse – talking to himself: '*Molodtzy rebiata, molodtzy*' [Brave lads, brave lads!].

7   My Brother Tolo

Insecure in the streets, I preferred to stay at home and read while looking out into our yard below. It was useless to prepare for school in September as all schooling was forbidden by decree. General education was also forbidden for Poles and Byelorussians but, unlike Jews, they could get some elementary and vocational training. Clandestine schooling was to be punished by death for Jews, deportation and forced labour for Poles and Byelorussians. The Germans were bent on uprooting the local intelligentsia and using these conquered peoples as sources of cheap, unskilled or semi-skilled labour.

Dad worked at the Jewish hospital which the Germans had segregated from hospitals for non-Jews. Yet he remained very popular with the peasants and, since his services were no longer available at the 'Aryan' hospital, many Poles and Byelorussians were coming to our home, where he installed an office and performed minor surgery. Carts and horses stood on Rydza Smiglego Street or in the yard. At a time when the population was feeling the pinch of food requisitions and money was losing its value, food was the only way a peasant could pay for a doctor's services. We had more food than we could consume. We had sacks of flour and kasha, we had butter and pork fat, which Mother quickly melted and stored in large containers. We had chickens and chicken fat, which she rendered with onions and bits of meat for a delicious spread for black bread. All this could be bartered for other, more luxurious commodities: sugar, cocoa, honey and tea. In short, we did not lack for food.

As we lived on the first floor of the house where Dr Max Heller had his own clientele on the ground floor, the patients, who were usually illiterate, often went to the wrong office. Dr Heller's father-in-law, a vigorous man in his seventies, did his best to abet this confusion. He stood in the yard for hours, engaging prospective patients in small talk in Byelorussian and redirecting them from the first to the ground floor whenever he could. One day, a peasant with an abscess on his posterior drove his cart straight into the yard, looking for 'this Jewish surgeon called Blumstein' of whom he had heard so many good things, to put an end to his misery. The good man was persuaded by Mr Zilberblatt to see his son-in-law, thinking that he saw Dr Blumstein. When he realized his mistake, he exploded with anger and ran out into the yard with his trousers down, leaving Dr Heller – who was not aware of his father-in-law's activities – completely nonplussed. The man poured out a torrent of abuse at Mr Zilberblatt, who was just about to intercept another prospective client. The scene was so comical that we all had a good laugh at the window.

We did not laugh very often. There was no news from Tolo, and Izak was considered dead. The last we heard was that Tolo and Sala Suchowlanski, another Jewish medical student from Grodno, had set out for home on foot two weeks after the fall of Lvov. This message was sent by a friend in Lvov through a Polish student who had travelled to Grodno by car with some Germans. We also learned that a massive pogrom was carried out by the Ukrainians after the Soviets withdrew from the city. Hundreds of Jews were slain with knives or shot in the streets. We knew that Tolo had escaped unharmed but how would he make it through the 400 miles of hostile territory separating Lvov from Grodno, infested with Jew-hating Ukrainians and German SS units which specialized in mass murder? We were already in the second half of August, and there was no trace of Tolo.

Every single night before going to bed Father would ask, 'Where is my sonny now, where?' and Mother would sob. The way from Lvov to Grodno leads through two cities with a sizeable Jewish population, Kovel and Brest-Litovsk. My parents tried to bribe a Polish policeman to go to Brest-Litovsk and enquire whether a certain Nataniel Blumstein had not perchance been apprehended or locked into the newly formed ghetto. But there was no news of Tolo. It was now over a month since he left Lvov. Fifteen miles a day should be easily feasible for a young man. As time went by, an insidious thought came creeping into our minds: Tolo had been murdered. Neither parent dared to say this openly, but Father's evening sighing and Mother's crying were hard to bear.

I loved my brother very much despite our substantial difference in age. We rarely played together, but when we did these occasions provided some of my happiest memories. When Tolo was confined to our home for disciplinary reasons he loved to play with my lead soldiers. Tolo was not very interested in studying. According to Mother, he was very capable but unfortunately under the influence of 'bad boys' like Oska Bronerwein or Dodek Myshalov, with whom he smoked cigarettes, played cards and chased after girls.

I secretly admired these 'bad boys'. They were so funny. Oska Bronerwein had perfect pitch and could play any melody he heard. Whenever he came to our house, he played on the piano all the latest hits of dance music and blues, all from memory. He also liked to play pranks and bad jokes on others, sometimes to his own detriment. I remember an incident with the sewer-man a few years before the war. Septic tanks were emptied by pumping the sewage by hand into barrels attached to horse-drawn wooden carts; the barrels were then emptied by gravity, or sometimes with huge ladles. Oska was always teasing the sewer-man, a Byelorussian whose name was Alexander, by shouting as he passed, for everybody to hear: 'Alexander, is the barrel full?' One day Alexander had had enough and replied, 'I will show you how full it is,' while throwing a ladleful of sewage in Oska's face.

Myshalov studied to be an officer in the merchant marine at Civitavecchia, in Italy. I admired his uniform and was proud that Tolo had such friends. In July 1939, when Tolo came home from France where he was supposed to study medicine in Lyons, I was so proud of him! He had a moustache like Errol Flynn's and sang the latest hits of Maurice Chevalier and Lucienne Boyer. I bragged: 'My brother is the strongest and the most clever, and he speaks fluent French!' And I sang, imitating him:

Elle avait de tout petits tétons,	She had very tiny nipples,
Valentine, Valentine.	Valentine, Valentine.
Elle était frisée comme un mouton.	Her hair was curly as a sheep.

I learned by heart the lyrics to these songs and boasted that I knew French, of which I actually did not understand a single word. Our hotel guests were full of admiration. 'What a precocious child; barely nine, and he knows French so well already!'

I thought now repeatedly about that unforgettable sunny August of 1939, when everything appeared so carefree at our hotel. It was full of happy guests; Father and Mother had finally paid off their heavy mortgage; the business was thriving with an affluent clientele from as far away as Cracow, attracted by Mother's inexhaustible energy and culinary skills. Our guests were entitled to seven meals a day, each with its distinctive Polish name, including two successive breakfasts, lunch, afternoon tea, dinner and a late evening snack called *wieczerza*. Is it any wonder that we needed the permanent presence of a medical doctor at our 'sanatorium'?

Druskieniki, a spa-resort set among thick pine forests, fields of heather, dreamy lakes covered with water lilies, with the Niemen winding its way between steep sandy banks, was becoming famous in Poland. Its salty mineral waters (*solanki*) were good for the kidneys and liver. It was also popular with young people on holiday. New dance halls emerged every year, some on the shores of nearby Lake Lot, and the beautiful Lake Ilgis on the Lithuanian border. An amusement park and a sports facility with a swimming pool, tennis courts and horse riding were completed. In the municipal park, full of flowerbeds and shady alleys, one could listen in the afternoon to an orchestra playing tunes from the *Merry Widow*, *Carmen* and other light classics. The small but rapid tributary of the Niemen at the forest of Poganka was diverted over some man-made waterfalls to provide the holidaymakers with cold-water therapy. The sleepy village of Druskieniki, so beloved by Poland's independence hero Jozef Pilsudski, was at last on its way to success.

And then in August 1939 came the bad news of the Soviet–German pact, and our hotel emptied overnight. The merry sounds of young laughter, of dance music reverberating from hotels, of horses and *droshkas* on cobblestones, disappeared. Silence spread over the spa, its walks, beaches, parks and forests. But the weather was more beautiful than ever and I had a new and unexpected companion, my big brother who was lonely after the exodus of all his friends. We walked to the banks of the Niemen through the pine forest adjoining our hotel. We bathed in its cool, swift waters. We dried in the warm sunshine. I gazed at the rapid streams curling around the large stones that emerged here or there from the water, glittering and sparkling in the sunshine. I watched Tolo choose a smooth, disc-shaped pebble, take it between thumb and index finger and throw it flat while giving it a spin with such a force that the pebble would bounce off the water surface many times before making a sinking splash. We called this 'making ducks'. The way Tolo could achieve eight or ten 'ducks' in one throw was for me a source of constant amazement and admiration. It was a joy to have my big brother all to myself.

On other occasions, we went to the forest of Poganka. The stifling summer heat was already gone but the air was still warm and a particular stillness descended on the woods, before the autumn winds would make their groan audible from far away. I loved to stretch near the steep banks of the Niemen and contemplate the crowns of those high, stately pines, listening to their whisper, the sunshine filtering through my half-closed eyes. From the Lithuanian side of the Niemen, the weak sound of a shepherd's flute was carried in on the breeze, now coming, now dying in the mutter of the forest and the rush of the fast-flowing river.

We hired a *droshka* with a coachman and travelled to the Lithuanian border, only 12 kilometres away. The beautiful lakes Ilgis and Lot were still shrouded in the morning mist. Fields of undulating blue and yellow heather were all around us. Long columns of storks and wild geese in orderly formations, squawking and cawing, were already flying south.

We moved from our big, empty hotel into a small house nearby, where I shared a room with Tolo. He taught me a lot of Polish *schlagers* and a hilarious French song called *Tout va très bien Madame la Marquise* [Everything is alright Madame la Marquise]. Tolo was then smoking like a chimney; I tried it several times, but it made me cough and I hated it. We played chess and draughts and cards. At night we had pillow fights until Mother and Father scolded us from their room.

During these unforgettable, carefree days of September

1939, I was oblivious to the world collapsing around me, I was so happy to be with my big brother. However, I never saw our sanatorium again, after it was taken over by the Soviets. I never again played with my brother. I saw him only on rare occasions when he was home from Lvov for vacations. Those September days in Druskieniki were always with me whenever I thought of Tolo. Where was he now?

I also often thought about the beginning of the war when we were in Druskieniki on 1 September 1939. We were sitting in our big, empty dining hall. As we listened intensely to the radio, hoping that somehow the gathering storm would dissipate, the solemn voice of the speaker from Warsaw announced that in the early morning hours German troops had crossed the border into Poland. A general mobilization was underway. Mother burst into tears. We were at war! I was very excited and curious. Who would win? I was not afraid of the Germans then but now, almost two years later, I knew who the Germans were.

There were renewed rumours of an impending pogrom, to be perpetrated by the special SS squads and the uniformed Lithuanian and Letton police battalions. The new Lithuanian National 'Army' were zealously helping their German masters with the systematic murder of Jews. A special technique was developed by the Germans. First a curfew was declared and Jewish quarters of the town were surrounded by the SS and their eager helpers; the Jewish population was then ordered to leave their houses and assemble in the town square or some other public space, often the yard of the central synagogue. The crowd was then led out of the town to a place where mass graves had previously been dug by other Jews or Russian prisoners. They were forced to line up next to the graves and mowed down with concentrated machine-gun fire. Rumours of unspeakable atrocities committed by Lithuanians and Lettons indulging in orgies of killing, which sickened even their SS masters, filled the town. Kaunas, Eishishki, Vilnius-Ponary, Riga and other localities were mentioned. We were watching with dread for any appearance of the yellow-brown Lithuanian uniforms which usually preceded mass executions of Jews. In his conversation with the *Judenrat*, the German *Kommandant* always dropped hints   that if the Jews 'behaved' – that is, gave enough gold and silver – no Lithuanians would be permitted in Grodno. When a new, very heavy tax was imposed on the Jewish community at the beginning of September every family did their utmost to pay the required sum. We all knew it was a matter of life and death. All of our gold and household silverware was taken away.

It was at that time, when tensions and fears were at their highest, that a very bad incident occurred in our apartment. I was at home with Mother one afternoon doing some maths exercises assigned by my father when I heard angry female voices and crashing sounds coming from the bathroom. Mother was always cleaning the kitchen, the hallway, the bathroom and the toilet, which Dr Kruglik also used but never cleaned. She treated Mother like her servant. I ran to the bathroom: Kruglik was sitting on top of Mother, punching her face with one of her powerful hands and clutching her hair with the other. Mother was bleeding; she was desperately trying to slip from under the huge woman, furiously pounding the heavy body with her fists. I saw red and jumped on Kruglik, and with both hands grabbed her by the hair and pulled with all my strength. I could hear myself screaming, 'You Byelorussian bitch, keep your dirty hands off my mother!' With one powerful blow, I was slammed against the wall by this Herculean woman. 'I will smear you all over the wall, you dirty Jew! I will show you who is the master here!' she screamed, and gave me another blow in the face. 'Just wait, the Germans will cut your throat. I will see to it!' She ran out of the bathroom, dishevelled, her face red, and disappeared into her room, slamming the door so hard that the whole apartment shook.

Mother picked herself up; an overturned bucket, a rag and a floor brush lay scattered on the wet floor. Her skirt was torn, her black hair a mess, covering her face that was all red from rage. Blood was oozing from her nose and from a deep scratch on one cheek. My nose was bleeding and we were both choking and gasping for air from anger and humiliation. We were still in a state of shock when Father arrived from the hospital. 'I was scrubbing the floor in the bathroom', Mother explained, 'when Kruglik arrived and ordered me to leave at once. I asked her to wait a moment so I could finish the job but Kruglik said that she was not asking me to leave, she was ordering me to leave at once. "I am not your cleaning woman," I said, "and I resent being addressed this way." Then Kruglik screamed that all Jews are slaves to Aryans and tried to throw me out of the bathroom.' But Mother, too, was strong, and the bloody scuffle ensued.

Father was outraged and immediately went to Kruglik's room, demanding an explanation. He was told that she would not speak to a kike and that she was about to leave to ask her German friends to throw us out of the apartment. This was too much for my father who seized Kruglik, dragged her through the hallway and shoved her through the front door so force-fully that she fell down the stairs, on to the landing. He slammed the door in her face. I was stunned to see Father's strength amplified by anger: much smaller than Kruglik, he had locked this giant woman in an embrace in which she seemed completely helpless. Out on the stairs, Kruglik was wailing in Russian, *'Niemtzy, druziya, spasitie! Zhidy menya biut, na matzu zarezat khotyat!'* [Germans, friends, help me! The kikes are beating me up, they want to slaughter me for matzoh!]. She ran into the street, calling for the Germans. Some interminable minutes passed, and then there was the noise of heavy German boots on our stairs. Three Germans wearing steel helmets and metal plates engraved with the word *Feldgendarmerie* hung around their necks appeared as Mother opened the door.

'Wo ist der Jude was hat die Frau geschlagt?' [Where is the Jew who beat up this woman?], barked the tallest, grabbing hold of Mother's arm, the other hand holding his opened holster. Father stepped out.

'I did not beat her up, I only defended my wife and child from this Bolshevik's fury,' answered Father in German. The tall German drew his Luger from the holster and directed it against Father's chest.

'Jude,' he yelled, *'weist du das nicht das fuer schlagen einer Arianer du wirst erschossen?'* [Jew, don't you know that for beating an Aryan you will be shot?]. My blood froze as I saw the big handgun directed against Father. Mother's face was white. Kruglik by now was at the scene, spewing hate and venom.

'Nu chto zhid, Youda Schwein,' she addressed Father with the only two words of German she knew. *'Ty teper zaplatish za svoiou mierzost!'* [Eh, kike, Jew swine. You will answer for your vileness!]. She continued yelling in Russian and spat in Father's face. He tightened his lips as he swept the spit from his cheek. Kruglik, by now completely hysterical, kept raving and ranting in Russian, all the time repeating *'Youda Schwein'*. The tall German hesitated at this display of insanity.

'Who is this woman?' he finally asked, still keeping Father at the point of his pistol.

'She is a Bolshevik and the former mistress of Ponomarenko, the Kommissar of Byelorus,' Father answered calmly in impeccable German. The German lowered his gun.

'Why don't you shoot this kike, what are you waiting for?' yelled Kruglik. The German hesitated and put his gun back into his holster. Mother was near collapse.

'You are under arrest,' said the German, addressing father. 'You come with us to the *Kommandantur*. You too,' he said to Kruglik, who could not understand that the German had decided to clear this case at headquarters; she looked more and more bewildered.

It was 3 p.m., and we could still do something. Mother, though in terrible shape with her swollen face, ran at once to the *Judenrat* to see Dr Brawer, who promised to insist on Father's immediate release as an 'indispensable surgeon'. After several interminably long hours Father was back home. He told us that while they were being lead to the *Kommandantur* he made it plain to Kruglik that if she did not withdraw her vicious accusations and cease her attacks against us he would expose her as former Party member and mistress to Ponomarenko under the Soviets. These few words whispered as they were led through the streets considerably cooled her thirst for revenge, because, in her new identity, Kruglik claimed she had been persecuted by the Soviet regime and was a great friend of the Germans, 'liberators of the Byelorussian people'. She immediately withdrew all her complaints and Dr Brawer's prompt intervention ensured Father was home by the evening, and we thanked God. We were completely exhausted but we went downstairs to the Hellers for supper to celebrate my father's safe return, which was nothing short of a miracle.

As mid-September approached, we started our preparations for winter. Wood and coal were brought to the cellar by Father's patients to ensure warmth and comfort through the cold months – though we were less and less certain we would still be in our apartment. Incredibly, Izak returned almost two months after he had disappeared in Kaunas and we had given up hope of ever seeing him ever again. He came from another world. We did not believe our ears and eyes, but there he was! He was very sick and was running a high fever. We did not recognize him. This overpowering man looked miserably thin and lifeless. He had lost over 60 pounds, he was sallow-grey, and only his eyes glittering with fever were lively like before.

He had been taken off the street in Kaunas with many other Jews in a round-up by the Lithuanian police. They were transported outside of Kaunas and incarcerated in a place called the Seventh Fort, part of a fortress system built under the tsars. An SS officer and his Lithuanian interpreter came to address the crowd. The Germans were looking for specialists to work in some industries taken over by the Wehrmacht. Although he had never seen a cannery, quick-witted Izak registered as *Handwerker-Konserwen Meister* [artisan-cannery specialist]. His powerful frame, and the Germans' need for canners, saved his life. While most of the others – men, women and children – were immediately massacred, he was temporarily spared. At first he worked as a labourer under terrifying conditions: 25 men to a cell without sanitation, surviving on less than 500 calories a day and brutalized daily by the Lithuanian guards, but he was alive. Then he was detached as a *Konserven Meister* to the food service of a military hospital, though he was taken back to the prison every evening. Realizing how much the Germans valued furs, the ever-resourceful Izak managed to attract the attention of the chief physician at the hospital by spreading rumours that before the war he had owned a warehouse full of pelts.

One day Izak saw the German director of the hospital accompanied by his young wife, and decided to take a gamble. He approached the Polish nurse who supervised him and told her that if the director would let him go to Grodno, to see his family for one day only, he would get a karakul coat for the director's beautiful wife and a nice fox fur for the nurse. The furs, he claimed, were in Grodno at the home of a woman with whom he had been in business before the war. This gamble could have easily cost him his life as the whole story was concocted out of desperation. The nurse spoke to the director who rapidly agreed. Escorted by a Lithuanian policeman and a German officer, Izak made the short trip by car to Grodno. He directed them to Mrs Roznatowska who luckily was at home. She understood the situation in a flash and, while playing along, immediately called *Hauptmann* Riegel. Still second-in-command at the *Kommandantur*, Riegel was overjoyed. He came at once in his DKW and gave the Lithuanian and the lieutenant a regular tongue-lashing: '*Ich habe den Mann uberall gesucht; wo haben sie ihn versteckt?*' [I was looking for this man everywhere; where did you hide him?] he yelled. He ordered both of them to go back to Kaunas and took over Izak as his 'personal prisoner'. There was nothing the Lithuanian and the lieutenant could do; Izak had outsmarted them.

The High Holidays approached but the mood was sombre. The Lithuanian and Letton auxiliaries were unleashing their bloody fury and, with German blessing, were slaughtering the Jewish communities of Lithuania, Latvia and north-eastern Poland. They were doing the dirty work of the German SS *Einsatzgruppen*, which now operated deep inside Russia, behind the front lines. News from the front was still bad; Father lost hope again and repeated gloomily in Russian: '*Razval! Razval!*' [Collapse! Collapse!].

This was a miserable and fearsome time as we all felt a sense of isolation and abandonment. The days were getting shorter, the evenings and mornings were dull and grey. We lived with fear and with fear we slept. Every evening was a painful experience. I had the impression that despite all our brave talks into the night we had lately given up hope of ever seeing Tolo again. Before falling asleep, Mother always sobbed and Father sighed mournfully, 'Where is our sonny?' I did not sleep well either. I was no longer going out for fear of being humiliated or, worse, separated from my parents in a round-up. I was deeply fearful of nights and early mornings, during which, we were told, round-ups and executions occurred. In the gloomy evening atmosphere of our bedroom I prayed for our lives and for Tolo's safe return – acutely conscious of the hopelessness of our situation. 'What have we Jews done to be humiliated and mistreated this way?' I asked myself. 'What kind of satanic incarnation are these big blond "Aryans" with *Gott mit Uns* engraved on their belts? And those Lithuanians and Latvians too cowardly to fight at the front, but killing women and children in the rear? Were we not once a proud and independent nation in Palestine?' I dreamt of a powerful Jewish army, which would restore our pride and mete out justice to our tormentors. I repeated and repeated these thoughts in my head until everything began to lose sharpness and coherence and I started to fall asleep.

'Tolya! Tolya! Tolya!' I opened my eyes and recognized Mother's frenzied cries. It was still dark, dawn barely filtered through the curtains. Mother, half-asleep, was sitting on her bed screaming in Russian: *'Tolya, Tolya, on zdies! Tolya, moi Tolya!'* [Tolo, Tolo he is here! Tolo, my Tolo!]. Poor Mother, she is losing her wits, I thought. *'Madamchen*, it's not even six. Go back to sleep, please,' Father implored. But Mother was already standing in the middle of the room, listening intently to a muffled clatter of cart wheels on cobblestones. It was a market day, when peasants converged on the town to sell the quota of fresh produce and food allowed by the Germans. Mother stood there, transfixed, now whispering, now crying 'Tolya, Tolya...'. And then she let out a piercing scream: 'Tolya, he is here, he is here!' She ran out of the room in her night-gown, all dishevelled, oblivious to the world with her heart-breaking scream of 'Tolya, Tolya, Tolya!' Father jumped out of bed, trying belatedly to stop her, but Mother had already thrown our heavy entrance door wide open while continuing to scream 'Tolya, Tolya, Tolya!' The faint sound of a cart and of some barely audible voices rose from the court-yard, and after a while the muffled sound of boots on our stairs. Mother was out on the stairs, clutching the ramp. Suddenly she let out a piercing, blood-curdling scream: *'Tolya prishol, Tolya prishol!'* [Tolo came, Tolo came!]. The next thing I saw – I could not believe my eyes – was a tall black-bearded *muzhik* in a filthy, lacerated sheepskin coat and heavy felt boots, all torn and crusted with mud. He was holding Mother in his arms. Her whole body was shaking convulsively, she was sobbing 'Tolya, Tolya ... Tolya prishol'. Another, shorter, similarly dirty *muzhik* looked on with visible satisfaction. He was Sala Sukhowlanski, the other student from Grodno and Tolo's travel companion. Tears of joy glistened in Father's eyes. Tolo had come home! Sonny was home!

Tolo was difficult to recognize; he looked worse than one of the homeless beggars one could see next to the Brigitska church on Sundays, but he was back and in one piece. After we had calmed down a bit, Mother went to prepare a hot bath for him. The peasant who drove him for nearly 60 miles, from Lomza, was paid handsomely and left with Sala, who was in a hurry to get home. Tolo was literally skin and bones. His clothing crawled with lice and fleas, and he stank. Mother brought from somewhere a big box with a hermetic lid and his infested clothing was thrown into it. His underwear was burned in the big kitchen stove. Tolo spent a very long time in the bathroom but when he emerged I could recognize him again. He was unbelievably thin, with sores covering his feet, but he was indeed my *stary* [old guy], my term of endearment for my brother.

It was past seven, the mid-September morning was grey and rainy. Kruglik's powerful step pounded the hallway; she was going for her morning bath. It was remarkable how tame this woman had become. It was understood without words that from 6 to 7.30 the kitchen was hers, while later it was Mother's. We also let her use the bathroom and kitchen first on weekends. Sometimes Mother and Kruglik shared the kitchen without speaking a single word. I was sure that the morning commotion had disturbed Kruglik, but she did not react in her previous ugly way. She was scared: Father had clipped her wings all right.

I was now sitting in our dining room and staring at Tolo devouring an omelette of four eggs, sandwiches with sausage and cheese on black and white breads, all washed down with strong sweet tea. He ate and ate and ate, and I was so happy to see him at last. Father was kissing Mother, they both looked radiant. This was the first day of real happiness in our family in a very long time.

8 Tolo's Story

Tolo's trip from Lvov to Grodno was quite extraordinary. He covered over 700 kilometres in two months, almost all on foot and over half of it through very hostile territory.

Unlike Grodno, Lvov held out before the German assault. It was evacuated by the Soviets in an orderly fashion a week after the German attack and was occupied by the Germans almost two days later. During those 36 hours a bloody pogrom was staged by the Ukrainians. Lvov's 400,000 inhabitants were a mix of Poles, Ukrainians and Jews, with a smaller number of ethnic Russians. Poles and Ukrainians displayed an understandable mutual animosity, but as much as they hated each other they both hated Jews even more. In particular, of late, the Jews were accused of sympathy toward the Soviets. Exceedingly Catholic, nationalistic and rural, the western Ukrainians fiercely resented Soviet domination, the expropriation of their rich agricultural lands and Stalin's persecution of their farmers.

As the Soviet troops withdrew from the city, Tolo had the opportunity to evacuate east; he was very friendly with a Red Army officer and, even more so, with his wife Masha – my lusty brother was her companion during the long absences of her husband. Masha literally begged Tolo to leave Lvov with her, but he decided to remain in the room which he was renting from a friend of the family, Mrs Rita Charlap. Fearing bombardments and a long siege of the city, the Charlaps had left their apartment for the countryside a few days into the war. Tolo was alone in the big apartment under the watchful and greedy eyes of the Ukrainian custodian and his wife.

On the morning of the Soviets' departure Tolo came back early from a tearful farewell with Masha. As he entered the building he saw the janitor's wife at the gate. Some time later, while shaving, he heard angry shouts in Ukrainian, '*Zhidy vidsilia ghet!'* [Kikes out of here!], and the sounds of breaking glass, fists and tools beating against doors. A crash was followed by a woman's scream; the banging and shouting increased in intensity; a few shots rang out nearby. A pogrom! Tolo bolted the door and leapt to the window, half of his face still covered with foam. He saw a large number of men – a few armed with rifles, most with sticks, butchers' knives and axes – breaking into the house across the street. The big iron gate of the house was being forced open with crowbars and axes. Windows were smashed and some men were climbing to the first floor, into the Kaplan's apartment. Tolo heard Mrs Kaplan screaming, *'pomiluite!'* [have pity!], and the crash of breaking furniture. Repeated shots were fired in the street. He could already hear voices at the gate of his house and banging against the door of the Jewish neighbours on the ground floor.

It was much too late to leave. The rampage was growing in intensity as more Ukrainians were joining in the pogrom. A woman's voice was again pleading for mercy, and was stilled by a shot. An infant was crying. He heard Ukrainian profanities amidst the noise of rifle butts and axes beating against locked doors, then the loud voice of the janitor's wife, 'Boys,' she yelled, 'there is a kike hiding on the first floor.' Tolo was ready to jump from the bathroom window, but it was too late. The yard below resonated with Ukrainian voices and the janitor was pointing out the windows of Jewish apartments.

Tolo was trapped. As he leapt towards the kitchen, he dashed by a small utility room with a water-storage tank: it was only about one-quarter full. Miraculously, he managed to squeeze inside; he could fit only by crouching and pushing his knees up against his chin. His feet, ankles and calves were under water. His buttocks were wet. He somehow managed to replace the heavy lid. He was now in total darkness. He froze as he heard the entrance door slowly giving in to the furious assault of crowbars and axes. His heart was beating madly. He heard angry Ukrainian voices behind the front door: *'Vykhody zhid sukin syn!'* [Get out, you s.o.b. of a kike!]. After what seemed like an eternity, the door gave in and the sound of boots and harsh Ukrainian voices filled the apartment.

'Where are you kike, answer or I'll kill you!'

'Under the bed, look under the bed,' a drunken voice yelled.

'He is not under the bed, the old devil! Nobody in the cupboard! Where is this filthy kike hiding?'

'And I am telling you that he is hiding in the apartment,' the voice of the janitor's wife was more assured than ever. 'I saw him myself this morning when he came into the apartment,' she insisted.

There were at least three of them. They were turning the place upside-down, throwing things around, breaking furniture and windows. They were drunk and obviously more interested in violence than looting. One of them entered the bathroom. Tolo's blood froze and his heart stopped. '*Iogo tut nemaie*' [Not here], he yelled. Cold sweat covered Tolo's forehead as the Ukrainian entered the little utility room before moving on to the kitchen. Tolo held his breath and forgot that he was squatting, folded in half, his knees shoved into his chin, his head against the cast-iron cover. All his muscles were cramped and aching, he had a painful stitch in his right side, but he remained as if made of stone. The Ukrainians were enraged. Tolo could hear them swearing, breaking glass and china, and the janitor's wife asking them to spare things she wanted to take for herself. '*Zbig do bisu sukyn syn!*' [He escaped to the devil, the s.o.b.!], they yelled and left the apartment.

Tolo breathed more freely but he decided not to take any chances. He could still hear screaming and shooting outside. Hours went by; the street noises faded. Tolo lost all awareness of time. He was still afraid of the janitor's wife; he could hear her coming and going to steal, but maybe also to check whether he was there. When he finally crawled out during the night, he was in agony from his tortured muscles and ravenously hungry but there was no question of moving around in the kitchen. He locked himself in the bathroom and stretched out in the bath. After the ordeal in the water tank this was a heavenly place. He fell asleep. He woke up to the sound of nearby machine-gun fire, instantly ready to crawl into the water tank again. The shooting continued for a few minutes more, then Tolo went back to sleep.

The next day, the streets were calm; the Germans were entering the city. Loudspeakers summoned the population to cooperate with the Wehrmacht and register with the *Kommandantur*. Some normality returned but during the brief period of the city's self-rule the Ukrainians had murdered thousands of Jews – men, women and children. It was by far the bloodiest pogrom Lvov had ever known.

Tolo cautiously ventured into the street and joined the crowd for registration. He met at the gate the janitor's wife, who seemed dumbfounded. 'Glad to see you,' she said with a forced smile.

The next few weeks were hectic. Jews were ordered to wear armbands with a Star of David and rumours spread about the formation of a ghetto. Food was becoming scarce as peasants began to hoard supplies. Long queues formed at shops that had something edible to offer.

Tolo had no resources and his life became uncertain. He decided to go home to Grodno, some 750 kilometres to the north. There was no public transport; no trains or buses. He would be crossing hostile territory. There were rumours of Ukrainian pogroms all over eastern Galicia and the western Ukrainians met the German armies as liberators; in towns and villages women threw flowers into the path of German soldiers, men volunteered for service in the Ukrainian militia units. This was *Kulak* [wealthy farmer] country, with its rich black earth, the granary of Poland and Russia – yet an unhappy land coveted throughout history by Tartars, Muscovites, Cossacks, Turks, Poles, Austrians, Soviets and recently twice by Germans. From time immemorial the population had endured murder, plunder and rape. And always Jews were accused of 'treason' and paid a heavy price. Some of the bloodiest pogroms took place in western and south-western Ukraine. During the civil war that followed the October Revolution, Grandfather Blumstein had been savagely beaten and never fully recovered.

In 1920, Poland annexed the western part of Ukraine including Lvov, while the central and eastern parts remained in the Soviet Union. Ukrainian nationalism was repressed by Poles and Soviets alike. Stalin's repression of the *Kulaks* in 1934 resulted in millions of deaths through starvation, deportation to Siberia or executions by the NKVD. The rage of the populace again focused on the Jews. The German *Einsatzgruppen* found enthusiastic partners in murder among the Ukrainians.

To be recognized as a Jew in the Ukrainian countryside could easily mean death for Tolo. It was safer to keep away from villages and to walk along the main highways where frequent military patrols maintained some semblance of order. Tolo teamed up with another medical student from Grodno, Sala Sukhovlanski. They sold all their possessions at the market, except the clothes on their back and what they could carry in a small bundle; they obtained the required travel permits at the German *Kommandantur* – a *Reise Ausweis* with a big *Jude* stamped on it. They were obliged to wear their Jewish armbands at all times.

They set out at dawn and walked along the Lvov–Kowel highway. Most of the traffic was horse-drawn buggies or peasant carts filled to overflowing with hay and rye – it was already harvest time. The only motorized vehicles were German military patrols and convoys. Tolo and Sala avoided Ukrainian villages and towns and walked without their armbands, fully aware that, if caught by a German patrol, they could be shot. But they were more afraid of the Ukrainian peasants whom they were constantly meeting on the road. The flat country provided several kilometres of perspective in all directions. Whenever a military vehicle appeared, they swiftly donned their armbands which they removed as soon as the Germans disappeared.

Sala was of average height, with Slavic features: blond and blue-eyed, not even a Ukrainian or a Pole could take him for a Jew. Tolo, on the other hand, looked Jewish. He grew a beard and a moustache to hide his Jewish features but his dark eyes and black, curly hair betrayed him. Conversations with peasants were led by Sala while Tolo kept a low profile. They were both claiming to be Polish students from Lvov, on their way home to Grodno. Their immediate destination was Kowel, then Brest-Litowsk, both cities with sizeable Jewish populations. They hoped the Jewish communities would help by providing some respite, and food for the remainder of the trip. By the time they reached Brest-Litowsk they would be out of Ukrainian territory, and more then halfway to Grodno. Once in Byelorussia, the danger – though far from over – would be reduced, given the less anti-Semitic disposition of the Byelorussian peasant.

They walked in daylight, at first covering 30–40 kilometres a day then, as they grew more tired, only 20 or 30. They avoided large villages and cautiously approached small hamlets, always at dusk, to ask for food. They slept in haystacks and barns and left at the crack of dawn. Tolo stood behind Sala, who did the talking and bargaining with the Ukrainian peasants; he played dumb as his black unshaven stubble grew longer and, in the twilight of the evening, tried to hide his face. They often slept in the fields rather than risk entering a Ukrainian village.

They dreamt of a hot meal and a bath. After a week on the road, they were only some 25 kilometres from Kowel, which they were hoping to reach before dusk when they were stopped by a German motorcycle patrol: two *Feldgendarmen*, one on the motorcycle, the other in a side-car with a mounted machine gun. The driver asked for their papers and examined them and their bundles carefully. He looked with disgust at the two dirty, smelly, bearded Jews. The German in the side-car kept his machine gun pointed at them.

'You accursed Jewish louse, don't you know what washing is?' he lashed out. The driver took out a whip and assailed Sala, covering him with blows and pushing him into a ditch. He then turned on Tolo just as a military convoy of cars and trucks appeared. The German for some unexplained reason jumped on the motorcycle and left. Sala was a mess: his shirt was torn open by repeated lashes, a blow to the head had injured an eye and his scalp was bleeding profusely. He was trembling all over and could only get up with Tolo's help. The military convoy passed them, raising clouds of dust. Nobody paid much attention to the two bearded, dirty Jews, the two *Untermenschen* [sub-humans] walking along the ditch.

The hot midsummer sun was above their heads. Sala's scalp was bleeding; they were both thirsty and the scorching heat was making them dizzy. They did not have the strength to continue on to Kowel and decided to risk entering a hamlet they saw at some distance off the road. They still had some money left, enough to pay a peasant for a loaf of bread, a jug of milk and a place to get some rest. On the dirt road to the village they met a cluster of peasants working in the field. The men wore voluminous trousers and white Ukrainian shirts and were cutting rye, swinging their scythes in a wide circle. The women, dressed in traditional multicoloured babushkas and skirts, were stacking the harvest. A *chlop* [Ukrainian peasant] approached them. He became very suspicious at the sight of the blood covering Sala's face and asked in Ukrainian if they were not 'Reds'. 'No,' Sala answered in Ukrainian, 'we are not "Reds", we are Polish students from Lvov going home. We got into a fight with some bandits who wanted to rob us and one hit me hard over the head. We want to wash, and get some food and rest. We will pay you well.' The peasant hesitated a moment, then shouted 'Marya, Marya'. A woman approached. Seeing Sala's bloodied face, she crossed herself.

'How much would you pay?' the *chlop* asked.

'Ten roubles for both of us,' answered Sala.

'No way; 50 roubles!' the peasant said. They settled on 30 roubles, paid in advance.

'Marya, show him the way,' the man said and returned to work as the others watched the newcomers from a distance.

'Come with me', said the woman. The village was one of those poor hamlets on the north-western confines of Ukraine which were not blessed with the wonderful black soil, the rich *tchernoziom* on which everything grew and prospered. The woman led them to a small hut, an *isba*, at the edge of the village. She lit a fire under a big pot of water and told them to sit at the table. She brought black bread, salted lard, an onion and a jug of milk still warm from the cow. '*Isty, budesh vmyvatsa pyrnyshe*' [Eat, you can wash later], she said.

After the meal, the woman brought two large wooden troughs and put them on a bench outside the hut, near the deep water well. She filled one trough with hot water and the other with water from a pail chained to the well. She gave them clean rags to dry themselves and a small clay pitcher for rinsing. They washed with their own soap. Tolo carefully washed around Sala's wounds. This took some doing; the head wound, though superficial, was very painful. Sala's eye was swollen and blue. The welts on his torso were red and inflamed. They changed their torn, blood-stained shirts and underwear for the dirty clothes they carried in their bundles. After they had washed, the woman led them into the barn where two cows and a horse were feeding on straw and hay.

'Here,' she said, handing them a ladder, 'climb into the loft. It's full of straw and you will be comfortable.' Soon, they were blissfully asleep and dreaming of home.

They were awoken by the creaking of a door and voices in the barn. A pale moonlight crept through the attic window; Tolo's watch was showing 2 a.m. They were still figuring out what was happening when a big head appeared at the top of the ladder and a man pushed himself up, soon followed by another. *'Nu zhydy davaite ghroshy!'* [Eh, kikes give up your money!], one of them said in Ukrainian, brandishing a knife in his right hand. The man behind him held an axe and a large army torch. Tolo and Sala retreated towards the window: Tolo first, trying to hide his face, then Sala, who was not afraid to show his 'Aryan' features. Sala emptied his pockets, which contained 20 roubles, swearing that he was a Pole and a friend of the Ukrainian people. This unexpected flurry of Ukrainian took the men by surprise; there was a moment of hesitation as they bent to the floor to grab the money. Tolo leapt through the window and landed on a big haystack just below the barn. He picked himself up and in a flash was running across the freshly mowed field towards a large swathe of uncut rye. Nobody was following him, but Tolo continued sprinting until he had reached the rye.

The entire landscape was bathed in silver moonlight. After a hard day of harvest the village was fast asleep, even the dogs did not bark. Suddenly, he saw a silhouette falling to the ground, jumping up and running. Thank God, it's Sala! He is escaping! Nobody was following him either. As he came close, Tolo saw that he had no shirt on. Sala had narrowly escaped death as the approaching Ukrainian demanded that he take off his clothes. He knew they would murder him once naked, as they did not want to mess up wearable clothes. First he took off his watch and threw it on the floor; then, fast as lightning, he took off his shirt and threw it in the face of the peasant. This unexpected move made the Ukrainian stagger backwards, giving Sala enough time to jump from the window and sprint through the field.

They waited, covered by tall, dense stalks of rye ripe for harvest. They waited for a very long time before cautiously advancing towards the road in the direction of Kowel. The road was empty but for a few military vehicles, their dimmed lights visible from afar – they ducked into the ditch, waiting for the vehicles to pass. At daybreak they hid in a corn field at some distance from the road, and waited for dusk. The following night they cautiously entered the suburbs of Kowel and hid in the cellar of a shelled house. Next morning, Tolo went to look for the *Judenrat*. The Jews of Kowel were still free to walk around the city, wearing an armband. At the *Judenrat* Tolo explained the situation and was given clothes for Sala. He brought them in a large briefcase in full daylight without being bothered. The *Judenrat* provided them with food, shelter and some money to continue their journey home, and Sala received medical attention. They stayed in Kowel a few days before moving on.

As previously, they walked along the main road but now they slept mostly in fields and ditches. They were happy to leave Ukrainian territory behind them. As they approached Brest-Litowsk the landscape changed; lush fields, ablaze with the colours of sunflowers and poppies, abundant in every kind of grain, became more sparse, yielding to clover, potatoes and cabbage. Villages became shabbier, domestic animals fewer and thinner, even people looked smaller and poorer with their grey, torn sheepskins. They spoke a dialect more familiar to Tolo. They were also friendlier and hated the Germans. Tolo and Sala became more and more trusting; they even openly ventured into villages and were given food and shelter. Tired, hungry and dirty they reached the city in five days.

Brest-Litowsk, a garrison city on the eastern bank of the River Bug which separated the German and Soviet parts of occupied Poland, was the lynch-pin of the German attack on the Soviet Union in June. It was occupied by the Germans even before the start of the invasion on 22 June. Under the Soviet–German trade agreement, freight traffic flowed routinely between the two countries. On the evening of 21 June, trains arrived as usual at the freight station and crack German infantry in full battle-gear poured out from the unlocked doors of the carriages. Within a few hours the city of Brest-Litowsk was in German hands, with Soviet personnel still sleeping. Many Soviet officers were shot in their pyjamas as they tried to join their units. However, the fortress outside the city offered a ferocious resistance, throwing back multiple German assaults. The outnumbered and outgunned Soviet garrison held the fortress of Brest-Litowsk, well into July. There were almost no survivors. It was a new kind of resistance and a new kind of war, never previously encountered by the Germans and gave a foretaste of things to come.

Furious at the Soviet resistance, the Germans had decimated the large Jewish community of Brest-Litowsk during the early days of the invasion. Since then, the community had been left alone. Tolo and Sala were placed by the *Judenrat* in two separate homes. They planned to stay only two or three days but were dissuaded from moving on, as the only way to Grodno was through the woods and swamps of Kobryn or Pruzhany which formed the north-western corner of the giant Pinsk-Pripet marshes. They were told that remnants of General Pavlov's defeated Soviet armies were roaming the forests, actively helped by pro-Soviet villagers. Villages giving shelter and help to partisans were being burned to the ground by the Germans. In the warm August evenings they could clearly see a faint red glow in the easterly direction–Pripet villages burning. Terrible stories circulated about mass slaughter by Germans in black uniforms, about village churches packed with women, children and old people set ablaze, about mass executions of the Jewish populations of the Pinsk-Pripet towns and *shtetls*. To go on foot north-east of Brest-Litowsk was to risk being shot by the Germans. Tolo and Sala were restless but they were persuaded to wait until some calm returned to the countryside.

They finally took to the road after almost three weeks as things became somewhat quieter in the Pinsk-Pripet area. They still had a long way to go before they reached home. They decided this time to avoid the main roads with their German patrols and to proceed at night slowly, through the fields, keeping a distance from the road. They slept in the forest during the day, occasionally in a barn. The villages were poor. Tolo and Sala did not have meat or milk for days. They changed the story they were telling, saying that they had been arrested, then had escaped from the Germans and were going home. Both were now hardened by experience and knew how to avoid trouble.

One day, as they rested at the hut of the *Soltys* [village elder] in a village near Pruzhany they were approached by a few men in sheepskins, armed with grenades and pistols, who told them to leave right away because a detachment of Germans in black uniforms was in Pruzhany and moving in their direction. Tolo and Sala followed the men, who set out across the fields into the nearby forest. They marched eastwards for many hours, well into the night, through a swampy forest, and came to a small village. They were sheltered in a barn and collapsed with exhaustion. In the morning, they were taken to the *Soltys*. The village – about two dozen straw-thatched huts and stables forming a single street – was surrounded by a dense, forbidding forest. A few meagre cows grazed in a small meadow. Tolo and Sala could not believe their eyes when they saw a big red flag with a hammer and sickle hanging from the entrance to one of the huts. 'This is the Town Hall, where the *Soltys* lives,' said one of their companions.

The *Soltys* was a stocky man with brown hair and an imposing moustache. He was wearing a grey *rubakha* [Russian shirt] buttoned at the neck, blue riding trousers and *garmoshki* [flexible, accordion-like Red Army boots]. His shirt was girded by a wide military belt with a five-sided red star on its buckle. He was a Soviet official! He greeted Tolo and Sala and invited them inside, offering them milk and black bread for breakfast. He was interested in their knowledge of German troop movements. He then took some *makhorka* [very coarse tobacco roots] from a metal box, spread it on a precut sheet of newspaper and carefully rolled it into a small tube. Stretching out his tongue he licked the border of the tube to hold it together, put the flat end in his mouth and lit a match. Soon he was contentedly inhaling the smoke, filling the room with an acrid stench. He then addressed the newcomers.

'Comrades, you are in the free Soviet partisan territory. No Fascist invaders have ever set foot here, and if they do they will be received in style. We are looking for strong and healthy men. Will you join us?'

Tolo and Sala said that they were heading home and could not abandon their old parents in their hour of need. The *Soltys* fixed his blue eyes on them. 'Comrades, we know you are Jewish,' he said. 'The Germans are systematically killing Jews;

special German army execution squads are sent to murder entire communities. I have first-hand information about these atrocities. The Germans want to exterminate a part of the population of the Soviet Union and enslave the rest. The only way out is to fight these ruthless animals with all our might. Maybe your families are already dead, maybe they are going to die soon. If you go to your home town you are walking into a mouse-trap. You are not going to help them but will only die with them. It is not for me to tell you what to do, but I would jump at the opportunity of joining the Red Army partisans.'

Tolo and Sala thanked him for the offer, but insisted on continuing their journey home. They resumed their trek in the direction of Slonim, a town with a large Jewish population, about 150 kilometres from Grodno. Leaving behind them the Pinsk-Pripet marshes they were greatly impressed with their visit to the Red villages, with the devotion and faith of these poor peasants, even now after the collapse of the Red Army; with their pride and with their hatred of the Germans. It was good to know that this huge area of forest and marshes was not really under German control. What a contrast to the Ukraine.

Tolo and Sala walked with renewed vigour, despite their exhaustion. They were coming closer and closer to home. But the awful strain of their journey made itself felt. The September nights were already cold; they had run out of money; they were hungry and filthy, their shoes were torn and their feet covered with blisters. One thought was pushing them on – they were every day getting closer to 'home, sweet home'. As they approached Slonim, they learned that German Army special killing squads had decimated the Jewish community in August and rumours about another pogrom kept them away from the city in which they had hoped so fervently to find some rest and shelter. They decided to stop in a small village in the direction of Volkovysk. By sheer luck the *muzhik* whose house they entered had heard about Father, who had performed surgery on his aunt. The name of Dr Blumstein was recognized by the rural population all around Grodno, as far as Volkovysk and Slonim. The most difficult part was to convince the peasant that Tolo was indeed the son of the famous surgeon from Grodno. The man was illiterate and nobody in his household could read Tolo's name on the German *Ausweis*. He was very suspicious and only after Tolo gave his aunt a few details about Father's clinic did he believe him. Tolo and Sala promised him a big reward if he would drive them the remaining distance to Grodno. They spent the night in his barn and set out the next day. The peasant placed them on top of a cart packed with hay. They could easily pass for poor migrant labourers. They covered the remaining 100 kilometres in two days, stopping overnight in a village quite near the city. There, Tolo learned from farmers who knew Father well that our apartment had been shelled and that the family now lived with Dr Heller in a house nearby.

We were now, all four of us, together, but unsure of tomorrow. We were terrified of a pogrom every evening and every morning, but together. Father arranged for Tolo to work as a nurse's aide at the Jewish hospital and life returned to 'normal'. Tolo, as usual, brought with him a number of songs. They were Polish songs sung in student taverns in the slang and drawl of Polish Lvov. They were racy and funny and I learned them by heart as we sang together. How good it was to have my brother back.

9 Still Free in the City

The isolation of Jewish communities throughout eastern Poland and the occupied portion of the western Soviet Union grew worse daily. Travel between cities was forbidden for Jews and became increasingly difficult for the Aryan population. There was no telephone, no post, and newspapers were strictly censored. We lived on a diet of rumours.

The Lithuanian, Letton and German SS commandos continued their bloody work. After Kaunas, Baranowitche, Lida and Wilno, massacres occurred in Slonim. The communities of Minsk, Kaunas and Wilno were hit again. Entire towns on the vast territory of *Ostland* (Eastern Land) became *Judenrein* [cleansed of Jews]. Details of these gruesome killings were brought back by travelling Poles and Byelorussians. Rumours were spreading that the Grodno *Kommandantur* would soon 'invite' a Lithuanian execution squad to deal with our community.

Just before the High Holidays, three important changes affected our lives. The 'good' news was the incorporation of Grodno into the Third Reich; the city was no longer under the jurisdiction of the *Baltic Reichskommissariat*, the eastern expanse destined to be colonized by Germans. We speculated that this was good because the Germans 'would not allow the Lithuanian police units to perpetrate massacres on the territory of the Reich itself'. The bad news was that all Jews were to wear an ugly yellow patch in the form of a star of David on the upper-left side of the torso, on front and back. The star had to be made of yellow fabric some three to four inches in diameter. In addition, Jews were forbidden to use pavements and had to walk in the gutter. Our humiliation was complete.

The community was again subjected to payment of a ransom. This time a number of prominent members of the community from all walks of life, with the exception of

101

medical doctors, were taken hostage by the Gestapo. If the *Judenrat* failed to pay the ransom in full within three days, the hostages would be shot. Unfortunately, the community was already bled dry by previous ransoms. Only half of the amount was raised and the hostages were shot.

These were very bleak High Holidays for our community. Neither Father nor Mother were observant Jews; this time, however, we all went to hear the *shofar* at the Great Grodno Synagogue near Peretza Street. The synagogue was full, and the community was mourning the hostages. One could hear sobs, the plaintive chant of the *cantor* and the hum and murmur of prayers. I looked with some bewilderment at the ranks of men wrapped in their prayer shawls, swaying in the trance of the *Shma Israel*. I was filled with rebellious thoughts: that *Eloheinu* was not worthy of being courted with so much fervour, that we Jews should be like all nations and have our land, our country, a haven, something worth living and dying for.

It was hurtful to see the satisfaction of many Poles at our new mark of shame, the yellow patch; as if our humiliation somehow made up for theirs. I much preferred the Soviets left stranded in the city. It was easy to recognize Soviet women in the street. They wore *babushkas* and 'Soviet style' clothes and often gave me a friendly, compassionate smile. In some eyes I could see dismay at the sight of my yellow patch and our humiliation of walking in the gutter. This warmed the heart and uplifted the soul. It was important to know that there were some human beings who felt empathy – that we were not a universal object of contempt. I sometimes thought of my friends Kolya Murashov and Galya Rybak: where were they now?

The news from the front continued to be bad. After victories in the bend of the Dnieper, in the Ukraine, the German armies swiftly advanced into the Don-Bass coal-mining region. Soon, the whole of the Ukraine would be in German hands. Mother often spoke about Uncle Lolya and Grandmother. As the battle approached the Don-Bass, she prayed that they would move east from the little town of Zugress. The Germans claimed over five million Soviet prisoners and the destruction of 80 per cent of Soviet armour and aviation. Hitler boasted that, before the year's end, he would review the parade of German troops in

Red Square. And yet...the German advance on the central front before Moscow was slow; encircled Leningrad was holding out despite repeated assaults, and the German forecast of its imminent fall was not materializing. The surrounded city of Odessa was in its third month of siege with no sign of surrender. Bitter fighting was raging in the Crimea where the fortress of Sebastopol was holding fast. It was significant that since August the Wehrmacht had stopped the summary executions of Soviet POWs because in the battle of Smolensk the Russians had managed to take scores of German prisoners. Yet the fate of Soviet POWs in the custody of the Wehrmacht remained horrible. In Grodno the Soviet prisoners were herded into the camp of Kielbasin, a few kilometres from the city. Peasants living in the vicinity reported that every morning truckloads of emaciated corpses were removed from the camp. The prisoners were left to die a horrible death from starvation and disease. Surely it would have been better to be murdered outright, as in the first weeks of the war.

October brought with it still more distressing rumours about the slaughter of Jewish communities all around us and behind the front in the Crimea and eastern Ukraine. Mother prayed for Lolya and his safe escape. We were expecting some words of condemnation from the civilized world, from the Pope, from England, from Roosevelt. Every day we devoured German newspapers for a sign of America's protest. Fantastic stories circulated about an offer by the Germans to let the Jews out of Europe to...Madagascar! However, nothing happened. America and Roosevelt, our only hope, were silent; the Pope was silent. It was not a good omen; the world did not seem to care.

With the beginning of October, as the nights were growing longer, came the first cold spell. Being out of school was a new sensation. At first I found it very exciting but soon I realized that somehow life was passing me by and I grew restless. Father tried his best to teach me some maths, but his mind was preoccupied and he had little patience. When I could not understand things which appeared simple to him he quickly lost his temper, calling me a 'cat's brain' and scaring me. I did not look forward to our little algebra and geometry sessions. Beside these maths exercises, I passed my time reading thrillers. I was especially fond of thrillers by Edgar Wallace, Nasielski, Romanski, Marczynski and Maurice Leblanc. I also tried my hand at writing a thriller with my friend Shlomo Pajes. This was my favourite occupation during those nights. It provided me with an escape into an imaginary world of action where I could trade my helplessness for freedom.

During one of our writing sessions with Shlomo, an incident occured that made my parents incandescent with anger: Shlomo broke one of the only two intact windows in our apartment. Following the heavy damage inflicted on Grodno by German bombing in June, almost every house in the city centre had broken windows. Window glass was impossible to replace and, with the cold season at our doorstep, broken windows were covered with ugly plywood, edged with felt and nailed to the frame. The two undamaged windows were our only source of daylight. One was a large picture window located at the end of the long corridor, next to the staircase. It had miraculously escaped the bombing blasts. One day, Shlomo hoisted himself to sit on the windowsill and pushed out the precious glass which shattered into a thousand pieces. My clumsy friend swiftly disappeared. Boy did I get it! We covered the opening with a pegboard that provided scant protection against the chilly autumn winds and rains. The entire apartment became darker and colder.

To add to my misfortune, I caught a cold and became partially deaf as a result of fluid accumulating behind my eardrums. I always remembered with dread my frequent childhood ear infections. Dr Rywkind would be called to pierce my eardrums and drain the pus. The infections of earlier days were gone by now but this deafness after colds had become commonplace. Dr Rywkind treated it by blowing air from a bulb through my nostril, while making me swallow water. It was unpleasant but it worked. Now, I had to see him regularly. He lived on Zamkowa Street, close to the Jewish quarter of the city and the synagogue. I liked Dr Rywkind; he was a big, heavy man with a bright, smiling face and blue eyes, and his skull was shaved like my father's. When visiting us, he often sang in a strong sonorous voice his favourite Russian song, *'Shiroka strana moia rodnaya!'* [Wide is my beloved country!] He had diabetes and always took his tea with a small tablet of saccharine. A born actor, he would first tell me a story or a joke whenever he had to do something painful. I laughed and the procedure did not seem to hurt so much. When I got my cold, I had not seen Dr Rywkind for some time, and he appeared less cheerful than usual, but his treatment was effective. I recovered my hearing.

In October, the Germans ordered the Jewish population to give up all their furs. The collection was to be made by the *Judenrat*. Jews were expressly forbidden to wear fur coats, which all went for the winter relief of the German Army in Russia. The officers of the *Sicherheitsdienst* (a branch of the Gestapo, known as the SD) insisted winter supplies be delivered promptly and in great abundance, lest we get a 'visit' from an execution squad. Since the Germans were clearly preparing a winter campaign, this order revived our hope that, maybe, the Soviet Army was not as completely finished as the *Voelkischer Beobachter* wanted us to believe. Nevertheless, few among us expected Russia to survive; all we hoped for was that the Germans would get a very bloody nose.

At the end of October, a decree was issued ordering all Jews of Grodno to be resettled in two special parts of town surrounded by barbed wire. These areas were called ghettos. The transfer was to be effective as of 1 November. From that time onwards no unauthorized Jew should be found outside those areas on penalty of death. Only six hours were allotted for the transfer into the ghettos. Anyone caught on 1 November moving before noon or after six o'clock would be dealt with on the spot. It was obvious that the order was issued to force us to abandon most of our possessions. We all started feverishly to prepare for the move. It was not a small task. The majority of Grodno's 25,000 Jews lived outside of both areas designated for the ghettos and now had to be squeezed into a space which provided housing for at most 5,000 inhabitants. Ghetto I (or Ghetto A) was situated not far from the city centre, bordering on Zamkowa and Dominikanska Streets. It included all of the old Jewish quarter with the Great Synagogue and was already densely populated. Ninety per cent of its inhabitants were Jews, mostly poor. Ghetto II (or Ghetto B) was located further from the city centre, on the other side of the railway track. The area was called Slobotka and was inhabited almost exclusively by Poles. Slobotka was the poorest part of Grodno, full of slums and shabby wooden houses. The Poles were promised relocation into vacated Jewish apartments in the residential centre of the city.

Ironically, we greeted this bad news almost with relief. We reasoned that we would at long last be living among our own kind, without the humiliation of walking in the gutter and the daily fear of being assaulted by Germans in the street. We would be trapped, but weren't we already? We were living in the city but were afraid of walking its hostile streets. Humiliation and constant abuse often ended in tragedy: families were separated for ever in sudden street sweeps by the Gestapo and their Lithuanian helpers. Determined to live or die together we were now virtually under self-imposed house arrest. The grown-ups minimized their trips out. I gave up seeing my playmates. Even at Shurik's, a ten-minute walk from home, I felt extremely insecure away from my family. A creeping fear of impending doom took hold of me whenever I was outside. Now, at last, we would all be together, albeit behind barbed wire. We would be free to walk on the *trottoir*, to visit each other without fear of a 'sweep'. We hoped that by removing us 'out of their way' the Germans would forget about us and maybe leave us in peace. We comforted ourselves with illusions that massacres occurred only in towns where Jews were not separated physically from the Aryans; not within a ghetto on the territory of the Reich.

Izak, however, did not agree. Having lived through hell in Kaunas, he was very sceptical. He was appalled that we were almost pleased to go into the rat-trap, as he called the ghetto. 'Why are we submitting like sheep and going willingly into the trap?' he thundered. A conversation with him was always depressing. Having regained some weight, Izak looked almost like himself again; his strength and vitality had come back. 'Jews, do not walk into the trap!' he shouted. 'Disperse! Go into the forests, there are not enough Germans to hunt you out!'

This was easier said than done. Where were we to go with our children, mothers and grandparents? The peasants in the countryside were at best indifferent, at worst hostile. It was impossible to survive in the forest without weapons. Cold weather had set in very early that year. As communication between Jewish communities was almost non-existent, the Germans could easily repress one by one any attempts to break out into the forests. They would murder all those remaining behind in the city: grandparents, parents and children. How many could survive in the forest without help from the Poles, Byelorussians or Lithuanians? There was no alternative. We heard rumours that a group of bold young men and women had gone into the forest, but here nobody contemplated any resistance. After all, living in the ghetto was better than dying in the forest.

The Germans started preparations for the resettlement into the ghetto by erecting high poles connected by several rows of barbed wire. Although most Jews chose Ghetto I, we decided on Ghetto II, which was much less crowded. With Dr Finkel – the other Jewish surgeon – moving into Ghetto I, it was natural for us to move to Ghetto II, so that each ghetto had a surgeon. Exceptionally, we got permission from the *Judenrat* for a three-room apartment that we were to share with another physician, Dr Pinhas (Paul) Klinger and his wife Miriam (Marysia), who came to Grodno in 1939 as refugees from Lodz. We found such an apartment on Jerozolimska Street in a small, somewhat dilapidated one-storey house. We were allotted two rooms of about 20 square metres and the Klingers another bedroom. We shared a tiny kitchenette. This was a lot of space, since the average allocation for a family was not more than a room. There was no bathroom in our tenement and the toilet was in the yard.

The Poles who lived in this flat were to move into our big apartment on Rydza Smiglego in the city centre. All these arrangements took place in an atmosphere of panic, since the move was announced only a few days before the November deadline. People were frantically running, trying somehow to secure a place to live and also take care of their belongings. The Germans were deadly serious about the six hours given for the move and their threat that anybody caught transferring possessions outside the allowed time-frame would be shot. In contrast to the Jews, the Aryans living on the territory of the ghetto had much more time to vacate their tenements.

This was a feverish time. Mother called on our Polish acquaintances and friends and was literally giving away our possessions. It was also, we realized, our last chance to talk to our Christian friends, and maybe entrust them with a few of our cherished family souvenirs and mementos for safekeeping. Mother gave *Pani* Marta and other friends our linen, the tablecloths from Druskieniki embroided by Nadia, our family photographs, my lead soldiers and stamp collection, most of our valuable books, our porcelain, dishes, kitchenware, and many, many other things. They were packed in big cartons and taken away. A lifetime of work and memories! It was heartbreaking to part with my lead soldiers and my stamp collection, but I was told that this was the only way to preserve them for 'after the war'. Mother cried when packing up some of her memorabilia: family pictures, two cartons of albums with souvenirs of Druskieniki, of trips to Italy, to Paris, to Vienna, to Zakopane – hallmarks of a happy life. There were old pictures of Father in the full regalia of a surgeon-captain of the Tsarist Army, taken in 1916 when he was decorated in St Petersburg, and of Uncle Eliasz in his beautiful uniform of the Hussars. Mother kept a few small photographs – of Grandfather Boukhin before he died in 1938, of Grandmother and of Uncle Lolya. We kept only the most basic necessities and clothing; the rest would be safer outside the ghetto, we thought. We never saw most of our possessions again.

Father hired a peasant with a four-wheeled horse-drawn cart for 1 November. We paid a very high price because, under the circumstances, coachmen and carts were at a premium. The Poles had already moved their belongings into our apartment a day earlier, leaving us their rather modest furniture, including beds and several mattresses. In exchange, we left our pieces of furniture that had survived the bombing. Father donated his medical furniture and instruments to the future Jewish hospital in Ghetto II. Interestingly, the Germans allowed the *Judenrat* to move hospital equipment before 1 November. We speculated that they were afraid of epidemics and wanted to have medical facilities in place before the move.

And so came the day for the move. The morning was grey, big snow flakes were falling in clusters from a pallid sky. They melted quickly, turning to slush. It was the first snow of the season, wet and dirty; the cold was damp and penetrating, such that makes people wish they could stay home in front of a roaring fire. We had to move quickly to transport whatever we could. The distance from our apartment in the centre of the city to our new tenement on Jerozolimska Street was about two miles. We could make at most five to six trips if all items were pre-packed and not much time was lost on loading and unloading. Tolo, Father, Mother and the peasant worked feverishly. We loaded the cart to the very top and carried on our backs whatever we could. Tolo went to our new dwelling first and stayed there to unload, while Father and the peasant loaded the cart at our old apartment. Mother helped packing, while I was charged to commute with the peasant, keeping an eye on him. The first thing we moved was food: flour, sugar, butter, cocoa, potatoes and other root vegetables, dried peas and beans. Next we carted wood and coal, then bedding and whatever else we could manage to transport.

The whole city seemed to be on the move. Already from our apartment window we could see people walking beside loaded carts and buggies, people with suitcases, with pillows and packages, people with dogcarts and wheelbarrows, all loaded to capacity. But this stream became a mighty torrent as soon as we reached the main thoroughfare on Brigicka Street leading, in opposite directions, to both ghettos. There were hundreds of people with yellow patches guiding horses, carriages, carts, wheelbarrows and bicycles, carrying mattresses, pillows, beds, cupboards, tables, chairs, cooking utensils, and thousands of other items precariously secured. All were moving towards the ghettos. The town reverberated with the sound of wheels on muddy, wet cobblestones. Poles on the pavement observed this exodus with interest, some with undisguised pleasure. The wet snow continued to fall, adding to the sense of frustration and gloom.

More than 65 per cent of Grodno's Jews went to Ghetto I. Most of my friends, including Shurik and Mirek, most of my parents' friends; Aunt Ada, Izak and Grandmother were there too. Isolated from my friends, I had the impression that a chapter of my life was over. What playmates and pals would I have in our new place? How would it feel to live behind barbed wire? The peasant, trotting beside the cart, was urging his horse on with an occasional crack of the whip and a loud 'vioo'. He was totally indifferent to the sight of the crowd and was humming some tune, visibly satisfied with the handsome profit of this unusual opportunity.

Walking over the railway overpass we found Skidelska Street divided down the middle with a row of high wooden poles. The barbed wire was still wound on huge spools set down in the slush. Polish policemen in their navy-blue uniforms and caps with visors, armed with rifles, were patrolling the streets, helping the green-uniformed German *Schutzpolizei*. The stream of people now divided into rivulets leading into the side-streets to the right of Skidelska, already in the ghetto. The streets were full of suitcases, boxes, mattresses and furniture between which people were rushing and running. Many simply dropped whatever they had carried, rushing back to their old abodes for more. Quick! Quick! Before the fateful six o'clock deadline! We turned on to Jerozolimska and arrived at our destination. Tolo was waiting to unload and we returned to our apartment for the next load to be moved. This was repeated several times before we all packed for the final trip to our new tenement behind the barbed wire. We awakened our old faithful German Shepherd, Asio, from his deep slumber near the stove. All four of us said farewell to our city streets. It was already pitch dark but a mass of people was still on the move. The snow had stopped, the air was damp and foggy. As we crossed the railway overpass we saw that Skidelska Street, the ghetto's boundary, was illuminated. All the street lights were ablaze and additional lights had also been installed by the Germans for the occasion. A white, milky haze hung over the ghetto. We turned on to Jerozolimska and reached the small one-storey wooden building. Our flat was to the left of the entrance. We unloaded, paid the peasant and walked into the tenement. It was exactly six o'clock.

10   *Ghetto II*

We entered the flat, with its low ceiling, through a short hall-way. On the left just next to the entrance was a kitchenette, and on the right a small bedroom which was taken over by Dr and Mrs Klinger. A small room located off the living room became our parents' bedroom. In the right-hand corner of the living room stood a cast-iron stove for coal and wood. The stovepipe divided at right angles at the ceiling. The two branches went through the walls into both bedrooms; one stove was thus heating the whole abode. A cupboard and a small sideboard stood against the wall adjacent to the Klingers' bedroom.

We lit the stove. The flat was small and heated up fast. We all worked feverishly to assemble our beds, shift the cupboards and furniture, and organize our belongings. Tolo and I were to sleep in the living room. We installed our beds against opposite walls. I slept under the window looking out on to the street, Tolo next to the stove, against the wall of our parents' bedroom. In the middle was a large square table with several chairs. The house had a small backyard with a storage shed, half of which belonged to us, and a shabby outhouse. Utterly exhausted, we left our wood and coal in a big heap in the yard, to be stored later.

It was late into the night when we finally sat down for a light supper and tea. It was good to have the Klingers with us. We knew them already from their visits to our old apartment a short time before our move. Originally from Cracow, in the late twenties they moved to Lodz where Dr Klinger, an eminent specialist of sexually transmitted diseases, had an important medical practice. They fled the German advance in September 1939 and settled in Grodno, expecting every day to be arrested and sent to Russia, like so many other refugees from German-occupied Poland. But the Germans caught up with them first.

A charismatic man in his mid-fifties, Dr Klinger was tall, handsome and of athletic build. With his high forehead, aquiline nose and forceful gaze under bushy brows, he exuded intelligence and energy. Abundant, wavy, salt-and-pepper hair added even more stature to his imposing presence. He was by far the most interesting storyteller I had ever met. He captivated us with stories of his adventures as a medical officer in the Imperial Austrian Army during the First World War. Stories about their flight from Lodz in 1939 were spellbinding. His German, which he interjected here or there, was impeccable, without a trace of foreign accent, a tribute to his Austrian upbringing. He was treated with respect by some Germans who wondered about this Jew who spoke such a distinguished, literate *Hochdeutsch*.

Dr Klinger had published a book called *Vita Sexualis* before the war. For having had the audacity to cite statistics indicating that Germans as a nation have an unusually high proportion of sexual aberrations, including sadism and fetishism, he was summoned to the Gestapo and viciously beaten. His life was spared only by a miracle, maybe because of his impeccable German and the intervention of Dr Brawer of the *Judenrat*.

I was so fascinated by his stories that it was a treat to have him living with us. His wife Miriam, or Marysia, as he called her, was a very quiet lady with a slight hearing problem. I saw her coming alive only when talking about their 17-year-old son whom they had sent to take refuge in England just before the outbreak of the war. Her voice broke with emotion describing their farewell at the pier in Gdynia. A few letters reached them in Grodno. He was in Coventry. When the city was massively bombed by the Luftwaffe, the Klingers lived through a thousand agonies. Since then, they had no news but they were confident that their son was alive and well.

On this wintry, wet night of November 1941, as we all gathered around the table with a steaming pot of tea, near the fire crackling in the stove, exhausted and chilled to the bone, we felt somehow more secure being separated from the hostile world of Germans and Gentiles. The fire sputtered and danced in the stove; Asio slept peacefully. I had the impression that he was the only one glad of the move to our cramped quarters. He curled up in a corner next to the stove, enjoying our company and snored lightly.

Dr Klinger said that the Germans, mindful of their winter campaign, would provide the ghettos with food and medicine. They could ill afford starvation and epidemics on the doorstep of the Reich, in a city which was an important railway centre and a stopover for troops on the way to the front. I was only half-listening, wondering who my new playmates would be. Most of my friends were in Ghetto I.

Coming into the ghetto I saw the new Jewish police for the first time. They wore blue armbands with a *Judische Ordnugsdienst* ['Jews' Order Service'] logo on them. They carried short wooden clubs, these were the only 'weapons' allowed by the Germans. I was excited to be on 'Jewish territory'. I fantasized that their clubs became rifles and heavy weapons and that we were fighting and winning a battle against our tormentors. The warmth of the stove finally got the better of me, and I fell asleep at the table. Mother put me to bed as the grown-ups continued their conversation into the night.

The next day was also snowy and foggy. In the daylight, I realized the ugliness of our new abode. Both bedrooms were dark, with minuscule windows looking out on to the yard. The outhouse had no running water or electricity. We had to wash either at the kitchen sink or in a basin, with water heated on the stove. In the apartment opposite to ours lived a *Judische Ordnugsdiens*, a young man called Sam, his wife Rosa and their baby. Rosa's parents, a gentle, quiet couple, lived with them.

Rows of shabby wooden houses like ours extended for maybe a kilometre across the width of the ghetto. The ghetto itself was some four kilometres long, encompassing a number of streets parallel to ours, surrounded by a waste-ground the size of several football pitches. A small concrete building with thick walls stood in the middle. It was an abandoned ammunition dump of the Polish Army. This was to become our 'Central Park'. Beyond it, the wooden shacks and slums continued for another few hundred yards before hitting the barbed wire.

Fifty yards down our street, on Skidelska, workers were finishing stretching double rows of barbed wire between thick wooden poles some two metres high and ten metres apart. These poles separated Skidelska into two parts: one in the ghetto, the other in the city. The entrance gate to the ghetto was located a few hundred yards from our street, in Skidelska Street. It was guarded by German *Schupos* and Polish 'navy-blue' policemen. They manned the gate from a little shack with a stove. Two *Judische Ordnungsdienst* were also there on duty, but outside, in the cold. There was no mixing of Germans and Jews, even at the ghetto gate. German *Schupos* and Polish police with rifles slung across their backs patrolled the area along the newly erected poles.

It was for me a shock to see that I was behind barbed wire, confined by the force of arms. It reminded me of Grodno Zoo, where the animals were fenced in, the dangerous ones behind iron bars. It was beyond my understanding why I should be behind bars like a dangerous animal. I knew from my experience in the Polish school that I was a Jew and as such an object of contempt and hate. Consciously, I never accepted the guilt thrown at me by the Christians; I felt pride at belonging to an old people which gave to the world its first moral code of behaviour, the Bible. This pride was my father's gift to me. However, unconsciously I must have wondered about it because on that day, caged behind this barbed wire, I asked myself for the first time: 'Am I guilty?' Guilty of what? I did not know. This thought that somehow, somewhere I had sinned, we all had sinned, and for this guilt we were deprived of our freedom, was torturing me and kept haunting me.

A new decree was issued by the Germans and posted on the wall of the *Judenrat* office in our ghetto: No Jew should approach the barbed wire to within less than ten metres, under the penalty of being shot. All Jews within the ghetto must wear the yellow patch just as before in the city. Why we should wear the yellow patch in the ghetto, among Jews, defied logic. But orders were orders.

Within a few days, Jewish workers were leaving at 6 a.m. through the gate of the ghetto for factories in the city. They marched along the road in long columns escorted by German and Polish police with rifles. They followed a specified itinerary. Upon their return in the evening, they were searched by the *Schupo* and Polish policemen, for food or other items. A handful of Jews were issued special permits to cross the city. Most were employees of the *Judenrat* serving as liaison between the two ghettos. Provisions were brought into the ghetto through the gate and distributed through the *Judenrat*, which was responsible for all commerce with the outside. Father, Dr Klinger, Dr Heller and others went about the installation of a hospital; supplies were inadequate, there were no anaesthetics, no sulphamide antibiotics, no vaccines. Only some anti-typhoid vaccine and some insecticides were delivered on time.

There were, of course, no schools; any instruction for children or adolescents in the ghetto was strictly forbidden and punishable by death. I was idle and I found in the street many other children of my age also at a loose end. I soon struck up some friendships. There was Danya, whom I had befriended already a few months ago and who lived with his aunt a few houses down the street. We were happy to meet again. He joyously exclaimed in Russian: 'Sasha, you are also here, in cage number two!' He always spoke almost as a grown-up. When he mentioned the Germans, his pale, delicate and sensitive face twitched with disgust.

'Those Fascists make animals out of us, but you will see, our army will not give in, they will soon come and deliver us.' He never lost faith in the Red Army, he dreamt about his father fighting and coming to deliver Danyousha, from hunger, misery and humiliation. Danyousha...he was only 11, but had already tasted a lot of bitterness. His aunt was without resources and they lived in misery. Mother saw that Danya was hungry and often invited him for a meal or a snack. One evening she also invited his aunt. We all sat at supper by our stove on a cold November evening. Father was now again full of admiration for the Russians. *'Molodtsy rebiata!'* [Magnificent lads!], he exclaimed. 'The Germans pay dearly for every inch of Russian soil near Moscow.' This beaten army was now offering a heroic resistance. From the Black Sea to the outskirts of Leningrad the Germans were getting a very bloody nose indeed. In the south, Rostov was holding out; Odessa fell only after three months of savage fighting; on the central front, the battle raged near Moscow. Hitler's juggernaut – approaching the capital city from west, north and south – was stalled. The German press reported bitter fighting around Toula, Mozhaisk, Kaluga, Kalinin, all along the 200-mile-long front. In the north, the Germans had clearly been stopped at the gates of Leningrad despite almost three months of furious assaults on the surrounded city.

German casualties were very heavy. Jewish railway workers reported that long military trains full of wounded soldiers passed by every day and every night. Military hospitals in the city were filled to capacity. This explained the German concern about epidemics. *Der Voelkischer Beobachter* and other German papers carried pages full of obituaries, all for officers and soldiers fallen in recent fighting. Dr Klinger called these pages *Wesoly Kacik* [Joyous Corner] and we graded newspapers by the size of the 'Joyous Corner'. The 'best' carried the longest lists of obituaries. The obituaries almost always ended with, 'fallen for the Fatherland and the much beloved Fuehrer'. This was the part of the paper we took strength from – the longer the pages of obituaries the better we felt.

This stiffening of resistance along the front boosted our spirits and gave us hope. Father was on his emotional roller-coaster again. He, who barely a month ago had been anticipating a Russian collapse, was bursting with optimism. 'I do not see how the Germans can now avoid a winter campaign in Russia,' he cried jubilantly. Father logically expected a swift German retreat from Russia, to shorten the lines of supply, before the real winter set in. He was already thinking about our possible escape through the front lines, which he thought would be close to Grodno. '*Molodtsy Riebiata!*' was the motto of these days.

Danya's aunt, who before the move into the ghetto had been in contact with other Russians, told us about the unspeakable plight of Soviet POWs in the camp of Kielbasin, where hundreds died daily of starvation. 'I am praying for my Yakov that if captured he would rather be shot as a Jew than taken to a POW camp as a Russian. I hope that our soldiers will treat these German sadists the same way, but I know they will not because only very few humans are capable of such bestiality.' Mother as usual had a weep for her family in Russia and we did our best to convince her that they had ample time to evacuate.

We asked Mother to sing. She was not in the mood, but she consented, to our delight, to hum a few Russian songs and we all joined in. And so, encouraged by the news, warmed by a good meal and the crackling fire in the stove, dazed by our songs, we all went to bed almost happy.

The next few days brought tension again. The Gestapo requested from the *Judenrat* another sum of money and more winter clothing for the German Army. SS and Lithuanian murder squads were specifically mentioned. We were forced to part with anything that had a small fur collar, our muffs and much of our wool clothing. The tension was compounded by an incident at the gate to the ghetto where one worker was savagely beaten by a *Schupo* for smuggling in a few eggs and a sausage in his haversack, provisions given to him by his boss. Similar and worse incidents – workers shot for a loaf of bread or an egg – soon became quite frequent as famine made itself felt in the ghetto.

The end of November and December were very cold and snowy. We were glad to have wood and coal for heating and cooking. I enjoyed those evenings around the table, near the stove, listening to Dr Klinger's marvellous stories and jokes. He was an excellent actor and performed while telling his stories. In one of them he played a teacher in one of those Jewish schools where classes were held in Polish. Sliding his reading glasses down to the tip of his nose, he peered at us intensely as he entered the 'classroom'. Suddenly grasping a long ruler, he struck the class register with all his might, screaming '*Shaaa!*' He then sat down and checked the student roster while staring at the class over his glasses.

'First, all precious stones stand up!' he yelled. 'Brilliant, Burstein, Diamond, Edelstein, Granat, Perlman, Perles, Rubin, Rubinstein, Safir.' After a brief pause, he yelled again: 'All precious metals, up: Guld, Goldstein, Goldman, Goldberg, Goldblatt, Goldteller, Korngold, Silber, Silberberg, Silberblatt and Silberpfenig!' He continued: 'All fruit trees and fruits, stand up: Apfel, Apfelbaum, Birnbaum, Kirschbaum, Pflaumenbush, Pomeranz, Traubensaft and Zitrone. Next, dishes and food, up: Butterman, Fishman, Fleischman, Fleischhacker, Kugelman, Nudel, Pfankuchen, Zemmelman and Zitronenfish.'

On another occasion, he acted out his impression of, a doctor of venereal diseases examining a Hasidic Jew. The Hasid is in his traditional garb and very uneasy, whispering in Yiddish into the doctor's ear, *'Vouees? Vouees?'* [What is it? What is it?]. The doctor's answer into his ear is also a whisper: *'Louees, louees!'* – which is the vernacular term for syphilis.

During these long, winter evenings people paid us visits. Dr Heller, who lived next door, came to play chess with Father and usually won, leaving Father in a very bad mood. Tolo's friends came to play bridge and *belotte*, a French card game. There was Dr Rusota, a refugee from western Poland trapped in Grodno. He had graduated from medical school in Genoa, in Italy, and when he happened to have a good hand he hummed Italian songs. Another refugee, Mr Madner, a medical student from Warsaw, came with his pretty young wife, who was also a bridge player, and their two-and-a-half-year-old son, Mareczek. The Madners lived in one room with another family of three. They were happy to come whenever they had the opportunity to escape their cramped quarters. Father and Mother were usually in bed at half-past-ten, while Rusota, Tolo and the Madners stayed on for bridge, after having rocked Mareczek to sleep with a monotonous lullaby: *'Moj Mareczek zloty poschedl do roboty i wrocil z roboty moj Mareczek zloty'* [My golden Mareczek went to work and came back from work, my golden Mareczek]. The toddler sucked his thumb as he was falling asleep on Tolo's bed. I liked these long evenings of bridge. I tried to look over Tolo's shoulder and learn without much success, the basic rules. 'One diamond,' Tolo announced. 'Two spades,' called Rusota. As the bidding went on, the nervous drumming of fingers on the table was mixed with humming. Tolo hummed the latest hits of Maurice Chevalier, Rusota hummed the famous hits of Tito Schipa, *Vivere* or *Parla mi d'Amore*. I stayed with them until my eyelids closed by themselves, falling asleep on my bed.

Lively political and strategic discussions took place around our table by the warmth of our stove. At the beginning of December it appeared that the Soviet Army, far from being beaten, still remained an organized and equipped fighting force. In the south, the Germans were thrown back from Rostov and retreated over 50 kilometres to the Mius River. This was the first serious setback of the 'invincible' German Army. A few days later we learned from German newspapers that a general Russian offensive had started near Moscow along a front of several hundred miles. The German armies were 'withdrawing in orderly fashion to previously prepared positions' – a code phrase for a serious defeat. Kalinin was retaken and soon it became obvious that several important breakthroughs had been achieved by the Russians. The spearhead of this offensive, which opposed Yeremienko and Zhoukov to Von Bock's *Heeresgrouppe Mitte*, were the tough Siberian troops just brought in from the Far East, whom the German papers called the 'White Devils' because of their white camouflage. Father was jubilant; he already saw the Germans withdrawing at least to the Minsk-Baranovitche area, some 200 hundred kilometres from us. We were now becoming convinced that the Russians would hold out and, with the help of the British, beat the Germans. We all speculated that with their first massive defeat the Germans would become less cocky about their final victory and therefore less reckless towards the populations of the occupied territories and, of course, us Jews. But the ultimate morale booster was the entry of America into the war against Germany. Now it was clear to us that, with the material wealth of the US, the tenacity of the British, and the heroism of the Russians, the fate of the German Reich and of the madman at its helm was sealed.

The weeks of December passed in excitement. We were all uplifted by the good news. I had new friends: Monia Butenski, Lutek Niemcewicz, Izio and Danilko Dubinski and, of course, Danyousha with his delicate blue eyes staring at the cruel world of Westerners. Sometimes, though we were both behind the same barbed wire, I felt ashamed for the Germans who confronted Danya. They represented in his eyes the Western 'culture' – *Die grosse Deutsche Kultur*, as *Tante* Thea used to say. What *Kultur*? Fighting half-starved children like Danya? Organizing a world into masters and sub-humans?

I was raised in a prosperous bourgeois home. My father spoke fluent German and French. He instilled in me a strong admiration for Western values, for the ideals of the French revolution which, he said, stood for the best in mankind: *'Liberté, egalité, fraternité'*.

Danya was full of quiet irony. He never articulated it clearly, but I knew what he thought: 'Is this what your Western culture has ultimately produced? Murdering entire populations, reducing entire nations to the condition of slavery and bondage?' His pale, almost transparent, lips twitched with a bitter smile. I felt ashamed for the West, for my ideals, for admiring the French revolution, for idealizing Napoleon, for *Tante* Thea and Pastor Plamsch. I tried to tell him, 'Our liberation will come from the West – England, America.' But Danya had other ideas: 'The West is corrupt and greedy, the Germans are their representatives, all of Europe works for them! It is "sub-human" Russia who will liberate mankind from war, oppression and poverty, because it knows the bitter suffering of the oppressed.'

Most of our time, however, we spent sledding, as snow was very abundant that year. We dragged our sledges on to our single little hill in the ghetto, off Artyleryjska Street, overlooking the 'Central Park' of Slobotka. We would slide down together, the icy wind biting into our faces. It was so much fun! It was good to come back home to a warm room, arranged by Mother into a cosy dwelling. A hot, savoury meal was always waiting for me, the fire was crackling in the stove and, come evening, Dr Klinger would tell his wonderful stories. Today was Hanukkah and a small blue light shone in some windows. A smell of cooked linseed oil hung around a few houses. I had a treat of potato latkes with sugar at Lutek's house. He lived in one room with his nine-year-old brother Izia, his mother and his aunt, Mrs Sofnas. Lutek's father had died two years earlier and his mother, a seamstress, provided for the family.

At that Hanukkah celebration at Lutek's I met Julek Herschfeld, a boy of 15, very short and physically underdeveloped. Lutek was the opposite of Julek: tall, blond, athletic and exuberant; his smiling face exuded confidence. His curly hair was always in disarray. He was the boisterous youngster of Jerozolimska Street and most boys were afraid of the physical strength of this 14-year-old. Lutek had a special relationship with Julek; he was very gentle and liked to discuss the scholarly things in which Julek excelled. I came to like Julek and appreciated his knowledge of history, especially the Napoleonic campaigns, which he knew so well. I was reading *Les Miserables,* and I found in Julek someone with whom I could discuss that fascinating period. Julek was also very good at chess, and was always winning. In our tournaments I didn't have a chance. Unfortunately, some boys taunted him and pointed their finger at him in the street. It was painful for me to see this, and to see the hurt on Julek's face. Lutek and I engaged in street battles to chase away those cruel young louts.

Another of my new friends was Monia Butenski. He was also 15. When he smiled he showed a row of big, uneven teeth; his smile reminded me of the French comic Fernandel. We called it 'Monia's smile' and poked fun at him. He had the ungainly body of a teenager. He was in love with a pretty girl of 16, Rysia Balaban, who didn't even so much as look in his direction. Monia suffered because of this, but we cruelly poked fun at him, singing: *'Monia tu, Monia tam, kocha Rysie Balaban!'* [Monia here, Monia there, he loves Rysia Balaban!].

We became used to 'our' ghetto, and the barbed wire appearing brutally from behind a house or a tree did not surprise or shock us any more. 'Here we shall be until one glorious, beautiful, sunny day the war will be over and we will be out of our cage.' I tried to imagine how this would come about. The Germans will simply pack up and run. The Russians will come and open the gates of the ghetto and we will run towards the soldiers, kiss them, wave flags and be free again... Maybe the British and Americans will come... I can see many planes in the sky, hundreds of them and thousands of parachutes opening above our city... We will greet them with flowers, sing American and English songs.' My eyes filled with tears. Would that sunny day ever come?

Dreams! After the good news of America's entry into the war and of the German retreat near Moscow, in January came the realization that the Russian offensive was spent and the front stabilized many hundreds of miles away from Grodno. We were uplifted by the firing of a number of German generals and the sacking of the Supreme Commander of the Wehrmacht, Marshal von Brauchitsch, a clear sign of the Fuehrer's wrath over the defeat and failures of the German Army in their autumn offensive. The Germans were pushed back some 100 miles from Moscow, but Hitler decided to stay put. Many cities near Moscow became surrounded fortresses, *Igelstellungen* – hedgehog positions, as the Germans called them, and the Soviet offensive just petered out. The German retreat to the Minsk-Baranowitche line predicted by Father did not materialize, the situation became stationary. The winter was exceptionally cold with temperatures reaching −25° to −30° centigrade. Jewish workers coming back from the railway told of many trains full of frostbitten Germans. Occasionally, furtively daring to glance across the barbed wire, we caught sight of a German soldier with a civilian multicoloured shawl around his neck – ear-muffs and a lady's muff wrapped around both hands. The stern military figure of the 'Master Race' transformed into a raggedy-doll, the 'Winter Fritz', as they were called in the Soviet press. The German papers were full of such figures, praising their heroism in −40° weather.

This was the work of the bravest general of the war, General Frost. I could not understand why everybody was saying that this very cold winter was so hard on the Germans, but nobody said that it was also hard on the Russians, as if Russians could by some magic escape frostbite. It was the Germans after all, not the Russians, who were the 'super-humans', weren't they?

My birthday came on 13 January. I was 12 years old and Father decided that I should have private lessons in mathematics, Polish and Hebrew. One day, a short young man with a shy appearance came to our home. His face was unusually pale; his small, reddish, watery eyes were deeply recessed. His upper lip was covered with a rusty-red stubble. In this arctic cold he wore a shabby raincoat with a thin lining, an old hat with ear flaps and torn mittens. His whole body quivered when he entered our warm room and tried to move his cold-stiffened fingers by the stove – a pitiful sight. Mother explained that he was Salomon Breitner from Warsaw, that before the war he had been a student at the Language and Literature Department of Warsaw University and that he had been a refugee in Grodno since 1939. Mr Breitner was to come regularly three times a week for two hours of lessons. To be undisturbed, we would have our lessons in my parents' bedroom. I was not exactly enthusiastic about the idea of having private lessons intruding on my playing with my new friends or on kibitzing the bridge players, but I could hardly argue my case with Father. So, I submitted.

Salomon – or Sala, as we called him – came regularly and we noticed at once the depth of his misery. He was working outside the ghetto in the tobacco factory. The pay that Jewish workers received was just enough to buy the loaf of black bread a week, but he could get something to eat either from Germans or from Poles. He could also buy food or some other goods from Poles and barter in the ghetto. He, like others, took chances by smuggling. It often happened that 'good' guards were at the gate. This meant that the *Judische Ordnungsdienst* could bribe them into looking the other way and enabled people like Sala, half-starved and half-frozen, to bring into the ghetto something to sell, allowing many a family to keep afloat. There were, however, days when the *Schupo* guards or the Polish policemen at the gate were new, or included a particular scoundrel. Jewish police organized a secret system whereby the incoming columns were given advance notice of an inspection or a specially vicious guard. Workers and the *Ordnungsdienst* communicated by sign language. When alerted, the workers shed their prohibited goods right on the street, some swallowing whatever they could before reaching the gate. Everybody knew the risk of smuggling food into the ghetto, but most had little choice. The bold and the resourceful could somehow survive, but Sala was neither. Most of the time he was starving and freezing. I could tell from his face what kind of 'catch' he had brought from his work. Mother took care of Sala as best she could. Three times a week before my lesson he ate supper with us and afterwards always took with him a little package of food. We were very privileged, having brought food with us, and even here in the ghetto, Father occasionally saw patients from the outside. They received special permits for admission into the ghetto hospital, simply because there was no experienced non-Jewish surgeon in Grodno. The only non-Jewish surgeon was a very young Byelorussian doctor by the name of Nitchiporuk, and some more influential Aryans did not trust him enough. Of course, they paid with all sorts of delights, such as sugar, butter or honey, that the Lord bestowed on human beings to enjoy.

11   Our Life in the Ghetto

Days and weeks of our first winter in the ghetto passed uneventfully, divided between playing with my friends, my lessons with Sala and long evenings of watching Father and Dr Heller locked in their eternal chess struggle or Tolo and his companions playing cards. It looked as if for the time being the Germans were leaving us alone.

Dr Heller was beating Father about three times out of four, putting him in a bad mood. I often wondered why my father played with somebody so obviously superior to him if he resented losing so much. The spectacle of these two bald men staring at the chessboard, their fingers drumming against the table or making convolutions in the air, describing hypothetical moves while muttering something completely incoherent, was so hilarious that I had to bite my lips not to burst out laughing. Their intense concentration never lasted long. As soon as one of them got an advantage, his face relaxed and a sort of sound filled the air. Both men were practically tone-deaf; all they were capable of was some buzzing. One had to know them well enough to recognize a sort of melody. Whenever Father was winning, he hummed off-key something that vaguely resembled the overture of Moniushko's opera, 'Frightening Manor'. Dr Heller had another tune that I could never properly identify. As soon as the situation on the chessboard changed, the tune changed. At any moment one could know without looking who was on the ropes. A tie was usually mute. Being the underdog, Father accepted a tie gracefully while Heller had his mood spoiled henceforth. But when Father won, the garbled humming of 'Frightening Manor' exploded into a loud 'papa, parappa, parappa, parapappa-rappa, parappa, parara...', or was sometimes replaced by even more off-key whistling. I loved to see Father win. He enjoyed it so much.

On other evenings I would watch our bridge players, Rusota, Tolo, and the Madners; sometimes the Klingers or Mrs Heller joined in. A young woman in her early thirties, Mrs Heller, who usually came with her three-year-old daughter Helcia, was on the heavy side. I joked unkindly that she must sit on two chairs lest she overflow and hit the floor. Here again, the air was heavy during bidding. But most of the time the room was filled with the humming of Rusota's Italian hits or Tolo's Maurice Chevalier songs. They at least were in tune!

On the rare occasions when Tolo was home alone, he would tell me about his love adventures in France. What a wonderful country it was and what splendid girls! I was particularly impressed with a story of his about making love to the daughter of a French Army colonel in Lyons, how the girl was crazy about him, how her father locked her up in her room and how Tolo climbed the walls of the house to join her in her bedroom. I was proud of having such a brother and bragged about him to my friends. Whether this story was true or not did not matter – I believed it, and all girls in the ghetto were crazy about my handsome brother.

One day in March as I was playing with my friends outside, we saw people running in panic, screaming in Yiddish, 'Go home, hide, Gestapo!' It was too late to run home. We froze behind the wooden fence in Lutek's yard; we could peek through the holes in the boards without being seen from the deserted street. On the corner of Skidelska Street we saw two Germans in leather coats with fur collars, wearing the much dreaded SS caps. They were with two Jewish policemen and two other people, a woman and a young child. A car appeared and a civilian carrying a tripod and several cameras emerged. One of the Germans was shouting orders in the loud guttural screeching of which only Germans are capable. The woman, dressed almost in rags, was made to undo her hair and let it fall in disarray. The German shrieked again and the woman knelt in the muddy gutter. She was kicked and rolled into the mud and melting snow. My heart was racing. Are they going to shoot her? But no shots were heard. Instead, the woman was helped to get on her feet by the two *Judische Ordnugsdienstmen* while the civilian was installing and adjusting his equipment. The child was then also rolled in the gutter.

In their dirty and pitiful state, the two were repeatedly filmed and photographed by the civilian. One uniformed German was also taking pictures with a Leica swung around his neck. The scene lasted maybe ten minutes, after which the Germans left in the car, slowly turning the corner of Skidelska towards the gate. The Jewish policemen with the two subjects also disappeared. For days to come I saw before my eyes the German photographer and the poor woman and her child rolling in the mud of the Jerozolimska Street gutter. We were told that in Ghetto I the same crew went into a rabbi's house, made him dress in the traditional garb, made him dance, and then cut his beard while taking pictures.

This is how they leave us in peace! I was again day-dreaming, imagining us, the dirty and the abused, organizing an army. We had real weapons and burst out of the ghetto firing on anything green and black that moved. I was personally killing the SS man who struck the woman. I was tearing him apart with salvos from my submachine gun. Cowards, how proud they are of beating women and children.

The first timid sunshine of April was here. The air was fragrant with the promise of spring. Storks and flocks of other birds were coming back from the south in long formations. The air was filled with cawing and squawking. Ice and snow were melting and water was gurgling in the gutters. The inhabitants of the ghetto became more lively, the streets full of people enjoying the warm sunshine. After almost six months in their squalid environment people were pale, their clothes worn out and mended. Young women and girls still tried to provide some colour, and it was a pleasure to look at them strolling along our *Ghetto Zwei Promenade*, which included Jerozolimska and Narutowicza Streets. Tolo was the Don Juan of the ghetto and could be seen often with different girls at different times. Lutek, Monia and myself spied on them. The trail led us to the hospital door. Tolo worked as a male nurse at the Jewish hospital where Father was the surgeon. On Mondays and Thursdays, when on call, he often disappeared with his conquests into a small private room which had a cot for male nurses on night duty. Tolo was furious with me and beat me in style on several occasions, but spying on Tolo was out of my hands since he provided such an attractive target for my pals.

Between lessons with Sala, playing with my friends and spying on my brother, time passed quickly. At the end of May an order was issued by the Germans that all dogs owned by Jews should be given up for collection by the Jewish police and ultimately for extermination. We did not want to give up our Asio, our faithful friend for 13 years, a family member, to be shot by the Germans. Father found a solution. The *Ordnugsdienstman* Sam who lived opposite had a brother, Zalman, who worked in a military hospital right across the street from the ghetto. He befriended there a German cook who agreed to keep Asio in his kitchen. We were relieved; what could be better for our faithful old friend than to be in the warmth of a hospital kitchen? When the fateful day came, Father took Asio on a lead right to the barbed wire on Legjonowa Street. Walking up to the wire was forbidden but luckily the whole street was deserted, with not a single *Schupo* or Polish 'navy-blue' in sight. On the Aryan side of the wire was the German in his uniform, waiting for the dog. Asio was a stocky animal but managed to squeeze under the wire. Father handed the German the lead as I silently observed the scene from a distance. The German squatted and gave the dog a pat on the head, then stood up and pulled on the lead. Asio anchored his legs and refused to budge. The German tried again and again to make him move, but Asio was stubborn and still very strong for his age. He seemed to be saying: 'I am a Jewish dog and I want to stay with my master here in the ghetto.'

Sensing the danger of the situation, Father shouted in an angry voice, 'Go over there at once, at once!', and forcefully pushed the dog under the wire towards the German. Asio turned his head to look at Father, lowered his tail and let himself be dragged by the German to the Aryan side of the street. He looked once more at his master who still angrily commanded him to go, lowered his head, curled his tail between his legs and dejectedly followed the German, without even looking at Father. I burst into tears. Father was silent but I could see his eyes were wet too. Four days later, Zalman, the brother of Sam the *Ordnungsdienst*, told us that Asio had died. He let himself starve to death.

Meanwhile the month of May was in its full splendour, the few chestnut and apple trees and the single lilac bush of the ghetto were in bloom. I spent my time outdoors. We played handball, we played chess, and also cards – *oczko* and poker. We were, of course, at the same time, spying on various couples and on Tolo. We forgot the reality of our situation and lived in the world of dreams and wishes where we kept our dignity intact and, in this sense, I was fortunate to be a child. But in the evening, when I was alone, when everything was still and the moon rose in the sky, bathing our house and Skidelska Street with its long line of poles and barbed wire separating us from the world in its silver light, reality came upon me like a stab in the heart. I resented the moon being always on the other, the free side of the wire and asked myself interminably the question... why? Why so often in my child-hood was I compelled to wrestle with the outside world trying to make me different and guilty?

I remembered an episode from before the war. I was just coming out through the gates of my school when I saw a crowd of boys surrounding and mocking a man. His move-ments were uncoordinated, he drooled and his glassy eyes stared without expression. The boys were jeering and poking at him, like a swarm of biting flies. I felt terribly sorry for this poor man and angry at the boys who tormented the unfortu-nate because he was different and helpless. So are we now, different and helpless. I saw the Germans as this tormenting crowd of boys. But wait, you tall, blond, blue-eyed Aryans, the world will not belong to you. It will belong to the short, the brown-eyed, the black-haired, the downtrodden, and the hungry. They are already stopping you at the gates of Moscow, Leningrad and Sebastopol. I was brooding again; closing my eyes, I could see the flashes of Russian guns a thousand kilometres away.

But waking up from my day-dreaming, the only Russians we could see were Soviet POW's, and their fate was so much worse than ours. Once I had a furtive glance at a small column of prisoners being led by German sentries on the other side of Skidelska Street. They looked so miserable, unshaven, skin and bones, in scraps of clothing, many without shoes, their feet enveloped in dirty rags against the cold of the snow. The camp of Kielbasin was a most sinister place. The very word Kielbasin evoked horror in the local population. Jewish work-ers at the *Heeres Bauamt* – the army construction site with a carpentry shop near Lososna, not far from Kielbasin – told horrifying tales about cartloads of dead prisoners leaving the camp every night; about messages written in blood on the walls of the barracks. The only way to leave the camp alive was to be taken for dead along with piles of corpses on a wooden cart driven by a special burial squad of POW's to a burial ground a few miles away. The German Army was starving millions of Soviet prisoners to death. Dysentery and typhoid fever were rampant. The prisoners were simply left to die. Father, having spent two years in a POW camp in Germany during the First World War, did not believe these stories, always saying that they must be exaggerations. Unfortunately, they were true.

We were elated to learn that the Russians had started an offensive, retaking Kharkov from the Germans, but our elation soon turned to disappointment as we read that the Russians were trapped in a 'cauldron'. The Germans claimed hundreds of thousands of Soviet prisoners and dead. We were crushed when in June the German Army resumed its offensive towards Stalingrad and the Caucasus. None of my father's forecasts came true. The front was being pushed further and further away from us. Meanwhile, rumours circulated about the deliberate starvation of hundreds of thousands of Jews in the Warsaw Ghetto. We thought with anxiety about the fate of Lenka, Rysio, Eliasz and Sonya, about our friends, the Chorazyckis and the Alapins.

For us in Grodno June passed in relative calm. In July, however, a few young men and women escaped from our ghetto. Rumours spread that they were joining the partisans organizing in the forests near Grodno. They left without being noticed. Yet one afternoon a detachment of *Schutzpolizei* marched straight into the ghetto and arrested a number of hostages. Some were well known, lawyers, social activists, school teachers, members of the *Judenrat*, and some *Ordnugsdienst*. I happened to be playing in Lutek's yard when we saw people running in the street. '*Daytche in der gass!*' [Germans in the street!] someone shouted in Yiddish. I ran home, where an anxious Mother waited for me. In a few minutes the street was empty. Suddenly I heard harsh German voices. My heart pounded. 'They are coming here,'

Mother whispered. A sound of boots, first against the pavement, then closer, then next to our house. Instinctively, we pulled inside the room, away from the door and windows. A loud knock on our neighbour's door. Strident voices could be heard from Sam's apartment: *'Schnell, los, los, los.'* The Germans left after a few interminable minutes. We heard a woman's voice in the entrance: 'Sammy, they took Sammy!' It was Rosa, Sam's wife. We opened our front door and there stood Rosa in shock, with their baby in her arms. 'They took Sammy!' she cried. In a few days the bad news came that the hostages had been shot, Sam amongst them. Officials of the *Judenrat* were warned by the local chief of the Gestapo, Errelis, that in the event of another escape attempt from the ghetto he would invite a special SS execution squad, the so-called *Einsatz Kommandos*, to liquidate the ghetto altogether. We all wondered how the Germans had heard of this escape. The fact was that, shamefully, we had some Jews collaborating with the German police. Some employees of the *Judenrat* and some *Ordnungsdienstmen* had special passes allowing them to walk in town and visit German police headquarters. It was clear that informers were at work in the ghetto.

The anniversary of the German invasion came and went without our taking much notice. Soon we were in the midst of a hot July. Nadia had been dead for over a year and we had been in the ghetto for over eight months. As difficult as it was for many people, we somehow survived. People were trying to fight despair and gloom. Some new songs were composed and became popular. One of them, sung by young people, went like this:

Ghetto jeden, ghetto dwa –	Ghetto one, ghetto two –
Bardzo smutna to gra.	A very sad play.
Zydow on wywozi, Polakom on grozi.	He deports Jews and menaces Poles.
Nie wiemy co jutro nam da.	We wonder what tomorrow will bring.

We sang some Russian love songs and I imitated Tolo:

Ty pomnish sad a v niem	Do you remember the orchard
moya liubimaya?	and in it my beloved?
Tsviela tcheremkha akh,	The bird cherry tree was
kak ona tsviela!	blooming, oh how beautifully
	it bloomed!

We often asked mother to sing, but she invariably refused, saying 'Caged birds do not sing.' In the steaming heat of July, I day-dreamed of kayak trips with my father, of bathing in the Niemen, of picking berries in the forest. It was the season of the wild strawberries and the thought of fruit made my mouth water. There were a few vegetables grown in the ghetto, cucumbers and onions, but there was no fruit whatsoever.

It was in the stifling heat of a July afternoon that I was sent by Mother to take a small package to my father at the hospital. The hospital stood on a narrow street on the opposite side of the ghetto, not far from the place where our Asio had been given to the German cook. The barbed wire ran along the middle of the street, dividing it into the Aryan and the ghetto sides. As I approached the hospital, I saw on the Aryan side of the street a boy of my age, dressed in shorts and a brown shirt with a black tie and a swastika on his arm. He was coming in my direction. I stopped to look at him with curiosity since I had never seen a *Hitler Junge* before. The boy spotted me, turned his head the other way and continued walking. I also resumed walking and we approached each other on opposite sides of the street. As we were level with each other, separated only by the width of the narrow street, the boy suddenly ran up to the barbed wire. I saw for a second a pleasant face and short blond hair neatly parted on the side. But the lips were twitching in a spasm of contempt and disgust. Before I could grasp a thing, I felt something wet on my cheek and on my leg. All this was so sudden that when I realized what had happened, the boy was already disappearing behind a house gate. I stood stunned, dangerously close to the wires, wiping spit off my face and burning with rage and humiliation. I did not say anything to anyone. I was shaken not only by the event, but by my passivity. I asked Father after dinner: 'Are we really a people of cowards and parasites to be hated so much?' I wanted again and again to understand what was happening to me. Father never ran out of patience to repeat how proud I should be to be a Jew, to belong to an old nation that gave the world its moral code. 'We are always,' he added, 'at the forefront of humanism. We were never cowards – the Maccabees, the defenders of Jerusalem and Masada, the settlers of Palestine, Trumpeldor, the Jewish Brigade, so much heroism and courage! We will always be hated by the forces of darkness: those who suppress freedom of worship, the pagan Babylonians, the Greek and Roman tyrants, the medieval Church and the Inquisition, and all those who want to have an easy answer to difficult social problems. They all found in us a scapegoat. The fact that we are weak, dispersed and without a country, makes us an easy target. This is why we strive to have a country in our homeland of old Palestine.'

He was convinced that we could rebuild a 'land of milk and honey', that we could live in peace with the Arabs, sharing the land with them. 'Having been strangers in so many lands, we shall know how to live with others. There is no reason,' he continued, 'why Palestine cannot become the Switzerland of the Middle East.' It was my Father all right, the eternal optimist. I looked at a map of Palestine in my school atlas and my heart expanded when I imagined that maybe some day we would have our own country and our Jewish Army would march against our oppressors.

As if to answer my dreams, something extraordinary happened: that evening the lights went out and the siren sounded. Allied planes! Whose planes? Russian or British? We listened intently to the feeble drone. The full moon made the night clear and everything visible for miles around. We stood in the street, our hearts beating with joy and anticipation. We stared at the sky, praying for bombs, but the planes flew very high; soon their drone subsided and the siren sounded again. The alarm was over. The whole of the next day everybody in the ghetto talked about the planes. It seemed that the *Schupos* at the gate had become panicky at the sound of sirens. Several *Schupos* ran inside the ghetto convinced that no bomb would fall on the Jews. The 'master race', such lions against women and children, became like chickens. The planes never came back but the ghetto was now awash with rumours of all kinds. Rumours about separate peace negotiations between the

Soviets and the Germans whereby the Germans would with-draw back to the old border, to Brest-Litowsk. We would be free! Rumours about Roosevelt's intervention in favour of the Jews and a proposal to evacuate them to America. The sad fact – but we did not know it then – was that FDR, Cordell Hull and the entire State Department paid no attention to our plight, about which they were very well informed.

Unfortunately, the Red Army was further than ever from us. According to German newspapers, the Wehrmacht was marching into the Caucasus, approaching the oil fields of Maikop; it was also reaching the outskirts of Stalingrad on the Volga. Baku's oil fields were cut off and the Soviet Union was denied the fuel necessary to continue the war. The British were chased by the Africa Korps all the way to Alexandria. The Japanese were beating the Americans in the Philippines and the 'impregnable' British fortress of Singapore fell to the Japanese in 48 hours. We were all stunned at the military ineptness of the Allies, which stood in such contrast to the ferocious resistance offered by the Red Army. We started seri-ously to doubt whether militarily the Allies would ever be capable of defeating the Germans and the Japanese. Father and Dr Klinger worried as they leaned over a big map of the Soviet Union. Dr Klinger was pessimistic, his duodenal ulcer was acting up again. He was on his rice diet, looking gaunt and sick.

During July and August we had 'visitors' in the ghetto – German soldiers, usually on the way to the front from their leave in Germany. They came to see 'strange sights in the East', including the sub-human species, these *Untermenschen* caged behind the barbed-wire fence. They came in groups of three or four, Leicas hung around their necks, taking pictures. The streets emptied instantly when people got wind of such a visit from our *Judische Ordnugsdienstmen* at the gate. However, in one such foray, a band of Germans managed to grab a young girl in the street before she could get away, then carried her off in a car and smuggled her through the gate. They drove her into town, gang-raped her and threw her into the street the next morning. The girl was arrested as a Jew tres-passing outside the ghetto and would have been shot had the *Judenrat* not managed to buy her back at the last minute. The

German soldiers evaporated, as they could have been prosecuted for *Rassenschande* [defiling the race]; for a German, having sexual relations with a Jew was a criminal offence.

At about the same time Father accidentally cut himself with a scalpel during surgery. The wound on his palm, between the thumb and the index finger, was small but the scalpel had just been used on a patient for cleaning out an infection. Father knew what this could mean to his hand. He immediately operated on himself and disinfected the wound with whatever was available to him. When he came back home from the hospital his hand was completely wrapped in a bandage. I saw that he was worried. The situation became quite alarming when the next day his hand swelled and he began to run a fever. Father decided that another cleaning out of his palm was necessary and went to the hospital. A paramedic performed the procedure under his supervision. On the third day after the accident, his arm became swollen and reddish-blue veins ran up to his armpit and he was running a very high temperature. Dr Klinger, Dr Heller and Dr Rusota all agreed that if the hand were to swell some more and show signs of gangrene, he should ask for permission to go at once to Ghetto I to have the hand amputated by Dr Finkel. I prayed for my father's hand. On the fourth day, the fever fell and the swelling slowly started to recede.

Very disquieting news about the Warsaw ghetto started to spread in September. There was talk about people being loaded into cattle trains and transported to an unknown destination. Rumours had it that Jews were being taken east – 'resettled in the *Ostland*' – and put into camps to work for the German Army. Some of these tales were spread by the Germans themselves. Asked directly at the *Judenrat* they confirmed that yes, Jews were being sent to the east into labour camps and yes, they were working hard but they were better off than in the ghettos. We knew from sporadic contacts between our workers and some Aryans that the conditions in the Warsaw ghetto were atrocious: people were dying by the hundreds daily from hunger, cold, typhoid fever and dysentery. Mother and Father said that Lenka and Rysio had made a mistake going back; they would have been so much better off with us.

Deep inside ourselves we all felt uneasy. We feared that sooner or later Grodno Jews would also be 'resettled in the *Ostland*'. It was rumoured that in such labour camps the men were castrated so that no Jews could reproduce. I was filled with dread, believing that death would be preferable to castration and slavery. Father was strangely silent, Mother filled with fear, and our friends apprehensive and nervous. Fear was with me now even in my games with Lutek or Danya: fear of death for myself and my loved ones. It was ever-present despite German denials, oppressing, augmented by the stifling heat of the end of summer and the monotonous sound of *Schupos'* boots on the pavement along Skidelska's fence. God, how I wanted to live!

News from the front seemed encouraging. It seemed as though the Germans could not take Stalingrad, although the *Voelkischer Beobachter* boasted that Stalingrad was in German hands. But Dr Klinger, an expert in reading between the lines, was sure that the German summer offensive at Stalingrad had stalled without achieving its objectives. Unlike in 1941, there were no claims of *Kesselschlachts* and tens of thousands of prisoners. There were just communiqués about bitter street fighting. It was obvious, as Dr Klinger said, that the Russians had withdrawn in orderly fashion and were hanging on tenaciously to the city. In Africa, Rommel was blocked at El-Alamein and was now in full retreat. Father was on his roller-coaster again; he was of the opinion that the German strength had almost consumed itself. Dr Klinger was much less optimistic, saying that we lived in a time of total war and total murder. He opined that in the future, after Germany was defeated, a special medal would be forged in our honour: the 'Medal of the Ghetto'.

'If we survive,' he added with a bitter smile, 'we shall wear it with pride and bequeath it to our children, for it will remind the future generations what evil human beings are capable of. It should provide a warning of the instincts lurking in the dark recesses of the human soul, a warning to the human race before it destroys itself. If I survive,' he continued, 'I will write a book about this period. I will call it *Nosilem Zolta Late* [I Wore the Yellow Patch].'

But Dr Klinger was changing. His ulcer attacks were more

frequent, his diet more and more restricted to rice, oatmeal and milk, which were not easy to find in the ghetto. In the nine months that we had lived together I had seen him change from a cheerful and vigorous man to a man subdued by illness. His complexion was sallow and his features drawn.

Even my carefree brother was preoccupied. He was now more than ever absent from home at night. Mother and Father did not question him about it. I knew exactly where he was going and even with whom. It was not difficult to have an affair; it was one of the few joys of life left. He was lucky to have access to the little room at the clinic. Many young people took turns for their romantic encounters at the abandoned arsenal house in our 'Central Park'. The ghetto youth were intent on living for the moment, trying to extract some pleasure amidst the shabbiness of our lives. The small wasteland of the Slobodka, with the pathetic ruins of the old arsenal, gave to many a young couple an escape from the harsh reality and the strangling fear for the future.

The High Holidays were approaching in an atmosphere of gloom intermingled with expectation. Among persistent rumours about the liquidation of the Warsaw ghetto we were grasping at straws with every bit of encouraging news – still hoping against hope for some German decency. We still wanted to believe the German explanation of the 'resettlement in the east'. We expected to hear rumours that trains filled with Warsaw Jews were going east, through Grodno, but there was none of that. We were encouraged by stories about the 'good life' of Jews in Hungary, who, we were told, were free. We took this as 'proof' that there was no central plan for our destruction. And yet, deep down, big and small, rich and poor, we all sensed our doom in spite of the calm prevailing here, in our ghetto. The calm before the storm.

By the end of September we read in the *Voelkischer Beobachter* a brutal speech of Hitler. The speech referred to the *Ausrottung* (extermination or eradication) of the Jews. The sentences that stood out for us were: 'When I spoke in 1939 at the Reichstag, the Jews laughed me out. Countless are laughing no longer and those who still laugh perhaps in time will also stop laughing.' Dr Klinger analysed the speech carefully and concluded that the word 'perhaps' (*vielleicht* in German) suggested that some negotiation with the Allies concerning our fate was underway and that this was Hitler's way of saying, 'if you do not satisfy my conditions the Jews who have not yet been dealt with will be so in time'. It was a frightening speech.

We drew our strength and hope from reading aloud the 'Joyous Corner' which was getting longer and longer, often with several pages of obituaries for Germans fallen on the Eastern Front, confirming the extraordinary intensity of the battle for Stalingrad. *'Molodtsy Rebiata!* They are bleeding those scoundrels white!' Father shouted. The Germans were throwing more and more resources into the fight but were unable to dislodge the Russians. Papers such as the official organ of the *Waffen SS, Das Schwarze Korps*, or the mass circulation weekly *Das Reich* described the ferocious battle for every inch of the city, silently acknowledging the extraordinary tenacity and self-sacrifice of the Red Army soldiers. In the Caucasus, the Germans were also stopped short of their objective even though the swastika was planted on the summit of Mount Elbrus. Leningrad was still holding out, after a whole year of siege. In Africa, after reaching the vicinity of Alexandria at El-Alamein Rommel was pulling back into Libya – and what Father called 'the Rommel–Montgomery tango' had changed its direction again. Nobody here was taking the African front seriously. Father, Klinger, Heller and Rusota were all convinced that the Allies were not sincerely fighting the Germans; that their military ineptness was a ploy to bleed the Germans and the Russians simultaneously, calculated to help the Russians just enough to prevent their collapse but not enough to ensure a swift victory. All saw in it the British diplomatic perfidy at work: 'to strike a balance' and 'to divide and rule'.

It happened suddenly one evening when we were just ready to sit down to dinner. We heard forceful knocking on the door. Mother opened the door, two *Judische Ordnugsdienstmen* and two *Schutzpolizei* with helmets and rifles entered our flat. Surprised, we looked at them with fear. *'Wo ist der Arzt Chaim Blumstein?'* [Where is the doctor Chaim Blumstein?] asked one of the Germans in a commanding voice. Father stepped forward. *'Mitkommen!'* shouted the German. Father took his jacket and cap from the cupboard, kissed Mother and said casually, 'I'll be right back.' The Jewish policemen stood in the entrance with sad expressions on their faces. They seemed to say, 'Forgive us, we are only doing our job.' All this lasted a few minutes and we hardly had the time to realize that Father had been arrested and might never come back. Mother ran immediately to see Mr Zadai, the chairman of the *Judenrat* of Ghetto II, who told her that Father had been arrested by the Gestapo and taken to the SD headquarters in town. He had no idea as to the reason for Father's arrest, and said there was nothing he could do and that we should wait for the outcome. Mother came back in tears and I was crushed by fear. A Jew arrested by the Gestapo was as good as dead. I knew that my father would not take abuse from the Germans, just as he did not take it from the Soviets. Only here, it would be certain death. I would not see Father again...

We had Dr Klinger to comfort us. He reminded us of his own arrest the previous year. If he, who had tarnished the 'master race' in his book *Vita Sexualis,* questioning the sexual and mental sanity of many Germans, had come back, there was no reason why my father shouldn't. This was of course rationalization. We knew what state Dr Klinger had been in when he was brought home from the Gestapo. He had had to be carried, had stayed in the hospital and convalesced for days. He never mentioned the horrid experience of the Gestapo interrogations. Why had Father been arrested? Were there any grounds for singling him out among the 50 ghetto doctors? We tried to hypothesize in vain. Rosa, the young widow, came over to comfort Mother. She knew only too well what it meant to have your husband arrested by the Gestapo.

We spent a sleepless night. I was with Father, seeing him beaten, tortured and even shot. Tolo came back late. He had not been at home at dinner time and did not know about Father. Trying to hide his anguish, he sat there, coughing and chain smoking. I could see his cigarettes glowing during the whole terrible night. Dawn came and I fell into a deep sleep. When I opened my eyes, grey daylight filled the room; it was late morning. It was raining outside, a fine October drizzle, harbinger of the autumn rains. It was difficult to face life without Father; I was convinced that I would not see him again and the world was an abysmal pit of gloom.

There was an uninterrupted stream of visitors, and I realized how many good friends we had. To me all their discussions, theorizing and sympathy were rather irritating, but I knew they brought comfort to Mother. Tolo went to the *Judenrat* to contact some *machers*, employees of the *Judenrat* who were in contact with the German police or the Gestapo. They could get information nobody else could obtain and exert some influence nobody else could. Above all, they knew who, when and how to bribe. Some took good advantage of their privileges by exacting heavy fees for their services. They claimed they had to buy their way around the greedy Germans. Some were arrogant, aware of their position of power. Sometimes they also sincerely tried to help. Particularly powerful among *machers* were those with direct access to the Gestapo officers, such as Gestapo *Kommandant SD Obersturmfuehrer* Heinz Errelis. The three we knew were Shulkes, Bass and Sarnacki. We knew Bass better than the other two and Tolo went to ask him to plead for Father's release. Bass promised to help us and told Tolo to return that evening. In the evening, Tolo came back from the *Judenrat* with good news: He said that a handsome gift for Errelis would be necessary to plead for Father's release. We promptly agreed. We were encouraged by the conversation with Bass. The fact that a ransom was mentioned was a hopeful development. Another tense night passed. The following day, we got news that officials of the *Judenrat* in Ghetto I had also intervened on behalf of Father, pointing out his indispensible services as the only surgeon of Ghetto II.

In the evening, 48 hours after his arrest, the unbelievable happened: the door opened and there was Father. He was shaky on his feet, his face was drawn, grey stubble covered his head and cheeks, which I had always seen close-shaven. His shoes and trousers were covered with mud from walking in the gutters. I threw myself on him, hugging and kissing him profusely but Father did not respond; he took a few steps, removed his coat and dropped heavily into a chair. He did not respond to Mother's kisses either, he did not speak. His blue eyes looked into the distance, beyond the people in the room. He was very pale and droplets of sweat covered his forehead. We all became silent, sensing that something quite terrible had happened. Father remained still for a long while and then kissed every one of us very tenderly. Mother whispered, 'Musik, Musik, what a state you are in!' After a long while Father spoke. 'There were moments when I was sure that I would not see you again and moments when only the thought of you kept me from committing the irreversible. Thank God we are together again!' This was all he said about his 48 hours in the hands of the Gestapo. We never learned what had happened to him, except that cuts and bruises covered his back and torso. He fainted while getting ready for bed and we ran to fetch Dr Butenski, Monia's father. He examined my father and ordered him to stay in bed for several days because his heart condition had worsened.

The day after Father's release, two Jewish policemen came to remove our beds. Embarrassed, they said that they were following orders from the chief Gestapo interrogator, the sadistic *SD Sharfuehrer*, Kurt Wiese. They told us what Wiese said about father: *'Der Jude wahr frech'* [The Jew was arrogant]. 'He must be taught a lesson, he was lucky that I did not shoot him. Remove his bed and let him and his family sleep on the floor for six weeks. I will check on it.' The Jewish police removed all our beds. As I feared, Father had not given in to the abuse of the SD henchmen. It was, as he said, only the thought of us that held him back from spitting in the faces of the SD torturers.

Father told us the reason for his arrest a few days later. It was a letter written by my cousin Lenka from Warsaw, asking Father to send her some of her belongings that she had left with us. The letter somehow found its way to the Gestapo, who took it for a coded message and wanted to know what 'secret code' was involved: what articles of clothing stood for gold and what for silver, etc. Given the state of isolation of the ghettos of Poland under Nazi rule it was difficult for Lenka to know about our conditions here in Grodno, just as it was for us to know about conditions in the Warsaw ghetto. A stupid letter could have easily cost Father his life.[1] This was as much as we ever learned from Father about the Gestapo episode.

---

[1] 'We later learned that Lenka escaped from the Warsaw ghetto during the summer of 1942 using 'Aryan' identity papers. Shortly thereafter, she was denounced, taken to Gestapo headquarters on Aleja Schuha, tortured and murdered. It is possible that Father's arrest was related to that event.

The misty drizzly days of October were here. The *raspoutitsa* was in full swing. For the next few weeks every once in a while, the Jewish police inspected our tenement to ensure that Wiese's orders had been followed. Although we slept on the floor, we outsmarted the Gestapo by hiding two of our mattresses in the storage shed during the day and bringing them in just before going to sleep. Father was very tired, he always went to bed as early as it was safe to do so. Many people came to congratulate him on his miraculous return and this was also tiring for him. He was visibly changed, tense and withdrawn. He appeared preoccupied by some ever-present and difficult problem. He barely touched food; he did not play chess, he did not laugh; and the off-key Monioushko's overture to *The Terrifying Manor* was no longer heard. Even Dr Klinger's jokes and stories did not produce much effect. He kept repeating to himself, *'Soukiny, pra-soukiny, pra-soukiny syny!'* [s.o.bs, arch-s.o.bs, arch-s.o.bs!].

Rumours of the liquidation of the Warsaw ghetto had persisted since the end of August and they were the object of heated discussions and speculation by our friends at bridge. Especially worrisome to all was the fact that, notwithstanding German assurances about the work camps for Jews in the *Ostland*, there was no talk of trains with Jews going east through Grodno. It was hard to imagine transports of many thousands of people over a period of three months without the railway workers somehow getting to hear of them. After all, Grodno was an important railway centre, the marshalling yard for all trains going north-east from Warsaw and from Germany. Of course, transports could also go east through Brest-Litovsk, but there was no talk of such trains either. The conclusion was that these trains must have been discharged of their human cargo before reaching Grodno.

The optimists assumed that these work camps were located somewhere in eastern Poland, the pessimists feared that SS execution squads were unloading and gunning down Jews from western Poland in a manner similar to the way they operated on the territory of the *Ostland* and in the Baltics. Until his arrest Father angrily refused to believe that such a wholesale murder could be sanctioned by the government of a nation considered as civilized, but the 48 hours at the

Gestapo had changed everything. Father actually started to believe the unbelievable: that a genocide of the Jewish people, directed and supervised by the German government, was underway. He never spoke about it, but I think that his arrest and torture by the Gestapo in a perverse way may have saved our lives.

One evening, Sala came to my lesson bringing disturbing news: Some young people were about to leave the ghetto for the forests and join the Red Army partisans. Rumours about Russian partisans organizing in the wide stretches of forest north-east and east of Grodno were brought into the ghetto by Jewish workers who had occasional contacts with their Byelorussian or Polish colleagues. Every now and then, they could have a chat with an Aryan friend while being led through the streets. Some would unobtrusively slip into an Aryan friend's apartment and stay there for the night, rejoining the column of workers the following morning. Such forays into the world of the Gentile were not without risk but they were possible whenever Polish police provided the escort instead of the Germans. It was easier to buy them off.

Sala told us that the decision to escape was taken in the wake of rumours about imminent transports from the Grodno ghettos. I was proud of being taken into Sala's confidence. Sala was torn by indecision. He was a young man of weak constitution. His grey complexion, small size, sunken chest and watery little eyes inspired little respect for his martial skills. He was always giving the impression of shivering from his feet up to his short reddish moustache. To top it all, he limped from a leg wound incurred during his flight eastwards in 1939. His whole little person aroused compassion in me, and I could not see how Sala could last long in the rough conditions of winter in a forest. And indeed, Sala decided to stay in the ghetto. He convinced himself that things were not as bad as the *panikmachers* [spreaders of panic] were making them out to be.

But the conditions in our ghetto were quickly deteriorating. After a year of being more or less isolated from the world at large, we were short of everything and, above all, of wood and coal to keep warm. Almost all private stocks of combustibles had been consumed during the long, cold winter of 1941/42.

Most of the wooden fences and trees had been chopped up and burned and there was no coal. Some supplies of coal were promised by the Germans but, since Ghetto I had priority over Ghetto II, the prospects for keeping warm that winter were very slim. We were still lucky to have some wood and coal left from the previous winter – maybe enough to get us through November. Most people were in a much worse predicament. Hunger crept into many houses and the *Judenrat* could not cope. Lines of hungry people grew longer every day. Mortality rates among older people were staggering. On Skidelska Street, every day, long wooden carts carried bodies to the cemetery. They at least had gained their freedom. Danyousha, my Russian friend, was getting sick; he was coughing and his delicate, almost transparent complexion became grey. His forehead was often covered with sweat and his blue eyes glimmered with fever. Danya's aunt Rosa was sick; she was unable to get up to fetch some ration cards from the *Judenrat*, and their tiny room was freezing cold. I felt for Danyousha and often took him home with me, but not often enough. He repeated in his impeccable Russian to my mother, 'Tatyana Pavlovna, you will see, the end will come, we shall prevail over those Fascist swine, we are already winning.' He had increasing attacks of spasmodic coughing and Father suspected some serious complication in his condition.

'Danyousha, sit down, have some tea, stay for supper,' we urged, but Danya always refused because he wanted to go and take care of his aunt. He thanked us for everything, put on his thin, patched overcoat, took the bundle of food Mother had prepared for him and disappeared coughing into the cold dampness of the street.

12   The Gestapo Takes Over

On 2 November 1942 – in ominous confirmation of recent rumours – Jewish workers assembling at the ghetto gate in the early morning were not allowed out and were detained there for hours. The ghetto was surrounded by a detachment of German Special Police and the gate control passed from the District Police, the *Schutz Polizei*, to the much-dreaded SD, or *Sicherheits Dienst*. *Obersturmfuehrer* [SS lieutenant] Heinz Errelis, the chief of the SD in Grodno, took over the control of both ghettos.

An eerie quiet descended on the ghetto. The streets were singularly empty. Occasionally, one could spot through the window a passerby with the blue armband of the *Ordnugsdienst*. Everyone else was inside with their families, and a heavy heart. The sense of impending doom hung over us; my throat constricted after hearing the bad news. So this is it. Shall we survive together? Shall we be separated? My mouth was dry, I did not want to survive my parents or my brother. I did not want to witness their deaths. If we had to die, I wanted us to die together. And yet... maybe it was true that we would be sent together as a family to a work camp in the East, just as the Germans were promising. I was not afraid of labour, I was almost 13 and I was strong. Maybe they would leave us in peace. Maybe these awful rumours about mass executions, about castrations, were just spread by anti-Semites who derived joy from our fear. Dear God, keep us all together there in the east, I prayed.

Father and Tolo went to the hospital to get some more information. Dr Klinger was in bed with another ulcer flare-up. I was strictly forbidden to leave home. Through the windows I could see a small stretch of barbed wire on Skidelska. A heavily armed soldier, clad in the green uniform of the Special Police, was pacing along. Special Police had replaced the more

144

complacent *Schupos* and the navy-blue caps of the Polish police.

My Father and Tolo confirmed that our ghetto was under the control of the SD – the Gestapo – and that completely new rules concerning the movement of people both within and outside the ghetto limits now applied. Each ghetto had its own *Kommandant*. Ours was a certain SD man named Otto Streblow, while the *Kommandant* of Ghetto I was Father's sadistic interrogator, Kurt Wiese. The number of Jews working outside the ghettos was drastically cut and only the most 'useful' were given permits to work in town, under the watchful escort of the Special Police. The ghetto was to receive electricity and water only two days a week. Our quality of life had sunk to a new low.

Ghettos in *shtetls* around Grodno had also passed under Gestapo control. The handful of people who were still allowed outside no longer received their permits from the District Police *Kommandantur*, but only from the Gestapo. Such permits were issued to a few *Ordnugsdienst* men and to the 'contact men' with the Gestapo, called *Verbindungsmaenner*. The gate was now controlled not only by the German Special Police but also by the Ghetto *Kommandant* Streblow, who installed an 'office' next to the gate. A similar arrangement was operating at the gate of Ghetto I on Zamkowa Street. There Kurt Wiese took personal control of the incoming workers.

The next day, while Father and Tolo were at the clinic, we heard a knock on the door and there stood a Jewish policeman with…grandmother! The old woman looked completely bewildered. She was shivering. We were stunned. How did she get here? What had happened to Izak and Ada? The *Ordnugsdienst* man, who was a friend of Izak, explained. Grandmother had been brought to the *Judenrat* by Izak and Ada. Izak had told his friend that they were leaving the ghetto and begged him to bring Grandmother to us. Izak's friend concocted a story about Grandmother being sick, needing to join her son in Ghetto II. He got a permit – approved by Wiese – from Rubinczyk, the chief of the Jewish Police, to escort her to her son in Ghetto II. We still did not fully understand.

Before he could continue, Grandmother began to cry. 'Esterka, they left me all alone. I do not know where they have disappeared, they took me to an office [she meant the *Judenrat*] and left me there. But he is so nice, this charitable man,' she pointed to the *Ordnugsdienst*, 'he brought me to you. I am so happy to see you, my children. What can I do, an old and crippled woman? It is a terrible word, the word "war", my child, so terrible!'

She was sobbing from happiness. She had come as she stood there before us, in her light coat and a kerchief around her head; she brought nothing with her, not even the bare necessities. But all this was irrelevant, she was with her family and her old wrinkled face slowly relaxed as she wiped tears from her eyes. 'I am so happy to see you! I am so happy to see you!' she kept repeating.

The policeman gave Mother a note from Izak. 'I will not let us be trapped here like rats,' Izak said. 'We are leaving the ghetto. Do not wait! Escape! Run! You are all condemned to die! I knew that already in Kaunas, over a year ago. Do not wait! Itchke.'

This was easier said than done. Izak was a country boy from Marcinkance. He grew up in the forest, he knew the peasants, their customs, their mentality and could even speak their languages. He also knew Polish, Byelorussian and Lithuanian peasants from corners as far west as Suwalki, south as far as Volkovysk and Slonim, and north and east as far as Druskieniki, Lida and Eishishki. He was a real local, with many Polish friends in the city.

'*Molodetz!*' said Father when he came home. Izak was one of those men who are free no matter the circumstances. It was a bold move to leave a warm place in the ghetto for the unknown when winter was just knocking at the door. This mentality ran deep in some *shtetl* Jews who lived in communion with nature. He did not know then that on the very same day half of the Jews in his native Marcinkance chose to run for the woods rather than submit to the Germans. The German and the Polish police opened fire. Many young men and women died, including several of Izak's closest relatives, but some reached the woods and among them several of Izak's 11 brothers. They eventually joined the Red Army partisans and fought the Germans. Four of them survived the war. But this was still far into the future.

Grandmother was entirely lost. Her severe deafness was a barrier separating her from the world. She was 76 and her memories were still from the First World War when her town of Ciechanow had been bombarded and burned by the attacking Germans. She had been shell-shocked and lost a good part of her hearing. For as long as I could remember her she was not entirely aware of what was happening around her. She was a very quiet woman, content to read her book – over and over – and dream of the past. Her deeply recessed and now darkened eyes glowed when she repeated, 'Straszne to słowo wojna, moje dziecko! – How terrible is the word "war", my child!' I looked at her sitting next to the iron stove and warming her stiff, bony fingers, staring lifelessly through the slits of the stove into its red glow. The day was fading and in the twilight her wrinkled face and her shrivelled, helpless silhouette appeared so sorrowful. Suddenly, the great misfortune of this good woman who had struggled all her life to bring up her family, to give an education to her four children, who had lost her hearing, her home and her husband to the savagery of one war only to be thrown into another, much worse, without even knowing what it was all about, occurred to me in all its cruelty. Tears filled my eyes; with all my heart I kissed my old grandmother and she smiled at me with her toothless smile, the first smile since she had arrived.

The next day, a decree to the Jewish population was issued by the Gestapo and signed by the *Obersturmfuehrer*, Heinz Errelis. It itemized the rules concerning *Die Umsiedlung der Judischen Bevoelkerung* [the resettlement of the Jewish population]. The Jews of Grodno were to be moved to *Arbeitslagers* [work camps]. The Jewish population was to cooperate fully with the German authorities in this move. The ghetto was placed under a daily curfew from 7 p.m. to 6 a.m. The *Judenrat* was to draw up lists of families to be moved in successive transports to the work camps. German and Polish police, assisted by the *Judische Ordnugsdienst*, were to ensure the orderly departure of transports from *Sammlungspunkten* [assembly points] to the railway station or to the camp of Kielbasin, which would function as a temporary transit camp before resettlement. A strict curfew was to be imposed during the transport operations. Unauthorized presence in the street would be punishable by death. During each operation, people would be required to be at the ready in their tenements, with their personal belongings packed, including warm clothing and valuables.

The decree further stated: 'After their names have been read out by the authorities, people must evacuate the premises rapidly and in an orderly manner. They will assemble in columns in the middle of the street and wait until ordered to depart for the *Sammlungspunkten*. On the days of transport, no Jew will be allowed outside of the ghetto and all work permits will be temporarily suspended. Any infringement to the orderly execution of the Resettlement to Work Camps is punishable by death.'

The sombre news spread fast and people heatedly discussed the situation on every street corner, but the streets quickly emptied upon the appearance of German Special Police patrols in full gear, with helmets, rifles and fixed bayonets. We were now hopelessly trapped.

At the same time, news began to filter through that Jews from the surrounding *shtetls* – Indura, Skidel, Luna, Pozeczki and others – had been brought into the infamous camp of Kielbasin, which had been emptied of the last sick and starving Soviet POWs a few weeks ago. It was ready now for another shipment of 'sub-human scum'. The camp was placed under two sadistic SD men: Rinzler and Schott. The Germans requisitioned four-wheeled peasant wagons and buggies from nearby villages and ordered the peasants to drive the Jews to Kielbasin, some five kilometres from Grodno. The move was to be completed within 24 hours and families were given very little time to pack; people were shot for lack of swiftness. The panicked Jews left most of their meagre possessions to the onlookers and to the Polish 'navy-blue' police who supervised the move. As the day progressed, an incessant stream of peasant carts, buggies and wagons of all kinds overloaded with people and belongings, poured into the wire-fenced gates of Kielbasin. Inside, a mixed detachment composed of German Special Police with bayonets and rifles at the ready; attack dogs and Polish police kept a close watch on the operation. An icy wind and freezing rain pierced through man and horse. Greeted with shrill German cursing and the ferocious barking of attack dogs tugging at their leads, they were assembled in the camp and then literally thrown into the freezing barracks still pervaded by the smell of death and horror inflicted on the Russian prisoners. Rinzler and Schott were seeing to it that orders were swiftly carried out, using two steel-spiked whips on anybody who got in their way. They shot many people for 'dragging their feet'. The inferno had opened its gates in Kielbasin, engulfing 20,000 stunned Jews from the *shtetls* around Grodno.

Events unfolded quickly. It was announced that transports to work camps would start from Ghetto II and Kielbasin within a few days. According to Errelis, some of these camps were located in Silesia and some in the east. The list of names for the first 5,000 Jews to be 'resettled' from Ghetto II was drawn up by the *Judenrat*. The Jews in the ghetto were divided into two groups, the *Nutzliche Juden* [the 'useful' Jews] and the others. 'Useful' Jews performed work that was either important outside the ghetto, especially to the German Army, or indispensible inside the ghetto. To the Germans, deathly afraid of epidemics spreading to the outside, most medical doctors belonged to the latter category. Clearly, *Nutzliche Juden* were to be spared deportation for the moment. Ghetto I, with the main administrative offices of the community, was spared liquidation at this time. However, a few thousand Jews from Ghetto I were ordered to Kielbasin to make space for *Nutzliche Juden* who were to be transferred from Ghetto II to Ghetto I.

Panic seized the ghetto. Everyone wanted to know if their name was on the lists of transports drawn up at the *Judenrat*. The 'contact men' with the Gestapo became omnipotent. They carried some weight with the SD and had direct access, if not input, to the 'lists'. Sometimes they could also bribe the Gestapo men. People were soon besieging them, offering jewellery, gold and money, anything, to avoid 'resettlement'.

Wild news about an imminent 'second front', about the Americans pressuring the Germans to stop the persecution of Jews, about ongoing peace negotiations between the Allies and Hitler circulated with an intensity augmented by despair, only adding to the frenzy of people trying to escape the transport.

Streblow, our ghetto *Kommandant*, was a young man in his mid-twenties. He wore a leather tunic and a green cap with skull and crossbones, the insignia of the SD. In addition to his pistol, he often carried a thick leather whip studded with iron spikes. On the second day of his tenure as *Kommandant* of Ghetto II, he whipped a young Jewish policeman who was too slow for his liking. The poor man was taken to the hospital where his deep cuts and lacerations had to be stitched by Father. A few days later Streblow showed up in the ghetto just before curfew and caught a teenage boy who had forgotten to affix the yellow star to his jacket. Without a warning or a word, Streblow shot the youngster through the head, point blank. Shortly after this incident, a group of workers assembled during the late morning at the ghetto gate. Their employers had promised to let them recover the tools they had left at their workshops in town in the wake of the ghetto's closing. Unexpectedly, Wiese and Streblow appeared. Without a word of warning, they fired bursts of sub-machine-gun fire into the crowd standing on Artyleryjska Street. It was a terrible slaughter. Many people were killed and many wounded. The SD men disappeared after the shooting, only to reappear after a while. They approached a young *Ordnugsdienst* who was wounded in the leg. The man had taken off his boot and was sitting on the step of a house, waiting to be taken to the hospital. Streblow shot him dead. Wiese and Streblow then proceeded to the hospital where Father and his staff were busy taking care of the wounded. Among the injured was a seven-year-old girl who had just happened to be walking with her mother on Artyleryjska Street during the shooting. Wiese ordered the child to be carried out of the clinic and placed on the pavement. Father pleaded with him for mercy for the child. Wiese did not speak, he pulled out his Luger and shot her dead. Father carried the dead child back to the clinic. What was even more wrenching for my father was that the child was the daughter of Mr Heller – not the doctor – a man whom he knew personally. I learned about this tragedy much later – my parents wanted to spare me anxiety and tried, often in vain, to hide disturbing events from me. The dead from the slaughter were buried in a small yard transformed into a makeshift cemetery. Proper funerals for the victims were forbidden by the Gestapo.

From that time on, Wiese and Streblow were called the

Schlaechters, or butchers in Yiddish. Their appearance sent everybody running for their lives. The street emptied and *Der Chef* could pass, nonchalantly touching the top of his impeccably shined Prussian riding boot with his whip. When the two *Schlaechters* visited our ghetto together, they amused themselves by entering some tenements and terrorizing the families. Once they ordered a watchmaker to stand with his head against the dial of a wall clock and began competing to shoot out the numbers on the dial. This gratuitous brutality had the clear aim of terrorizing us, and was not a good omen.

I prayed for some miracle to happen. I was forbidden to leave home and had only permission to play with Lutek, Danya and Monia, who were my closest neighbours. We were often interrupted by people suddenly rushing down the street, shouting '*Der Schlaechter* is coming, run away, hide!' From the four of us, only Danya could expect to be on the first transport. Lutek said that his mother paid almost all her savings to be taken off the transport list. Monia's father was a physician and therefore 'useful'. He knew that he would not be on the first transport. Father was also told that we would not be on the transport list. Danya and his sick aunt were on the ghetto welfare rolls and by the criteria of the *Judenrat* certainly not indispensable.

How were they going to survive in a work camp? Danya, so weak and frail, his aunt very sick. Danya was not afraid. He told me once: 'I hope they send us far to the east, closer to the front, to *nashikh* [our people]. I will escape. If they kill me, so be it, but I will not put up with this. Aunt is very sick, she will not survive the trip, but I'll escape!'

'Did you hear, Tatyana Pavlovna,' he addressed Mother, 'those Fascist swine cannot take Stalingrad, they are beaten. *Nashi* [our troops] are beating the hell out of them. Please God, maybe I will live to see them run! They are all brave against helpless women and children, but in the field, bayonet against bayonet, they run like rabbits!'

At home, Dr Klinger and Father now stopped their conversations as soon as they saw me approaching. They wanted to spare me anxiety, but I knew in my heart that *Umsiedlung* would mean the grave for most of us.

It was getting dark. It was snowing with the heavy, wet

snow of the first snowfalls. The transport was due in a few days. When I came back home from Lutek's, I found Mother in a state of agitation, her eyes red from crying. Father was not home; he had left just a few minutes ago. 'Why did he have to go just before curfew?' I asked. 'He has an emergency at the clinic,' was the answer. I became nervous and concerned when the clock struck seven o'clock and Father was still not back. We had no electricity and in the dark my mood became even more desperate. Mother and Tolo tried to calm me down by saying that he was probably sleeping over at the clinic. This did not surprise me; my father had lately been working around the clock, taking care of the wounded. But then why wasn't Tolo at the clinic as well? I felt that the grown-ups as usual were hiding something from me.

The next morning Father was still not home and I became very agitated. Mother finally took me into her confidence. Father had decided to establish contact with Dr Docha in Zukiewicze, near Indura, 30 kilometres away. He was waiting for a propitious moment to pass under the barbed wire and escape the watch of the Special Police patrols. Yesterday's heavy snow and poor visibility had provided such a moment. Father was now convinced that escape from the ghetto was the only way to avoid the 'resettlement', but knew it had to be organized in order to succeed.

I admired my father's courage; I had never admired him so much and never had I been so terrified, for him and for us. The ghetto was guarded day and night by patrols ready to fire on anything that moved close to the fence. Patrols were now also operating within the ghetto and one could easily be shot for transgressing the curfew. Father was very well known by the Aryan population in town and also in the villages around Grodno. He could quickly be denounced. Even if he succeeded in crossing the city, how would he make it to Indura? How would he make it back? I was at home pacing the room, watching the clock, listening to every knock on the door. Every shadow moving by the window made me nervous. The Germans had made it a point of informing the population that a Jew caught on the Aryan side would be summarily executed. The Aryan population was awarded a special bounty as an incentive to denounce any Jew outside the ghetto. Thank God, so far nobody had spoken about Father being caught and this was a good sign.

The day passed and then came another curfew and another night. I could not sleep; I feverishly imagined father shot, his body lying in the mud next to the ghetto fence, or being only wounded and fleeing with police dogs behind him, or denounced by a Pole, taken to the Gestapo and tortured. I dozed on and off, escaping into dreams and then snapping back to harsh reality again. I could sense that Mother was awake; smell the stench of Tolo's *makhorka* cigarettes and see them glowing in the dark. And then the door opened; Mother reached it in one jump. Father was back and in one piece! Dear, dear Father, all wet, covered in mud, but in one piece! In the flickering light of the candle I looked at the clock; it was 3 a.m.

Father did not say much, he was very tired. His short overcoat made from Scottish tweed was torn in several places and he was all covered with mud, as he had had to crawl quickly under the barbed wire of the fence. To leave the ghetto he had had to wait for over two hours near the hospital for the change of the police patrol whose movements he had previously studied for several days. The fog and the driving snow made it so much easier. The short coat he wore had never had an affixed yellow patch and was therefore a 'pure Aryan' coat without the pale spot betraying a removed Jewish star. He walked from the fence to the nearby cemetery, where he spent the night protected from the snow by some roof. Luckily, it was not that cold.

By dawn Father proceeded towards Indura, first on foot then on the daily bus from Grodno. This was very risky but his Aryan features did not betray him as a Jew and nobody recognized him on the bus. He arrived at Docha's home before noon. For the way back Docha ordered his coachman Mikhalko, a good-natured Byelorussian peasant, to harness two horses to the cart and drive Father to Grodno. The foul weather drove the few Germans at police stations along the road to stay inside. Mikhalko left Father in town after dark.

Walking back to the cemetery, dad had a mighty scare. A Polish boy ran after him, yelling, 'You Jew, what are you doing here? Give me your wallet or I will turn you over to the police!' Father did not flinch and snapped, 'Go away you little hooligan or I will grab you by the scruff of the neck and take you to the police myself!' The boy disappeared, swearing. Father's self-control, his Aryan looks and his flawless Polish made the boy doubt his own judgment. But the incident demonstrated the principal danger lurking on the Aryan side – the innate talent of Poles of any age for 'sniffing out' a Jew. Father waited at the cemetery until well past midnight for an opportunity to crawl under the barbed wire back into the ghetto. He ran down Jerozolimska Street, cautiously ducking from time to time to avoid being spotted by German patrols.

And then came the evening of the transport. At exactly seven o'clock the dark ghetto streets were suddenly flooded with light. For the first time since the ghetto was created all street lamps were ablaze. Projectors and spotlights installed at several points near the fence were sweeping the streets. At the same time electricity was restored to the houses, although water remained cut off. Our house stood in the strong beam from a projector located near the fence on Skidelska, flooding the lower part of Jerozolimska Street with light. The scene was frightening and unreal. Though not on the first transport list, we were gripped by fear of what would happen next. We all sat in silence around the table with the Klingers, and waited. Our supper was cold and unfinished. Only Grandmother sat serene in her corner, her hands crossed on *War and Peace*, whispering, 'How terrifying is the word "war", my child, how terrifying!' Each minute lasted an hour. Finally they came: the rumble of boots on the street, at the gate, the pounding at the neighbour's door, hoarse German voices, Yiddish voices, a woman's voice, the cries of a baby. They entered the tenement of Rosa, Sammy's wife. She left with her one-year-old baby. How would she manage? How would the child survive the trip? People were leaving neighbouring houses, assembling in the middle of the street to the accompaniment of the harsh *'los ... los ... schneller ... los ... !'*

The night was clear and cold and I saw through the window, in the stark brightness of street lights and projectors, many people with suitcases, bundles and knapsacks, holding children by the hand. There was Rosa with the child in her arms. She walked straight, with a warm kerchief over her head, keeping the child snugly wrapped up, close to her body.

Her father and mother followed, loaded with bundles and suitcases. They were being helped by an *Ordnugsdienstman*, doubtless a friend of Sammy. They all quietly joined the others. A number of Jewish policemen helped arrange the crowd into a long column under the orders of a few German Special Police and Polish 'navy-blues' with rifles at the ready. Everything proceeded in an orderly fashion. People were now being taken from the big house where Monia and Danya lived. I strained to see Danya and thought I caught a glimpse of a small silhouette helping a bigger one, but I was not sure. There was too much light, and Mother ordered me away from the window. How would he manage with his sick aunt? I felt miserable. 'Why am I left? Why do I have a father who can protect me, and he doesn't? Goodbye Danyousha, will I ever see you again?' I had a lump in my throat and tears collected in my eyes. The crowd was in the street for some time; then orders were given and the column moved, slowly disappearing towards the *Sammlungspunkt*, somewhere near Artyleryjska Street.

The next morning was beautiful and cold. After almost a week of foul weather the sun shone brightly in a cloudless sky. I went to see Lutek. Mrs Niemcewicz greeted me.

'Glad to see you Alik', she said. 'My nephews are all gone, so is my sister, in this awful cold.' Her eyes were very sad.

'And Mrs Sofnass?' I asked.

'Gone also,' Lutek replied.

'God only knows how she will survive the trip, she was so frail,' his mother added.

Lutek was sad that Frieda, a girl he liked very much, had been taken as had the Dubinski family with Izia Dubinski, his best friend. I was thinking of Danya: Where was he now, where was he going?

In the evening, Tolo brought the news that my teacher Sala Breitner had also been taken. It seemed as though everyone had been deported. Father and Dr Klinger discussed the brutal way in which the transport had been assembled. The SD men had all been at the *Sammlungspunkt* – Wiese, Streblow, Rinzler, Schott and their commander Errelis – beating, shooting and instilling terror. The sick, some brought on stretchers, were packed in with the healthy as if a quota of Jews was to be delivered to the work camp regardless of their physical condition.

The ghetto now was to be shrunk to half its previous size. The entire stretch beyond our 'Central Park', including the ammunition dump, was to be evacuated and resettled in the remaining half. The abandoned area was to become temporarily a no man's land where neither Jew nor Gentile was allowed. Anybody found there would be shot on sight. Any property left in the abandoned area belonged to the Reich. Workers leaving the ghetto to work at German installations in town were warned that smuggling food into the ghetto was punishable by death. There was practically no food and no fuel. On most days there was no water or electricity. We remembered the words of Hitler in his September speech: *'Unzahlige lachen schon nicht mehr'* [Innumerable Jews are no longer laughing].

We took comfort at the sight of Jewish workers in escorted columns going to work outside again. At least there was still some contact with the world; some newspapers would be coming into the ghetto with them. Work outside the ghetto was a privilege; one could at least eat on the job, get a piece of decent bread. The ghetto bakeries were supplied with the most disgusting quality of flour, mouldy and filled with a powder that looked and tasted like sawdust. The bread had the consistency of clay. One had to be careful eating it and remember to chew it well, as one could easily choke on a wood splinter, or worse. We started now to feel the pinch. All the 'goodies' from Mother's pantry – the salted butter, those pails of rendered lard with fried onions, those sacks of flour and kasha, jars of honey and boxes of cocoa, all the wonderful things that kept us going for more than a year – were gone, except for some rendered lard [*smaletz*]. My breakfast and supper consisted of a few pieces of the heavy clay-like bread with *smaletz* and weak tea without sugar. The midday meal was invariably a heavy dried bean or yellow split pea soup, with more clay-like bread and a sliced onion. I was never hungry, but I dreamt of the good times, of a roast goose or turkey, of chips, hamburgers and, above all, of chocolate! Where did they disappear to, the Wedel chocolate bars and Plutos' chocolate-covered halvah which I had loved so much before the war? I would even easily settle for the Soviet chocolate candy *Mishka Kosolapyi*. But I was lucky not to go to bed hungry when so many children around me were starving.

It was still light when columns of men coming from work on the outside halted on Skidelska along the ghetto fence and at the gate. Each column was escorted by several German and Polish policemen. Every haversack was checked and many a worker was submitted to individual body checks. Suddenly a shiver ran through the column as the phrase '*Der Schlaechter* at the gate' travelled from man to man with lightning speed. Streblow was at the gate, and *Der Chef* [the chief] was in a bad mood. Two men were taken aside and beaten by the Special Police for smuggling bread and lard. Streblow approached, nonchalantly playing with his long, spiky whip. '*Verfluchte Schweine!*' he screamed, raining lashes on the two huddled men. 'How many times do I have to repeat that nothing can be smuggled into the ghetto?' He drew his Luger. A shot rang out, one of the men clutched his abdomen and slid down onto the cobblestones. Like a bolt, the other man took off, zigzagging as he ran. Streblow fired a few more shots but kept missing. '*Verdammt nocheinmahl!*' he swore as he dashed to his 'office', grabbed his *Maschinpistole* gun and opened fire in the direction of the running man, hitting workers who stood between him and the escapee. The running man was hit and fell, tried to get up, waved his hands and then fell motionless as Streblow continued to fire, still screaming '*Verfluchte Schweine!*' Several men lay on the road in the mud, some motionless, others screaming for help or moaning in pain.

'*Los...los...*' The gate now opened and a stream of workers poured inside. Streblow was at the gate, whip in hand, his cap with skull-and-crossbones askew over his forehead. Father was summoned to the clinic. Tolo and other nurses accompanied by Jewish policemen were sent with stretchers to pick up the six wounded men and the two dead. Streblow was now in a state of rage, waving his whip and hitting anyone within reach and whose face he did not like. Tolo tried to look away from the *Schlaechter*, but the SD man noticed and applied a powerful lash aimed at Tolo's face. Tolo managed to duck and turn his head away; the spikes hit him across the shoulder and only the thin end of the whip reached the corner of his left eye. That night Tolo came home with a dressing on his eye, which was swollen and blue from a large haematoma. He had a red welt on his neck and the shoulder of his overcoat was ripped open by Streblow's blow. His eye swelled so much that he could not open it and had to apply compresses which Mother prepared around the clock.

Dr Klinger had managed to get hold of a copy of the *Voelkischer Beobachter* and studied it carefully. The Germans claimed they had won the battle of Stalingrad, yet their communiqué referred to bitter fighting in the city. The major piece of news, Allied landings in North Africa, was very disappointing. This was not the eagerly awaited 'second front', a full-fledged battle front along the Atlantic coast of Europe; it was only a preparation for a possible future second front somewhere in the south of Europe. We were nevertheless excited, hoping that the Germans, facing America's powerful resources, would realize the war was lost and relinquish their terror against us. On the Russian front, beside Stalingrad everything was quiet, the usual lull in the fighting due to the *raspoutitsa*. With the frost coming any day now, we were expecting a big winter offensive by the Red Army.

In the flickering light of a kerosene lamp Dr Klinger read the paper in his vibrant, impeccable German, injecting a few thoughtful comments in Polish. After reading the news reports, he read from the 'Joyous Corner', pages and pages of obituaries of Germans fallen at Stalingrad. It was becoming clear that, although at the pinnacle of her conquests, Germany could not be victorious. But how long would it take to bring Germany to her senses? Could we hope to survive?

We had lured ourselves for over a year into believing that the slaughter of Jews in the *Ostland* – in Latvia, Lithuania and the Ukraine – was the result of sporadic outbursts of violence by locals, undeniably carried out with German help and blessing, yet not a deliberate, centrally orchestrated governmental plan to exterminate our people. For us, in Grodno, the year just past in the ghetto had been a welcome pause from the devastating pogroms raging all around us in the summer and autumn of 1941. We had, therefore, deluded ourselves into believing that we were relatively secure, here in the Third Reich. That belief was shattered now. Everybody felt that a centrally planned action was being executed with customary German precision. And all this talk about 'resettlement in the east', with plenty of food and good living conditions in *Umsiedlungs Lagers*, sounded particularly unconvincing.

Father came back from the hospital the next evening well after curfew, escorted by two *Ordnugsdienst*. He was dead-tired after having spent over 24 hours without sleep, operating and taking care of the victims of yesterday's incident. He would not talk. Tolo was on his bed, his eye puffed up and hurting badly. I could not get to sleep and peered through the window drape: Jerozolimska was dark, not a single street light on, only a sky full of stars. I thought about our future, our future so aptly described by Lenskii in the wake of his duel in Pushkin's *Eugene Onegin*.

What does the future hold for me?
In vain my eye tries to behold,
In thick mist it is shrouded.

I asked myself a million questions. Why are the poor, the downtrodden, the powerless and the sick the first victims of divine wrath? I ardently believed in God. He was my shield and my hope, not just the God of the Jews, but the God of all people. For me God was a warm feeling of justice, compassion and love, and I was now engulfed in inner turmoil, questioning His very nature, if not His existence, when I needed Him the most. That turmoil was to last for years to come and was never to be finally resolved.

My thoughts came back to earth. Tomorrow there would be no water or electricity. It was amazing how fast we adapted to these new conditions. On days with running water we filled up a big tub, enough to wash and drink for the whole week. During these 'fat' days Mother cooked for the remainder of the week. A thick yellow pea soup and a bean soup quietly simmered on the stove and filled our tenement with a delicious smell. We also got used to the light of a kerosene lamp and a newly acquired acetylene lamp – the cutting edge of high technology! It shed a pleasant, bright, greenish light but reeked of acetylene generated by the drip of water on a calcium carbide stone.

Some of our friends were back; Dr Rusota, the Madners and Julian Schiff were again coming for bridge. They stayed till 9 or 10 p.m. in defiance of the curfew. They all lived close by; the Madners were now in Rosa's empty flat, Rusota and Julian one house down the street. The Madners and Julian often stayed to share our meal of black clay-like bread with *smalec*, onions, salt and hot tea. After supper I played with Mareczek. He was a delightful child. I loved to make him laugh and show his recently acquired baby teeth. I chased him around the room, crawling on the floor between the chairs and the table, and every time I caught him he would burst into laughter. I also carried him on my shoulders, galloping around the place, or took him on my knees to sing *'Jedzie, jedzie pan, na koniku samm, a za panem chlop, na koniku, hop, hop, hop!'* [The master rides all by himself on a horsie and behind him a peasant on a horsie, hop, hop, hop!]. He laughed and laughed. Sometimes I envied Mareczek: he was like Grandmother, only much happier.

Our life was rapidly reaching some new level of normality and we prayed that our tormentors would leave us alone. We could manage. Happy rumours were already circulating that the transports had been suspended because of acute shortages of rolling stock. Rumours also persisted about an expected change in German policy against the Jews because of pressure from Roosevelt. How we wanted to believe that powerful America would exert her influence to help save us!

Mother's birthday on 18 November came with the first frost of the year and we all prayed for an end to the transports – wishful thinking. Bad news came from Ghetto I where three people, a young woman and two men, were publicly executed by Wiese and Streblow for leaving the ghetto without a permit. Their bodies were left hanging from balcony rails on Peretza Street for days. Wiese and Streblow also continued to shoot Jewish workers at the ghetto gates for trying to smuggle in a little food.

The camp of Kielbasin now included Jews from both Grodno ghettos, in addition to Jews from surrounding *shtetls*. Jewish policemen in contact with workers from Kielbasin told about the dreadful conditions there, about the sadistic psychopath SD Rinzler, who was the *Chef* of Kielbasin. Rinzler was a strange man, apparently quite educated, even able to read Hebrew. He was older than his other Gestapo cronies but he, even more than the others, enjoyed humiliating his victims before finishing them off. He ordered people to sing cheerful songs, to crawl in the mud to kiss his feet, to drink a quart of burning alcohol or to eat excrement before shooting them. He picked out young girls, ordering them to his quarters. He sometimes made them run outside naked and shot them afterward. His 'tricks' were inexhaustible and every day several people were humiliated, mutilated and eventually murdered.

Rinzler was also a sentimental man, he loved classical and romantic music. He was always on the lookout for musicians to play Schubert, Schumann and Bach for *Herr Kommandant*. Having found a few musicians, he proceeded to set up a small orchestra; after a few days, he shot a violinist for allegedly making a mistake, leaving the others in mortal fear. The orchestra played chamber music and also Jewish folk tunes, which Rinzler apparently liked. He especially enjoyed *Yiddle Mit Dem Fiddle* and often had it performed at the entrance of the camp when he was searching the Jews coming from their work outside. It was an unreal sight: the camp dominated by a watch tower, Special Police sentries with dogs patrolling along the barbed wire, Rinzler with a whip raining down insults and blows, singling out victims for execution, while the orchestra played the joyous tune of *Yiddle Mit Dem Fiddle*. The camp of Kielbasin under Rinzler was the antechamber of hell; Rinzler was feared even more than Streblow and Wiese.

Before the end of November news spread that Ghetto II, our ghetto, would be liquidated, with the exception of a few hundred *Nutzliche Juden* who would be transferred to Ghetto I to join those who had been transferred there earlier. A feverish siege of the *Judenrat* and, above all, of the *Verbindugsmaenner* ensued. Father went to the *Judenrat* several times and was assured that we would be on the list of people to be transferred to Ghetto I. Lutek's mother was also assured they would be among the last Jews to join Ghetto I. She had given everything she owned, all her family valuables, to bribe the SD men for herself and her two sons. Julian Schiff did the same, hoping to be part of the last 'lucky few hundreds'.

Evenings at home were a time for debating and interpreting

the course of events. Father was good at strategy while Dr Klinger excelled in the subtleties of the German language. Together, they were experts at reconstructing the news from hidden facts and the half-truths provided by the German press. It was in this feverish atmosphere of panic that Father got hold of a copy of the *Voelkischer Beobachter* – and what a copy it was! After careful analysis of the paper, Father and Dr Klinger both concluded that the German Sixth Army at Stalingrad was 'in the bag'. Father, the eternal optimist, was jubilant. He repeated over and over in Russian, '*Razval iouzhnovo fronta!*' [Collapse of the southern front!]. He saw at once the strategic implications of this breakthrough: 300,000 Germans were being 'bagged' in Stalingrad, and 800,000 Germans embroiled deep in the Caucasus were in grave danger. With spearheads reaching as far as the oil fields of Maikop and Groznyi, the German armies in the Caucasus were at risk of being cut off by a swift Soviet thrust towards Rostov-on-the-Don. 'If the Russian advance in the Donetz continues,' Father went on excitedly, – 'another 800,000 scoundrels will soon be "bagged" in the Caucasus! *Molodtzy rebiata, molodtzy!*'

At the beginning of the Russian winter, the German southern front was collapsing. The news could not have been better. Everything now seemed possible; a major German collapse, maybe even an end to the war. People were desperately giving up everything for a chance of joining the last 'lucky few hundred' to be transferred to Ghetto I. People dreaded above all the terrible conditions of the journey to the camp, the cold, the crowding, the lack of food and water, the awful stress. There was still some hope that '*Umsiedlung*' meant hard labour rather than total extermination; nobody seemed yet to realize fully the extent of German perfidy.

The transports took place late in the evening or at night. The Germans did not wish to expose their own soldiers, on their way to or from the front, to the grizzly sight of Jewish transports. Come morning, people were already packed into the cattle trucks, the heavy doors slammed shut and locked. The train was often dispatched to an auxiliary track where it waited for hours, sometimes days, for military transports to pass. The jam-packed, frozen, exhausted, thirsty, hungry people screamed in agony for water, for a gulp of fresh air. These screams were left unanswered, the guards were trained to be indifferent to Jewish suffering. It is this part of the *Umsiedlung* that we all feared the most. Once the door was locked it was opened only after the arrival at the destination, and this could take many agonizing days.

It was the fact of transporting very sick people, who most certainly could not survive the trip, that Dr Klinger found to be the most disquieting element, and he became increasingly convinced that the *Umsiedlungslagers* were death traps.

13   *Ghetto I*

Although Father was assured that we were on the list of the last transfer, things were often unpredictable. Evacuation of Ghetto II was carried out by the *Ordnugsdienst*. Jewish policemen ordered us out of the house. Tolo and Father dragged big suitcases filled mainly with the remnants of our pantry supplies. A small crowd was already assembled in the middle of the street. We saw Mareczek perched on his father's shoulders, bemused to see all these folks, looking happy to have an unexpected ride. We were ordered to assemble in columns of six. Here was Monia Butenski with his family; Dr Max Heller, Mrs Heller holding little Helcia by the hand. In the distance I saw Lutek with his mother and Izia. The sun was bright in a cloudless sky; the snow crackled under our feet; it was cold and many were trotting on the spot to keep warm. At last we moved in the direction of the *Versammlungspunkt* on Artyleryjska Street, just opposite the gate, where a long column of people were already waiting. Suddenly a murmur ran through the column. '*Die Schlaechter* – Be careful,' said an *Ordnugsdienst*, 'they are all here – Streblow, Wiese, Rinzler and Schott – and they are in a bad mood!' We came to a sudden halt caused by a commotion further down at the gate. We were too far away to see but later learned that a man had been shot by Streblow for having a fur collar on his coat; he may have forgotten that all furs had been commandeered for the German *Winterbesorgung*.

We proceeded forward after a wait. As we approached the gate, the *Ordnugsdienst* split us into several shorter columns and we found ourselves shoulder-to-shoulder with people from different streets, all converging towards the gate. The crowd was ordered to a halt and was now forming a half circle with the ghetto gate at its centre. German police and Polish 'navy-blues' with rifles at the ready were watching us at the gate. Wiese, Streblow and Schott, whips in hand, oversaw the operation, pacing along the columns. Wherever they appeared hats and caps came off instantly; we were bowing to our masters of life and death. Streblow walked by us and, my terror notwithstanding, I took a peek at the *Schlaechter*. He paced the column, whipping those who were not quite in line. The holster of his pistol was open and he could shoot anyone at any moment.

The *Verbindugsmaenner* arrived at last accompanied by an officer of the *Ordnugsdienst* with his silver-trimmed blue armband; he held a loudspeaker and a list. They positioned themselves near the gate and prepared to read. A *Verbindungsmann* read from the list in alphabetical order and the *Ordnugsdienst* repeated each name through the loud-speaker. My throat constricted as the first names rang out. Every person called proceeded under the stern eye of two German policemen and Wiese, who stood right by the gate. After crossing the gate the people were being assembled on the Aryan side of Skidelska Street, keeping off the pavement. My tension increased as names beginning with 'B' were being called. 'Dear God,' I prayed, 'let our names be on the list!'

'Blumstein Chaim, Blumstein Estera, Blumstein Nataniel, Blumstein Aleksander, Blumstein Fryda,' the loudspeaker yelled. Thank God we are going to Ghetto I, I thought. I looked around and saw Mr Madner with Mareczek on his shoulders. He smiled and said, 'You are lucky.' We were now trotting in line towards the gate, all five of us, past Streblow on our right, past the *Verbindugsmen* and the officer of the *Ordnugsdienst* on our left, under the eye of Wiese and the German policemen. *'Los...los...gehe schon!'* I was crossing without looking left or right, my heart was pounding as I knew what could happen if I attracted Wiese's attention.

'Hier, stillgestanden!' yelled a *Schupo* as we joined a small group of people waiting on the Aryan side. We stood there as other names were being called and the small column grew in size. The roll call reached the letter 'H', and no Heller was called out! Why was Dr Heller staying? Why? 'Klinger Pincus, Klinger Miriam.' The names rang out from the loudspeaker. Here comes 'N', but no Niemcewicz, Lutek is not coming! Why? Had not Mrs Niemcewicz given all her valuables to be

allowed to stay? And where is Monia? Only then did I realize that 'B' had passed without his name being called, yet his father was a doctor!

Soon the roll-call was over. We were a few hundred lucky people. On the other side of the barbed wire stood a large crowd looking at us with undisguised envy. All my friends were there: Monia, Lutek, Juletchek...Somewhere there were also the girls we admired so much, Rysia Balaban and her sisters. The Hellers were there, and the Madners with Mareczek, and Julian Schiff despite all the bribes he had paid. How convinced he had been that he would be among the lucky ones!

As I stood there waiting, my thoughts wandered to our new life in Ghetto I. My best friend Shurik Lampert was there, as well as Mirek Tropkrynski, Rita Gitis, many of my parents' old friends – Rosa Gitis, the Birgers, the Starovolskis, the Jezierskis and the Rywkinds. We had not seen them for over a year.

'Nah...Los...Los...gehe schon!' I was pushed in my back with a rifle butt. An old *Schupo* was nagging me to advance at last. I was frozen stiff, not feeling my feet any more. We moved slowly towards the town centre, along Skidelska, over the railway overpass. In the distance I could see many trains in the marshalling yard to our right, towards the Central Station. Which of these trains would transport our friends into the unknown?

When I was free, every time I passed over this bridge I loved stopping in the middle to lean over the barrier and wait until a train engulfed me and the bridge in an acrid, hot cloud of vapour and black smoke. *Tante* had struggled to take me away from this dirty but fascinating spot.

The snow squeaked and crackled, the temperature was well below freezing. We now crossed into Brygicka Street towards Batory Square, Zamkowa and Ghetto I. Brigicka was one of the main thoroughfares of the city, a busy street. It was a market day and the pavements were jammed with multi-coloured crowds of peasants in sheepskins and babushkas, and city dwellers, some with fur collars and hats. A small crowd of onlookers formed on the pavements to watch the long column of Jews led by German and Polish police. They were staring at us, people marked with the yellow patch of shame, dragging along suitcases, bundles and knapsacks, stumbling, sliding on the slippery, grey snow over the cobblestones of Brigicka Street, to the tune of hoarse, *'Schneller... schneller...los!'*

I looked at the crowd and noticed their reaction to us. Most appeared pleasantly amused, some looked indifferent, a few women crossed themselves. I felt very angry, humiliated and lonely. I sensed that many of these 'Aryans' were rather happy to see us downtrodden and abased. I remembered again the poor feeble-minded man of Orzeszkowa Street and the fun my schoolmates at the *Cwiczeniowka* had jeering at him. He was as helpless as we were now, and I felt that day as he must have.

At the corner of Brigicka and Batory Square I passed on my right a young woman with a red beret and ear muffs. She wore an old blue coat, maybe a size too large, and torn *valenki*, the Soviet felt boots. Her big blue eyes looked directly at us, and they were filled with...tears. I felt at once the flow of warmth and compassion emanating from her. It said everything that could be said about this despicable spectacle of the humiliation of human beings by their fellow man. Her shabby clothes, different from those of the surrounding Polish burghers, betrayed that she must have been a Soviet Russian, a *Sovietka* trapped in 1941 behind enemy lines. In this crowd, she seemed the only one with a warm, human heart.

We were now on Zamkowa Street, approaching the gate of Ghetto I. Suddenly, out of nowhere, Kurt Wiese appeared next to our column. I passed so close to him that I almost brushed his coat; I saw his hard face with steel-grey eyes below the Prussian military cap, with the skull-and-crossbones insignia of the SD. We halted at the gate and were again summoned one by one by an officer of the *Ordnugsdienst. 'Blumstein Chaim, Estera, Nataniel, Aleksander und Fryda, los...'* We proceeded under the close scrutiny of Wiese and his boss Errelis. We were now on the other side of the barbed wire in Ghetto I, in 'cage number one' as Danyousha would have said. Where was he now?

Ghetto I was a very crowded place: 13,000 people, 25 per cent of Grodno's population assembled in barely five per cent of the city space. The entire ghetto consisted of a single main street, Peretza, and a few adjacent streets with the Great Synagogue on one of them. People lived in dreadful conditions, often two families to a room. The *Judenrat* was very strict in partitioning the living space and we went there to register. The *Judenrat* was located in a three-storey building just near the gate close to Zamkowa Street which, like Skidelska in Ghetto II, was divided into two parts by a barbed wire fence. Our friend Dr Rosa Gitis took our family in. We said goodbye to the Klingers to whom we had grown very attached. We were sure to miss each other.

Rosa Gitis lived with her 15-year-old daughter Rita at the very end of Peretza Street on the first floor of a two-storey building. The two tiny rooms in the apartment were occupied by Rosa and Rita, and Lena Lampert with her son Shurik. Rosa and Rita slept on a couch in the first, somewhat larger room, which also contained a table and four chairs. The smaller room was occupied by Lena and Shurik. A minuscule kitchenette, bathroom and a toilet, off a tiny entrance hall, completed the apartment. I was happy to be under the same roof as my best friend Shurik but I could not see how nine people could all fit into this tiny space. The problem was eased by Father and Tolo who found two folding camp beds, allowing us all to squeeze in. Grandmother slept on one of the camp beds in the room with Rosa and Rita. Lena gave her bed to Mother and Father and slept on the other folding bed which was deployed at night in the passage between the rooms, while Grandmother's camp bed blocked the passage to the tiny hallway. Tolo slept on the floor in the kitchenette, his calves and feet stretching out into the hallway. I slept with Shurik on the floor on his mattress in a head-to-feet arrangement. After dinner, the table and chairs were piled legs up in the tiny bathroom, on the sink and stove of the kitchenette and on the toilet, while every inch of available space was used up for sleeping. This arrangement worked as long as nobody had to go to the bathroom at night. An urgent call of nature meant that I had to step over Shurik, stumble over my parents' bed, then stride over Lena's bed to get to the living room. I then had to stride over Grandmother's bed to access the tiny hallway and stumble over Tolo's feet sticking out of the kitchenette. Finally, after reaching the toilet, I had to remove the chairs stacked up on the seat, putting them carefully over Tolo's feet in the hall. To return to sleep I had to do all this in reverse. Needless to say, we could rarely get a full and undisturbed night of sleep and I often thought of the 'luxurious' conditions we had in Ghetto II.

Rosa could probably have acquired a smaller family for this impossibly tiny apartment, but she was a very dear friend. She insisted we come. She was waiting at the ghetto gate to greet us. I heard her saying to Mother, 'Tanya, we are all in the same boat' and adding in Russian, *'V tesnotie no ne v obidie'* [In cramped quarters, but welcome]. Dear Rosa, she did not have it easy. Dr Izak Gitis, her husband, had died just before the German invasion. Rosa had had to survive that loss and console Rita who, at the vulnerable age of 13, was shattered. She had to make a living, cope with the events, the transfer to the ghetto and the terrible fear of tomorrow. All this happened in such a short time.

The crowding was especially painful to Grandmother. She was bewildered and frightened. She constantly asked Father: 'Motek, what has happened to you, can't you make a decent living any more? Can't you live like a *mensch*?' Father then shouted into her ear: 'It is war, Mother, war!'

This overriding argument calmed her down for a few minutes while she muttered, resignedly, 'Yes, it is a terrible word the word "war" my child, a terrible word!' An hour later, she would come back at my father with the same question. She became especially upset at night when sometimes she could not control her bladder or her bowels. Mother took care of these accidents; she washed Grandmother and changed her bedding. The kerosene lamp was lit, we all had to get up and reshuffle the position of chairs and table to clear the access to the toilet and bathroom. Accidents like this deprived us all of sleep, but nobody complained.

Father and Tolo were assigned to work at the ghetto hospital which, for lack of space, was located on the second floor of the Great Synagogue, close to Peretza Street. The synagogue was a large three-storey building situated next to a sizeable yard. The prayer hall and the women's balcony, supported by columns, occupied the ground and first floors. The second floor and parts of the first had been assigned in better times to religious administration. Now they were painted in white, beds were installed and the rooms were transformed into a dispensary hospital. Services were held on Fridays, Sabbaths and holidays in the big prayer hall, with the chief rabbi, the cantor and a full congregation. It must have been a weird experience being sick there listening to the prayers and psalms reverberating throughout the building.

Father was appalled by the conditions he found at the hospital; the shortages, the overcrowding and lack of hygiene, all much worse than in Ghetto II. Although the Germans dreaded contagious diseases in the heart of the city, Ghetto I was in the throes of an epidemic of spotty typhoid fever. The disease, carried by lice, was spreading with lightning speed in the camp of Kielbasin where it had killed thousands of Soviet POWs before latching on to the new occupants of the barracks. It was next imported from Kielbasin by people who had managed to bribe their way into Ghetto I. The disease was intensifying despite availability of some German-supplied anti-typhoid vaccine and all the efforts deployed to halt it. The number of sick people was staggering and there were not enough hospital beds. Father and Tolo were soon caught in the whirlwind of the fight against spotty typhoid fever.

The overcrowding and discomfort did not affect me all that much. I managed to sleep quite well and I was happy to spend my days with my friend Shurik. We played chess in daylight and in the evening in the flickering light of a petroleum lamp. This beloved game was ideal for our situation. We were deeply absorbed for hours, while occupying only a small portion of our living space. To play a good game exercised our brains and gave us a sense of accomplishment. It was difficult to do anything else, even more to walk and play outdoors in the crowded streets of the ghetto. Frequent German patrols crisscrossed the few streets, and to collide with one of them could mean death. But even forgetting the German police, there was nowhere to run. Every few hundred yards one came against the barbed wire or the ghetto wall. Above all, we stayed home to escape the ghastly sight of poverty and hunger that kept the ghetto in its iron grip. Before the war, the historic Jewish quarter, in which Ghetto I was located, had been home to the poor Jews of Grodno. Now one encountered on every block small children in rags, with their hungry black eyes, blue from cold, stretching out their little bony hands begging for food. I began to appreciate how well off I had been in Ghetto II.

A few days after our transfer, I was with Mother on Peretza Street when we caught sight of an old woman, all in rags, standing against the wall and begging for food. It appeared to me that I knew her from somewhere. As we approached, Mother recognized her and she recognized us: it was Chaya Sora, the chicken lady! She must have been well over 80! I remembered her from better times; she used to come to our house, selling kosher chickens. Her toothless, mumbling Yiddish was difficult to understand. Liouba, our cook, always gave her some hot tea with milk and a sweet bun. She used to sit at the kitchen table and dunk her bun in the tea to make it easier to chew. Now there were no chickens to sell and Chaya Sora had to beg for a piece of bread, for a few *groszen* to survive the bitter cold! Mother gave her some money and Chaya Sora cried and cried. No, there was no fun outside. It was better to play chess with Shurik, to talk or to play cards with Rita and Shula Neuman, a former schoolmate of Rita's.

Here, as in Ghetto II, the curfew was in the early evening. Water was available three days a week while electricity was permanently cut off. Mother cooked on a small alcohol stove called a Primus. We all shared whatever we had and ate together. We drank tea with saccharine as sugar was not available. All our 'delicacies' from Ghetto II were gone but we still had a few jars of rendered lard, some flour, some dried peas and some onions which we had dragged from Ghetto II. We survived December on these staples and even planned a 'feast' for the New Year.

While Shurik and I were busy at chess, the grown-ups spent the long wintry evenings playing cards. Father, who detested card games, liked solitaire and would spread his cards on the bed while Tolo, Rosa, Lena and Mother played a French card game, 'belotte'. Rita and Grandmother read their books. Sometimes Father brought *Der Voelkischer Beobachter* and read aloud to us. The news was very good. The Eastern Front was on fire. The Red Army passed to the winter offensive. The Sixth German Army was completely surrounded at

Stalingrad. The Don and Donetz fronts were collapsing and the victorious Russians were approaching the city of Rostov-on-the-Don to seal the fate, Father expected, of Von List's Army in the Caucasus. This could mean a loss for the Germans of at least another half a million men or more, a loss which could bring with it a collapse of the entire German southern front and an end to the war! We were elated by these magnificent victories and wondered how it was possible that after the debilitating defeats of 1941 and 1942 the Red Army was still so vital.

Father was again convinced the Germans would now be forced to slow down their persecution. But there was no breath of hope as new orders were issued for the liquidation of the camp of Kielbasin. A few people who succeeded in bribing Rinzler and transferring to the ghetto told horror stories about the unbelievable sadism of Rinzler and Streblow, now switched to Kielbasin. Public hangings, torture and humiliation were daily occurrences. The liquidation of the camp was continuing under the whip of the SD men, the German and Polish police, to the tune of Rinzler's orchestra and the barking of attack dogs, as the terrorized and frozen inmates proceeded towards the railway station of Lososna to be dispatched to an unknown destination.

At long last, many began to get convinced that *Umsiedlung* meant death. Young people talked about escaping to the forests. But how? The ghetto was patrolled around the clock along its entire perimeter. Inside the ghetto there were those who for fear or profit could denounce them to the Gestapo. And if that was not enough, the city beyond the ghetto was full of Polish informers – the *Szmalcowniki* – with a particular, uncanny flair for sniffing out Jews. The rural Polish and Lithuanian population was hostile to us, the Byelorussians indifferent at best. Assuming that one could brave the bad weather and reach the forest, how could one survive without shelter, food and weapons? Only with weapons could one take food from the peasants and weapons were difficult to obtain. They were either hidden by the peasants who obtained them from retreating armies, or in the possession of the *Armia Krajowa* – the AK [underground Polish Home Army]. The peasant kept weapons to protect himself from marauders while the AK was no friend of the Jews; some claimed that its right wing was secretly dedicated to the extermination of Jews in Poland. Red Army partisans provided the only hope for the Jews, but they had barely started to organize. Some young people tried to find them, but most of the time such attempts ended in tragedy.

In the ghetto, things were getting wild. The SD men made frequent visits and amused themselves by shooting anyone they chose. Wiese was murdering people left and right, especially at the gate on Zamkowa Street where long queues of workers waited in the arctic weather to be searched.

Wiese was a strange man. Rumour had it that he was a barber by profession; he was always well groomed and his fingers were manicured. Like Rinzler, he was sentimental; he liked flowers and his dog. Unlike Rinzler, he was a family man, according to people who sometimes worked at his house, but as soon as he stepped into the ghetto he became a cold-blooded murderer. We could never understand this schizophrenic behaviour, displayed by so many Germans. It seemed to us that everything German was a fake; their maudlin sentimentalism was to us as cheap as their convictions, their hatred as artificial as their friendship. To me they were human machines, superbly efficient robots, perverts. They became the most despicable people on earth, people without a soul. My beloved *Tante* Thea and Pastor Plamsch receded in my memory into darkness.

The last days of 1942 caught us all in a gloomy mood. We were afraid to imagine what 1943 would bring. Snow fell on the last day of the year as we were thinking of the millions of people who were celebrating the coming of the New Year – people who were having a good time. We thought of America, the lucky land where Jews were free. People would be dancing there, the champagne flowing! We thought of Switzerland, another lucky land. God, what wouldn't we have given to be there. But never mind, we would even settle for Hungary. Hungarian Jews, we were told, were not living in ghettos. We decided to forget our daily pain and meet the New Year hoping for the best.

After the curfew, we all sat around the table in the dim light of the petroleum lamp to a 'feast' Mother had prepared on her

Primus stove. It consisted of succulent, crisp potato latkes, a lot of them, deliciously fried, covered with a thick layer of sugar, which Father had brought from somewhere. Rosa found two bottles of sweet apple wine. We ate the pancakes, drank the wine and became mellow. Rosa, Lena and Rita begged Mother to sing something, to defy Hitler. It was crazy, I had not heard Mother sing for a very long time, but here in this atmosphere of gloom, with misery, starvation and death surrounding us, she sang. She sang songs from her Russian repertoire in her beautiful voice, then continued with a string of sad Jewish songs, *Oif dem Pripetchek Brent a Feierl, Sterndl, Sterndl* and, of course, *Eili, Eili*. We all burst into tears. Then we sang some Soviet songs, all of us together. We sang *Katiousha*, we sang *The March of the Red Air Force* ('Higher and higher is the flight of our birds'); we sang *The Song of Moscow*. It was like a heady wine, it gave us strength, it was like a defiance of the accursed Germans. Yes, it is the Red Army beating those murderers, yes our freedom will come from the east! I was all flustered with emotion and fell asleep on that last night of 1942 dreaming of meeting our German tormentors with rifles and bayonets.

The very next day we were reminded brutally of our desperate situation. The camp of Kielbasin was liquidated. The remaining inmates were being transferred from Kielbasin into the ghetto. I was on Peretza when the half-dead and frozen skeletons from Kielbasin arrived. I watched a procession of pitiful figures dressed in tatters, dragging their frozen feet in the snow and mud. Small half-skeletons/half-children with hungry eyes, blue from cold, clutched their bony fingers around a walking skeleton of a parent. Many horse-drawn carts and sledges squeaked past me, with the sick, the dying, and those shot on the way. Escorted by German police with rifles and some *Judische Ordnugsdienst*, they all proceeded towards the Great Synagogue to be taken in charge by the *Judenrat*. A skeleton approached the pavement and grabbed the hand of a bystander with a moan in Yiddish, 'Brother, a piece of bread, I am dying of hunger and thirst.'

'*Nah, los du Verfluchte!*' the *Schupo* spotted the man and pushed him back into the crowd with his rifle butt. I couldn't swallow and my throat constricted at the extent of this misery:

I had never seen anything like it. They were coming on foot all the way from Kielbasin under the whip of Rinzler, Streblow and Wiese. Many who could not walk fast enough were executed on the spot, their bodies thrown on the carts together with the sick. Suddenly a whisper ran through the crowd on the pavement: *'Der Schlaechter!'* The pavements emptied in a second as everybody ran for shelter. I had not far to run and stumbled into the entry, colliding with Mother who was going out to have a look at the people from Kielbasin. When she saw my stricken face, she asked, 'Was it that terrible?'

Father and Tolo were at the hospital in the synagogue with more work than could possibly be handled. There were many sick and dying, mostly with spotted typhoid fever or dysentery. Some were so dehydrated that nothing could be done for them. There was a shortage of beds and medicine, and no appropriate food. Father was in charge of triage. Tolo was in a team taking care of delousing – removing and disinfecting clothes, distributing disinfected clothes, dispensing hot water. The SD men avoided the hospital, they were obviously afraid of catching typhus. This was a blessing for the doctors and nurses who could at least work in peace.

As he was making his rounds among the sick, Father's eye suddenly caught the burning gaze of a skeleton of a man. Father could not place him and paused for a minute. Then the sound of his Yiddish-accented Polish, *'Panie doktorzu, panie doktorzu'*, shook Father to the core. He shouted, 'Leiba! Leiba!' Dear Leiba, the caretaker of our property in Druskieniki, was here; nothing but skin and bones, his deeply sunken eyes lit by fever. Father at once examined him: advanced dehydration from severe dysentery; he was dying. Father directed him to a bed in the section reserved for the very sick; he tried to keep him alive, but Leiba did not want to live. *'Panie doktorzu,'* he said, *'meine Krasavitze* ['my beautiful one', as he called his wife] went with little Sheine [his small daughter] with the last transport from Kielbasin. Moishe-Leibka [his son] was shot in November in Porzeczki when he tried to escape the transport...I somehow remained because I was very sick...they hid me in the infirmary barracks... I have nobody left and nobody to live for... I see *meine Krasavitze* every night, *Panie doktorzu,'* he whispered. 'She calls me...'. He clutched Father's hand, 'I want to be with her...' The next day our faithful friend, good Leiba from Druskieniki, was dead. When Mother learned about his death she cried. A whole period of our life, a happy period, was connected with Leiba. That evening Father's exhausted face appeared infinitely sad in the flickering light of the oil lamp. We were all in mourning for Leiba. There was silence. Only Grandmother, with her eternal book in her hand, kept whispering 'What a terrible word is "war", my child, what a terrible word!'

The next evening Kurt Wiese was again at the ghetto gate, terrorizing the long column of incoming workers. Because of the desperate hunger in the ghetto, workers increasingly took chances, bringing in a hidden piece of bread, an egg or a sausage. Wiese knew that and he personally conducted the search of anyone who seemed to him suspicious or nervous. That evening he paced the long incoming column, the end of his whip stroking the heel of his Prussian boot. 'Du!' [You!], he barked, poking a teenage boy with the tip of his whip, ordering him out of the column. 'Du,' he barked again, poking another. Finally, six people were assembled and made to strip naked in the guard room. A man named Kimche, a father of four, had a quarter of a loaf of white bread hidden under his belt. Wiese ordered him out of the guard room to stand against the barbed fence in full view of the incoming workers. Kimche told him that this bread was for his sick child and begged him to spare his life. Two pistol shots and Kimche sank to the snow mortally wounded.

When rumours spread that another transport was imminent and that lists were being prepared at the *Judenrat* for the next few thousand to go, our desperation reached its peak. There was not a trace, not a letter, not a greeting from all those thousands who had been sent to the 'work camps' in November and December: *Umsiedlung* meant death. The stories dispensed to their Jewish workers by some 'good' Germans – about work camps with decent conditions where families stayed together, where 'work-loving' people were unharmed, and about the Fuehrer who would send the Jews after the war to Madagascar, where a Jewish State would be proclaimed – were taken for what they were: fairy tales. People were now desperately looking for poison. The price of cyanide, morphine, arsenic, strong sleeping pills, even rat poison, sky-rocketed. These items became more valuable than gold or diamonds. Many carried them in their pockets. People were ready to commit suicide rather than endure the agony of a transport. Rosa Gitis told us that now that she was convinced we were going to our death she would poison herself and Rita, rather than go willingly. This was her way of defying the Germans.

Many also tried desperately to buy themselves out by bribing the Gestapo through the *Judenrat Verbindugsmaenner* and higher officers of the Jewish Police, who were rumoured to have become fabulously rich. People envied these relatively secure positions, but at the same time despised them for their dirty job of cooperating with the Gestapo. They were called *schwarze ikheses* [black eminences]. Some people bowed low to them on their passage and tried to ingratiate themselves, almost as if they were Gestapo. I was very glad to hear reassurances from the *Judenrat* that Father was 'useful' and that we would be among the last to go. Dr Finkel and Father were the only surgeons in the ghetto, but how much were such assurances worth? I remembered Julian Schiff, who bribed, got 'assurances', and yet was still taken.

Wiese and the *Judenrat* were drawing up the lists for the next transport. It was made known that people would be summoned by an apartment roll-call. They were to assemble in the streets with their most precious belongings and proceed to the Great Synagogue, from where they would be taken to the trains. The transport from the ghetto was scheduled for the middle of January, around the time of my birthday.

Today was my birthday, 13 January. I was 13 years old. Under a happier sky I would have been a Bar Mitzvah. Mother cried at the mention of my birthday. I could see her anguished eyes looking at me, not able to protect me from my destiny.

In the tense afternoon before the transport we were four teenagers sitting around our table: I was playing chess with Shurik, next to us Rita and her friend Shula Neuman, the daughter of Dr Neuman, were doing a jigsaw puzzle. Shula was expert at reading cards; according to Rita, she was a fortune teller. Shula was not only pretty, she was full of mystery. Her deep-set, misty brown eyes somehow looked beyond the present; this was perhaps why she exerted such a fascination on those who knew her. She paid little attention to me, three years her junior whom she doubtlessly considered childish. This was irritating, as I secretly liked her. But that afternoon was different; the four of us sat around the table, snow was falling and darkness invaded the room, though it was still more than two hours to the curfew. We begged Shula to lay out her cards and predict our futures, to tell us what 1943 had in store for us. 'Are you not afraid of it?' she asked, but we begged her again.

'Shula, please lay out your cards, please!' So Shula laid out her cards; first came Shurik, then me, then Rita. Shula did not speak, she placed the cards for each of us, then turned her intense gaze toward me.

'Alik,' she said 'you are the only lucky one, you are going to survive 1943!' She looked at me with astonishment, packed the cards and left. I will never forget the frightened, sad look of Rita, while Shurik dismissed the whole thing as nonsense. He was too rational to pay heed to fortune tellers.

All the street lights in the ghetto lit up without warning at six o'clock. Electricity was restored to our apartment. It was a weird and scary feeling for us, so used to the weak yellow light of a petroleum lamp or of a candle, to be suddenly flooded with all this brightness. An *Ordnugsdienst* came for Father and Tolo to escort them to the hospital at the synagogue where all medical personnel were mobilized. Soon after they left, we heard a noise of heavy boots on the staircase: two *Ordnugsdienst* and one German policeman came into the apartment. The officer of the *Ordnugsdienst* read from a list: 'Lena Lampert with her son Alexander – take your personal belongings and join the transport in the street.' Frantically, Lena and Shurik packed their suitcases and a knapsack. Mother and Rosa squeezed in the last of our bread, a jar of lard and a small jar of sugar. I do not remember how they left the apartment, whether we even said goodbye to each other. We were in a state of shock, grateful to have been spared this time. I looked through the window, trying in the glare of projectors to catch a glimpse of Shurik and Lena in the crowd. Frightened, Mother pulled me away from the window. 'Are you crazy? Do you want to have us shot?' she screamed.

After the street noises had receded, we switched off the lights and went to bed. My mattress was unusually comfortable; because my old friend Shurik was not there, I could stretch my legs and turn – the whole mattress was mine. But I could not sleep. Occasionally, in the distance one could hear faint pops that sounded like shots. I tossed and turned, thinking of Shurik. Where was he now? Standing in the yard of the synagogue, walking with Lena through the snowdrifts to the train? Packed mercilessly into a cattle truck? Where were Father and Tolo? Would they come back home tomorrow? From the cot in the next room came the plaintive voice of grandmother: 'How terrible is the word "war", how terrible!'

In the morning, Father and Tolo came back exhausted and profoundly shaken. The medical staff had been summoned to accompany the sick who were on the transport list and had to be delivered to the train. All the *Schlaechters* were on hand, Wiese and Streblow with their whips and sub-machine guns at the ready. The snow stopped falling and the temperature dropped steadily. The big prayer hall of the synagogue was crowded to capacity.

The sick were taken down on stretchers and loaded on two lorries provided by the Germans. The numbers had to tally but in the confusion a few of the very sick, who would undoubtedly have died during the journey, were hidden by medical staff inside the hospital. There were young mothers with babies in the crowd. They were not allowed on the lorries and had to proceed on foot all the way to the train. Some old people could not walk and could not bear the long hours of waiting in the frost. Some collapsed in the yard, some in the prayer hall of the synagogue. They were shot to 'keep the procedure orderly'. Tolo and the other nurses had immediately to clear the floor of the bodies.

Among the thousands waiting for hours in the cold were several pregnant women. Tolo was particularly shaken by the fate of a young woman who the night before had given birth. It was plain that the baby and the very weak mother could not possibly survive the journey. Dr Birger and Father begged Wiese to leave the woman and her baby. Wiese was adamant: she had to go! And so she went, pale, tottering, without a word, to join her husband in the hall of the synagogue, her newborn baby cradled in her arms.

After hours of confusion, waiting, beating and shooting, the escorted columns marched off. They marched through Zamkowa towards the Niemen and the Lososna railway station, avoiding the centre of town on which an early curfew had been imposed. The march, as we learned later from a few *Ordnugsdienst*, was horrible. The Germans, in a hurry after a sleepless night, were in a very bad mood. *'Los...los... schneller!'* A pregnant woman who could not keep up with the quick pace of the column was shot. The road to Lososna was strewn with bodies. A red trail marked the snow from the Great Synagogue all the way to Lososna station. At dawn, a German police truck picked up the bodies and delivered them to the train. The numbers had to tally.

The blood stains were scraped off the synagogue walls with bleach on the order of Wiese who, despite a sleepless night, was again spreading panic in the ghetto the next morning.

Except for Shurik and Mrs Lampert, almost all our friends remained. The Gitises, the Birgers, the Klingers, the Rywkinds were still here. Nobody harboured any illusions, even the most naive. Some people were feverishly building hide-outs in cellars, in attics or between walls and stocking them with what food was available to them. Information about such a shelter was worth a fortune. Information about a contact on the Aryan side was also invaluable. Overall, however, despair was rampant and people were looking more and more to suicide to avoid unnecessary suffering. Our ship was sinking rapidly with no safety rafts available.

The next day, news of yet another transport spread like wildfire. Only some 5,000 Jews were to be left in the ghetto and all the others had to go. A list of the 'indispensable 5,000' was being drawn up at the *Judenrat*. The transport – or *Aktion*, as the Germans called it – was to occur within a day or two. After their announcement, Wiese and Streblow felt in a 'joking' mood and sent to the hospital for a bottle of a 90-proof alcohol. Wiese then made an employee of the *Judenrat*, an old man, drink a large glass of the alcohol at gunpoint. The man collapsed and Wiese and Streblow left the *Judenrat* laughing.

We hardly had time to breathe before the next transport came in the horrifying glare of street lights and projectors. Mother packed the bare necessities and the food we would need for the trip. She gave every one of us a piece of Tolo's 'lucky shirt', the dried-out fragments of the membrane that covered Tolo at birth, which she kept as a talisman. For a moment I saw her eyes full of tears and fear: they were blessing me and Tolo. We were now all ready, sitting around the table with Rosa and Rita, waiting for the inevitable to happen. The yellow pea soup was getting cold; nobody was hungry, except Grandmother who did not realize what was going on. Father was very pale; he had thought there would be a few weeks of respite between the transports that would give him time to plan our escape, but he had been caught by surprise. We were trapped.

At nine o'clock we heard a loud knock on the door. Two men from the *Ordnugsdienst* entered the apartment with a list. They read out the names of our family. 'All those whose names have been read are to follow us at once.' We kissed Rosa and Rita goodbye, took our bundles and followed the policemen. In the middle of the street we joined a large group of people. We were ordered to wait in the glare of the street lights and projectors as other groups joined the crowd. It was very cold and my feet were getting numb. A long column formed and moved along Peretza. We were ordered to turn left into a side street and stopped before a single-storey house which in better days was used by the 'Maccabi' sports club. Two very large rooms that looked like former exercise halls were already crowded with people, some standing, some sitting on the floor. To push oneself forward, one had to elbow, shove and stride over bodies. We finally found an empty corner where we squeezed on the floor. Bewildered, Grandmother was constantly asking father 'Motek, what is going on? Why are we here?' We did not know why ourselves until several *Ordnugsdienstmen* came to summon to work all those who were considered indispensable by the *Judenrat*. Father and Tolo were among them, as well as other doctors and medical personnel. They were escorted to the hospital at the *Versammlungspunkt* at the Great Synagogue. The policemen told us that we were the lucky ones. 'Everyone who is not here or in a few shelters like this one will be deported tonight or tomorrow.'

The hall reverberated with noise. People still kept arriving and soon it was difficult to stretch on the floor without bumping into other bodies sitting or trying to lie down. I was stretched on the floor, my head against the wall, using my coat as a blanket and my knapsack as a pillow. I was very tired, but too excited to fall asleep. Mother, her back against our suitcase and her legs outstretched, was supporting Grandmother who was falling asleep. At my feet, a young woman was desperately trying to pacify with her breast a crying baby. Further away, a bearded man with a skullcap and a prayer shawl stood *davening*, rhythmically swaying back and forth: '*Shma Isroel...*' Somebody was moaning, somebody searching. A high-pitched, anguished voice in Yiddish cried, '*Cyla...Cyla... Vo byst ty?'* [Where are you?], someone sobbed. It was difficult to sleep in all this hubbub. In the middle of the night, the doors to the building were locked. Suddenly someone yelled, '*Shaaa! Shtill!*' and as the din subsided for a while, one could hear outside shots followed by short bursts of sub-machine gun fire. They were all coming from the direction of the synagogue. I instinctively grabbed Mother's hand; Father and Tolo were facing the *Schlaechters* in the hospital-synagogue. Sporadic shots continued throughout the night, all coming from the same direction.

It was an awful night, and bitterly cold. I dozed off, but was constantly woken. Mother, who did not close an eye, told me that I was waking up screaming; I had nightmares. There was still some hot tea in our thermos bottles; it gave me some physical comfort and helped me to drowse off. In the morning we were told to remain in the shelter until the transport was over. There were at least a thousand people in the shelter and only one toilet. Grandmother had trouble controlling her bowels and bladder, and she was miserable. She cried and we cried with her.

The doors were unlocked in the afternoon and we were told to assemble in the street. Part of our luggage was left in the shelter. The glare of sunshine on snow blinded me. It was a glorious winter day, such as used to give us so much joy. I closed my eyes. A silver-trimmed *Ordnugsdienst* read to us a decree from the Gestapo to the *Judenrat* announcing that as of yesterday only half of the ghetto could be inhabited by Jews, the other half was to become a no man's land. Anybody caught there would be executed.

Our former abode was in the no man's land and we had to look for a new shelter within the confines of the 'new' half which included the area near Zamkowa, the upper part of Peretza and the section adjacent to the Great Synagogue. The ghetto was a sorry sight. Empty houses, some with broken windows, stared at us. The streets were littered with broken glass and debris. Here and there, a body lay prostrate on the glittering snow. From a distance they looked like huge black birds shot by a hunter; up close they resembled grotesque rag dolls. I counted four bodies on our short way to the *Judenrat*.

At the *Judenrat*, we met Father and Tolo. Tolo's eyes were filled with horror. His coat was torn and his hair dishevelled. I had never seen my brother in such a pitiful state, not even after his journey from Lvov. At that time he was dirty and skinny but his eyes were full of excitement and life. This was something different altogether. Father looked exhausted and gaunt. How overjoyed we were to see them! We kissed and kissed, happy to be among the living.

Father had a plan; he wanted us to find shelter in the building of the *Judenrat* on the side where the windows faced the Aryan side. With 80 per cent of Grodno Jews already deported, most of the *Judenrat* building stood empty, including some offices located on the second floor, their windows overlooking the walled yard of the Garrison Church on the Aryan side. Our family was allowed to take such an abandoned office. The room was spacious, with tables, chairs and a cast-iron stove in the corner. A bitter cold hung over the room. Father and Tolo soon brought two iron beds with mattresses taken from an empty apartment across the street. They also brought from there an axe and tools including a small hand-saw, a metal wash tub and some cooking utensils. We chopped the furniture from the adjacent offices to make a roaring fire in the stove. We brought snow from outside and heated it on the stove. The tub of water was placed on the stove and poor Grandmother had to be washed from top to toe after her accidents at the shelter. We stepped outside, and

Mother washed Grandmother before anyone else was allowed to wash.

We warmed our chilled bodies and came back to life. Only then, as we settled down and relaxed a bit, was Tolo able to tell us, slowly, and with pain, the horrifying story of the previous night. They had arrived at the hospital just before columns of people from all parts of the ghetto appeared at the synagogue. The synagogue was entirely surrounded by German Special Police. The Gestapo were out in force; they were all there, sub-machine guns and whips in hand. They were shooting to scare people. Wiese was particularly ferocious, in a very foul mood because earlier in a narrow street a young Jew jumped out of a house entrance brandishing an axe. Were it not for the quick reaction of a *Schupo*, who shot the man before he could apply his blow, Wiese would be dead. After that incident, all hell broke loose. Wiese entered the house and shot a number of people, including a small child. He now displayed particular cruelty wherever he appeared. The other SD men did not lag behind him and soon Peretza and adjacent streets were littered with bodies.

The cold was bitter and the big prayer hall overflowed with people. Tolo and other hospital staff were helping to move the sick on the list from their hospital beds to the trucks supplied by the Germans. Presently, while waiting by the stretcher of a sick man, Tolo saw Rosa and Rita Gitis in the hall of the synagogue. Taking advantage of the prevailing confusion, he somehow got them to the first floor, into the hospital section. They were placed on the ground, given blankets and hidden among the sick while Father took care of a wounded boy who, in defiance of German orders, had been smuggled into the hospital.

In the meantime, the first column to be marched off to the trains was formed in the synagogue yard. Mr Jezierski, a friend of Father's, a proud man and an organizer of Jewish self-defence units at the time of 1935–36 Polish pogroms, was in the first row of the column. The Germans this time wanted to inject some 'fun and music' into the dismal picture of lines of starved and resigned families. Pots and pans were brought from an abandoned household nearby and, under Rinzler's supervision, a 'show' was promptly improvised. Mr Jezierski

and a number of prominent community members in the first
few rows were ordered to trade their hats for cooking pots.
Pans and metal lids were to be used as cymbals. Everybody
was ordered to sing *Yiddle Mit Dem Fiddle*, those in the first
row to beat their 'cymbals' and perform dancing movements
to the amusement of the SD men and *Schutzpolizei*. When an
older man refused to dance, he was shot by Rinzler, the music
lover. The column then started their painful six-kilometre
journey towards the Lososna station, an unreal procession –
the orchestra of pots and pans, the familiar, harsh German
orders, *'Schneller! Schneller! Los!'* blended with the weak
singing of *Yiddle Mit Dem Fiddle*.

And then they came again, people from other streets,
converging on the synagogue. Again cries, shooting, blood
splattered on the walls; the nightmare was far from over. This
time, Wiese and Errelis entered the hospital and ordered all
the sick on their feet. The sick tried desperately to get up for
fear of being executed. But the reverse happened; those who
could not stand up were left, while those who did were
ordered downstairs. Rosa and Rita, when ordered out of the
hospital, swallowed their overdose of sleeping pills. Going
down the stairs, Rita was unusually pale and swayed on her
feet. Tolo was in the hall and made his way towards them.
Rosa said in Polish, 'our fate is sealed now'. Tolo understood
what had happened when he saw them both on the truck for
the sick: Rita in a half-sitting position was limply tilted over
her mother's shoulder. She must have been already unconscious, while Rosa, pale, with her eyes closed, was falling into
eternal sleep. Rosa and Rita Gitis, our dearest friends, were
true to their promise; they defied the Germans. Dr and Mrs
Klinger were also taken. Neither Father nor Tolo saw them in
the crowd.

It was difficult to bear; we all cried thinking of our friends as
we sat at the table and finally had some hot tea. We sat
gloomily around the cast-iron stove, a family that until now
had escaped the transport by a miracle. We knew that the next
time it would be our turn.

Night was falling, red shadows from the fire were dancing
on the wall. God, how I wanted to live and escape my fate!
Father started to talk. 'Listen,' he said, 'it is high time to act,

we are all condemned if we do not. We shall try to escape even if it costs us our lives. I have chosen this forsaken office of the *Judenrat* as our living quarters for a good reason: its windows are only a few yards from the Aryan side.'

Indeed, the windows of our room overlooked the wall surrounding the yard of the military Catholic Church – *Kosciol Garnizonowy*, or Garrison Church – where masses for the Polish troops used to be held before the war. The ghetto wall, a stone wall topped with barbed wire and broken glass separated us from the churchyard.

'Luckily,' Father continued, 'being on the second floor, we are well above the wall. All we need is a rope ladder long enough to reach the churchyard when thrown from the window. Maybe the Germans will give us a couple of weeks' respite.' He stopped, looked at us and continued. 'It is impossible to hide the escape of a well-known doctor in a population so dramatically reduced, and we know the insane energy which the Germans deploy to hunt all escapees. With the police alerted, we may never make it to our final destination. The first to escape the ghetto will be Alik and Esterka,' he pointed to me and Mother. 'I will try to make an arrangement with an *Ordnugsdienst* to guide you through a passage to the Aryan side. But if I can't, you will have to use the ladder at night and hide in the church until morning. Early in the morning, you will cross the town and report to our contact in the suburb. Tolo and I will stay behind in the ghetto to quash any suspicion of your escape. After a week or two,' Father continued, 'we shall follow by a similar route and, with luck, will join you at our destination.'

I had not the slightest idea of that 'final destination', but I guessed rightly that it was arranged by my father's friend Dr Antoni Docha. Of course, Father was very secretive about it and never mentioned his name.

'So, beginning tomorrow, Alik, your task will be to make us a long rope ladder. Eight yards at least. I have brought you some rope and tools.' Father showed me a roll of thick rope. He pointed to the hand saw, axe and a pocket knife brought that afternoon from the neighbouring house. 'We shall use as rungs the legs of these chairs and tables which we have chopped for the stove.'

So this was it; we were trying to do something. I could not sleep; my eyes remained wide open. Reflections of the fire in the stove flickered on the ceiling. My thoughts wandered from Rita, Rosa and Shurik to Dr Klinger, to Izak and Aunt Ada somewhere in the forest. What was Father's destination? He must have organized all this during his daring November escape. How would we succeed? Izak and Aunt Ada had not yet been discovered. We had heard nothing and that was a good sign. So there was a chance...but that was at the beginning of November, before the first transport, before the Germans were on high alert. I wanted so much to live; I would make the ladder as quickly as possible. Grandmother was snoring loudly, fast asleep after the ordeals of the previous night. Poor Grandmother! It was obvious that she could not escape with us; she would have to be abandoned. She did not understand what was happening. She was convinced that everyone, including her son, had gone mad. But the word 'war' explained everything to her. I knew that Father would wait until the last minute before abandoning her. What would happen to Father and Tolo if they waited too long?

I set to work on my ladder. Father showed me what I was supposed to do and I measured and sawed with gusto. With my pocket knife I carved in each wooden rung two large grooves for the rope. I carefully fastened the rope into the groove around each rung and spaced them less than a foot apart. For me, it was a work of precision and I enjoyed it immensely; it gave me the feeling of finally doing something to counter our inevitable fate, a feeling of defiance. It took several days but at last the ladder, with a great number of rungs, was finished. Two long dangling pieces of rope for securing the ladder were left at each end. I proudly reported to Father on a successfully carried-out assignment.

During the evening, a young Jewish policeman came to our room to discuss something with my parents. He knew the Klingers personally and claimed he had seen them on the transport. He told us that Dr Klinger injected himself and his wife with a lethal dose of morphine just before being loaded into the cattle trucks. Both collapsed and were thrown into the truck with the sick. He got this information from a friendly *Schupo* who was struck by the perfect German spoken by Dr

Klinger before he collapsed. The *Schupo* had also told him that the transport was heading towards a work camp in Silesia named Auschwitz. It was the first time that I had heard this name mentioned. We were used to the name Malkinia, a small town between Warsaw and Bialystok, being mentioned lately as the destination of transports.

A small number of friends were still in the ghetto. Dr Birger, the director of the hospital, was here with his wife and their two daughters, Gala and Iza. The Tropkrynski family was also in the ghetto. I was happy to learn that Mirek was still here. Nobody knew where the Neumans were. The family had disappeared and we speculated that they were in a bunker or a hide-out. A large part of the ghetto, including the flat where we had lived with the Gitisses and Lamperts, was now in no man's land, separated by a hastily erected wall of wooden boards and barbed-wire fences. Only police, including the *Ordnugsdienst*, were allowed into the no man's land. The Germans knew that some Jews were hiding there and were searching systematically from house to house. Errelis had ordered that anyone discovered in this zone be handed over to the Gestapo for interrogation, meaning torture before death.

But I wanted to get out! Cooped up in the room for days I needed an outlet for my youthful energy. Having found Mirek, we soon began to play in the street drenched by sun and snow. I was aghast to realize how little space we had now. Peretza was cut in half, and most of what remained consisted of a few narrow, winding streets in the historical ghetto where we had to stay out of the way of the ever-present German patrols. I had a great idea: to play at the old ghetto cemetery. The cemetery was tiny and densely packed with old tombstones with weathered Hebrew lettering, but it was the only space where we could play without fear of the Germans. The cemetery was surrounded by an old brick wall and had only one entrance, on a side street leading to the synagogue. A long, one-storey brick building with a shingled roof was both a funeral parlour and a morgue but everything now was abandoned. The people from the *Hevra Kaddisha* burial society were gone and nobody cared. We ran between the tombstones, played hide-and-seek, pelted each other with snowballs. Mirek wanted to peek inside the morgue. We decided to tiptoe in. The wooden door opened slowly with a creak. A peculiar musty smell like 'old curtains' hung in the air. Sprawled corpses were arranged against the wall, looking like big stuffed dolls. They probably had been shot a few days ago, during the terrible night of the 'transport of the 10,000'. I became very scared and wanted to leave, but could not 'chicken out' in front of my friend. Near the entrance was the body of a young woman; she was lying on her side, her long fair hair covering her face like a mysterious veil. If it were not for her pale blue colour, she could have passed for sleeping. Next to her, an old man was sprawled on his back; he had lost one shoe and his big toe protruded from a torn sock. He also looked peaceful in his sleep. Other bodies nearby were covered with blankets or rugs. Mirek was curious, he wanted to peek under the blanket. We approached the body of a man whose head was covered with his coat. Mirek took off the coat and dropped it with a scream. The head of what must have been a middle-aged man, was a bloody pulp! We left that dreadful place running and did not stop until we reached Peretza.

Workers were finishing putting up the board wall that separated the ghetto from the no man's land. We slowed down in fear of the German patrols. The image of the man with his head half-gone haunted me in my sleep for many days. 'God, if I have to die, let it be quick through the heart,' I prayed. For the next day or two we felt an irresistible force dragging us, Mirek and myself, to the little cemetery. The corpses were still there. We got used to them and played our snow battles among the tombstones.

14   Escape

The young *Ordnugsdienst* visited us again. Bewildered, his voice hoarse with agitation, he told us about a hide-out that the Germans had discovered in the no man's land, and the horrible death of the eight people within it. They had been beaten, lined up against the wall and shot.

The Germans were enraged, they were mad; Von Paulus' Army at Stalingrad had capitulated and black flags flew around the city. The *Schlaechter* were running wild. On the first day of February, Wiese and Streblow paid an unexpected visit to the *Judenrat*. They brought a few bottles of *samogon* – 90-proof moonshine – and sent for the president of the *Judenrat*, Dr Brawer. Wiese ordered the old man and two other employees to drink a whole bottle each without stopping. The *Schlaechter* stayed for a few minutes to see the effect, and left amused. Dr Brawer collapsed and was transported to the hospital to have his stomach pumped. He said to Father who was attending to him, 'My days are numbered. Wiese is playing with me like a cat with a mouse and will shoot me at the next opportunity.'

The same evening Father told us that Mother and I would have to escape in three days. He outlined his plan: we would meet the young *Ordnugsdienst* on Peretza at 6 p.m., two full hours before the curfew took effect on the Aryan side. As an *Ordnugsdienst*, he was familiar with the old ghetto border and the new no man's land, and would guide us safely to the Aryan side. In return, we should take charge of his sister-in-law, a young widow named Frania.

A very resourceful and energetic young woman, Frania had volunteered a few days before to follow up on the contact worked out by Father and Dr Docha in November. She secretly left the ghetto and came back with good news: everything was ready. We were all now bound together. According to our young *Ordnugsdienst* friend, we had a good chance of making it since, for the moment, no new transports were contemplated and German vigilance had slackened. The main difficulty would be for us to pass over the bridge across the Niemen where a round-the-clock watch for Jews and smugglers was kept by the Polish 'navy-blue' police.

Mother frantically prepared for our departure. At night, she laid out all our fortune on the bed. It was considerable: 900 green US dollars! She divided the 50, 20 and ten dollar notes into three parts of 300 dollars and sewed two of them into Father's and Tolo's overcoats, under the lining at shoulder level. She kept 300 dollars for both of us and placed a piece of Tolo's 'lucky shirt' with each portion. And as she worked she was crying. For two whole days I prepared myself mentally for the moment of our escape, but as the time approached I became very uneasy. Above all, I did not want to be separated from Father and Tolo, afraid of never seeing them again. I feared being caught and tortured. I watched our unsuspecting Grandmother, to whom now in our frantic rush to escape nobody paid much attention. She was, as usual, with the book on her knees asking Mother 'Esterko, what is this fuss about? Are you afraid of a search?'

'Yes Mother, yes,' answered Mother. Soon Grandmother forgot what she was asking and serenely stared anew at the pages of her eternal book.

'Motek, you have to promise, you will follow us soon and not wait too long – you have an obligation to us!' Mother implored. She was afraid that Father would stay with Grandmother as long as he could, and then it might be too late. But we both knew that Father would not abandon his helpless mother without a knife at his throat. I frankly did not believe that I would see my father and brother again.

The fateful evening came. We left with Father to meet our young friend. Tolo stayed behind. Mother and I both wore old coats with the yellow patches removed, the fabric cleaned so thoroughly that every trace of the patch was gone. Mother wore a very large woollen babushka shawl wrapped around her shoulders. It covered her face, except for her eyes and the tip of her nose, protecting her from the biting cold and concealing her Semitic Mediterranean features. I did not need to hide my face; it was so 'goyish', I was told, that even a Polish anti-Semite could not 'sniff me out'. Darkness was falling rapidly, and we had to hurry: crossing the no man's land could take a long time, and from there to our final destination at the Vorstadt we had to cover several kilometres before curfew. We walked briskly towards Peretza and entered a corner house located just before the no man's land. In the courtyard I recognized the tall silhouette of our *Ordnugsdienst* friend and, beside him, a huddled-up female form holding a bundle in her arms. A baby! Nobody had told us about a baby. What if it cries and attracts the attention of the police? How would Docha react to this? How could we accommodate a baby in our hide-out? This was not a part of our deal. As we stood there stunned, Frania said, 'This is my little Ilana. Oh please, please do not worry! Siewko promised to find a home for her.'

Time was precious and we had to get going. Our destination was the house of Dr Docha's gardener, Mr Siewko, who lived in the middle of the Vorstadt, the western suburb of Grodno on the other side of the Niemen. We finally agreed that mother and I would proceed first, arm in arm, then – at least 20 yards behind us – Frania with her baby. The baby was awake in her mother's arms, bundled up in blankets protecting her from the cold and the biting wind. In the twilight, she looked at us with her big brown eyes without crying. 'Let her stay quiet,' we prayed. Our young friend gave us the signal to proceed. My parents kissed goodbye and with a heavy heart I kissed my dear father. We followed the *Ordnugsdienst* along Peretza and then turned right into a small blind alley blocked off by a wooden fence with several rows of barbed wire stretched along it. The *Ordnugsdienst* cut the barbed wire with a pair of pliers and, with a strong push, he pivoted the boards of the fence, uncovering a crevice large enough for us to squeeze through. On the other side of the fence the blind alley led through the no man's land to an empty house that abutted Dominikanska Street, on the Aryan side. 'It is too risky to enter this house,' our friend warned. 'Go to the house on your left and get into the courtyard. You will see on your right the old ghetto wall which now separates the no man's land from the Aryan side. There is a hole in the lower right-hand corner, big enough to squeeze through. After that you will be in the yard of a normal Aryan house on Dominikanska Street. You should be able to walk out into the street through the front gate without arousing suspicion. Be careful of the German patrols on Dominikanska and of the Polish police on the Niemen bridge. Good luck!' We squeezed through the space in the fence and proceeded into the no man's land. Behind us, Frania's brother-in-law pivoted the boards back into place.

The die was cast; there was no return. We walked rapidly through the alley. All the houses were deserted, some open windows staring emptily at us. Everything was deathly silent. Our steps were muffled by the snow, but in my anguish I could hear them squeak. The few minutes it took us to reach the house on our left seemed like an eternity. The door opened easily into a short hallway that led into a yard. We all gathered in the hallway before our next leap. I went into the yard to explore the former ghetto wall. The yard was small, covered with frozen rubbish and abandoned bottles. The snow increased visibility and I could see distinctly the wall studded on top with pieces of sharp broken glass separating us Jews from 'normal' human beings. On the other side was the yard of a large house adjacent to Dominikanska Street. There were lights on in many of the windows. The sound of traffic and human voices was coming from Dominikanska. I inspected the wall; a hole leading right into the yard of the tall house on Dominikanska was clearly visible in the right corner, behind a heap of snow-covered rubbish. I signalled, and Mother and Frania came out. We looked back towards the darkness and the ghastly silence of the condemned ghetto before pushing easily through the hole. We crossed the small yard and assembled under the entrance by the heavy gate separating us from the street. My heart was pounding. We had to get into the street without alarming any inhabitant of the house or arousing the suspicion of any passersby. I cautiously tried to push the gate but it appeared to be locked. 'My God we are lost! If they find us here they will turn us over to the police.' Mother joined me and we pushed and swayed the gate, trying to keep it from squeaking. Frania, with Ilana in her arms, could not help us; she was concentrating on trying to keep the baby from crying. From behind the gate came the noise of the street:

loud voices in Polish and German, the trotting of hoofs on the snow, bells from passing sleds, laughter – the rhythm of the free world. I was consumed with fear, but we were at the point of no return, and the appeal and smell of life was so strong. At last the gate started to squeak and give way; the more we pushed, the louder the noise. 'If we do not attract attention now we never will,' I thought. The gate finally yielded and opened with a wild screech. My heart stopped beating but nothing happened.

We remained immobile in the passageway for a few minutes before walking into the street. It was essential to look calm and resolute as we joined the other pedestrians, first Mother and myself linking arms, then Frania with her bundle some 30–40 feet behind. We had a firm agreement: should one party be caught, the other would proceed as if nothing had happened and deny any connection. As we marched out of the gate on to the pavement, we almost stumbled into a German *Schupo* patrol. My heart stopped, but I grabbed Mother by the arm and started to speak loudly in perfect Polish with the drawl characteristic of the Kresy (eastern part of Poland), laughing loudly. I knew that I had a 'perfectly Aryan' appearance and that I could make my Polish impeccably 'goyish' too. I had learned that at the *Cwiczeniowka*. Even a Pole with a highly developed 'nose' for Jews would not suspect me immediately, and certainly not the two Germans in the patrol. The main thing was not to appear frightened and not to be hesitant; Father had drummed this into my head and I constantly rehearsed it in my mind. The two Germans passed by without paying the slightest attention to us and we quickly mingled with the crowd of people rushing home in the biting cold before the approaching curfew.

Mother huddled even more into her babushka shawl so that hardly any part of her face was visible. I, however, exposed my face openly to the cold, conscious of my 'Aryan' looks. We passed Dominikanska, turned left on to Batory Square, leaving the entrance to the ghetto on Zamkowa far to our right. I suddenly felt exhilarated by the open space, by the sight and sound of horse-drawn sledges with their little bells, by young voices, by the sound of laughter. How different from the grey, haggard and resigned faces in the ghetto. People here walked energetically, they were rushing with purpose to warm, lighted homes; some carried small packets and bundles, doubtless containing delicious bread and other good things to eat. We passed a few German soldiers arm in arm with their sweet-hearts. The mere feeling of walking through the vast stretches of the town, without the yellow patch, on the pavement with dignity, without bowing to the German uniforms, made me feel giddy with elation. I filled my lungs with gulps of frosty air and felt the whole meaning of being free, like a bird defying gravity, spreading its wings and admiring the beautiful world. The Garrison Church with its high steeple was now behind us. On the other side, only a few hundred yards from here, Father, Tolo and Grandmother were trapped in their dark room at the *Judenrat*. Would I see them ever again?

We accelerated our pace, we had barely an hour to curfew. We had been warned of the tight control held by the Polish police on the bridge. They were much more adept than the Germans at 'sniffing out' a Jew. We turned into the streets sloping down to the bridge across the Niemen. They were dimly lit and almost empty, and it was frightening to be here suddenly alone. I continued to talk loudly, always accentuating my local Polish drawl of the Kresy. Hiding my anguish, I simulated a happy voice. Mother was silent, her Russian accent could easily attract attention and her Semitic features would give us away immediately. We could hear small steps in the distance: it was Frania following us. The baby in her arms was quiet and fast asleep.

As we approached the bridge, the destruction of this part of Grodno became evident, the result of German bombing. We passed the empty shell of a large building, the ruins of the Seventh City Hospital where Father used to be Chief Surgeon and where he almost burned to death on the fateful day, 22 June 1941. The police barrage on the bridge was visible from afar. Farm vehicles and sledges were being stopped and searched for meat, lard and vodka. Coming closer, I saw two Polish 'navy-blues' inspecting the inside of a peasant's sledge using torches, and checking his papers. Another policeman stood on the pavement and occasionally beamed his torch into the faces of passersby. It was here that ghetto fugitives were being caught so often. We had no papers. Should they stop us, we would be arrested immediately. Fear clutched my throat again, but we continued to walk fast. There were fortunately other people on the pavement, all walking fast, braving the icy wind from the river. I talked some nonsense in my 'goyish' drawl, occasionally bursting out with forced, nervous laughter. I played my part very well. We passed the policeman with the torch, who did not even try to shine it on us. We crossed the bridge and I sighed with relief as we continued our fast walk on the other side for at least another hundred yards before I turned around. Frania was marching right behind us. Ilana did not cry, she was probably still asleep. Nobody bothered us, thank God!

This part of Grodno, the Vorstadt, was utterly devastated during the brief but intense fighting in June 1941. It was not easy to find the names of streets all in ruins, with walls pockmarked by shell fragments and broken, twisted lampposts. We had another half hour to the curfew to find our destination off Lososianska Street where Mr Siewko lived. It would become very dangerous to walk about after curfew, but to ask directions from the occasional passerby would be equally dangerous. Luckily, Frania had been here only a few days ago and vaguely remembered the way, but that was in daylight while now it was pitch dark. After a lot of turning around, we spotted on the wall of a house gutted by fire a sooty, scratched plate with – we guessed – 'Lososianska ul.' written on it. Frania said that it was the wrong end of the street. Siewko lived at least a few hundred yards away. We advanced slowly, stopping at each inhabited house, lighting matches to see the number. Many houses did not have numbers and some numbers were unreadable. It was getting late, barely ten minutes to curfew. We had to ask somebody for help. There were no passersby. We decided that, with my 'Aryan' looks, I would enter the first inhabited house and ask for directions. This was dangerous, but to stay in the street after curfew was even more so. I rang the bell and a female voice asked me what I wanted. Through the closed door I shouted, 'Could you tell me, ma'am, how to find number nine of Lososianska Street, I have to get there before curfew.' I did not try to explain. While keeping the door slightly ajar, the woman cautiously gave me directions; she did not even look at my face. We walked some distance before finally arriving at our destination. The house at 9 Lososianska was damaged and appeared uninhabited but the entrance door was intact. I rang the bell; it was 8 p.m., the start of a curfew on the Aryan side.

A woman opened the door, her face hidden in the darkness. I asked with my best accent of the Kresy, 'May I see Mr or Mrs Siewko?'

'This is she,' the woman answered, 'are you Alik?' Mrs Siewko let us all in and locked the door behind us. 'Follow me,' she whispered. Bypassing a dark staircase, she stepped into a courtyard and showed us a very small house with dimly lit windows. 'This is our house,' she said. 'Come right in; it may take you a while to warm up, but then I must take you down to the cellar.'

The room we entered was poorly furnished. An old couch stood against the wall and an oval oak table with a few chairs was in the middle. A tall, slim, middle-aged man greeted us; he was Mr Siewko, Dr Docha's gardener. He was obviously made very tense and uncomfortable by our presence. Mrs Siewko, a tall, fair-haired woman, would have been pretty if it were not for her worn features. They led us through two bedrooms into a little pantry. Mr Siewko squeezed in three chairs and we all sat to warm up and relax. Ilana was still sleeping in Frania's arms. Frania gingerly put her on the floor to rest her arms and gasped with relief; Ilana was heavy. The baby woke up and looked around. She twitched her mouth and started to cry. Only now could I see her features; she had a pretty delicate face, dark curly hair, big almond-shaped brown eyes and long black eyelashes. Her Jewishness was difficult to hide. Mrs Siewko looked at the baby with undisguised kindness, picked her up, rocked her gently and smiled. It was obvious that she was a warm-hearted woman. She had a small child of her own, which made things easier. She changed the baby and then brought us three bowls of steaming, thick potato and millet soup. I hadn't even realized how cold and hungry I was.

Maria – that was her name – said that tomorrow her husband would go early to Zukiewicze to tell Dr Docha of our arrival. 'Until he sends someone to take you to your hiding place, only Alik can sleep here. The baby can stay here for the night and we will put her in the crib with mine. You,' she addressed Mother and Frania, 'will have to go across the yard down into the cellar of the burned-out house. I will give you blankets and you will have to huddle together to keep warm. It's much too dangerous to keep you here. People sometimes visit us unexpectedly and you both look unmistakably Jewish. The Germans are raving mad, they have suffered a tremendous defeat at Stalingrad, black flags are flying all over the city, road controls are stricter, and with the liquidation of the ghetto the *Schupos* are looking for Jews everywhere. We cannot take any chances.'

So we separated, Mother and Frania with blankets and a petroleum lamp into the cold of the cellar and I, the lucky one, remained inside to sleep in the warmth of Siewko's living room. I stretched on the sofa; I was exhausted but I couldn't stop thinking of Father, Tolo and Grandmother left trapped in the ghetto. Would they have time to escape? The news about the German defeat somehow did not strike a chord, Stalingrad was so far and there was no Father to rejoice in happy expectation of a German collapse. Soon I was fast asleep.

Somebody shook me. 'Alik, time to get up!' A small electric lamp was piercing the darkness of the room. I saw Maria looking at me. I had a hard time returning to the real world. It was cold. Suddenly I was wide awake and sprang up from the couch. It was 5 a.m. The little flat was full of activity, Mr Siewko preparing to take the bus to Indura, Maria changing the babies. I dressed and went out into the darkness to see Mother and Frania. The penetrating cold lashed my face and made breathing difficult. How had they survived in that cellar? Maria joined me, holding a petrol lamp and leading the way. It was a deep cellar, down two flights of stairs. A heavy lock hung on the door. The cellar was damp, but warm compared to the arctic conditions outside. In the dim light of the lamp we could see Frania stretched on a blanket. Mother was sitting against the wall, she had not slept a wink, afraid of the many rats and mice. The candles and matches lay there untouched as the women had been frightened of signalling their presence. Both were chilled to the bone and very happy to get into the house to warm up for a while. We were given some delicious 'Aryan' black bread and a *bavarka* – hot water with milk and sugar. Soon Maria took both women back to the cellar, this time with the baby as it was impossible to keep Ilana in the house during the day. As for me, I was lucky; Maria allowed me to crawl under the bed and stay there.

The Siewkos had visitors. Listening to their voices and looking at the shape of their shoes I tried to imagine their faces; it helped to pass the time. Soon, I became very hungry and sore from my folded horizontal position on the hard floor, but people were constantly coming and going and there was no way for me to come out. Time stood still.

At 5 p.m., Siewko returned from Zukiewicze and I was allowed to crawl from under the bed. Frania, mother and the baby came out of the cellar. They were in a sorry state; cold and hungry, and the baby cried all the time. To pacify her, Frania gave Ilana her breast, but the baby bit her and Frania cried from pain.

Siewko reported that Dr Docha would have a hiding place for us but not for the baby. Under no circumstances could he take the baby, as she would be the end of us all. Someone would come tomorrow to take the three of us to our destination. Frania refused to part with the baby, even if it cost her her life! Fortunately, a childless couple lived close by, Siewko's niece Marta Kowalewski and her husband Tadeusz. When Frania had visited a few days ago, she had begged the Siewkos to help her find a home for Ilana, and Marta had agreed to take the baby. However, this arrangement was a strict secret between the Siewkos and Marta; her husband was not to be told that the child was Jewish. The man did not like Jews and had to be made to believe that the child was Christian and had been abandoned.

'Will he denounce Ilana if he finds out?' we asked. Maria reassured us. She knew the man. 'His bark is worse than his bite,' she said. 'He is very religious and will probably accept the child as a gift from heaven. They will, of course, baptize the baby and name her Halinka.'

After our supper of black bread and *bavarka*, the Siewkos went to make the final arrangements with Marta while her husband Tadek was on a night shift at work. We sat squeezed in the pantry in the dark; Mother, overtaken by the warmth of the house after the exhausting night and day in the cellar, was napping. The baby, now changed and fed, was wide awake, but remarkably quiet. The silence was only interrupted by Frania's sobbing.

The Siewkos came back after a short while. 'Everything will be fine, Frania!' Maria exclaimed. 'Don't cry, everything is set! We have to deliver the baby without arousing any suspicion. This may not be easy,' she continued, 'as their neighbour across the staircase is a *Volksdeutsch* [ethnic German] named Kammerer. He has six children and works as a supervisor at the Grodno tobacco factory. He has little to do with the police or Gestapo, although, like most Germans in important positions, he is a member of the Nazi party. The Kammerers are decent people but the problem is that many Germans, even some uniformed Nazis, come to visit him. Should he or a visitor notice something suspicious, everything could be lost.'

To protect Marta it was decided that the baby would be placed in the middle of the landing between the two neighbouring doors. 'When the child cries, we shall let the German discover her first,' Maria explained. 'Marta will come out a few minutes later and only then "discover" the child herself. There will be a letter explaining that the child is illegitimate, and imploring the good people to take her into their care and raise her as a good Christian. It is probable that Kammerer will have nothing to say when Marta cries out "Jesus has heard my prayers and sent me a little girl from heaven!"' Maria added.

The plan was good, provided the 'package' could be delivered without incident and no suspicions aroused. We had to do it the next day, just before our departure. The main entrance to the house would be left open and I could do my 'delivery' without being noticed. I had to do it, partly because of my 'Aryan' face, but mostly because Frania was hysterical with grief. If caught, I would try to concoct a story that would not implicate the Siewkos and their niece. I did not even want to think about such an eventuality. All highly agitated, we prepared to spend our second night at the Siewkos: Mother and Frania in the cellar, Ilana in the crib and I on the sofa, ready at any time to plunge under the bed in the next room.

In the early morning, after Frania and Mother returned to warm up, we all went to the cellar with the baby to wait for the arrival of Dr Docha's coachman, Mikhalko, who was to come before noon with his sleigh full of sacks of potatoes. We were to leave as soon as 'Operation Halinka' was over. Huddled together, we tried to keep warm in the cellar. Frania held Ilana tightly in her arms, tears streaming down her face, unable to speak. Her sobs intensified as the time of separation approached. Maria gave us the green light around noon. Both Marta and Tadek, her unsuspecting husband, were at home. Maria gently took Ilana from Frania's arms. The baby was crying and Frania was seized by convulsive sobbing which could endanger us all should a stranger step into the house. It was best for her to stay in the cellar with Mother, who tried to calm her down. I followed Maria into the flat. Maria fed Ilana, changed her and put around her neck a medallion of the Virgin and a small silver cross. She wrapped her in a thick, worn blanket. A cardboard poster around her neck said in big letters: 'MY NAME IS HALINKA. MY MOTHER IS DESTITUTE AND CANNOT FEED ME. DEAR VIRGIN MARY, GIVE ME A MUMMY AND A DADDY WHO WILL LOVE ME AND MAKE ME A GOOD CHRISTIAN. MAY GOD BLESS THEM FOR IT!'

The 'package' was ready for delivery. Maria went first to check the street. Soon she was back, waving for me to come. Ilana, clean, warm and fed, was now quiet. I took the heavy bundle and crossed the yard. The snow and wind hit me in the face, Ilana started to cry. 'Not now, for heaven's sake,' I prayed. I was lucky. The street was deserted except for some pedestrians far away. I turned right and soon I was standing before a small house divided into two apartments. I pushed the front door ajar and found myself on a dark staircase with a short flight of steps. My eyes, well used to the darkness of the cellar, could easily see the doors of both apartments facing each other across the landing. Ilana was so heavy! Thank goodness she had stopped crying. I climbed the stairs on tiptoe and delicately positioned the 'bundle' on the landing, exactly in the middle between the two doors. I placed her face up with the poster over the blanket for all to see. The baby remained quiet. I reversed my steps, praying that she remain quiet. Back in the street, I walked with composure the short distance to the Siewkos' house. They were all waiting for me in the cellar; Mother, Maria and Frania. Frania was in a sorry state, she sobbed and cried, repeating over and over, 'Ilana, Ilana my child.'

By now Mikhalko had rested, and was getting impatient. He came into the cellar. 'The snow is getting worse,' he said, 'we had better get going if we want to cross the German road controls at Kopciowka and Indura before the curfew, or we will be in big trouble.' Though I had seen him a few moments ago feeding the horses in the yard, I had hardly noticed him in my excitement. He was a short, moustached *muzhik*. He spoke the Byelorussian peasant dialect and made the sign of the cross every few minutes. He wanted us to leave immediately, saying that the few carts on the road after dusk risked being extensively searched at checkpoints. It was close to 1 p.m. and we needed at least four hours to pass the Indura checkpoint. This could bring us close to curfew. But Frania refused to budge before finding out what had happened to Ilana. We waited in the cellar until Maria somehow managed secretly to communicate with Marta.

'Everything worked out fine,' she said. 'As soon as you left, Alik, the baby started to cry and Mr Kammerer came out with his wife. "Do not touch," he shouted to his wife, "it may be a bomb!"' Ilana kept crying louder and louder. By then Marta and Tadek were out on the landing. Marta kneeled down and opened the bundle. 'A child!' she shouted, 'a little girl!'

'The German lifted Ilana from the floor and read the poster aloud. He looked at the baby and shook his head. "She is very pretty, you know," he said to his wife. "This baby comes from a good family, she is well dressed and clean, a real cutie. Her mother is surely a teenage girl from a good home seduced by a scoundrel; there are so many of them nowadays." He sighed looking with concern at his teenage daughter who came out together with a few other Kammerer children to see what the commotion was about. "The baby is pretty." He looked at Ilana again, trying to hush her by rocking her back and forth. "What shall we do, Magda? We have six, let her be the seventh."

'Marta intervened. "Herr Kammerer," she said, 'you have six of your own and we have none. I prayed to the Holy Virgin to send me a child and I truly believe that she has heard my prayers. Tadek and I will love this child and accept her as our own."

'"Well," said Kammerer, "if you want the child that much let her be yours, but we shall celebrate this. Let's open a good bottle of wine!"'

By now everything was ready for our departure. Mikhalko was getting very impatient, even angry. He was muttering something in Byelorussian and it was difficult to know if he was grumbling to himself or to the two mares, Dobrynia and Malynia, who were finishing the fodder in their nosebags. They were harnessed to a sleigh full of sacks filled with potatoes. 'You have to get into one of those, they are big enough for you to fit in,' he said, showing us a pile of empty hemp-cloth sacks. The time had come! We all bade farewell to the Siewkos. I saw Mother handing something to Mrs Siewko. I learned later that it was 50 dollars, a substantial fraction of our fortune.

'Get into the sack, I will help you stretch on the bottom of the sleigh.' Mikhalko smiled as Mother tried clumsily to get into her sack and lift herself to a sitting position on the cart. 'I'll cover all of you with sacks of potatoes. Even if there is a search, the Germans will not notice a thing unless they use dogs or their inspection spikes. But they do it rarely, only if they are on high alert.'

The prospect of being skewered at the inspection station sent a cold shiver down my spine. I remembered last summer with Lutek and Danya. We were at the ghetto gate on Skidelska, watching an inspection of carts loaded with cabbages and potatoes for the *Judenrat*. I remembered how the German drove the long, thin, sharp iron bar all the way through the cabbages to the bottom of the heap and then carefully inspected the tip of the spike, repeating this operation in different places before letting the carts pass. I preferred not to think what could have happened to someone hidden under those cabbages.

I stepped right into the sack and pulled it up to my waist. Mikhalko lifted me and helped me to stretch out in the bottom of the cart. I brought my knees to my stomach and he pulled the sack over my head, tying it loosely with a piece of rope. We were now side by side, Frania next to me and Mother with her head touching my knees. The sacks full of potatoes came on top of us layer by layer, carefully spread around by Mikhalko. I was weighted down, surrounded by darkness and a musty smell. It was uncomfortable but bearable.

A push, a pull, a tug – the sleigh squeaked, and off we went. Mikhalko cracking his whip. *'Vio-o, poshli, staryie tchertoviny!* – Vio-o, let's go, you old she-devils!' He ordered his reluctant mares to move against the driving snow and the wind. *'Vio! Vio!'*

Siewko opened the gate, relieved to see us go. *'Dowidzenia!* – goodbye,' he said. It was Saturday, 6 February 1943.

The hard boards of the sleigh pushed into my ribs and the damp smell of earth and hemp filled my nostrils. Fortunately the ride itself was smooth, the sleigh gliding on the deep layer of fresh snow which covered the road. We were on the highway to Indura. All my thoughts and prayers were now concentrated on the two checkpoints, one some 15 kilometres from Grodno at the village of Kopciowka, the other – not far from our destination – at the small town of Indura, manned by the Polish police and less feared by the locals. The cold was penetrating and soon I was frozen stiff. I could hear the voice of Mikhalko broken by the wind. *'Vio, vio staryie kobyly!* – Vio, vio, old mares!',* he shouted as he cracked his whip. Frania was sobbing. I tried to doze off but the cold kept me wide awake. We travelled for a very, very long time before I heard Mikhalko telling us in a tense voice that we were approaching Kopciowka and should be completely still. He betrayed his anxiety by lashing out at the horses and swearing in Byelorussian. When we came to a halt, I stopped breathing altogether. A German voice made my blood curdle.

'Was hast du da?' He repeated in broken Russian: *'Shto ma-iesh?* – What have you there?'

'Kartoshka, bulba, Herr Polizei – Potatoes, *Herr* Police,' answered Mikhalko.

The voices were made faint by the gusts of wind, but I could hear the German swearing *'Verfluchtes Donnerwetter!* – Damn this weather!'

'Los, gehe schon – Move it, be off already,' he barked. Mikhalko smacked his whip. *'Vio tcherty, poiekhali!* – Vio, you devils, go!' We moved off; the inspection was over. We were later told that the Germans had been drinking schnapps in their warm control booth on the road. They had not even bothered to step out and look at the cart. The German had opened the door of the booth just long enough to ask his questions and had then stepped back into the warmth.

We now had to pass the other checkpoint at Indura; but the Polish police were even less inquisitive and we passed without stopping. A big weight was lifted off my chest; the heavy sacks of potatoes suddenly appeared light. We had made it through the checkpoints! In no time we would reach Dr Docha's village at Zukiewicze. The sleigh was gliding smoothly, and Dobrynia and Malynia trotted almost joyfully, or so I thought from below the sacks. I tried to doze off, but the cold and the pain in my toes and fingers were unrelenting. The wind was still strong and I could hear a whisper of pinetrees; the road must have been cut through a forest. Everything was quiet; Frania's sobs had subsided since Kopciowka and Mother was completely silent.

By now we had been buried in the sacks for about four hours; we were covered with a thick crust of ice and snow. I dreamt of a warm fire and hot soup. I recalled the story of *The Little Match Girl* from the big illustrated book of Andersen's fairy tales which *Tante* Thea brought me from Koenigsberg for my seventh birthday and read to me so many times. This sad story always made me feel for the poor match girl, even though her death, dreaming about a warm fire and food, must not have been a horrible one. I was alarmed at this thought. I did not want to die of cold.

It was pitch dark when we arrived at Docha's little estate in Zukiewicze. The snow was still falling but the wind was weaker. Mikhalko helped us crawl out from under the sacks He himself looked like *Died Moroz* – the Russian children's 'Grandpa Frost' – all covered from head to toe with a crust of icy snow, with icicles hanging from his moustache. My feet were hurting, every move was painful. Mother was helped by Mikhalko. The three of us staggered into the house, while Frania remained on the sleigh. She did not want to remind the doctor of her existence before Mother could explain things to Docha. After all, he may well have sent Mikhalko for the Blumsteins alone, and Siewko's story about Docha agreeing to hide Frania could have been a fabrication: not surprisingly, the man wanted to get rid of us at all costs. We would eventually have to tell Docha about Frania but this was probably not the right moment for her to show her face.

We entered a hall with a broad staircase leading up to the

living quarters. Dr Docha was expecting us. He appeared hassled and very tense. To top everything, his wife Janina had just given birth to a baby girl and was still recuperating. She came out briefly in her dressing-gown to see us. In the dim light of a petrol lamp I could only see her silhouette, but Mother said that Janina was a beauty, a real madonna.

Docha told us that we should proceed immediately to the village of Staniewicze, some ten kilometres from his estate. A patient of his, a poor peasant named Edward Staniewski, and his wife Aniela, had agreed to hide us. They lived on an isolated farmstead at the edge of the village. As he visited his patients regularly, he would see us in a few days without evoking any suspicion among the neighbours. But for us to remain with the Dochas even for an hour might lead to catastrophe.

We had no choice but to proceed with our trip. We returned to the sleigh; this time we alternated walking and riding on top of sacks. We were the only ones on the road. We were all dead tired and frozen. We turned off the main road and followed a narrow track. The snow stuck to our faces, blinding us, but the wind subsided. In spite of the surrounding whiteness it was impossible to see further than a few yards away. After what seemed an eternity, we turned abruptly off the road on to a small path and heard at once the barking of a dog. The mares whinnied and stalled, the going was rough as the sleigh sank into deep snow. Mikhalko swore as the barking intensified. After a few minutes, we saw on our left the outline of a barn and a stable. We came to a halt before a small, miserable hut all covered with snow. Mikhalko got off the cart and advanced towards the hut, his legs sinking calf-deep into the snow. The dog was now straining at the chain that tied him to the entrance door, barking furiously. Somebody yelled, 'Tsatsus, quiet! Quiet!' The door of the hut opened with a creak.

'*Khai budzie pokhvalony Yesos Khristos!*' [May the name of our Lord Jesus Christ be hallowed!], said Mikhalko.

'*Na wieki wiekow, amen!*' [For ever and ever, amen!], a voice answered.

Mikhalko entered the hut and the door closed. The barking, which had briefly changed to yelping, resumed afresh. The dog was barking at us.

Soon we entered a dark vestibule leading to a small *isba*. I was overwhelmed by the humid warmth which puffed into my face and pleasantly surrounded my frozen body. Inside the main room, in the right-hand corner, a kerosene lamp stood on a heavy, rectangular table flanked by a long bench. The room was maybe 15 by 9 feet, with a low ceiling. On the left against the wall stood two beds separated by a door leading to a back room. In the weak, flickering light I saw a bearded man lying in the left corner bed. A big picture of the Virgin Mary hung on the right wall, while another of Jesus hung on the back wall, above the man's head. The room had no floor, only a layer of hard clay with some yellow sand lining the junction between the clay and the wall. A stocky woman stood next to us, shaking snow off her sheepskin. She helped us to remove our ice-encrusted coats and blankets and left them in the dark vestibule between the front door and the *isba*. Her gait and her voice radiated energy. She lifted the lamp from the table and placed it on a hook on the ceiling. The light fell on her face. She must have been in her forties, a sturdy peasant with hair pinned into a knot at the nape of her neck. A thick, straight nose, high cheekbones and a wide mouth gave her a slightly coarse appearance. Her deep blue eyes, which fixed us with their intense stare, betrayed resolution and intelligence.

She invited us to sit at the table and disappeared into the other room from which a strong smell of cabbage emanated. The fragrance was heavenly and the thought of a hot borsht made me salivate. I was coming back to life! The man in the bed began to talk to us. 'How was your trip?' he asked. He spoke in Polish, with a strong Byelorussian accent. Looking at him, I noticed how thin he was; his face was drawn, pale and wasted. Greyish-black hair, cut short, covered his head. He had a small, greying beard and a moustache. Deep-set blue eyes, small but lively, looked at us. He was lying on his back. From the ceiling hung a long leather belt, the use of which became clear to me when he grabbed it to lift the upper part of his body, his face betraying considerable effort and his mouth twitching in pain.

'Helka!' he yelled, 'come here!' A girl of maybe 15 or 16 came from the back room. She was pretty, with soft, straight features, blue eyes, long fair hair bound into a thick plait, and well-developed breasts. 'Bring me my *makhorka* and paper!'

'Yes Uncle', the girl replied and disappeared for a minute, coming back with a box. The landlord opened the box and stretched on the lid a small sheet of thin paper which he filled with coarse tobacco roots. He then rolled a cigarette which he promptly lit, taking in a deep breath of smoke. The unpleasant, acrid smell of *makhorka* hit my nostrils.

The landlady appeared with the borsht. We all ate voraciously. I savoured each spoonful of the thick cabbage soup with potatoes and beans, which spread warmth and life into my frozen body. Helka looked at us with undisguised curiosity. The landlady now introduced herself: 'I am Aniela Staniewska, and this is my husband Edward. We are part of the village of Staniewicze which is inhabited by the *szlachta* [noble folk] of this county.'

She looked at Mikhalko with contempt; he was, in her opinion 'only a peasant'. We were later very amused at this distinction between the Polish peasants, poor as they were, who referred to themselves as *szlachta*, and the Byelorussian peasants, whom they contemptuously called *chlopy* (peasants). The Poles were fiercely Catholic and anti-Russian, whilst the Byelorussians, for the most part, were Orthodox and pro-Russian. Despite their similar looks, similar Byelorussian dialect, similar poverty, their toiling the same soil of limited fertility, their antagonism was strong – sometimes leading to violence and vendettas. Thus we did not expect Mikhalko to stay in the hut any length of time. He left immediately, saying that we should expect Dr Docha's visit in a few days.

After eating I became overwhelmed by the urge to sleep; I was ready to drop dead on the floor. We were led to the back room by the landlady – *Gosposia*, as we called her in Polish. She sternly warned us that we were to be permanently confined to this little room, to avoid being seen by an unexpected visitor. 'We have to be very careful, nobody knows you are here and things should stay this way. The moment you are discovered, you'll have to leave at once!' she said. 'If the Germans catch you here, it will mean death to our entire family and an end to our village!' We knew that she was right.

The small room, also lit by a kerosene lamp standing on a table in the corner, was crowded. On the left side of the door was a huge peasant stove made of fired clay bleached with lime. A metal door shielded the big opening used for loading the wood and for occasional baking. The chimney ran through the ceiling, but the stove's massive body, at least five feet long, reached only to about shoulder level, thus creating a warm loft where two short people could sleep. On the other side of the doorway was a small cooking range on which most of the daily cooking was done, its flue connected to the main chimney. Whenever the oven was lit, the central wall of the hut remained warm. Next to the main body of the stove was a wooden barrel used for kneading dough. A large armoire that reached to the ceiling stood opposite the stove. There were two windows in the back corner of the room. Hela's bed stood against the back wall, its foot by the cooking range. Hela was now to sleep with *Gosposia* in the main room, while Mother and Frania took over her bed. I was assigned to the loft on the stove, somewhat short for a grown-up. I climbed up, using the kneading barrel as a stool. *Gosposia* gave me a quilt and some pillows. Embraced by the warmth of the stove, I fell instantly asleep.

15 Staniewicze

The loud cry of the rooster began to wake me. I turned over and smiled in my sleep; I was out of the ghetto and was no longer doomed to the horrors of the transport. The rooster repeated his long, shrill *cocoricoo*. I pulled the covers over my head and continued voluptuously to slumber, feeling after yesterday's trip every little bone in my body. I heard *Gosposia* getting busy around the house, and slowly opened my eyes. Daylight was already seeping into the room. Climbing down from my oven loft, I looked through the window covered with beautiful designs painted by the frost. After yesterday's storm, we were in for a sunny day. We all got up and dressed rapidly. There was very little washing. Water was brought in from a deep well a few yards outside the house, and it was icy.

As a rule, *Gosposia* lit the big stove while Hela took care of the animals. But today was Sunday, and *Gosposia* carried out both jobs as Hela went to church and then visited her mother, *Gosposia*'s sister Mania. The farmstead was poor; comprising about six acres of land with one cow, one horse, three pigs, a few sheep, a rooster and a few hens. Edward, the *Gospodarz* (landlord), could barely walk and *Gosposia* had to be the main breadwinner, taking care of everything from sowing to harvesting.

After lighting the fire, *Gosposia* brought salt pork, potatoes, black bread and a few eggs. I looked at this splendid food with widened eyes. I had not seen an egg in more than a year and I had not tasted such delicious black bread since we went into the ghetto or even before. I was starved and could hardly wait. The fire in the big stove crackled merrily. *Gosposia* fried the salt pork in a big cast-iron pan, then sliced cooked potatoes and added them to the pan. They fried with a spluttering sound and gave off a delicious smell. When the mixture of lard and potatoes was crisp and brown, she broke some eggs and threw them over the contents of the pan. I devoured my portion, relishing the aroma and crispness of bacon, the delicious velvety taste of fresh country eggs and the crunch of freshly fried potatoes. I savoured the rich, thickly sliced, fragrant, black country bread, which had nothing in common with the clay-like substance, filled with husks and sawdust to which I had become accustomed. How good it was to be in the country!

Gosposia was glad the fresh snow had covered the sleigh tracks leading to the farmstead, so the inquisitive neighbours wouldn't ask, 'Who on earth visited Aniela last night?'

'There are some individuals in the village who spend their time, especially in the winter, sitting at the window and peering into their neighbours' houses just to spread gossip. These people we must dread like poison,' she said. 'Before we do anything, we must first think about their reaction.' She went to the living room and peered through the upper part of the window which was free of frost. 'Everything is OK,' she exclaimed, 'nobody is around, you can come and look at our village.'

Inside the room, Edward, having said his morning prayer, was just finishing breakfast. He was sitting in bed, his legs on the floor, cutting pieces of bread and small pieces of salt pork with his pocket knife. He ate from the blade of his knife which he wiped with a cloth at the end of his meal.

Looking from the main room window, I realized our situation. The farmstead, though technically a part of Staniewicze, was actually located between two villages, Staniewicze to the north and Yarmolicze to the south, about one to two kilometres from either. It was accessible along a path from an unpaved road running between the two villages, now covered with snow. From the main room window one could see the village of Staniewicze and a portion of the road from Staniewicze to Yarmolicze; one could thus easily see anyone moving in our direction from Staniewicze. From the back room window we could see a sizeable portion of the Yarmolicze side of the road and spot anyone coming from there. Any traveller on the road could be seen from our windows, giving us enough time to hide. However, the path joining the farmstead with the road was shielded from view

from either room by the barn and the stable. Most of the traffic along the road was between the two villages. Few were
interested in the poor farmstead of Edward and Aniela but,
because we could not see the junction of the path with the
road, we had to hide whenever a traveller was spotted on the
road or risk being surprised by somebody coming from
behind the barn.

'Here comes Hela,' said *Gosposia* looking out of the window.
Something was indeed moving against the white of the snow
and I marvelled at what excellent eyesight *Gosposia* must have
to be certain of the identity of the moving object at such a
distance.

'In the winter we can spot everything moving around the
farmstead, in the summer it is another matter,' said Aniela.
'But the war will be over by summer. Ziutek said the Germans
had a terrible defeat in Russia and are retreating in panic.'
Ziutek Kulikowski, I learned later, was a young man involved
in the local Polish underground, the AK. He was also Mania's
lover. We soon found out that Hela was the child of *Gosposia*'s
unmarried sister Mania. Childless, Aniela and Edward had
taken the girl in and treated her like their own daughter. As
Edward was increasingly crippled by sickness, Hela became
very useful on the farm.

Now we needed to organize our stay here; we had to create
a hiding place that would conceal us from visitors to the hut.
We shifted the heavy armoire to the back wall next to the
oven, leaving just enough room behind the armoire for a
short, narrow bench. We were lucky: the armoire fitted the
space between the oven and the opposite wall perfectly. We
could now squeeze behind the large cupboard by sliding from
the top of the oven loft and then standing on the bench.

All this was accomplished in a hurry, with Hela's help, and
it was not a moment too soon. At about 2 p.m., the alarm was
sounded by *Gosposia*: a visitor! It was Sunday, after all. A
village woman called Olga was proceeding slowly in her
sleigh. Hela warned us that such a visit could last the whole
evening. We hid behind the cupboard. We climbed one by one
on the kneading barrel, then on to the oven loft and from there
down on to the bench, pressing our bodies between the wall
and the armoire.

Hela and *Gosposia* brought their spindles into the big room and sat down to spin just as Olga was entering the hut. We heard her voice, *'Niech bedzie pochvalony Jezus Chrystus'*, and the voice of the *Gospodarz*, *'Na wieki wiekow, amen'*.

Some time passed. The wheels of the spindles hummed merrily. Dusk was slowly falling and it was getting pitch dark behind the cupboard. We stood pressed against the wall. I tried to stand still, holding my breath. At first it was easy, but as time passed I became restless. I had to scratch my back and I tried to do this slowly, without making a noise. Then I had an irresistible urge to clear my throat. An attempt to do this softly made Mother panic, and she grabbed my hand and squeezed it so hard that I almost screamed, but Olga, oblivious to the passing of time, was spreading the village gossip as we all prayed for her to leave and to end our ordeal. At last, we heard Olga saying goodbye. We waited impatiently for the door to close behind her, but we still could hear her voice. She was twiddling and twaddling without moving. She belonged to that breed of people who cannot give up gossip of their own free will. I could see that Mother and Frania were suppressing an urge. Mother made desperate efforts and almost cried but Olga was still standing in the door, blabbing in her Byelorussian dialect. At long last the door closed and the dog Tsatsus barked as *Gosposia* accompanied Olga outside.

Gosposia called us out of our hiding. Olga had stayed for nearly five hours! We still waited a short time before *Gosposia* gave us the 'OK' signal after checking that everything was clear outside. It was a frosty night. The black sky above the snow-covered thatched roofs was sprinkled with myriads of stars. We went behind the stable, hugging the walls, looking cautiously around before running quickly to relieve ourselves behind the barn, while *Gosposia* stood her watch on the path to the road. We agreed that if she spotted somebody from afar she would hum or whistle the popular Polish song *Jak to na Wojence Ladnie* [About the Uhlans] – this would mean 'proceed cautiously back towards the entrance'. In case of unexpected and acute danger, she would start swearing at the horse; we would then remain pressed against the back wall of the barn.

After five hours behind the cupboard it was so good to be outside. Against the whiteness of the snow Staniewicze appeared as a dark mass of huts, while on the opposite side of the road the village of Yarmolicze could hardly be seen at all. Tsatsus was circling me and wagging his tail; he understood that we now belonged to the household. The few minutes passed and *Gosposia* was already calling the dog, 'Tsatsus, Tsatsus!' – a code word for getting us back into the hut.

In the hut, Edward was in pain and we tiptoed past his bed into the back room. Supper consisted of black bread fried with salt pork, and *bavarka*. What a supper! Since our arrival I could not get enough of all these wonderful things. We all ate in silence, emotionally drained and physically exhausted by Olga's long visit. Frania had recovered a little of her appetite, but she was still very depressed. Her eyes were red. She cried silently, so as not to provoke *Gosposia*. It was clear that until the end of our captivity she would not have any news of her baby.

The vestibule, which formed the windowless entrance to the *isba*, was used for storage of all kind of junk – chests, boxes, barrels, ladders and tools. One could also climb from there to the attic by means of a ladder. *Gosposia* occasionally used the vestibule as a privy for her sick husband, to spare him walking to the 'official' spot behind the barn. She now installed in permanence a black-enamelled pail with a tight iron lid, which we called *sagan*, to be used for nature's calls. It became indispensable during the day and during moonlit nights when going behind the barn was too dangerous. We placed the *sagan* behind a barricade of big wooden chests to shield the person squatting there. One of us was assigned to the chore of cleaning and emptying it behind the barn at night.

As the days succeeded one another, I could not stop thinking about Father, Tolo and Grandmother left in the hell of the ghetto with the *Schlaechters*. I prayed that Tolo and Father would not wait too long and would escape when there was still time. I was overwhelmed with gratitude to God, for I remembered at night my silent prayers in the ghetto that we might escape somehow when I felt instinctively that we were all sentenced to die in the transport. Mystical thoughts came to me mostly at night or in the evening. In the adjacent room *Gosposia* snored and below my loft Frania sobbed. Howling, of dogs in the village or maybe wolves looking for food, could faintly be heard from far away. On stormy nights the wind would moan around the farmstead, raising pillars of snow which by the morning would have piled under the windows, blocking the entrance to the hut.

I kept asking myself why we, the Jews, were chosen to suffer. Was it possible that we had to endure this tragedy because we had not followed the teachings of another Jewish prophet, Jeshu from Nazareth? It was impossible to believe this. If indeed he was ever-loving and ever-forgiving, why did he not forgive us for the blunder of our ancestors? I was overwhelmed by feelings of gratitude and love. I glanced at the picture of Christ hanging on the wall above Edward's bed. In the penumbra of the flickering petrol light, he gazed at me with sweetness. In the evenings, before the rapidly spreading dusk, I looked from our bedroom window at the beautiful red sunset and I prayed to God to spare my father and brother. I was emotionally devastated. As always on such occasions, I poured out my feelings by writing poetry. And now, at Staniewicze on 9 February 1943, my tears mixed with ink as I wrote my poem, *Ode to God*.

O Boze, oderwani jestesmy
   od swiata, uratowales nas,
Ale ze wzgledu na moja
   trzynasta rocznice urodzin
Uratuj nam Ojca i Brata
I w swej boskiej opiece miej
   ich i nas codzien.

O Lord, cut off from the world
You have saved us,
But for my thirteenth
   birthday, I beg thee Lord
To save my father and brother
   and extend Your protection
To us all.

Modle sie do Ciebie O Wiekuisty,
Lzy mi splywaja po twarzy,
Przychodza na mysl strony
   ojczyste
I brata postac sie marzy.

I pray to you O! Eternal,
Tears stream down my face,
I think about home
And see as in a dream my
   brother's silhouette

Leze i mysle godzinami
Probuje zasnac, lecz razem z
   snami
Przychodzi jakas nocna zmora
I nie zasypiam ja z wieczora.

My thoughts do not leave me
   for hours
I try to doze, but with my sleep
A nightmare comes
And I am awake.

To slysze powolne tykanie zegara	Now I can hear the slow beat of the clock,
To psa szczekanie mnie budzi	Now a dog's barking awakens me,
I mowie sobie: to sen, to mara!	I want to believe that all this is but a nightmare!
Tu widze ich widze w tym okropnym piekle!	Here, here I see them in this hell!
Tyle mysli przez glowe mi przelata	So many thoughts run through my head,
Gryze, mietosze poduszke placzac wsciekle	I bite, I pound my pillow crying madly
O Boze! Uratuj nam Ojca i Brata.	O God! save for us my father and my brother.
Oto stysze jada sanie w oddali	I hear a sleigh in the distance,
Okropna sciska mnie trwoga	Terror clutches at my throat,
Wolam wszystkich aby sie chowali	I summon all to hide
I cicho sie modle do Boga.	And I pray, whispering, to the Lord.
Zasypiajac koszmarnym snem	When overcome by nightmarish sleep
Modlitwa blagalna z mej duszy ulata:	A prayer escapes my soul:
Wesprzyj nas Boze na ramieniu twem	Lend us Your strong arm O Lord!
Uratuj nam Ojca i Brata.	Save my father and my brother.
Gdy z rana zlociste slonca promyki do okna wpadaja	In the morning when the playful sunshine falls through the window
Platajac figle, lechocza mile, Barwami teczy graja	And erupts in myriads of colours,
Wtedy zal ogromny dlawi moja dusze	Then grief and sorrow grip at my soul.
My meczennicy, nie dla nas slonce; dla nas katusze	There is no sun for us martyrs; only torment.

Staniewicze

Nasze cierpienia trwaja dlugie
  miesiace
A nawet wiecej, lata
Wiedz wynagrodz o Boze serce
  cierpiace
Uratuj nam Ojca i Brata.

Zostawieni w piekle okropnym
  tym
Ich los dostal sie w rece kata

Wiec rozgrzesz ich dusze
  i w ucieczce pomoz im
Uratuj nam Ojca i Brata.

Po pelnym dniu cierpien,
  gdy slonce zachodzi
I na niebie oznacza sie ksiezyc
  blady
W seledynowej swiatla powodzi,
  widzialem Ciebie Boze!
I u Ciebie-m zasiagal rady

I wtedy gdy ziemie spowijal
  mrok
I otulala ja nocy szata

I wtenczas o Boze przyrzekles mi

Ze uratujesz nam Ojca i Brata!

Our suffering endures long
  months and years.
Reward O Lord! an anguished
  heart,

Save my father and my
  brother.

Abandoned in this hell,

Their fate is in the hands of a
  hangman.
Forgive them their sins and
  help them escape.
Save O God! my father and
  my brother.

After a day of anguish,
  at sunset
When the moon faintly
  appears in the sky,
In a blue flood of light
  I saw you O Lord!
I asked for advice and You
  gave me guidance

And then when twilight
  covered the earth
And when night's veil
  descended
You have promised me
  O Lord!
That you will save my
  father and my brother!

This poem came from the depth of my battered soul. I was thinking not only of Father and Tolo, but about Shurik, Monia, Lutek, Danyusha, Rita and Rosa, Shula, the poor crippled Juletchek, Mareczek, the Hellers, the Klingers, Leiba and Moishe-Leiba, and so many others; they were there high in the red glow of the wintry evening sky marching in an unending procession. O Lord! save my father and my brother!

We were expecting Dr Docha during the weekend, maybe with news from Grodno. After supper, Tsatsus started to bark furiously. We hid behind the cupboard and *Gosposia* went out to meet the visitors. Soon she was back calling us out of hiding. Docha entered the room.

'*Niech bedzie pochvalony Jezus Chrystus.*'

We were now trained to answer, '*Na wieki wiekow amen*'. I saw a man clad in a thick sheepskin, his head covered with a fur hat and ear-muffs, his face wrapped in a long woollen scarf rolled around the sheepskin collar. This attire made him appear portly and at first I recognized only his gold-rimmed glasses and his sharply protruding nose. He shook the snow from his boots and coat, took off his hat and crossed himself in front of the picture of the Virgin hanging on the wall. With a stern look, *Gosposia* ordered us to do the same. I hesitated for a moment but then followed the others kneeling in the direction of the picture. I could see Dr Docha folding his hands and touching them to his forehead. For a few minutes he was absorbed deep in prayer, then he rose and greeted us individually. His good blue eyes looked at me for a while. 'How are you, Aliczek, how do you like it here?'

At that moment, Mikhalko came in and asked *Gosposia* where he should put the provisions they had brought for us. *Gosposia* went out with Mikhalko while we showed the doctor our security arrangements. He warned us and *Gosposia* not to change her daily routine in the slightest; not to buy more food at the market than usual, or bake bread more often than usual. Any suspicion among the neighbours in the village might lead to disaster.

He was optimistic about the future as he said that the Germans had received a terrible beating at Stalingrad. He added: 'The Allies in Africa are finishing off Rommel and will soon create a second front in Europe, hopefully not too far from us, so that we can be liberated by them rather than by the Russians.' We never doubted that Dr Docha was a member of the Polish Home Army, the AK, and a staunch nationalist for whom Wilno and Lvov were sacred Polish cities to be reclaimed from the Russians. He was very pessimistic about the ghetto's survival. Having heard that German police from rural areas were being mobilized for some final *Aktion* in

Grodno, Docha was convinced that the ghetto was about to be liquidated and Grodno made *Judenrein* [cleansed of Jews]. He discussed with *Gosposia* the possible arrival of Father and Tolo. *Gosposia* and Edward were anxiously awaiting Father's arrival. They welcomed having a doctor at Edward's bedside; this was one part of their deal with Dr Docha. The other part was that Dr Docha would not charge them for his many house-calls, which the Staniewskis could ill afford to pay.

We stepped into our back room to allow Dr Docha to examine Edward and give him an injection. After he had finished, he ordered Mikhalko to get ready for the trip back. We asked Docha to have some soup with us but he declined, saying that this would not be wise because he was expected at the bedside of another patient.

'We should never give anybody any reason to suspect anything, but I will see you soon,' he said, putting on his winter gear. He kneeled, made the sign of the cross and brought his folded hands to his forehead. He stayed in this position for a few seconds, then left for another hut in the village, where a very sick man awaited him.

During the next few days, we continued to improve our security. We established a watch at the back window, dividing the shifts between the three of us. This was easy, as we were all confined to the back room. However, the main danger came from the entrance door in the front room and here we had a mighty helper, the clever black sheepdog Tsatsus, who was now kept attached to his kennel at the entrance door. The slightest barking sent us fleeing behind the cupboard, often for no good reason. Luckily, we soon learned that Tsatsus had one way of barking at strangers and another for chickens, pigs and members of the household.

With the fields covered by snow, *Gosposia* and Hela's main activity was to take care of the livestock and spinning. The spinning wheels hummed day and evening as both women spun flax and wool. They sat in the front room, close to the window, so that they could see the road from Staniewicze. On such occasions, Tsatsus was allowed inside, where he slept, biting and scratching his fleas, savouring the warmth of the *isba*. At night, he was again attached to his kennel and kept his watch on the sleeping farmstead.

We now had ample time to prepare ourselves for visits from the village, yet danger was always lurking. One Saturday a peasant walked into our room with his wife, surprised that Aniela had changed the location of the big cupboard. *Gosposia* quickly answered that the room was humid and that the proximity of the oven kept the wood of the cupboard dry, allowing the drawers and the door to fit properly. 'O-ho,' said the peasant, approaching the cupboard, 'you must have a lot of muscle, Aniela, to be able to drag this stocky beast!' And he wrapped his arms around the side of the cupboard. As I saw his big hand clasping the wood right next to my face, I almost died of fright. 'This is it,' I thought, 'we are lost!' But the peasant did not notice anything suspicious and left the room, joking with Edward about the Herculean strength of his wife. 'I would not like to pick a fight with you, Aniela,' he said, and everyone burst out laughing. This memorable visit lasted for hours, until late into the evening. We were petrified and Mother almost fainted when we were finally allowed to come out from behind the cupboard. *Gosposia* laughed at how she had dragged the half-drunken bastard hugging the cupboard out of the room. It was obvious that she was quick-witted and enjoyed danger.

Yet another frightening incident occurred during a visit by some village women. As we stood behind the armoire, I whispered something that made Mother nervous. I do not know why her nervousness appeared very funny to me and I tried to stifle my laughter; this in turn made Frania laugh. Frania's attempts at stifling her laughter appeared even more funny to me and I was just about bursting at the seams, and pushed a handkerchief into my mouth in an attempt to suppress my laughter. It was absolute madness. Fortunately, *Gosposia* and Hela, noticing something amiss in the back room, began to speak more loudly and our muffled laughter was not heard.

What a delight it was to stretch after a long visit and go outside into the frosty night air, behind the stable, to look at the immensity and beauty of the universe. But then *Gosposia*'s call for 'Tsatsus' would all too quickly remind us it was time to get back into our 'cage'.

After having slept soundly for a few nights, I now dreaded returning to my warm sleeping loft for I had discovered to my horror that it swarmed with bedbugs. I already knew this vermin from the ghetto and the flat we had shared with the Gitisses and Lamperts. But there they had nested in the wall and divided themselves among nine people, here they nested deep in the cracks of the oven where they multiplied and thrived. At night they swarmed all over me. I was their favourite meal. How I hated those red, foul-smelling, repugnant parasites! I became increasingly apprehensive of darkness, as they came in swarms only when the light was out. My sleep, which provided me with a few hours of happiness and freedom, was now challenged by bedbugs. I did everything I could to get rid of them. I washed and scrubbed the oven, poured petrol and kerosene over the cracks. This had a beneficial effect for a day or two, but then they came in force. I now dreaded the night more than the day.

Meanwhile, *Gosposia* was in a good mood because Mother had given her 100 dollars, a fortune for a poor peasant with only six acres of land. We had only 150 dollars left, and were counting on Father and Tolo's reinforcements to survive. But would they make it here? With the talk about the liquidation of the ghetto, I had nightmares about both of them being shot by Wiese or Streblow at the synagogue. I continued to write my poems and pour out my feelings on the paper of a grammar school notebook which Hela gave me.

Hela also brought me books from the small church library, including a book about the creation of the universe, written by a French priest and astronomer, the Abbé Mauraux. A big book full of illustrations, it contained a physical description of light, energy and matter. It had a chapter on life and its evolution, and much more. Having had my schooling interrupted for almost two years, I found many of Abbé Mauraux's concepts difficult to grasp but I understood the main point he was trying to make. He wanted to show that scientific inquiry leads directly to the proof of God's existence. I was fascinated by this book as it strengthened the mystical moods which were now increasingly taking hold of me.

Confined night and day to the back room, I wondered about our Jewish destiny and about the existence of God. The Catholic priests proclaimed from their pulpits that we Jews were punished by God for rejecting Christ, but what did I have to do with Christ's crucifixion? What did Shurik or Rita or little Mareczek or the midget Juleczek have to do with it? And what about those small children from Kielbasin going to their death? Why should Christ – the Jew from Galilee, the Christian God of Love and Mercy – take such a toll in suffering from his own people? But if our religion was right, why did the Lord let his people suffer so much? The logic of my thinking led me to the uncomfortable conclusion that there might not be a Christian God of Mercy or a Jewish God of Justice. Maybe the Soviets were right after all. Our teacher Clavdia Semyonovna, at the Russian middle school, had taught us that all this religious talk was 'opium for the people', dispensed by those in whose interest it was to keep them ignorant, nourishing their primitive instincts and irrational fears, making it easy for the clergy to amass treasures and power at the poor people's expense. And yet, there were moments when I felt an overwhelming love and gratitude towards a transcendent Being. I felt so small and insignificant, I felt that my suffering could not be in vain, that it was cleansing and redeeming; that there was beyond my limited understanding a Justice, a Love and Harmony that made this suffering worthwhile. Such moments were rare and more often I thought, 'You poor stupid boy, the fear of death makes you wish for a Protector, an ever-loving and ever-powerful Father. You have seen with your own eyes that there is no Justice and no God.' Torn and tormented, trying to 'prove' or 'disprove' God's existence, I climbed up to my loft at night praying to God for the safe arrival of Father and Tolo.

On 15 February, almost ten days after we had arrived at the farmstead, *Gosposia* returned from the village with terrible news from Grodno: the ghetto was being liquidated. Rumours in the village had it that the ghetto was burning and many Jews were being shot, hanged or burned alive. 'Peasants in the nearby Byelorussian village were saying that Dr Blumstein had been hanged by the Germans,' she told us. We went into a state of shock; Mother cried and I became numb with grief and helplessness. *Gosposia* grumbled, she was not pleased; after all, her deal with Dr Docha was for Dr Blumstein to take care of Edward at his bedside, and maybe cure him.

It happened a few days later. It was evening and the half

crescent of the moon was hanging above the village. In its pale light one could see far over snow-covered fields. On such nights we never ventured outside. We felt resigned and drained. I could not bear the thought of never seeing Father and Tolo again. It tore at my heart and would not leave me for a single moment. God had not listened to my prayers! Engulfed in an agitated sleep, I awoke suddenly to the furious barking of Tsatsus. There could be no doubt: someone was heading for our hut. I immediately jumped from the loft down to the bench and wedged behind the cupboard. Frania was already climbing on the loft from the kneading barrel and Mother was rushing behind her. *Gosposia* came to look through the back windows. *'Pani doktorowo,'* she told Mother, 'I recognize Mikhalko, but who are the others? Maybe you can recognize them?'

Mother crept out from behind the cupboard and cried out 'Motek, it is Motek! And there I think comes Tolya, Tolya...yes Tolya!' She burst into tears of joy. 'They are here! They are alive!' Five black figures were moving clumsily through the deep snow, cutting across the field. I could now distinctly recognize Mikhalko, Father and Tolo, but who were the other two people? Tsatsus was pulling at his chain, barking frenziedly at the approaching strangers. *Gosposia* went out to bring him into the hut, worried that his barking would attract attention in the village.

Not knowing who the two strangers were, we decided that only *Gosposia* and Hela would go out to greet them. We heard Mikhalko's deep voice at the door, *'Khai budzie pokhvalony Yesos Khristos!'* and *Gosposia* replying *'Na wieki wiekow, amen!'* – then Father's voice asking 'Where is my wife and Alik?' We threw ourselves in each other's arms. Father was unshaven, his stubble cold and prickly. The *isba* became illuminated with a yellow light as Hela lit the kerosene lamp. Father wore his short Scottish winter jacket, woollen knee breeches and a visor cap with ear flaps. His clothes were covered with snow and encrusted with ice. And here was Tolo in a long, ragged coat, an icy rag on his head for a hat. He was kissing Mother, who sobbed for joy, 'Thank God, Tolya, my son, you are here!'

In the vestibule just behind the door the two other people were shaking snow off their clothes. One was a young woman of medium size, with a big woollen babushka shawl wrapped around her head. She wore high rubber boots and a sheepskin coat. The man who accompanied her was rather short and stocky. He also wore a torn old coat hanging limply down almost to his feet, visibly much too big for him, a visor cap and old ear-muffs. They all looked pitiful – completely frozen, shivering and exhausted. They rubbed their blue, frozen fingers and ears.

Gosposia was not happy and grumbled to Edward in Byelorussian. 'Why the hell have they come with yet two more Jews? I have no room for them. There are seven of them now, Jesus Maria! Where will we hide them? Every additional Jew is a mortal danger to all of us! I will not stand for it! Tell the Doctor, I will not have seven people here!' she screamed at Mikhalko. 'Let him take care of it! First three, then five, and now seven! I will not stand for it! Tell him!' She was fuming. Then she exploded: 'Why the hell did you walk through the open fields in the moonlight? Do you want us all to be shot? Don't you know that people have good eyes? You could be spotted from miles away!' Her angry voice became plaintive as she raised her arms in desperation.'Why did I get involved with all these Jews? Jesus Christ, why did you send them to me?'

Gosposia was a good-hearted woman but, as we all quickly discovered, in her anger she could be terribly violent and insulting. Mikhalko tried to explain, saying the police were on high alert everywhere. It was much too risky to be on the road. He said he had left his sleigh in a friendly village the other side of Indura, and they had trudged the remaining 10 kilometres on foot through the fields. 'We have been walking for nearly five hours already and are half-dead from cold and fatigue!'

Gosposia calmed down. Still grumbling, she ordered Helka to make a fire and heat some buckets of water in the oven. One by one our travellers, including Mikhalko, took off their footwear and rubbed their feet with cold and then warm water. Father, whose shoes were in tatters, had the worst frost-bite. His toes were blue and open sores caused by friction covered his feet. And, as Tolo and Father sat on the bench, rubbing and warming their frozen bodies, waiting for a hot sweet brew with bread, the fantastic story of their escape from the hell of the ghetto started to unfold.

Staniewicze

The Eastern front on 22 June 1941 and on 22 June 1944.

225

16   Father's Story

On the morning of 14 February, after a respite of three weeks, the transports from Grodno ghetto resumed, this time in full daylight. Tolo and Father took Grandmother to the synagogue-hospital as they felt somewhat safer there than in our room inside the *Judenrat*. People were rushing to and fro, a few were making last-minute preparations for their hide-outs. At the synagogue, a detail of Jewish police tried to keep the area clear for the arrival of the crowd that was to be transported. Rinzler, Schott and Errelis were already there with their long whips and sub-machine guns. Special Police surrounded the area just before the first columns arrived, herded in by *Schupos* and the *Ordnugsdienst*. The synagogue and its yard eventually became jammed with people. The SD men were yelling commands to the *Ordnugsdienst* to keep people in columns, Wiese and Streblow were shooting into the crowd. The first long column began marching before noon towards the Grodno central railway station, in full view of Aryan passersby, who gathered along the pavements to gawk at the procession. All disguise was finally dropped.

Father, Tolo and Grandmother were still at the hospital on the upper level of the synagogue. At the end of the morning Wiese came in and ordered all staff and all the sick who were able to walk to go out into the square. Father walked with Grandmother, who was confused and dizzy. Everybody was lined up and two huge *Schupos* counted heads. A brief order rang out: 'All even numbers to the transport, all odd numbers back to the hospital!' It happened that both Tolo and father, with grandmother hanging on his arm, were even numbers.

'*Na, los!*' yelled a fat *Schupo* as he brutally pushed them into the crowd with his rifle butt.

Grandmother, who did not understand what was going on, looked at Father with bewilderment. 'Motek, what do they want from us?' There was commotion and yelling at the other end of the column – Wiese was beating somebody. A brief staccato from his *Maschinpistole* ended the commotion. The lifeless body of Dr Brawer, the president of the *Judenrat*, was sprawled on the snow near the wall of the synagogue. For him it was all over.

The medical personnel wore armbands. Tolo had an armband with an 'S' for *Schwester* [nurse] and Father with an 'A' for *Arzt*, or doctor. As they were standing in the crowd, Tolo spotted a woman on a stretcher just as the nearest *Schupo* was distracted for a moment by some incident. Tolo seized his chance. He darted out of the already moving column and stood beside the stretcher, displaying his *Schwester* armband. The woman on the stretcher was unconscious. As Tolo 'stood guard' by the stretcher, Father and Grandmother were in the crowd already advancing towards the Zamkowa Street gate and the train station. Suddenly a loud voice called, 'Dr Blumstein, you are urgently needed at the hospital.' It was the voice of Dr Solomon Birger, the director of the hospital and a dear friend of my parents. After a few seconds of hesitation, Father stepped out of the column, dragging Grandmother with him. A pair of brutal German hands grabbed Grandmother, separated her from Father and threw her back into the crowd.

'Nicht du, nur der Arzt! Du gehst ja zurueck!' [Not you, only the physician! You are going back!]

'Das ist meine Mutter!' [She is my mother!], Father protested.

'Mutter oder nicht, Sie werden sich schon treffen' [Mother or not, you will meet her soon for sure], joked the *Schupo*. The crowd was moving and Grandmother was carried along with the stream, her old wrinkled face looking for Father in desperation and crying 'Motek where are you? Where are you?' Father sobbed convulsively, but did not squander this unexpected opportunity. He had a family and a duty towards us to live. Grandmother could no longer be helped; he had stayed with her in the ghetto until the bitter end, but now it was the eleventh hour, it was his last chance. His face ashen, his heart torn to shreds, Grandmother's voice ringing in his ears, he looked at his helpless old mother being carried further and further away by the crowd.

In the meantime, Tolo was approached by Wiese who had

noticed him standing in front of the stretchers. 'Are you transporting the sick from the hospital?' asked Wiese.

'Jawohl, Herr Chef,' answered Tolo. 'This woman may be
contagious and the director told me to stand guard by her.'

'Contagious?' Wiese shouted, scared out of his wits. 'Take
her back upstairs to the hospital at once!'

'Jawohl, Herr Chef.' Tolo and an *Ordnugsdienst* carried the
woman upstairs. He saw Father talking to a stocky man with
dark hair and the silver-trimmed armband of a senior
Ordnugsdienst officer, still able to move freely within the
confines of the ghetto. Tolo, who did not know what had
happened to Father, was overjoyed to see him back at the
hospital. Father told him that Misha Wystaniecki – this was
the name of the *Ordnugsdienst* officer – would lead them
across the ghetto to our room inside the *Judenrat* building, to
escape as planned. In exchange, Father would give Misha
Siewko's address. That was the deal. The best time for crossing would be in the afternoon before dusk.

Outside the hospital the *Aktion* continued; the Germans
were getting ready to make Grodno *Judenrein*. Most of the sick
had already gone – on foot if they could walk, or in a police
truck – and had been taken to the train. Those who remained
were too sick to be moved at all, or contagious. Half of the
staff and doctors had also gone. Those who were still at the
hospital tried desperately to avoid being taken in the next
round-up. Forgotten in the commotion were the very sick,
considered as good as dead already. Some moaned softly,
some prayed in Hebrew, some lamented, calling for their
families; others, too weak to do anything, closed their eyes
and waited for the deliverance of death. One person who still
cared was the director of the hospital, Dr Birger. He moved
from bed to bed trying to alleviate suffering. A woman, who
had had a Caesarean section the day before, was running a
very high fever. There were no antibiotics and Father could do
nothing to help her. She begged the nurses and doctors to give
her poison to kill her, but nobody would do it, mainly because
poison was a priceless commodity.

As the afternoon progressed and the sun cast long shadows
across the hospital ward, the *Schupos* returned. Everybody
was ordered out. Taken by surprise, Father and Tolo, who

were still waiting for Misha Wystaniecki to take them to the *Judenrat*, found themselves again descending the same stairs and joining the crowd for the transport. From the square, they could hear volleys of sub-machine gun fire in the hospital. The SD butchers were finishing off the very sick in their beds. The yard and the synagogue were full of dead bodies. Even the *Ordnugsdienst* were now being shot at random. The smell of death was everywhere.

In the midst of the column, Father and Tolo were being pushed through one of the narrow ghetto streets towards the Zamkowa Street gate. Suddenly, the column halted. There was commotion and shooting. A *Schupo* ran forward, while another *Schupo* next to Tolo and Father remained in place. He stood there, staring at the crowd and at Tolo. Tolo had in his pocket a gold Swiss watch – a Longines entrusted by Uncle Lolya to Mother when she had visited him in Zugress two years previously. Lolya wanted to have it repaired in Grodno because spare parts were more readily available in the West. The watch was repaired but the war had made it impossible for Mother to send it back to Lolya. Tolo looked around and, seeing that the German was alone, pressed the watch into his hand.

The *Schupo* glanced at the watch, smiled and walked away – Tolo and my father bolted from the column and ran into the entrance of the nearest house. It all took just a few seconds. They waited for some time before crawling into an empty apartment where they hid with pounding hearts under the beds. They could hear again in the narrow street the raucous voices '*Los, los, gehe schon!*' The shouting and commotion died down after some time; the column was gone. Father and Tolo waited before venturing out into the street. Dusk was falling. They walked hugging the walls, wedging into every entrance and looking around before proceeding again towards the *Judenrat*.

A final leap across Ciasna Street and they were inside the *Judenrat*. It was completely empty. Their steps echoed on the staircase and along the corridor as they rushed to our room on the second floor. They found everything in its place: the rope, the ladder, the nails, the hammer, the knife. There was no time to lose; curfew was approaching. The window overlooked a six-foot-high brick wall with barbed wire and broken glass cemented on top. This wall separated the ghetto from the Garrison Church on the north side. On the south, the Aryan side, the church faced Batory Square and was enclosed by a wrought-iron fence with spiked railings through which the ghetto wall was clearly visible. It would have been safer to wait until dark before proceeding to secure the rope ladder to the window, but they had little time. Suddenly, Misha Wystaniecki, with his wife Rozia behind him, stepped into the room. Just a few minutes more, and Father and Tolo would have been gone. Now they were in this together.

The moment to escape was at hand. They removed their yellow patches and flung out the rope ladder with all the strength they could muster. It landed on the churchyard side of the wall. They climbed down the ladder very slowly, one at a time, painstakingly avoiding the broken glass on top of the wall, which took some doing. After landing, they raced for cover through the open yard towards the archway of the church and decided to proceed separately towards the Vorstadt and Siewko's house. Under the cover of twilight they had their chance, but first they had to get out of the fenced churchyard without being seen from the street. The only way to do this was to climb over the wall on the east side and bolt into the yard of an Aryan house that led into Dominikanska Street. Luckily, the top of the wall here was bare of broken glass. Tolo and Misha helped Father and Rozia. Tolo climbed next, and finally Misha who turned out to be very athletic. They were now in the yard of a private building. The gate was not locked. They stepped out into the street with determination and, mingling with the other pedestrians, proceeded separately towards the bridge on the Niemen. At the corner of Batorego, Father almost bumped into a woman whom he instantly recognized as an old patient of his. Her eyes opened in amazement. Father signalled her to remain silent by putting his hand to his mouth. She crossed herself and clenched her hands together in the sign of 'good luck to you!'

Their hearts were pounding as they approached the bridge, where the checkpoints had been reinforced because of the liquidation of the ghetto. It was getting very cold. Maybe this made the police on the bridge less vigilant. At any rate, they

1. Myself (left) and my brother as toddlers.

2. Mother before a recital at our Sanatorium in Druskieniki (summer 1935).

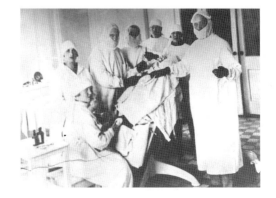

3. Father operating at our clinic in Grodno (1934).

4.   Mother with friends and guests at our Sanatorium in
     Druskieniki (1933).

5.   Blumstein family (Grodno 1935).

6.   With Mother at the Maccabi skating ring in
     Grodno (1936).

7. With *Tante* Thea Boehm in the garden of the Sanatorium in Druskieniki (1937).

8. First Conference of the 'Jewish State Party', Grodno (1934). (The young Menachem Begin – future prime minister of Israel – first on the right in the second row, standing against the wall; my father – fourth on the left in the second row, sitting against the wall.) From *Lost Jewish Worlds*, courtesy Yad Vashem, Jerusalem.

9. At the Niemen beach with father and Tolo, Grodno (1938).

10. Father, mother and cousin Lenka at the entrance to our house in Grodno (summer 1940).

11. Uncle Lolya mobilized as Surgeon-Major, Red Army (1941).

12. Moving into the Grodno ghettos on 1 November 1941. From *Lost Jewish Worlds*, courtesy Yad Vashem, Jerusalem.

13. Deportation from Grodno ghettos in November 1942. From *Lost Jewish Worlds*, courtesy Yad Vashem, Jerusalem.

14. The Great Synagogue of Grodno used by the Nazis as *Umschlag Platz* (winter 1943). From *Lost Jewish Worlds*, courtesy Yad Vashem, Jerusalem.

15. The hut of Aniela and Edward Staniewski at the village 'Staniewicze', where we hid from February 1943 until our liberation in July 1944.

16. The first page of my poem *Oda do Boga* (Ode to our Lord), written in hiding on 9 February 1943.

17. With my parents a few months after liberation, Grodno (autumn, 1944).

18. At the *Ichud* in Lodz (winter, 1946).

19. On Father's *Yourzeit*, Lodz Jewish cemetery – 6 July 1947. From right to left: my brother, my sister-in-law, mother and myself).

20. Ada and Izak Kobrowski, Austria (1949).

21. Aniela Staniewska (*Gosposia*) Staniewicze (1972).

22. Dr Antoni Docha at work, Sokolka, Poland (1951).

23. With Aniela in Staniewicze (June 1977).

crossed without being bothered and soon were at Siewko's door.

Siewko was alarmed at the sight of four Jews knocking at his door. He said that the Germans had the entire police force on alert, with frequent patrols criss-crossing the Vorstadt on the look-out for Jews. Several houses had already been searched and some Jews had been caught. There was no way they could stay in his house or even in his cellar, but he could show them to the ruins of a house some distance away where they could hide in the cellar. He would, of course, go to Zukiewicze to get instructions from Docha. There was still some time to the curfew and they followed Siewko to a street with many burned and bombed-out houses. Some had been razed to the ground. Siewko led them into the deep cellar of such a house.

For two days and two nights they hid in the most remote corner of the cellar. In the evening Siewko brought them some hot soup and hot tea in a Thermos. On the afternoon of the second day, they heard voices in Polish as a torch beam swept the cellar. A band of teenage hooligans were hunting for Jews. There was nowhere to hide and they were soon discovered.

'Eh, kikes!' yelled the leader. 'You are hiding here, eh? You want to escape death, eh?' He paused for a moment. 'There is no escape from death for you!' In the twilight of the cellar it was impossible to see his face. Surrounded by six thugs with drawn switch-blade knifes, Tolo, Father, Misha and Rozia retreated, their backs to the wall.

'Janek,' yelled the leader, 'you stay outside and run to the police station if any of them tries to resist. And you kikes,' he said, 'take out your wallets!' He approached Misha with his knife ready to strike. 'Hands up!' he ordered.

Misha tried to reason with him. 'Look, aren't you ashamed of what you are doing? I am a reserve officer in the Polish army and you are robbing me of my means to survive!'

This talk only served to infuriate the tall hooligan. With a thrust of his knife he ripped open the side of Misha's winter jacket. Rozia let out a strident cry and threw herself on Misha. One of the teenagers grabbed her and pushed her away into the corner.

'Now, Jews,' said the leader, swinging his knife, 'give us

your wallets and your money nicely, because we are getting very annoyed!'. To resist was futile as the police could have been alerted in no time. With their hands up, they let themselves be searched. The youths were thorough. They took Father's wallet with 200 dollars and Misha's wallet with 100 dollars. Tolo had no wallet, his 300 dollars were sewn into his coat. 'Now,' the leader ordered Tolo 'you take off your coat; everybody strips!'

'We are going to the forest,' Misha tried to argue again, 'how are we to survive in this cold without our coats? Have some human feeling, some compassion!'

'You dirty kike, give your coat or I will kill you!' The boy raised his knife. Misha threw down his coat but not before taking out the toothbrush which he kept in his pocket.

'Leave it!'

'No, I won't give you my toothbrush!'

'You want a bet, kike?' yelled the hooligan grabbing Misha's hand. The toothbrush broke and Misha threw it away.

A battle now developed between Father and another youth who was trying to grab his Scottish winter jacket. Father was a man on whom coercion could work only up to a point. This point exceeded, he transformed into a stone regardless of the consequences. This had happened under the Soviets, it had happened last October at the Gestapo, and again here. While Tolo gave up his coat with the 300 dollars sewn into the lining, Father, who unfortunately had transferred 200 dollars from his coat to his wallet, was holding on to his jacket in an outburst of anger and despair.

'Over my dead body will you take my coat,' he screamed. The leader approached Father and swung his knife, but Father did not flinch.

Suddenly, the leader shouted, '*Chlopcy* [boys], let's get out of here! And you damn Jews, don't think you have got rid of us. I promise you that you will die anyway. The police are looking for you and they won't have to look much longer!'

The six left the cellar, taking all their wallets, and Misha's and Tolo's coats with the money sewn into them. Tolo and Father were left with only 100 dollars sewn into Father's jacket. Misha, as we later learned, had the bulk of his money and valuables hidden so well that only a thorough inspection of his body could have revealed their location. Angry and shivering, they stood thinking what to do next.

They decided to change cellars as they were not sure whether the hooligans would return with reinforcements to kill them. They walked to Siewko's house in the dusk. Siewko was glad to see them; he had gone to see them an hour before and panicked when he had not found them in the cellar as he expected. Mikhalko was already waiting for them. After paying Siewko, they huddled together on the sleigh, Tolo and Misha wearing the old, torn coats that Siewko gave them. They did not try to hide; four grown people was just too much to hide under potatoes. The weather was good and they advanced speedily. Mikhalko drove through the German control post at Kopciowka while the four detoured through snow-covered fields to avoid the German police. Mikhalko waited for them at the opposite end of the village. This was very risky and Mikhalko did not want to push his luck any further. As soon as they reached a familiar Byelorussian village just before Indura, he left the sleigh and the mares with a friend and they all trudged for over ten kilometres through the deep snow, avoiding the villages.

17 All Together

After they had all warmed up with soup and *bavarka* we started to make room for everybody, seven people to be accommodated on less than nine square yards of space. Father and Mother squeezed on the wooden bed, I had to give up my warm loft to Misha and Rozia, who were short enough to huddle there, while Frania, Tolo and I had to stretch out on the clay floor between the window and the bed. It was uncomfortable, but so sweet to know that Tolo and Father were with us. I thanked the Lord for granting my prayers.

With the arrival of four additional people our lives were dramatically altered. We had to increase our vigilance and sentinels were posted permanently at both windows, in the front room and the back room, keeping a close watch on the Staniewicze–Yarmolitche road. All of us were assigned to this chore, the grown-ups alternating every two hours. I was frequently assigned to the much less important back window. In case of emergency, two people climbed on to the oven loft, hiding behind a small curtain which was hastily put up by our women; I crawled under the bed while four people tried to squeeze behind the armoire which could really only accommodate three.

It was obvious that this could not continue and we decided to dig a hide-out. After some discussion, we resolved to dig a hole approximately nine-feet long, seven-feet wide and five-feet deep under the vestibule. It would be covered with wooden boards and sealed with beaten clay to make it look like the rest of the floors. The hole would extend from the vestibule into the back room through a bottleneck emerging at the wall near the stove. The neck's opening would be just big enough to enable one person at a time to squeeze into the hide-out. It would be closed with a wooden cover full of small holes to allow for access of air.

This was a difficult project. Work had to proceed at night, with sentinels posted around the hut; dirt would have to be removed from the vestibule and hidden, planks be found and cut to size. Even though the ground in the entrance was not completely frozen, it still had to be broken with a pickaxe and shovels. The vestibule was confined within the hut and the noise we made was muffled, yet we had to beware of disturbing the stillness of wintry nights when sound could easily carry far.

Gosposia was burdened with three additional Jews to feed and shelter. Every one of us contributed to make the others' stay more difficult. The question of food was paramount. *Gosposia* could not freely provide the food that was needed. For the time being, we had enough money to buy food, but buying it at the Indura market would doubtless arouse suspicion. 'Aha, Anielka Staniewska is buying such quantities of food! Where does she get the money from? Why does she need all this food? Surely she must be keeping Jews in her house!' From mouth to mouth, suspicion would travel into Staniewicze, where the peasants were likely to report their concerns to the local police.

Baking bread was also a problem. Villagers knew how many times a month each family baked bread by the amount of smoke that rose from their chimneys; and even at night smoke was visible in the moonlight. We therefore insisted that Mikhalko bring us staples at night when Dr Docha visited Edward. Such visits would not arouse suspicion because Edward's sickness was known to everyone in the village, but they could not be too frequent either and could only imperfectly satisfy the needs of seven people.

Gosposia's bad mood did not improve much, notwithstanding Misha's attempt at sweetening the bitter pill of the three additional Jews with two five-rouble gold coins that he extracted out of a mysterious hidden place. Work on the hideout progressed very slowly and only during moonless nights. Luckily, the nights were still long and the sky overcast. We all worked hard at night and rested during the day. The women and I stood guard by the wall of the barn, scrutinizing the Staniewicze–Yarmolicze road. We took hourly shifts, as the winds of early March were icy. The whiteness of the snow provided for very good visibility and we had to be particularly careful. As the partly frozen ground was broken with a pickaxe and dug with a shovel, the dirt was taken out in buckets to the stable where it was spread and hidden under the straw. Planks were removed from random locations along the back wall of the barn and cut to size.

Digging was carried out so carefully that, standing guard some 50 yards away, I could hardly hear it. As I peered intensely into the grey mist of the snow-covered fields my thoughts sometimes wandered. Everything had happened so swiftly, unexpectedly and brutally. Like leaves in a whirlwind we had been seized and tossed about. Again before my eyes were Shurik, Lutek, Mirek; I saw Rita and Rosa, Dr and Mrs Klinger, I saw Grandmother with her eternal *War and Peace*, I saw Mareczek, sweet little Mareczek, perched on his Father's shoulders, I saw Danyousha with his delicately chiselled face and big green eyes. Where were they now? Who was still alive? The more I thought, the more my eyes filled with tears, tears of sorrow, and gratitude that I had been spared. These dreams were usually interrupted by the squeak of steps on the snow: Frania or Rozia coming to relieve me.

Our hide-out was almost finished when it happened. I was on sentry duty by the stable when suddenly Tsatsus went berserk. His barking exploded as he tugged at his chain. It was obvious: somebody was approaching rapidly through the fields towards the entrance. It was too late to sound the alarm, there was nothing I could do but press my body against the grey wall of the barn and make my way slowly towards its entrance. I pushed the barn door slightly ajar and, my heart beating wildly, flung myself into the hay, hiding behind a big stack. I heard a deep voice, '*Niech bedzie pochvalony Jezus Chrystus,*' and the voice of *Gosposia* answering, '*Na wieki wiekow, amen*'.

The visitor must have seen us. If he entered the hut and saw the tools and the moved earth, we would be finished. I could hear *Gosposia*, interrupted by the fury of Tsatsus' barking. 'Sorry...I cannot accommodate you...no way. My husband is very sick...contagious...People from the village...come... relatives...Wait here, he is on the bed pan...I will bring you a loaf of bread and some salt pork...' The stranger was arguing but his words were drowned out by the barking of Tsatsus. Had he seen us?

Again I heard, *'Niech bedzie pochvalony…'*, his heavy steps on the snow and the deep voice fading. The danger appeared to have passed. Presently *Gosposia* entered the barn; she whispered, 'Alik you can come out of the hay.' We all tried to guess if he had seen us. We learned that the man was from Lomza, some 50 kilometres away. He was fleeing the Germans because of some black-market problem and was looking for the partisans. He wanted to stay for a day but *Gosposia*, who had given him food, had refused him entry into the hut, saying that her husband was dying of a contagious disease and that soon she would have a house-full of relatives. Her sang-froid had saved the situation. The man was probably armed, he could have broken into the house and blackmailed *Gosposia*. I was very frightened; it was the second time that we had experienced such a close shave. Could we possibly survive until the end of the war, I wondered. We decided to finish our hide-out as quickly as possible even if this meant not sleeping at all.

The excavation was completed, the wooden boards positioned and caulked. A thick layer of clay was laid on top and compacted with a flat stone, leaving only a few small openings for air. It looked perfect. The bottleneck emerging at the bedroom side of the inner wall next to the big stove was reinforced with small boards to allow a body to slide through with ease. A cover with large holes for air was lined with some cotton wool and fitted exactly to the neck's opening. Since potatoes and sand already lined the walls of the *isba*, in case of emergency the opening could be camouflaged easily under a few layers of large potatoes. Some air seeped through the potatoes, supplementing the scant air from the small holes in the clay cover in the vestibule. Now that everything was completed, we dragged the big armoire from the back room to the vestibule and positioned it on top of the hide-out, so that no one could walk freely over our shelter. The interior of the hide-out was coated with a thick layer of straw.

The grand opening came when Misha sounded the alarm. We hastily descended into the shelter in pre-assigned order: Mother, Father, Frania, Rozia, myself, Tolo, and finally Misha.

We were all sandwiched in a sitting position – our legs outstretched, our backs against the wall – three on one side and four on the other. The hole was completely dark and smelled of damp earth and fresh straw. *Gosposia* secured the cover and dumped the potatoes on top of it. We remained there for an hour. We had enough air to breathe. It was perfect. *Gosposia* was satisfied as she opened the neck. 'Congratulations, men,' she said to Father, Misha and Tolo, 'the only way they can discover you is with dogs, as they will not be able to notice anything from outside or inside the hut.' She was wrong, however: a strong knock with a rifle butt on top of the shelter at the level of the vestibule floor emitted a hollow sound betraying the empty space below.

With the hide-out ready, we were now considerably more secure than during the previous six weeks when we had had two narrow escapes. The back room without the huge armoire now had more space. It was decided that two adults would sleep in the hide-out, to make it easier for the rest of us to hide in case of a night alarm. As the youngest, I was spared sleeping in the hole; as were Father and Mother, being the oldest. This left Misha and Rozia or Frania and Tolo alternately sleeping there. The hide-out was a dreadful, unhealthy place. It was raw and damp, and the straw lining it became mildewed even though we changed it frequently. Earth worms, small roaches and long earwigs quickly colonized the hole too. However the bedbugs did not like the cold dampness of the shelter, prefering the warmth of the room, and even though I was exempt from sleeping in the hide-out, I sometimes wondered where it was 'better' to sleep.

We were constantly practising to cut down the time it took us to disappear into the hide-out in case of alarm – the aim was for all seven of us to be hidden within two minutes, allowing less than 20 seconds per person. After a week of such exercises, we could pack into the hide-out in the middle of the night with our sleeping gear in under three minutes. First my bedding was thrown into the hole; next came Misha and Rozia's bedding thrown straight from the top of the stove. All this was done while the two people already in the shelter were spreading the blankets and pillows around. Then, the remaining five crawled in, in pre-assigned order. After the lid was put in place by Misha from the inside, *Gosposia* covered it with potatoes. In less than three minutes the room looked as if only one person, *Gosposia* or Hela, had slept in it!

18   The First Spring

The second half of March was a quiet period. The snow-covered fields became oceans of mud and the roads turned into quagmires. People stayed indoors rather than sink, and traffic was at a standstill. Peasants were busy preparing the seed for spring sowing and the tools for the summer and autumn harvests. Occasionally, a night frost made the roads passable again for a day or two but the spring sun always had the upper hand. The days were getting longer, the birds were returning and the mornings were filled with their chatter. Here and there the green stem of a snowdrop showed timidly through the melting snow. Flies started buzzing around the windows again. There was so much to be done. The ground had to be prepared for sowing and planting and every day the noise of work in the fields got stronger. We were increasingly on our guard.

As everything was coming back to life, strange new feelings and desires were also stirring within me. Looking at our young women, Frania, Rozia and Hela, I was troubled when they undressed next to me, not paying much attention to little 'Aliczek'. I could smell the scent of their bodies and it turned my head. I fantasized about being alone with one or the other, feeling guilty, sinful and ashamed of my thoughts. As hard as I tried to suppress such emotions, they always returned and my guilty feelings grew even stronger.

One day *Gosposia* brought scraps of German papers from the market at Indura; the merchants used old copies of newspapers to wrap food at the stalls. The paper was two weeks old, but for us it was an extraordinary treat and a link with the world. Father's forecasts were wrong once again: Von List's German Caucasus army had managed to slip through a gap at the town of Rostov-on-the-Don which Von Manstein was holding against furious Russian assaults. The Germans regained Kharkov in a powerful counter-offensive. The front stabilized on the Mius River, the Donetz River, and far to the east of Smolensk, many hundreds of kilometres away from us. Leningrad was still surrounded but holding out. Would this war never end? Germany was far from ready to crumble.

Edward suffered a lot; his left thigh was swollen and festering from open tuberculosis of the bones. He was unable to walk and often moaned at night. Father tried to alleviate his pain with injections and medications brought by Docha, which he often administered around the clock. He wanted to put Edward's leg in traction and asked Dr Docha to bring some weights and pulleys.

Food was constantly on my mind. I was growing and had a ravenous appetite. After the relative abundance of the first few weeks, food was becoming less plentiful. Our menu included black bread, potatoes, dried pea soup, barley, onions and cabbage. Salt pork was served only on Sundays. This fare seemed heavenly to me, but I was constantly hungry. Only the Staniewskis and Hela had some meat and fat daily. *Gosposia* liked me; she joked with me and even patted my cheek. With a smile on her broad, open face, she sometimes gave me a piece of salt pork, a sausage or a potato pancake. Meals were the focal points of my day but after licking my plate clean I was still hungry. I knew that my parents were giving me some of their food. 'Eat *funfurek*,' my father would say, 'you are growing and need the food more than us.' And I ate anything I was given and still wished for more.

I missed my friends and I was lonely. I could not share the grown-ups' enthusiasm for politics, I did not read old German newspapers. During the long hours between meals, I continued to struggle with Abbé Mauraux's book and the existence of God, for whom I yearned with all my being. I often addressed the Lord when sitting in our dark hide-out, my heart pounding and my fingers clasped in prayer. At times I thought about all those who had not been spared. Why not innocent little Mareczek? Why not Danya? Why not the others? I could not forget the blue, frozen, skeletal bodies of the children from Kielbasin. Their big, black, hungry eyes in their thin little faces continued to haunt me. What had they done to deserve this? On such occasions I felt like shaking my fist at God. On other occasions, looking at the picture of Christ in the flickering light of our evenings, I was fascinated by the sweetness, serenity and peace radiating from it. Overcome by mystical feelings I cried in gratitude and sorrow: for Christian love, everlasting love and forgiveness.

But where was it? *Gosposia* and Edward never tired of telling us what the priest reminded them of during Sunday sermons, that the Jews were punished for their foul deeds against 'our Lord and Saviour Jesus Christ', that their souls were damned for ever to burn in hell. The only way to redemption was conversion to the true Christian faith. *Zyd niedowiarek!* [Faithless Jew!]. Whenever Edward started on this topic, his mouth twitched with disgust and his small deep-set eyes glowed with hatred. He shook with anger against those cowardly, blood-sucking infidels. This mild and good man became hard to recognize and we rushed to get out of his sight until his anger subsided. *Gosposia* calmed him down, saying 'Be quiet Edward, we all know that Jews are deadly sinners, but don't get so excited about it.' Edward became utterly exhausted after such outbursts and would fall back on his pillows; but before long he would be his old self again, a mild and suffering man.

I could not, of course, accept their explanations, nor could I understand how a God of Love and Mercy could be so unbelievably cruel. This made me doubt the veracity and credibility of the Christian faith and I developed a love–hate relationship with Christianity. My relationship with the Jewish religion was not much better, as I could not accept that the God of Israel would not oppose what was being done to His people. In short, I could not understand God. But to reject His existence was too painful; hence, I settled into a spiritual no man's land. Whenever danger closed in – Germans driving through the village, *Gosposia* or Edward in a foul mood – I prayed fervently, forgetting my doubts. Whenever I thought about my people and Grodno, I shook my fist at the sky and the blasphemous thought came again and again: 'There is no God, Clavdia Semyonovna was right, religion is the opium of the people.' This inner conflict – between my ardent wish to believe and my inability to do so – continued to be a source of great torment to me.

Hela brought me books from the church on Sundays. She was the only one who knew how to read in the Staniewski household; *Gosposia* could neither read nor write, and Edward only a little. The books Hela brought were usually religious, the Old or the New Testaments, but a few were about life in the Polish countryside under the tsar. One of them, a love story between a simple farmer's daughter and a young nobleman, a *Panicz*, included a description of the village Jew and his family which made me very angry. The Jew was dirty, hook-nosed and spoke a broken Polish with a Yiddish accent. He practised usury, swindling the good, gullible peasants, compounding their misery. He was sly, cowardly and greedy, and colluded with the enemy. He and his family lived off the labour of poor villagers: cheating them, lying to them and fomenting intrigues for his benefit. In short, he was a perfect parasite. The peasants finally got together and chased the Jew and his family from their village. He asked for their forgiveness in broken Polish, but this was denied.

The whole month of April was a busy time for *Gosposia* and Hela. They worked very hard, almost without interruption, from 5 a.m. to sunset. The animals had to be fed, and sowing and planting were in full swing. The work slowed down somewhat when Easter was upon us and *Gosposia* decided to slaughter a pig. This was actually a clandestine operation as all meat had to be sold at a discount price to the Germans in Indura, but few peasants obeyed the law, and most hid at least part of their meat. Hence, the raids by German police in search of hidden meat and grain.

I had never witnessed the slaughter of a large animal, I had only seen Chaya Sora in our kitchen bleeding a chicken. The way the pig was killed looked horrible to me. *Gosposia* took a long, sharp spike, somewhat similar to the one I had feared so much at the Kopciowka police checkpoint. Soon we could hear the horrifying shrieks of the animal in the yard. I peeked through the window: *Gosposia*, sitting astride the pig, was running the bloodied spike through its back into its heart. The mortally wounded animal collapsed to its knees with ear-piercing squeals, which soon changed into faint yelps. The dead pig was then dragged into the barn and drained of blood. We were surprised when the body was taken to the hut and placed on the table in the front room, to be emptied and cut. First came the bowels, organs and brain: they were taken out in a big bucket to be emptied, washed and used – bowels for sausage casings, organs for delicacies. This produced such a stench that it was difficult to breathe without becoming nauseated and came to a peak when *Gosposia* and Hela emptied the gut to prepare it for stuffing. The stench permeated everything and we had no place to hide.

Gosposia and Edward visibly enjoyed our discomfort. 'Look at them, these faint-hearted city dwellers with their delicate noses; a little smell and they are ready to pass out! Especially those good-for-nothing city women who know only how to paint their lips!' My Father, who had an aversion to pork, suffered the most. He turned deathly pale, but bore up with his usual stoicism. It took nearly two days to separate the meat and the lard from the carcass, to cut it up, to salt, to prepare the stuffing and fill the washed gut to make sausages. Everything was inventoried – every sausage and every piece of meat and lard. They were then stashed away in a secret larder known to only *Gosposia* and Hela.

We were very thrifty with the meat and salt pork we bought from *Gosposia*. It was rationed and divided into seven parts. Even with half of my parents' rations it was not enough for me, and even less for my brother. We had fresh meat just once, when the pig was slaughtered.

The Polish countryside was beautiful in the latter part of April and May. The sun was warm and the fields were covered with a green cloak of young wheat and rye. Leszko Staniewski, a neighbour from the village, sang while he worked. His young, sonorous voice resonated for us all to hear:

Ja wole, ja wole	I prefer, I prefer
Slonce, las i pole…	The sun, the forest and the field…

How good it was to be alive and free, and I envied him his freedom. As for us, we had to increase our vigilance again. I kept watch for hours at the back-room window. A mild spring breeze filled with the scent of nearby forests came in through the slightly open window. This joy of nature coming to life after the long winter communicated itself to all of us, but nobody expressed it as directly as Mother who, for the first time in over five months sang again. We closed the windows and she sang beautifully with her warm but now muffled soprano. She sang pretty Polish songs of the spring by Moniuszko to please Aniela and Edward, but invariably Mother came back to her unlimited Russian repertoire – to Gritchaninov's 'Snowdrop'. Another song, about a poor little legless child praying to God to glue on a pair of legs in her sleep, made me feel heart-broken, for we too were all like legless cripples. Frania burst into sobs. Poor Frania cried all the time, saying her life had no meaning away from Ilana.

Gosposia told us that Hela's mother, her sister Mania, knew about us. It was probable that her lover Ziutek Kulikowski also knew. We wondered who else in the village knew and started to doubt that the secret could be kept from spreading. We dreaded being denounced, or simply killed in the night by fearful villagers anxious to get rid of the danger that we represented for the whole village. We all concluded that a weapon would give us a small measure of protection against village intruders. There were plenty of weapons abandoned by the Polish Army in 1939 and by the Soviet Army in 1941. They were hoarded by peasants who sold them for hard cash. When Mikhalko next came by with some provisions from Dr Docha, we asked him to get us a pistol.

A few days later, Mikhalko brought a big Browning pistol with a single magazine and eight bullets. We paid him an enormous sum, 50 dollars split equally between Misha and us. We now felt a little more secure and somewhat more in control; if we were to be discovered by the Germans we did not want to be beaten and tortured before being executed. Misha was to be the keeper of our weapon, given his military experience. We all agreed that, if discovered, we would not leave our hide-out – the first bullet would be for the first German to appear through the hole and then Misha would shoot every one of us, one by one, taking the last bullet for himself, or so he promised us. A pistol also provided us with some protection against villagers who might hesitate to provoke a shoot-out. I felt now that at least one German would pay dearly if we were discovered, but I preferred not to think about it.

Gosposia's sister Mania and her boyfriend Ziutek Kulikowski came to visit around Easter. Ziutek was a congenial fellow in his late twenties or early thirties. He was of average height, slender with dark hair. His pleasant face was rather well chiselled and sensitive, his demeanour more of a city-dweller than of a peasant. It turned out that Ziutek was a member of the underground Polish Home Army, the AK, which was directed by the Polish Government-in-Exile in London. Like all of us, he had high expectations for a swift German collapse. The eyes of most Poles were cast on London from where they expected a miraculous liberation by the Anglo-Americans. We all sat around the table, except Edward who was sitting on his bed. *Gosposia* brought some *samogon*, dried sausage, pork roast and ham, pickled cabbage and black bread. Ziutek had brought with him a very recent mimeographed AK news bulletin. The Warsaw ghetto was being liquidated, but the Jews of Warsaw were fighting the Germans! 'The ghetto,' said the bulletin, 'is in the hands of ZOB [the Jewish Combat Organization], but the Germans burn it block by block.' It was difficult not to notice that the bulletin stated the facts dryly and without comments.

Tragic though it was, this news elated me. At long last, after so much resignation and humiliation, we were fighting back! 'God,' I prayed, forgetting again my inner doubts, 'give them the strength to fight!' That night I could not sleep, with my eyes wide open I imagined the Jewish fighters in Warsaw killing Germans with grenades and machine guns. The German police and SS who were so used to killing helpless women and children, were now suddenly faced with fighters wielding weapons! At last our heroes were avenging all of us! I had a lump in my throat from elation and joy. I wanted to be among them and kill, kill, kill, those German sadists. I wanted to kiss my heroic brothers and die with them, avengers of our misery. I wept for joy. For the first time in a very long time I felt proud of being a Jew.

In the morning we began to worry again. Would Ziutek keep our secret or would he betray us, maybe to his AK companions? Despite Mania's assurances that Ziutek would not utter a word of what he saw, Aniela was worried. She showed her nervousness by becoming irritable and harsh, even violent. The first to be mistreated were our young women, Rozia and Frania: Both women tried hard to stay clean and this was anathema to *Gosposia*, who very seldom washed. She considered primping and washing a wasteful activity fit only for lazy city dwellers who passed their time looking at themselves in the mirror. Washing, in fact, was difficult; water had to be brought from the well to be heated on the stove which had to be lit. Only *Gosposia* or Hela could go to the well, which was located in full view of the village, and such sorties had to be kept to their usual number, to prevent arousing suspicion. Last, but not least, washing activities impaired our speed of hiding, making us all vulnerable to a sudden alarm. At any rate, that morning Rozia asked Hela for a pail of water and *Gosposia* yanked it from Hela's hand. She hurled insults at Rozia. 'You are parasites, only good for smearing your lips and powdering your asses like monkeys! What about honest work? But no, you are incapable of it! All you can do is smear your lips and your bottoms!' Rozia retreated to the backroom but *Gosposia* continued her vituperations. 'All these Jews and their women who do not fear Christ!' She ran out of the hut, grabbing a pitchfork in the vestibule. We could still hear her swearing and shouting in the stable.

When *Gosposia* came back, she was still in an angry mood. We suspected it had partly to do with money. Our reserves had already dwindled significantly. Misha, however, had a mysterious cache of valuables – Mother had caught sight of the bulging shape of a small pouch attached to his belt.

Misha claimed to be a reserve officer in the Polish Army. A native of Wilno, where he had practised law in the office of the famous criminal defence lawyer Andreev, his mentor, he became a high-ranking officer of the *Ordnugsdienst* in Ghetto I. He was not very talkative and kept pretty much to himself.

Our suspicions about the reason for *Gosposia*'s foul mood were correct. After receiving 50 dollars, she forgot her anger and the incident with Rozia. Several pails of water were brought in and heated for washing. However, our lack of confidence in Ziutek was not justified. Ziutek loved Mania, he was a decent man and a Polish patriot. He kept our secret.

19   The First Summer

May was rushing by. The air was full of delight from the lilacs which were in bloom all around the village. Cherry trees, linden and honeysuckle all added to this symphony of fragrance. Evenings and nights were silk-soft. Braving the danger, we sometimes opened the windows for a short time to fill our lungs with these balmy gusts. The rye, wheat and corn were growing fast but were still low, so that one could easily see anybody approaching the hut. Aniela allowed us to slip out cautiously at night and we took turns for a minute or two to stretch and fill our lungs with delectation; the fragrant air turned our heads like strong wine.

My brother made the most of these brief moments, disappearing every evening, sometimes prolonging his time so much that we asked ourselves anxiously 'Where did he go?' I could sense that something was cooking between him and Hela because, when he disappeared Hela would not be there either. I liked Hela not only because she was a pretty girl but also because she was nice to us. I have never heard a bad word about us from her. I enjoyed watching her returning from church on Sundays in her Sunday dress with her long blond braid falling down her back; her blue eyes were happy and she showed two rows of lovely white teeth when she smiled. She paid little attention to me or my insistent glances and smiles. For her, I was 'Aliczek', the little boy. But Tolo, a handsome fellow of 22, had a way with girls. He had enough tricks up his sleeve to turn the head of any girl, let alone a country girl like Hela.

I noticed that Tolo slipped out into the vestibule as soon as Hela stepped into the yard to feed the animals, bring water or do some other chore. There he would be, waiting behind the entrance door, hidden from view like a tiger stalking his prey. Once, I inadvertently caught him trying to grab Hela as she was carrying water through the entrance door. My sudden appearance scared my brother who threw me a dirty look and retreated inside the *isba*. From that time on, I knew that Tolo was courting Hela and I was jealous.

As the days passed, the rye and corn grew higher and higher, concealing the road from our view. It was becoming dangerous to be in the front room, since strangers could unexpectedly enter the hut. We relied increasingly on Tsatsus who was now permanently attached to the bench at the entrance. But even he was confused by the tall growth all around. We decided to minimize our presence in the front room, except for our window sentry. Besides, exhausted and drained by his illness, Edward was getting increasingly irritated by our presence This confinement to the back room was getting harder and harder for me to bear and as always, whenever I felt very strongly about something, I wrote a poem:

Nie dla nas sa	*Not for us*
Nie dla nas sa pola, nie dla nas sa laki	Not for us are fields, not for us meadows
Nie dla nas sa gaje, nie dla nas jest slonce	Not for us are groves, not for us sunshine
A dla nas nieszczescia, placze, rozlaki	But for us are despair and separation
Niedoli dlugie miesiace	The long months of misery
Nie dla nas jest wolnosc, nie dla nas nauka	Not for us is freedom, not for us learning
Nie dla nas sa kraje, nie dla nas jest zycie	Not for us is travel, not for us is life
A dla nas smierc straszna,	But for us a gruesome death,
Co wszedzie nas szuka,	Which looks for us everywhere,
I ponurego wichru wycie	And the mournful howling of the wind
Bo my nie ludzie, my potepiency	Because we are not people, we are damned
Czekamy swego wyroku	We wait for our sentence
Siedzimy w tym piekle jak stracency	Sitting in this hell like the doomed
I drzymy na odglos kroku	And shiver at the sound of a step

Wiezienie te dla nas przeklete	This damned prison
Ponurej wichury zew	This dreary wailing of the wind
Najmniejsze psa szczekniencie	The slightest barking of the dog
Mrozi nam w zylach krew	Freezes the blood in our veins

I pytam sie Ciebie o Boze!	And I ask you, O God!,
Czy skoncza sie cierpienia	Will our suffering ever end?
i kiedy?	
Gdy skoncza sie to o krajach	When it ends, then shall I say
I zyciu	to life:
To dla nas! powiem wtedy	It is for us!

Everything stood still. We had lost our faith in the Western Allies. We were convinced that Churchill was playing a clever game and wanted to bleed both the Russians and Germans to death. The snail-paced action of the Allies against the few German divisions of the Afrika Korps was in stark contrast to the gigantic battles taking place in Russia. The swift surrender of the Allies whenever the Germans or Japanese displayed military superiority – in Crete, Dunkirk, Singapore, Dieppe – compared very poorly with the heroic resistance of Odessa, Sebastopol, Leningrad and Stalingrad. I was constantly angry at the Allies for refusing to open a vigorous Second Front, and at Pope Pius XII, who issued a ringing condemnation of Communists but never condemned the Nazis while tens of thousands of us were dying every day. Father believed that a few words from the Pope in favour of us Jews would go a long way, encouraging more Poles to help and fewer to cooperate with the German police and the Gestapo. Countless lives might be saved. But there was no word from the representative of Christ on earth, only silence, which Father considered tantamount to condonation. To me Pius XII was a hypocrite continuing vicariously the dirty work of the Inquisition.

German 'wrapping' papers – the newspaper pages used to wrap food, which once in a while *Gosposia* brought from the market at Indura – were full of stories about the hell of the Eastern Front, about the bitter struggle for every foot of ground waged by German soldiers against those 'subhuman devils', the soldiers of the Red Army. The front pages were full of scenes of battles and Russian dead. The back pages were full of German obituaries. The 'Joyous Corner' continued to grow longer and longer. My thoughts turned in gratitude to those multitudes of grey-clad Soviet soldiers who, at an incredible price in blood and suffering, were breaking the backbone of this invincible German Army, the instrument of the most brutal and sick ideology that was ever invented by a human mind. The Soviet soldiers were my heroes. Forgotten was the time when Father was on an NKVD blacklist and when we trembled at the slightest knock on the door. Gone were the apprehensions which we all felt at life in a totalitarian state. The only phrase about the Soviets we could now say was, *'Molodtsy Rebiata!'*

Sometimes in the evening, stretching out on the clay floor before the onset of sleep's sweet oblivion, I closed my eyes and tried to imagine our liberation. It seemed almost incredible that such a thing could ever happen; that we would be able to go out into the open, enjoy the sun, the fragrance of the fields and orchards, the murmur of the pines in Druskieniki and a kayak ride with Father on the Niemen. My poor Father, he was looking very old. His face, covered with white stubble, had become drawn, his blue eyes sunken and veiled. The closely shaved skull of the surgeon was now covered with patches of snowy hair. He had lost a lot of weight; and his optimism, which had sustained us so often in the past, was now vacillating.

Time seemed to stretch out before us without end, just like the sea of wheat and rye around our hut. We were well into June and it was now nearly impossible to see anything travelling down the road. Only a trained eye could still spot a moving human head or people in a carriage occasionally emerging above the dense forest of stalks. We could be surprised at any time by an intruder emerging from the rye just a few yards from the hut. Especially dangerous was the back of the house where the rye was growing less than six yards from the window. The sentries in either room now had to move just behind the window, their bodies pressed to the wall without relaxing their vigilance for a second. The two-hour watches felt like an eternity.

Another problem was the *sagan*, our big black chamber pot hidden behind a barricade of chests in the vestibule. To sit (or

251

rather squat) on that pail was now becoming very risky. We agreed that anyone caught short should wait there, hidden behind the chests, until the immediate danger was over and only then proceed quickly to the attic, which could be reached from the vestibule by a ladder. The ladder would be put in place by Aniela once the intruder was well installed inside the *isba*, and would then be inconspicuously removed.

We could now stay in the attic instead of the back room. When we chose to stay in the attic we had to remain there for the whole day and be extremely quiet, as every step resonated in the rooms below. The attic had many advantages: it was open to fresh air, it was spacious, lined with straw brought in from the stable, and we all could stretch, read, meditate, even play chess or just sleep. We opted more and more for the attic. Misha and Father played chess on a home-made paper board with clumsy figures chiselled out of wood and I read Abbé Mauraux's book to my heart's content, fighting with myself about God's existence and day-dreaming about the sweet scent of freedom. The scent coming from the *sagan* below was far from sweet: it became nauseating during hot spells. We tried to use it only in the evening when the *sagan* could be emptied immediately behind the barn, but this was not always possible.

I decided to write a diary and my memoirs from the ghetto. I was strongly encouraged by everybody as they felt that, if we survived, the diary of a 13-year-old boy would be of considerable interest. For me it was a way to escape, a way of getting back at the Germans, a way to freedom. *Gosposia* used a trip to the market to sell some potatoes and cabbage as a pretext for buying me a pack of grammar school notebooks which, she said to the merchant, was for Hela. She also brought stacks of old newspapers, which she said she needed for the household and the barn. Most of the papers were several weeks old but a few were more recent. We literally devoured them regardless of their date; unless we got some news through Ziutek Kulikowski who listened to the BBC Polish broadcasts, but whom we met very seldom, our news was mostly very old.

This time we learned something very frightening: 12,000 Polish officers captured in Russia had allegedly been shot by the Soviets at the Katyn forest near Smolensk. The Germans were shedding crocodile tears about the officers, whom they might well have executed themselves. Father suspected that the whole thing was a German ploy to win over the Poles who, as much as they loathed the Russians, were not supplying the Germans with ethnic SS divisions for the Eastern Front, unlike the other conquered nations. The papers, full of grim pictures of unearthed bodies, accused the Red Army of the massacre. A long list of names was published. We recognized among them the name of a young doctor from Lvov, Simon Fleschler. I remembered Simon very well. He had come to our 'sanatorium' in Druskieniki in June 1939 as our house-physician for the summer. He had been mobilized at the end of August and left in a hurry, like so many others. He was short, slim, with dark hair and had an acute sense of humour. He knew how to imitate local accents and was a great story-teller, second only to Dr Klinger. I still remember some of his jokes to this day, as I remember his uncanny knack for improvising rhymes. I could hardly imagine Simon Fleschler as one of the bodies shown in the grizzly pictures of the German press.

Edward, learning from us about Katyn, went bright red in the face and had one of his emotional outbursts. 'The Bolsheviks are evil, they are against Poland, even the Holy Father spoke out against them. He did not speak out against the Germans. The Germans are not all that bad, they are the only ones who can squash those Antichrists!' This made us very uneasy because we knew that such outbursts led inevitably to ravings against 'those goddamn Jews who reap their just punishment for killing our Saviour'. Edward's health had improved lately. The traction device for his left leg and his hip, which Father engineered from some pulleys and rope brought by Mikhalko, was helping. He could now hop about on crutches for half an hour at a time. For the first time in many months he had been able to go outside to inspect the animals in the barn. He was visibly happy to feel in control again. These expeditions exhausted him, however, and afterwards he would sink into his bed in pain, supporting the sick limb with both hands. Father advised him not to overdo these walks, but so many things had to be inspected after so long a period of 'women's rule' at the farm. Poor landlord! I liked him in spite of his occasional temperamental outbursts. As the harvest season approached, Hela and *Gosposia* worked in the field all day, weeding and inspecting the crops. There was plenty to do and there were many peasants moving about the village. Seeing Edward out of the hut, people came to congratulate him on his recovery. The landlord proudly sat down with the visitors to a snack of *samogon* and sausage.

For us it was a difficult time. Half of us were hidden in the attic, the other half in the hide-out. People in the attic usually had no idea that a visitor was about to enter the *isba*. When this happened, the last one to disappear into the shelter pounded a warning – three strong knocks on the ceiling. This meant 'acute danger, do not move'. A single knock meant 'the acute danger is over'. Our fear was that German police might raid the village during such a visit, cutting off the people in the attic. If this occured, the only way out was to jump from the attic into the rye and try to hide in there.

The Germans were raiding the villages in search of meat, lard and grain amassed by peasants in quantities exceeding the allowed quotas. The search was thorough, sometimes using police dogs. It was already a year since German police had raided Staniewicze, despite frequent forays on some neighbouring villages. It was clear that our turn would soon come and the isolated location of our hut might attract suspicion. We knew only too well that Jews had been discovered during such raids; it had happened this winter in Mogilany, a nearby Byelorussian village. The village was burned to the ground, many villagers executed and all the young people taken as forced labour to Germany. Whenever the German police raided a nearby village we knew very quickly, because a sort of 'telephone by signals' functioned between villagers. As soon as *Gosposia* or Hela came with news that the Germans were in Yodkievitche, Eysmonty or in another neighbouring village, we all disappeared into the damp blackness of our hide-out. The rumble of potatoes thrown on the entrance made us feel as if we were being buried alive. We sat in complete darkness and silence, squeezed together, each thinking about what would happen if the Germans came to our hut. I imagined the course of events if we were discovered. We assumed that Misha would shoot the first German coming near the hide-out and then shoot us one by one. But what if he missed or if the German got him first? We would all be savagely beaten and tortured to divulge any names connected with our rescue. Then, we would be shot. It was the beating and the torture that I feared most and I prayed that Misha succeed in killing us all.

German raids on neighbouring villages were protracted affairs, starting in the morning and lasting into late afternoon or evening. Confined to the hide-out, we were given bowls of pea soup at midday by *Gosposia* or Hela, who worked in the field while keeping a watchful eye on developments. The *sagan* was removed. To forgo our natural functions was sheer torture, but somehow we managed to hold out. At the end of the ordeal, coming out of our blackness, blinded by daylight, stiff and numb from immobility, we were tortured by physical needs. Having reinstated our sentries, we then all took turns on the *sagan*.

As the days got longer and hotter and filled with fear, we slept less and less. By 5 a.m., as daylight inundated the fields, the sentries had to be in position at the windows. The stove loft was now a dreadful place to sleep, stifling and swarming with bedbugs. We had a new occupation: killing fleas. Their numbers had suddenly exploded and they devoured our flesh. We never had much problem with lice, whose population we kept under control by regular inspection of our clothes and sleeping gear. But our bodies were covered with flea bites and we were all like our faithful friend Tsatsus, scratching furiously. Our daily task was to kill as many fleas as possible. Sitting in the attic, we had plenty of time. We held competitions: who could kill the largest number? Sometimes a blood-gorged 'matron' was found hiding four or five 'baby' fleas under her body. They escaped, jumping in all directions. The champion was Misha who one day killed 265 fleas, a great feat.

I divided my time between killing fleas, losing at chess and writing my diary and memoirs starting in September 1939. Every morning I had to decide: Whether I would climb into the attic, where I could write without being disturbed, or stay in the back room and the hide-out? Away in the attic, I was not around when the landlords were taking their substantial midday meal and missed the tasty treats which *Gosposia* sometimes gave me – a piece of sausage here, a piece of salt pork there. In the attic we were handed our portion of bread and soup and no more. As I was always hungry, I often opted to remain in the hide-out, hoping that a treat might come my way.

The weakness of our position, being split between the attic and the shelter, soon became apparent. One day Mother and I were in the back room, Rozia was on sentry duty at the front window, while Misha, Father, Tolo and Frania were in the attic. A man suddenly emerged out of the rye and entered the hut. He stumbled into Rozia and we froze in the back room hearing, *'Khai budzie pokhvalony Yesos Khristos'* from an unfamiliar voice and *Gosposia*, Edward and Rozia – who did not lose her cool – answering, *'Na wieki wiekow, amen'*. It was too late to do anything. Even the door to the back room where I was with Mother, was half-open.

The young peasant was a Byelorussian from a village nearby, a farm-hand looking for work. He had been told in the village *Gosposia* might need some help as Edward was sick. He had decided to cut through the fields to the farmstead. We heard *Gosposia* saying she did not need help right now but would need some during the harvest. She invited him to sit down and carefully closed the door to the back room where Mother and I stood petrified, pressing our bodies to the wall. She presented Rozia casually as her sister's friend on a visit from Grodno and soon bade him farewell. Throughout the peasant's visit I was afraid that somebody would move in the attic as they did not know that a stranger was in the house – everything had happened so fast that there had been no time to warn them.

The alarm was over, but Aniela flew into one of her terrible tantrums. 'Go to hell!' she screamed. 'If you can't keep a proper guard then you should just go! I have had enough of keeping seven Jews in my house endangering everybody's life! Just pack up and go!' In addition Rozia got a dressing down from Misha, who always treated his wife with contempt, calling her clueless, clumsy and incapable of standing hardship.

The First Summer

Rozia and Misha were only recently married. She was a refugee, the daughter of a well-to-do businessman from Warsaw. She was college educated and had travelled to the United States, where she spent a year with relatives in Minnesota. She often hummed American melodies like *This is the Big Apple* and showed us the steps of the charleston and the jitterbug, which I considered ridiculous. Rozia had a good figure, brown eyes and dark, curly hair, but she had a very big nose. She was not pretty, although not without sex appeal. Mother criticized her for being silly and, curiously enough, her husband accused her of the same thing.

For all her shouting, *Gosposia* did not envisage throwing us out. For one, the intruder was a *chlop* from a far-away village. Aniela had not lost her cool and had handled the situation well. So had Rozia who, in spite of her slightly Jewish looks, spoke a very pure Polish. The *chlop* had shown no apparent curiosity. Also Aniela knew that Edward needed Father's care and was glad to have him around. And, finally, with us on the loose, she was afraid that if we were caught and tortured we would give her name to the Germans.

After this incident we decided not to split up any more, except for sentry duty. We often chose the attic during the day, ready if need be to jump into the tall rye below. At night we preferred being near the shelter for even the nights were full of danger. Young villagers roamed the fields and one could clearly hear their loud voices all around. Tsatsus, now attached day and night, kept a watchful guard. In the heat of the day we sweltered in the attic. Nights in the back room were not much easier. The stuffiness of the room was compounded by the stove, always in use during the day – for cooking, for heating water and, once every three or four weeks, for baking bread. It radiated its heat into the room at night because we kept the windows closed and the curtains drawn. Sleeping on the stove loft was now impossible and Misha and Rozia alternated with Tolo and Frania, sleeping in the shelter or on the floor next to me.

These summer nights were the most ghastly period of my life in Staniewicze. In addition to the oppressive heat and to the legions of fleas with whom we fought a losing battle, the old scourge of bedbugs made a powerful comeback. In the heat of the summer they multiplied in fantastic numbers. As

soon as the light was out, long columns of the repulsive creatures marched along the ceiling and let themselves drop onto
the floor, to get at us. It was like a smelly red drizzle dripping
from the ceiling. I squashed them on my pillow, on my face, in
my ears. They stank and I was nauseated. I envied the adults,
who somehow managed to sleep while I could not. I wanted
to sleep in the hide-out but Father was opposed, arguing that
it was better to be bitten by some 'harmless' bedbugs than to
compromise my growth and future health in the damp shelter.
I dreaded the approach of darkness as I knew I would be
unable to escape my nightly torture. At the first whiff of
bedbugs, I got up to spend the night sitting on the kneading
barrel where I was less vulnerable. The room was filled with
rhythmic breathing interrupted by an occasional snore. I could
identify everyone by the way they sounded in their sleep. As
my eyes closed and I swayed more and more on my seat I
considered going back to sleep come what may. But then I
recalled the smelly red insects bloated with blood and I
decided to wait until the first light when, contented by their
nightly feast, they disappeared into the cracks. Fortunately the
nights were brief, and with the first blush of dawn I finally
stretched out on the floor to catch an hour of sleep.

During these sleepless nights on the kneading barrel I had
plenty of time to reflect. Sometimes moonlight filtered
through the curtains covering the window. It cast a silver glow
on the image of the Virgin hanging above my parents' bed.
She smiled lovingly at me. For the umpteenth time, I mulled
over the arguments of Abbé Mauraux, and new doubts
increased my anguish. I thought about far-away America
where the Jews were free. My thoughts often took me to
Palestine where a new breed of Jew was being born, free and
proud, without trace of the cowardice and obsequiousness
displayed by some of our Jews. They were the antithesis of the
submissive *shtetl* Jew with his kaftan and *payes*, towards
whom I felt a certain disdain. Father maintained that the only
solution to our long history of wandering was to go back to
our ancestral homeland, Palestine. Father's dream was of 'a
little house on Mount Carmel' but he had remained in Poland,
attached to his businesses at the clinic and the 'sanatorium',
which only became profitable in 1939 when my parents paid

off their mortgage. How eagerly would he now drop everything to go to Palestine! I looked with sadness at his white
head and drawn, tired features. The dream was over. Could
we at least make it until the end?

And so the nights passed, fearsome, exhausting, endless.
Tired and sleepy during the day, I lost my appetite and could
not even write my diary. And then, suddenly, I had an idea. I
would dress in an outfit so tight that it would protect me from
my nightly tormentors. I dressed fully, my shirt tucked into
my trousers; long socks were pulled over my trouser bottoms
and another pair over my hands and over the long sleeves of
my shirt, both secured with string. Over my head and face I
donned a large, loose-knit scarf through which I could
breathe. I tucked it into the collar of my shirt and also tightened it with string. Frania helped me dress. My first
appearance in this 'diver's' outfit produced a general outburst
of laughter. But it worked! The bedbugs stayed away from me,
concentrating on my more accessible neighbours. After three
weeks of sheer torture and losing a lot of weight, I had won
the battle and slept again.

Frequent thunderstorms shook the countryside. Lightning
struck dangerously near and a house in the village was
burned down. If any of the thatched roofs at our farmstead
were to catch fire we would be discovered. We decided to pay
Gosposia to order an 18-foot lightning rod from the local
carpenter. We sat in the shelter as it was being installed. We
learned later that this event had produced a flurry of suspicion in the village. People wondered how Aniela could afford
an expensive lightning rod, but the illness of Edward, who
was bed-ridden and helpless in case of fire, provided enough
of an explanation to stop the gossip.

We feared a new summer offensive by the Wehrmacht but
since April things had been quiet in the east. A sign of Russian
as well as German exhaustion, this lull in the fighting
confirmed to us that the Western Allies were playing games,
waiting for both adversaries to collapse. Then, in the middle
of July, Aniela brought some two-week-old papers back from
the market with huge headlines. '*Erbitterte Panzer Schlaechte in
der Byelgorod-Kursk Gegend*' [Bitter tank battles in the
Byelgorod–Kursk area], exclaimed *Der Voelkischer Beobachter*.

'The biggest tank battle ever,' exclaimed *Das Schwarze Korps*. Thousands of tanks battling thousands of tanks, thousands of planes involved. The daily numbers of Soviet tanks and planes destroyed were fantastically high, in the hundreds. These numbers were possibly inflated but it was clear that a new and powerful German offensive was in the making. This news was depressing; it suggested that, in spite of its winter defeats, the Wehrmacht was still very strong. At least the front was alive again. We also took satisfaction from the news of Allied bombing of German cities. 'The British air-pirates and the American air-gangsters struck our cities again! Thousands of innocent civillians hit.' The papers were full of resentment and bitterness for the 'atrocities' commited by the Allied air forces. We speculated that maybe, just maybe, if they started hurting seriously, the Germans would slow down the geno-cide they were perpetrating on us. Maybe the Allies had given them a secret ultimatum: 'Cease your horrible slaughter of the Jewish people and we will not hit your population centres.' All this was wishful thinking, but we hoped against hope.

Another piece of good news was brought one evening by Ziutek Kulikowski who came holding a short bulletin by the Polish Home Army. 'A second front has been opened by the Western Allies,' he announced with enthusiasm as he saw us crawling out from our hide-out, where Tsatsus's barking had sent us in a whirlwind. We learned that the Allies had landed in Sicily and were fighting Italian and German troops. This was not the genuine second front we were expecting – a direct thrust into France or Belgium through the channel or, short of that, a landing on the southern coast of France or at least in the Balkans. It was very hard for us to witness the static nature of the Allied advance. The great news was that the powerful German push in the Kursk–Byelgorod sector had been beaten down. The Soviet Army for the first time started a summer counter-offensive on a broad front and, for the first time in the summer, the Germans were retreating. The Wehrmacht once again had been defeated on a grand scale. This was much more significant to us than the landing in Sicily, a rather limited affair on a distant island on which, subsequently, the fighting would last for over six weeks.

With this injection of good news after so many months of no

news at all, we could now talk to Aniela and Edward with more confidence in the future – something we had avoided for a long time. Our landlords reminded us often that we had come with the understanding that the war would be over soon. 'You have now been here for half a year and the end is not in sight,' they repeated. 'Maybe the Germans will win. You cannot stay here for ever.' As time went by, they became increasingly irritated and impatient.

Father was again full of enthusiasm, constantly muttering a familiar tune, *'Razval Srednievo Fronta!'* [Collapse of the middle front!]. He was full of confidence and told Edward: 'It is but a question of a few months before Germany asks for surrender.' Edward just shook his head, but was becoming less irritable. Things were happening, a bit too slowly to our liking, but we felt that finally we were emerging from the abyss of despair in which we had been buried since the traumatic winter of 1943.

Dr Docha and Mikhalko arrived one evening, bringing with them some salt pork, sugar and flour. We were as usual reminded to kneel in the front room while Docha and our landlords prayed. Dr Docha was rather gloomy, he talked at length with Aniela, then with Mother and Father. From their looks I understood that something was amiss. Dr Docha was pressing all of us to accept Christianity, pointing out that he had at heart the salvation of our souls for which he was risking his life and the life of his family. The only way we could thank the Lord was to embrace Jesus Christ through the Catholic faith. He was ready to baptize us. 'There are rumours all over the county that I am hiding Jews,' he said. 'We are alive today, but may all be dead tomorrow. There is no salvation for our souls outside the Holy Church and Jesus Christ.'

This undisguised pressure by Docha was a source of torment, especially to Father who became very pensive and withdrawn. With his thoughts far away from us, he often did not hear what he was being asked, he became forgetful and even sometimes declined the evening meal of soup and black bread. I was broken-hearted to see him thrown into a state of depression for the first time in my life. His face suddenly sagged and deep wrinkles appeared on his forehead. His eyes were covered with a veil of resignation. At night I could hear him tossing and turning whispering like a prayer, '*Konets, konets uzh poskoree!* – The end, the end, quickly the end! [of the war]'

I guessed instinctively what was eating him. He was a man of principle and could not accept the prospect of baptism. He did not have the flexibility of a survivor. None of us took Docha's demand that we convert as seriously as Father. Misha laughed it off, saying, 'if sprinkling with water can save me from death then I will shower with holy water from morning till evening'. Tolo considered all this baptism business a joke. Frania was also ready to do whatever was required to survive, her thoughts and tears were always for Ilana, of whom she had had no news. Mother was very disturbed, but resigned to comply. As for me, I was torn between my mystical inclinations towards Jesus and the humiliation of being compelled to do something which I keenly felt as a betrayal of my people, something which was so strongly resented by my parents. I had no doubt, however, that no matter how abject this act would appear to me I would submit to it if my life were at stake.

Only Father was opposed to conversion, with all his body and soul. He took to studying a map of the Eastern Front cut out from a German paper. Sometimes his lips moved in silence, as if he wanted to convince himself that we could all make the 600 kilometres through fields, forests and swamps to the front. Then, aware of the futility of such an attempt, he would sink glumly into other thoughts. I sensed how deeply the edge of what he considered a betrayal of his people and of himself was cutting into the essence of his being. I knew how he loved us and how he struggled with himself. I saw the terrible toll that this struggle took on him.

As the interminable, stifling month of July was at last drawing to its end, the memory of Docha's visit began to fade. We knew that he would be back and pressure us again to convert but we lived from day to day. *Gosposia* was very busy – the harvest season was at hand. She sharpened sickles and scythes, and assembled pitchforks and other tools. It was essential that wheat and rye be harvested rapidly on her six acres of land, then bundled and brought into the barn to beat the autumn rains. Threshing, storing the grain, ploughing the field and cutting the straw and hay for fodder, all these tasks had to be done before the rains. It was impossible for a woman alone with a teenager niece and a crippled husband to manage. Yet delaying the work would endanger the crops and attract attention; some villagers had already offered their services to Aniela in exchange for a portion of the crop. Having locals snooping around the hut would be extremely dangerous and we decided with *Gosposia* to hire a farmhand, the stranger from a Byelorussian village near Lunna who had scared us earlier in the year and whose wages we were to pay. This too was very risky, needless to say. With a stranger around the hut at all times, Tsatsus would accept him as part of the household after a few days. We had to be on unrelenting maximum alert, permanently confined to the hide-out during the day. The nights would be especially dangerous, since the farmhand, though sleeping in the barn, might enter the hut without warning.

For ten full days, hell was visited upon us. At 5 a.m., with the first crow of the rooster, brutally torn from the best moments of our lives, we were rushed into the raw, mildewy darkness of the dugout – to the fetid smell of earth and rotting straw mixed with the rank sharpness of human sweat coming from our unwashed bodies. Meanwhile Kostya, the farmhand, ate a hearty breakfast of bread, soup with potatoes and milk. The first few days were the worst as Kostya worked almost under the windows. The working party had a mid-morning snack in the field. Around noon, they came back for their lunch break, their scythes on their shoulders under the midday sun. *Gosposia* spread the table with sausage, salt pork, onions, pickled cabbage and cucumbers, black bread and drink. We could hear Kostya joking with Edward and the women as they all ate lunch. Kostya then took a short nap in the barn. Oh, how eagerly we waited for this moment to crawl out, stretch and partake of our bowl of *bavarka* with black bread. Only those who have experienced similar moments can understand the intensity of pleasure and relief that is provided by satisfying simple body requirements withheld for hours, for a large part my life now revolved around these moments of ecstasy: from bowl of soup to bowl of milk to a bowl of *bavarka*, from a piece of black bread with onion to a potato with salt.

As the days passed, Kostya worked further and further

away from the hut and we grew bolder, now and then releasing one of us to stretch in the room. Kostya was a jovial and very talkative fellow and it was very difficult for *Gosposia* to get rid of him in the evening after a few drinks of *samogon*. Sometimes he lingered until very late. It was apparent that the young lad had taken a shine to Hela, so *Gosposia* kept a watchful eye on him. It was considered a disgrace for a *szlachta* [gentry] girl, even one born out of wedlock, to be courted by a simple Byelorussian *chlop*. While we were nearly suffocating in our hide-out, we were comforted by the thought that the harvest was almost over. At the end of ten days, the six acres had been harvested and sheaves of wheat and rye lined the fields.

It was a Sunday and Kostya was leaving. After church *Gosposia* took out a clean tablecloth and served Kostya and Edward; Hela, her mother Mania and Ziutek were also there. *Samogon*, sausage, meat, bacon, sour cabbage and pickles were surely part of the feast. Edward was in a good mood, the sight of his harvested field had given a powerful boost to his morale. He hobbled around the hut and into the yard on crutches to have a look at the harvest and at the animals. The company was very merry and there was much joking and laughter. A delightful smell of fried bacon penetrated into our hide-out where we sat in total darkness.

Kostya was standing not far from where Hela was cooking. We could hear every word he said, probably looking at her. We almost smelled the *samogon* on his breath. We sat in silence, trying not to move. The shelter was suffocating; the potatoes had been placed over the lid and there was barely enough air for seven people. Our joints were stiff and sore from immobility, and pressing physical needs tortured us. The afternoon became evening, time dragged on and on.

After having eaten, with much joking and gossiping, the company sang some religious songs. *Gosposia*'s strong, slightly inebriated voice, detached from the rest and slightly off-key, sang a song we had heard time and again.

O Matko Swieta, opiekunko ludzi	O holy Mother, protector of people
Niech Cie placz sierot do	Let the cry of orphans earn

litosci wzbudzi	Thy mercy
Wygnancy Ewy, do Ciebie wolamy	The exiles of Eve, we beg you
Zlituj sie zlituj, niech sie nie tulamy.	Have pity on us, do not let us wander.

As they all sang prayers to the Virgin Mary, we prayed to the God of Israel to make Kostya go home. But soon the religious songs became interlaced with merry Byelorussian songs and Polish drinking songs. At last, and none too soon, our prayers were heard and a very drunk Kostya said his farewells to everybody and went staggering on his way.

The days that followed were anti-climactic. We could again place our sentinels at windows. Most of the wheat, rye and corn around our hut had been cut and visibility was again 50 yards. Although wide swathes of various crops still remained here and there, we had no problem spotting anyone approaching along the road. The *sagan* was back in the entrance. It was sweet and relaxing to go back to our 'easy' life, dividing ourselves between the attic and the back room. I could resume my writing, Father and Misha their chess games, Frania and Mother their knitting, and Tolo his clandestine courtship of Hela. *Gosposia* and Hela now worked around the clock to bring in the harvest before the onset of the rains. After dusk, when the twilight made it difficult to distinguish between shapes, Tolo and Misha rushed into the barn to help thresh the crops, but only after Hela and *Gosposia* had been moving around the farmstead for a while. Edward hopped to and fro giving orders and Frania or I stood guard behind the barn until complete darkness. Big sacks made of jute were filled with grain – they had to be remitted to the Germans before the deadline. The 'overflow' was hidden in a secret silo dug out in the barn. We had several alerts but were extremely lucky that nobody was caught by surprise.

When *Gosposia* went to Indura to remit her grain to the Germans, she came back with stacks of papers, some very old but some only two weeks out of date. We devoured them. The Germans were in full retreat: Orel and Bryansk had fallen to the Russians, Kharkov had been abandoned and fighting was going on around Poltava. The Wehrmacht practised a 'scorched-earth' policy, burning and destroying everything behind them – cattle, crops and villages. We could only imagine what they were doing to the civilians. On our front, there was renewed activity around the Smolensk area and in the direction of Vitebsk. This meant that the front was approaching, though it was still more than 500 kilometres away. At the same time the Western Allies had finally occupied Sicily. It had taken six weeks for the powerful Anglo-Americans to overcome a few German SS divisions and their demoralized Italian ally – this meant to us that the Allies were still not interested in winning the war. The Rommel–Montgomery 'tango' of North Africa would continue in Italy.

The hot nights of early September were perfectly still. However, during the day big Junkers trimotor transport planes with a black cross on their fuselage, flew over very low, rattling the huts. Something was going on. Could the front be closer than the papers reported? Maybe a new powerful offensive on the central front was in progress. Maybe a Russian breakthrough in our direction had materialized. At night we tried to get our ears close to the ground in the hide-out, hoping to hear the distant roll of artillery; in vain, everything was silence.

By the middle of September Edward had another relapse and was overcome by pain and exhaustion. Father ordered him to apply the traction device continuously. Edward descended into a very sombre mood and became very irritable. We tiptoed around the back room, trying not to disturb him. One day, our sentry at the front window spotted a man walking along the road and we quickly disappeared into our hide-out. Ready to jump into the shelter, our sentry would wait for Tsatsus to bark, signalling that a stranger had taken the path to our farm. In the absence of barking, the stranger would normally continue along the main road and would then be seen by the back-window sentry. The alarm would then be over and we could all crawl out. However, this time the stranger spotted on the road disappeared without emerging on the other side and Tsatsus remained silent. We stayed in the hide-out for over an hour. When one of us decided to crawl out to see what happened, he saw Edward peeking through the window and desperately struggling to leave the house on his crutches. He was red in the face from excitement and pain; sweat streamed down his cheeks. We could hear him yelling in his Polish–Byelorussian dialect, *'Anielka idi sioudy! Ja vidal etou zydowskouiou korovu. Bud ona prokliata eta zydowskaia korova!'* [Anielka, come here at once! I saw the Jewish cow. May the Jewish cow be damned!]. We could not understand what was going on but, when *Gosposia* showed up, Edward greeted her by hitting her with one of his crutches. We were scared out of our wits as a domestic scene erupted. Edward hurled insults at Aniela, accusing her of being a whore. Aniela was strangely silent. We all huddled together in distress. Would this end up by being once more 'the fault of these damned Jews, whose presence has only brought us mishap?' We kept silent as we crawled out of the shelter. The shouting eventually died down and we could hear Aniela sobbing. We kept out of the way and went to sleep with empty stomachs, still perplexed about the cause of this violent domestic quarrel.

Over the next few days, Edward was exhausted and irritable. We all huddled in the back room, except for the sentry, who sat by the front-room window without uttering a word. But then I forgot to be cautious and went into the front room to pace it a few times. Edward was sitting on his bed, holding on to his belt. Suddenly I felt a powerful, burning lash across my arm. In an instant I dashed into the back room: a broad red welt marked my forearm. Mother cried and I felt humiliated. Hela finally explained the reason for the scene. Edward suspected Aniela of having a lover whom he called *Zydowskaia korowa*, the 'Jewish cow'.

'Why "Jewish cow"?'

'Because many believe that cows belonging to Jews are often left to graze on other peoples' pastures,' she said.

'The man we saw disappear was Aniela's lover?'

'Yes,' Hela answered.

'Tsatsus knows him then, because he did not bark?'

'Yes.'

'Who is he?' Hela did not want to say, beyond divulging that he was married with children and that she did not think he knew about us. Now we had another worry: did the 'Jewish cow' know about us? Mania, Ziutek and now the 'Jewish cow'. The circle was widening.

The stifling heat of summer was over, so was the harvest; sheaves of wheat, rye and other crops were stacked in the fields like orderly rows of soldiers. They were loaded on to carts. The evenings, cool and clear but already dark, were still filled with activity. From far away one could hear the regular beat of flails and the crunching sound of hay-cutting. Everyone was in a hurry to beat the rains.

Work on the farm continued unabated. Now that the grain was threshed and hidden in *Gosposia's* secret silo, the straw, hay and clover had to be cut for fodder, the potatoes had to be dug up and garnered. The fields had to be ploughed and fertilized. It was a continuous chain of work until the first snows. Tolo and Misha helped in the barn, cutting hay and straw with a rotary knife that formed a spoke in an iron wheel equipped with a handle. One man grabbed the handle with both hands, rotating the wheel while the other fed the thick bundles of hay, clover and straw under the knife. The full strength of a grown man as he thrust himself forward was necessary to cut through the bundles. It also produced a cutting sound of 'tchak-tchack' which could possibly be faintly heard in the village. I wasn't strong enough to cut the hay, but I was useful as a sentry to observe the approaches and the road.

Since Edward's outburst, our landlords had both been irritable. The landlord, constantly suspicious, kept a watchful eye on Aniela, often hopping on his crutches into the yard, calling out *'Anielkaa, Anielkaa, gde ty?* – Anielkaa, Anielkaa, where are you?' Aniela, in turn, was driven to the brink. The tension was unbearable and was often discharged on us. Our women were, as always, the first to suffer – Aniela had a pronounced weakness for men. Mother, but especially Frania and Rozia, were the targets of her wrath, they were humiliated and reduced to tears. The situation was worsened by the fact that our money had almost gone. Misha proved to be very stingy and unwilling to part with even a penny. He often argued with Mother, who accused him of letting the situation with *Gosposia* fester to a point where she might throw us out. He argued that Father, as a doctor, would make a good living after our liberation while he, a *mecenas* (lawyer), would have to live on his savings.

We tried our best not to irritate our landlords. I confined myself to the attic where I wrote my diaries and memoirs. Father, also, started to write about Grodno under the occupation. His writings were a precise compilation in Russian of facts concerning German crimes and atrocities in our city, including statistics about the Jewish population, transports, and so on. He called his document 'Unprecedented Crimes Against the Jewish Population of Grodno' and hoped that this material would swell a future Act of Accusation against the executioners of our community.[1]

The news from the front was encouraging. From papers that were three weeks old, we deduced that the Germans were retreating from the Ukraine. Poltava had fallen and Mother was elated that her native city had been liberated. The Red Army had reached the Dnieper – and perhaps had already crossed it. On our front, the Germans had been thrown back some 150 kilometres west of Smolensk – to Orsha, 450 kilometres east of Grodno, still a distance we could not possibly cover without being caught. Italy had collapsed and the Allied front was somewhere in the mountains north of Naples. We were again disappointed by the limited scope of this second front.

The German police stepped up their inspections in October. German vehicles were taking to the road, passing barely 100 yards from us. Squeezed inside our hole for hours on end, expecting the worst, we prayed. It produced a sigh of relief when *Gosposia* or Hela shouted, 'They have passed by, they have passed by, they are heading for Yodkovitche!' This did not mean, of course, that they would not return to Staniewicze; but luckily Aniela was considered poor, and the crumbling, isolated farmstead did not attract much attention.

The Germans discovered here and there hidden grain and hidden meat or lard. Peasants were arrested and sent to Germany, sometimes entire families, to work in camps or factories. Rumours circulated that peasant girls were being sent to army brothels. Some fled to join partisan groups in the

---

[1] Father was logical and had an excellent memory. He later handed over this account, on the front line, to a Jewish major of the Red Army, following our liberation on 16 July 1944. The major promised to turn it over to the 'Anti-Fascist Committee in Moscow'. To my knowledge, the report was never published.

forest: the Poles to the AK, the Byelorussians to the Soviet Partisans, whose attacks on German communication lines and military transports grew bolder every day. One day *Gosposia* came with the news that a Jewish partisan detachment had been spotted in the forest near Marcinkance, some 50 kilometres north-east of Staniewicze. We thought about Izak and Aunt Ada who, if still alive, surely were somewhere near there.

It was at that time that some partisans made a daring ambush on a German rural police vehicle near Indura. They killed the *Kommandant* and severely wounded three *gendarmes*. This produced a terrible reprisal: 50 hostages were taken from neighbouring villages and shot. The village nearest to the ambush was burned to the ground and many peasants were sent to labour camps. The evening sky was aglow in the north-east. It made us very edgy; we knew only too well how this reminded our landlords of what could happen to them and to the village if we were discovered.

Gosposia and Hela were now employed in ploughing the field and fertilizing it with manure. The potato harvest was next in line. They were a bit late and most of the crop was ruined when the frost hit prematurely. This was a big misfortune as we relied on potatoes as our main staple. Then Krasula, the cow, became unwell and stopped providing milk.

I was so ravenously hungry that I ate anything in sight. I was growing fast, going through puberty. I waited for *Gosposia* to make some potato pancakes, fried crisp with oil or bacon. My mouth watered for hours in anticipation. She always gave me some tidbits. Ah, the wonderful taste of the fat, golden and crispy pancake! Sometimes I dipped my bread in the frying pan, sponging up the last drops of fat. Increasingly Mother and Father gave me some of their portions under the pretext that they were not hungry. Tolo, my brother, had his own way around hunger. He would lie in wait in the attic, ready to jump down to the vestibule as soon as Hela appeared through the front door. Hela kept pieces of dry sausage that she was certainly stealing for him from *Gosposia*'s secret larder. One day I surprised them in the vestibule. Tolo was hastily swallowing a big piece of sausage and almost choked when he saw the door from the *isba* opening – it could have been

Gosposia. I could not understand how neither *Gosposia* nor the landlord had seen the obvious: Hela was in love with Tolo. Jealous of him for seducing her, and furious at his reckless disregard for our safety, I started to speak to Tolo but he knocked me out. I fell to the ground and Tolo panicked, he raised me back on my feet and kissed me. He was very frightened. I did not utter a word about it to anyone.

The weather changed again. The *raspoutitsa* ravaged the fields; it rained non-stop. The clouds trailed in shreds, low and slowly, without end, on the flat horizon; the village and the road were hidden by mist. We again relied mainly on Tsatsus to warn us of strangers approaching and were constantly on alert. Ziutek Kulikowski came by on a foggy November evening, bringing us good news: the Russians had crossed the River Dnieper in several places and were pushing their pincers west of Kiev and into the Zaporozhie. Father was immediately jubilant. He believed that the German divisions in the bend of the Dnieper, as well as the Germans in the Crimea, had already been cut off. '*Razval youzhnovo fronta,*' he exclaimed again, '*molodtsy rebiata!*'

But Ziutek had not come to cheer us up – he handed Father a long letter from a man called Hillel Braude, whose family Father knew from Grodno. Hillel had lost his entire family. He had jumped from the train on its way to Malkinia (which we later found out was Treblinka) in February and was now hiding in the attic of a friendly peasant whom he had known before the war. The rest of the family did not know about him and Hillel was alone, he had been a prisoner in a corner of the attic for over half a year. His situation was desperate. Oh, how he wished to join us, to see some other human faces, to be with other Jews. Otherwise, 'life is not worth anything to me any more,' the letter concluded.

It was Ziutek's best friend Piotr who was hiding the Jew. His hut was in the middle of the village, and his brother was an anti-Semite. Hillel needed a new hiding place, but where could he go? As the cold season approached, Hillel was becoming more and more depressed. He became suicidal. One evening Piotr heard a commotion in the attic and rushed up. He found Hillel hanging from a beam, but fortunately still alive. Piotr cut Hillel down and promised to look for another hiding place for him. He spoke to Ziutek, who told Piotr about us but without divulging our whereabouts. He thought that Hillel would be better off with us. After all, he said, the punishment for hiding one Jew, seven Jews or eight Jews was the same: death. If *Gosposia* did not agree to take him in, Hillel would surely commit suicide or freeze to death in the attic.

We now had a dilemma. Taking in another person increased our risk of being discovered, but a fellow Jew was dying and we decided to try and convince *Gosposia* to accept another Jew even though she was already overburdened with seven. But how could we ask her to take in another penniless person when our money had practically run out? There were still Misha's hidden treasures, but he guarded them jealously and seemed to prefer hunger to parting with a few dollars. How could we credibly tell her after nine interminable months that the end of the war was near?

In spite of her occasional ugly outbursts, *Gosposia* was fundamentally a good and compassionate woman. This fact could have escaped a casual observer because she was very hard, just as her life had been. One of many children of a poor peasant family, she knew difficult times. She had known famine during the turbulent years of the First World War, and the birth of independent Poland was followed immediately by the Soviet–Polish war, a dark and difficult period. After the war Aniela's mother had died, and she had to work hard to help her family. She fell in love with young Edward from the neighbouring village of Staniewicze, but his family was opposed to the match because she had no dowry. Edward was forced to break with his family and remained to this day on non-speaking terms with his brother. But Aniela's dowry was her unrelenting energy and enthusiasm. They married, and both worked hard. It seemed that slowly their dreams were becoming reality – and then Edward became ill with bone tuberculosis. Dr Docha treated him but they did not have the money to pay him. The illness got worse and to make ends meet *Gosposia* had to sell some of her precious possessions – two acres of prime land, some pigs, a horse and a cow. She was now the only able-bodied member of the household and had to take care of the property. Then came the Soviet rule and she was forced to manage her property for the *kolkhoz*. They still owed Dr Docha quite a sum of money, which, incidentally he did not claim. This debt had contributed to our acceptance by the Staniewskis, who felt they could not refuse the favour Docha was asking of them – and besides, it provided Edward with a doctor right by his bed.

I liked *Gosposia*'s blue eyes gazing intensely from a sun-and wind-burned, wrinkled, rugged face, her strong white teeth showing occasionally through a rare smile. I liked her muscular arms wielding the scythe and her craggy strong hands. I knew that under the thick and hardened skin was a good and sensitive heart. The only way left to us was to appeal directly to that heart and hope that she would respond.

At first she reacted as if somebody had burned her with a poker. How could we even think about another Jew coming here when our own fate was far from settled? Maybe soon we would have to leave ourselves as more and more people were learning of our whereabouts. Her answer was a flat and a resounding 'No!', but we came back again and again, speaking of Hillel's suffering. We insisted the war was almost over and she would not notice the difference between seven and eight Jews. Slowly Aniela gave in, but she had to convince Edward. Another few days passed and Edward also reluctantly agreed. We sent a message to Ziutek through Hela: 'Hillel can come! We are waiting!'

20   Hillel

Ziutek brought Hillel to the farmstead at around midnight on a snowy night. In the dim light of the oil lamp through the half-open entrance door I recognized the silhouette of Ziutek, brushing wet flakes off his soaked sheepskin, and behind him the broad-shouldered figure of a tall man stamping his feet and shaking off the melting snow. *'Niech bedzie pochvalony Jezus Chrystus!'* the man pronounced upon entering the room. *'Na wieki wiekow, amen!'* everybody answered. One could discern a blond beard and reddish-blond hair lumped in disarray on his forehead. Water was streaming down his face, which remained in the shadow of the weak, flickering light. The man stumbled and a strong smell of *samogon* filled the room; he was very drunk. As he came closer, I saw a big, reddish Sarmatic moustache, so popular among the Polish nobility. His complexion was fair, and blue eyes stared at us in an alcoholic stupor. 'Shepetovka has been taken!' he exclaimed. 'Kiev is going to fall in a matter of days! The Germans are finished in the south!'

This was a joyous cry for a man who just a few days ago had attempted suicide. He released a long and powerful burp which filled the room with the foul smell of ill-digested food and alcohol. The warmth, the light, and so many faces staring at him had produced a powerful reaction. The food and alcohol he had had with Piotr to celebrate his rescue was obviously too much for his stomach. He clutched his chest and, before we could utter a word, ran outside. This was the strange entry of Hillel Braude into our midst. Ziutek explained that Hillel and his friend had drunk themselves almost to death when they had learned that *Gosposia* had agreed to take Hillel in.

Hillel integrated quickly. He was a very straight, decent, unhappy man, who had lost all his family to the January transport. He was not talkative and he rarely smiled. Hillel's parents had had a dairy store in Grodno, which gave him connections to the local peasants. Caught in the transport from Ghetto I, he had jumped from the speeding train. The guards had opened fire but Hillel managed to escape. Bruised and haggard, he had wandered from hut to hut. He was denounced once but had managed to flee again. After an odyssey during which he almost froze to death, he found Piotr, a friendly Polish peasant whom he had known before the war as a supplier. A good human being, Piotr agreed to keep Hillel in his attic, telling only his wife – his children and his old mother, who lived with them, were told nothing. Piotr's house was in the middle of the village and Hillel had to be extra careful. He could not move about and was confined to a small area of the attic. At the end of March Hillel had become very ill with pneumonia and had lost the will to go on living. Piotr cared for him as for his own brother.

Hillel had stayed eight long months in the darkness of the attic without seeing a human face other than Piotr's or his wife bringing him his food. All alone, he remained with his thoughts and memories, and the dreadful prospect of another winter in the attic. This had been too much for him and he had decided to end his ordeal. He had fashioned a noose from a piece of rope and fastened it to a beam by climbing on an old broken chair. Having watched Hillel closely for some time, Piotr had suspected that something tragic might occur and he reached the attic just in time to bring Hillel back to life. From then on Piotr was determined to find him a warmer and less solitary hiding place. He was a friend of Ziutek Kulikowski and had opened his heart to him, and this is how we had learned about Hillel. Is it a wonder that the two friends drank themselves nearly to death upon hearing the good news?

Our life revolved around waiting for the Russian winter offensive which we all hoped would finish off the Germans and liberate us. Father was adamant: 'Those bastards will never endure another winter in Russia! An imminent attack on the central front at Orsha will liberate us!' However, a momentary lull settled on the entire front and we all waited and waited for the big news, which did not come. The days grew ever shorter, winter was here and *Gosposia* was far behind schedule. The grain was still not completely threshed, the hay was only half-ready for fodder. The frozen remainder of the potato crop had to be gathered to feed the pigs. We all helped, in the evening after dusk.

I was often assigned to a solitary vigil behind the barn, straining my eyes to inspect the fields and the road, peering into the evening mist. The fields were now deserted, here and there covered with wet snow. I usually squatted behind a mound of snow at a small distance from the barn, so that, while it was difficult for anybody coming from the road to spot me, I could easily recognize an oncoming stranger even in the twilight. I could hear the monotonous 'tchak-tchak' of the rotary knife cutting the hay and the beat of the flails against the clay floor of the barn. It was cold but it felt so good to take in big gulps of wintry air, nestle into the sheepskin, given to me by *Gosposia*, and dream. My thoughts wandered into the past and the future. Sometimes I saw in the twilight many, many people advancing slowly along the road, carrying bundles and suitcases, holding infants in their arms, children walking holding hands. Some were on carts and carriages huddled together. Who were they? Where were they going? The long procession disappeared into the distance between the low-hanging, grey, shredded sky and the darkness of the fields and forests.

My dreaming was cut short by Rozia or Frania coming to relieve me or by *Gosposia* calling that work was over. One evening, it was particularly cold; a strong northerly wind numbed my face and chilled me to the bone. To take shelter, I moved closer to the barn. I huddled into the sheepskin and glued myself to the wall. Suddenly, I was frightened out of my dreaming by *Gosposia*'s angry voice: 'Ah, you little spy, what are you spying at? I will give you spying!' She walked towards me and menacingly raised her arm as if she wanted to strike me. I did not understand her anger. Through the darkness, I saw Misha coming out of the barn. 'Don't play the innocent with me,' she yelled in Byelorussian. 'Why are you spying on me? One word to the *Gospodarz* and I will blow your head off!' I finally got it: Misha and *Gosposia* had been alone in the barn without any work going on. I wanted to tell her that I was not spying, that I had only moved so close to the barn to protect myself from the icy wind. But it was useless.

From that time on, *Gosposia*'s attitude towards me changed. I was not 'Aliczek' any more. There were no more occasional potato pancakes, or pieces of sausage or salt pork for me. Misha was now often chosen by *Gosposia* to 'cut the hay'. It was obvious that he was 'sacrificing himself for the common cause'. Sometimes Hillel was chosen, and he too followed his fate with resignation. Tolo was spared, maybe because he was too young; so was Father, probably because he was too old.

The romance of Tolo and Hela grew stronger. Tolo was becoming bolder every day, in callous disregard for our safety. No loner satisfied with stalking Hela in the vestibule he followed her at nightfall into the stable where she went to feed the animals. One evening, coming back from my observation post, I knocked for fun at the door of the stable and saw my brother jumping out. He was furious and shook his fist at me. 'What a bastard he is,' I thought with envy, 'for endangering us all!' Hela's every move, every glance was now for him. Her blue eyes opened wide whenever he appeared! She was always trying to be near to him, she even moved her spinning wheel to the back room where they could exchange glances.

But another romance was also slowly developing. Frania, who cried so often, and Hillel, who rarely uttered a word, began to smile at each other and it would have not surprised me to discover that they were in love. A year ago in the ghetto I had been spying on young couples with Lutek and Monia, and following them almost to the Slobodka arsenal. Now, under my nose, there were couples who were in love or making love: *Gosposia* and Misha, *Gosposia* and Hillel, Tolo and Hela, and now Frania and Hillel.

21 Winter 1944

One day a blanket of snow covered the fields. Against it, one could be seen from afar and it became dangerous to leave the hut, even for a moment. I recalled the poem by Pushkin from *Eugene Onegin*:

Vstaiet zarya vo mgle kholodnoi	In the cold mist the dawn is rising,
Na nivakh shum rabot umolk	The hum of work died in the fields.
S svoiei voltchikhoiou golodnoi	With his hungry female
Vykhodit na dorogu volk	The wolf adventures on the road.
Yevo potchouia kon dorozhnyi	Sensing danger, the horse
Khrapit i putnik ostorozhnyi	Is snorting and the traveller
Nyesyotsa v goru na vyes dukh	Bolts up and rushes off.
Na utrvenney zarye pastukh	The shepherd early in the morning
Nye gonit uzh korov iz khleva	Stopped driving cows from the shed.
I v tchas poludennyi v kruzhok	At midday the horn does not call him any more
Uzh nye zavyet yevo rozhok	
V izboushke raspyevaya deva	Inside the hut the maiden sings,
Pryadet i zmnikh drug notchei	Spinning, and wintry nights' friend,
Tryeshtchit luchinka pyered niei	The splinter-lamp, crackles in front of her
I vot uzhe tryeshtchat morozy!	And already the frost is upon us!

The peace of the muddy *raspoutitsa* time was over. Christmas was approaching and we were getting ready for the ordeals of the long visits by *Gosposia*'s gossips, whom we could spot on the white snow from miles away.

It was getting colder and colder. Strong winds swirled in the snow, blocking the road and piling drifts outside. Our windows were covered with delicate frost designs. I liked storms because they meant peace and quiet – people not venturing outside, Germans drinking schnapps and keeping warm inside their police quarters. We could now bake bread at any time since a fire was crackling in the stove every day and nobody in the village would pay much attention to the smoke from our chimney. I especially liked evening storms as they produced a certain cosiness in the austere *isba*. Everything appeared mysterious and peaceful in the twilight of the flickering flame. The wind howled and sobbed, the hut shivered against sudden gusts, the Virgin smiled from the wall and the pictures of saints looked down at us. We all huddled together, eight people in the back room with drawn curtains: Tolo and Father playing chess on the floor, with Hillel interfering, Frania and Mother knitting on the bed and Rozia and Misha reading on the stove loft with a candle. I also sat on the floor, near the oil lamp, writing, observing the dancing shadows or just listening to the wind. At times the rattle of a broken board in the attic or the sudden thud of snow against the window would make us all anxiously look at one another, instantly ready to jump up and disappear into the blackness of the hide-out. We were like helpless forest animals, like deers scared of any sound and any whisper. We were all conditioned by months of fear to react in unison. We did not have to talk, our anxious glances were enough and we all knew what to do at any time of danger.

Hela and *Gosposia* spun their flax in the front room near the ailing Edward. Hela would often bring her spinning wheel into the back room and squash in with us under the pretext of talking to our women, but actually to look with loving eyes at my brother who would send her passionate glances in return. Occasionally a groan of pain would come from Edward on the other side of the wall. At times Mother would hum in a whisper a sad Russian song. I liked particularly the Ukrainian song about the falcon who soars to freedom or Tchaikovsky's lullaby:

Spi malyutka moi pryekrasnyi	Sleep my little beautiful
Baioushki baiou, baioushki baiou.	Baioushki baiou, baioushki baiou.
Tikho svyetit myesyats yasnyi	Quietly shines the gleaming moon
Baioushki baiou, baioushki baiou.	Baioushki baiou, baioushki baiou.

Now and then Father would whisper in desperation, *'Konietz, konietz ouzh poskoreye!'* [The end, make the end come faster!]. I forgot my unresolved qualms about God and His existence. I was writing, writing and writing with a frenzy. At such times I felt free and happy. No German could reach me.

Edward was very sick again, his summer recovery had just been a remission, and with the onset of bad weather he became feverish and was in constant pain. Father did his utmost, but there was little he could do. We were running out of food. We had run out of money. Only Misha had money stashed away, but he was determined not to spend any for us. He had resolved instead to go hungry with Rozia and to endure *Gosposia*'s foul moods. I waited impatiently every day for the eternal bowl of thick yellow pea soup and bread, but I could hardly swallow the frozen potatoes. Father and Mother had both lost a lot of weight. Mother, naturally a plump woman, was now skinny. Father's pot belly had long since gone, and his hair and beard stubble were white as snow. Their drawn faces expressed exhaustion, and both now looked very old to me. Only Father's blue eyes remained lively. In spite of our long wait for the 'end', he optimistically maintained that our liberation would come much sooner than we suspected. My dear Father, the eternal optimist, how wrong he could be! Hadn't he prophesied a complete collapse of the German Army after Stalingrad a year ago? I teased him constantly that when he said 'quickly' it meant at least another year.

At the end of December *Gosposia* brought a few German newspapers from Indura. The long-awaited Russian winter offensive had started in the south and the Red Army was relentlessly pushing the Germans beyond the Dnieper towards the Dniester and Romania. The former Polish border with the Ukraine would be soon reached. Germany had been bombed mercilessly by the Anglo-Americans. But none of this affected us directly: the central front was quiet, still west of Smolensk at Orsha, still 450 kilometres away. Nor was there a second front worthy of this name. The front in Italy, north of Naples, had not moved much since September.

We were puzzled and appalled that the civilized world had stood by and allowed the wholesale murder of an entire people. We felt betrayed and abandoned by everybody. We did not know that even at this late date England would still not allow Jewish refugees into Palestine, or that the US Congress was more than ever opposed to granting visas to the decimated Jews of Europe, but we sensed that nobody wanted us. Many Poles did not hide their satisfaction, they were pleased that an awkward minority problem was being 'solved' for them by their enemy, pleased that so much Jewish property was falling into their hands. Some cooperated enthusiastically with the Germans. An army of *schmaltzowniks* was at work: a Jewish life for 50 Reichsmarks.

Christmas and the New Year came and went. It was a poor New Year for all of us.

Baby [peasant women] and *kumoshki* [gossips] had started coming for long visits again. Some even brought their spinning wheels with them. The women spun or knitted, the men chatted, and we had to stay in the hide-out for hours on end – sometimes the entire day without so much as a bowl of soup or a glass of water. Once Rozia, who had a bladder infection, wet herself. She sat sobbing softly while the smell of urine spread in the hide-out. She continued to cry long after the visit was over.

Nights brought occasional relief. The black expanse of the sky, with its myriad of twinkling stars and constellations, was so beautiful. Father, an amateur astronomer, showed me how to recognize the constellation of the Great Bear, the Little Bear, the Milky Way of which our solar system was a part, the brightest star Syrius and the closest Alpha-Centaura, some 60 light years away. I learned to identify the planets – the largest Jupiter and the closest Mars, which I fantasized was populated by little clever and gentle Martians and a red flora. What a wondrous edifice was our universe! I felt elated about this world that was beyond the reach of the Germans. I would look at the sky and repeat the poem of Lermontov which Father often recited and which Mother had sung in better times; it expressed what I felt so well.

Vykhozhu odin ya na dorogu	I tread alone on my way
Skvoz tuman kremnistyi put blestit	Through the fog the road is bright
Notch tikha, poustynya vnyemlyet Bogu	The night is still, the desert hails the Lord
I zvyezda zvyezdoyou govorit	And the star is speaking to the star.
V nyebyesakh Torzhestvyenno i tchoudno	The heavens are solemn and beautiful
Spit zyemlya v siyanyi goloubom	The earth is sleeping in a blue aura
Tchto-zesh mnye tak bolno i tak troudno?	Why is it for me so painful and difficult?
Zhdou-l tchevo, zhalyeyou li o tchem?	Do I expect or grieve for something?
Ou-zh nye zhdou ot zhizni nitchevo ya	I do not expect anything from life
I nye zhal mnye proshlovo nitchout	And I do not grieve at all for my past,
Ya ishtchou svobody i pokoya	I am seeking freedom and peace
Ya-b khotyel zabydtsa i zasnout	I would like to forget and to sleep
No nye tem kholodnym snom mogily	But not with the cold sleep of the grave
Ya-b zhelal na vyeki tak zasnout	I would like to sleep for ever so
Tchto-b v grudi dremali zhizni sily	That life would slumber in me
Tchto-b dysha vzdymalas tikho groud	That breath would quietly swell my breast,
Tchto-b vyes den, vsyou notch moy sloukh leleya	That all day, all night my ear caressing
Pro lyoubov mnye sladkii golos pyel	About love a sweet voice sang to me

Tchto-b nad mnoyou vyetchno zelenieya	That above me, for ever green
Tyomnyi dub sklonyalsya i shoumyel	A dark oak would bend and whisper.

Yes, how I would have loved to forget, to sleep under that dark oak, its leaves rustling in the breeze, and then awake to our freedom! Would this all be only a bad dream or would it be the cold sleep of the grave? That was the question constantly on my mind.

Our situation was precarious. Father was afraid that Edward might not last until the summer. As long as Edward lingered on, Father was considered indispensable. What might happen after his demise was anybody's guess. We feared that we might be quietly 'disposed of' by the villagers, as more and more peasants knew about us. If *Gosposia* ever asked the villagers to help her get rid of the Jews and the terrible curse they could bring on the village, there was no doubt whatever that one stormy night we would all be murdered.

At the end of January, Dr Docha came with Mikhalko. They brought some food and some medicine for Edward. Docha had a long conversation with us. He brought some religious books and insisted that a higher purpose had been served by him saving us. He demanded that we follow the ways of the Saviour, who had saved us through Docha. We should recognize Him and embrace the Holy Church. We should read the Holy Bible and prepare ourselves to become Catholics. He felt that he had given us plenty of time to think already and was all set to baptize us himself. I had never seen Docha so determined, angry even. Only Father, whom I never saw praying or crossing himself, was spared reprimands as Docha could not bring himself to pressure him directly. 'But now,' he said, 'the time has come, He has saved you, showed you the way and you should in gratitude accept Christ.' Gone were the hints – it was almost 'convert or else!'

I had never seen my father in such a bad way as when Docha left. He felt deeply humiliated, repeating to Mother that he would rather die than convert. He insisted that we, the young people, should submit and live, but reiterated that he would open his veins rather than submit. Mother argued that the whole thing was a charade anyway, that conversions under duress were invalid, that Jewish law allowed conversion in the face of death. Father was not arguing, he was determined. I was bewildered. I could not comprehend why he, an agnostic who went to the synagogue only on Yom Kippur, attached such importance to the act of conversion. How could he be so stubborn?

Since Edward's relapse, *Gosposia* had been sleeping badly. She needed the entire bed for herself and sent Hela to sleep in the back room on the stove loft. Misha and Rozia were now off the stove, taking turns with Frania, Hillel and Tolo at sleeping in the hide-out or on the floor. I was still fighting the bedbugs, occasionally donning my 'diver's' suit, but when I found a bedbug in my morning gruel I reacted the way the adults did: I simply took it out with a spoon and calmly continued my meal.

Bedbugs became a part of my landscape but something else perturbed my sleep: my brother. Tolo was becoming more and more daring. Now that Hela was sleeping on the stove, it seemed to me that Tolo was 'sleep-walking' right up the stove during his nights on the floor. I decided to check on him and I fought to stay awake. Everybody was already asleep when I heard the slight squeak of a step on the kneading barrel. A slight disturbance on the stove...I checked... my brother was gone...I was stunned and bewildered, shaking with anger and jealousy. What would *Gosposia* say if she found out? What if Hela got pregnant? Should I wake up Mother and Father? They were fast asleep and snoring. I was torn between the hope of punishing Tolo and the fear that Aniela might wake up and come into our room at any moment. If she found out about this, she or Edward would surely throw us out!

I began to find it difficult to sleep again, staying awake at night, listening out for the slightest noise, whisper or heavy breathing coming from the stove. I did not know what to do, but was determined to spoil Tolo's pleasure; I would wait until the rascal was on the stove and then violently cough or sneeze. This must surely have scared the two of them out of their wits. I did it so often that my parents woke up at times. 'Alik, why don't you sleep, are you sick?' Mother would say. I had the impression that my parents knew everything, but could do nothing about it. It was only after Tolo returned from his 'sleep-walking' that I would fall asleep. I hated my brother and I had the impression that he hated me too.

One day he was standing in the vestibule, waiting for Hela and his piece of sausage or ham. I tried not to leave him there alone for too long and opened the door purposefully, pretending to go on the *sagan*. This sent him back to the room in a fury. But soon he became less and less impressed by my presence. I began to use stronger tactics: I would suddenly open the door to the vestibule, asking innocently, 'What is Tolo doing in the entrance for so long?' Father would call Tolo, reprimand him and warn him of danger. Once I opened the door to the vestibule so wide that he had to jump away from Hela. He came at me and struck me in the face with all his might. The dark entrance swirled around. The next thing I knew I was on the floor looking at the alarmed face of my brother. He helped me up and wiped the blood from my split lip. I was furious and did not want his help. I fantasized about getting bigger and stronger and teaching this reckless brute a lesson.

We thanked God every day for remaining undiscovered. We were always hungry. In the morning we ate a gruel made of coarse dark flour cooked with salt and water, sometimes with a touch of milk. It was called *zacierka* and it was tasteless. In the afternoon we had the eternal yellow pea soup and a slice of black bread with salt and onion. In the evening it was black bread again with hot water sometimes sweetened with some saccharine.

Docha had not visited for a while. That was a relief to me, because I now feared his visits. I resented the charade of kneeling and praying, and I dreaded Father's reaction. On Sundays we suffered through the long visits of *kumoshki*. In the evenings I wrote my diary and listened to the wind. It looked for a while as though the Germans had forgotten our village.

One day *Gosposia* received word that Edward's estranged older brother, Stakh, who lived in a nearby village, wanted to come to make amends. She was not overly pleased: there was no love lost between those two. Stakh was well off. He had been angry at Edward for marrying Aniela, who was poor and had no dowry. He also mistreated Aniela's sister, Hela's mother Mania. Both sisters had been on non-speaking terms with Stakh for many years and now, out of the blue, he wanted to come and make amends. 'What does he want from me now?' *Gosposia* asked. Stakh was coming to stay on the Saturday and Sunday and he would naturally sleep in the back room. He was apparently very nosy and Aniela was petrified, she did not trust Edward's brother at all. We decided to leave the hut before dawn and hide in the barn under the straw. It was the end of February and bitterly cold. We dug ourselves into the straw and the hay like animals looking for a den in which to hibernate. Time stood still. In the evening Hela, after feeding the animals, secretly brought us some lukewarm water with milk and black bread. The night was unending. I could not feel my feet. We took turns getting up and moving about to keep our circulation going – after all, it was unlikely that Stakh would be snooping around the farmstead in the middle of the night.

The next morning Hela came running into the barn. She was out of breath. The German *Feldpolizei* from Kopciowka were in Staniewicze, searching for grain. Barns and stables were being searched first, and thoroughly, because the farmers' secret silos and larders were usually there. We could not stay in the barn and we could not go back to our hide-out. Nor was it possible to escape through the fields without being spotted at once on the snow. We were lost!

But *Gosposia* did not lose her head. She started an argument with her brother-in-law that degenerated into a quarrel with insults flying both ways. She threw Stakh out of her home. We could hear his angry voice, 'Go to hell, you whore!' and *Gosposia*'s, 'Get out of my house and don't ever set your foot here again!' Soon the brother-in-law had disappeared from view and *Gosposia* signalled to us to come back into the hut. But this in itself was a risky business. How could all eight of us cross the open distance between the barn and the hut without being spotted from the village or the road? We crawled from under the straw and decided to dash across one at a time, two minutes apart. It was dangerous but we had no choice – the Germans were in the village and could be here any minute. And then, a miracle occurred. It started snowing; first a few snowflakes here and there and then more and more.

Soon it was snowing hard; it was difficult to see the village. We sped towards the hut, happy to be sitting in our hide-out once more.

We anxiously followed the advance of the Soviet Army. Ukraine was almost entirely liberated, the Red Army had crossed the Dniester into Bessarabia and was about to cross the Pruth into Romania. This produced a huge bulge which included the whole of Byelorussia, but the long-awaited offensive on the Smolensk–Orsha front had not materialized. In March, an air raid was staged on the Grodno railway station by a few Soviet bombers. The damage was minimal, but we were elated. Father said that it was a prelude to a Soviet offensive on our front. It was now certain that we were not going to be liberated by the Western Allies whose armies had been hopelessly bogged down since September in southern Italy. This meant, if we survived, that Father's dream of 'a little house on Mount Carmel' was merely a pipe-dream; we would be doomed to live in the Soviet Union. Father, in his optimism, predicted the formation of a Jewish state after the war, a federation where Jews and Arabs would live in harmony, side by side. He was convinced that the British would cancel their anti-Zionist policy: the Arabs were, after all, siding with the Germans. In the papers we saw pictures of the Mufti of Jerusalem in tête-à-tête with Hitler, reviewing the Bosnian SS battalions. 'There is certainly a Jewish Palestinian Division in the British Army. This cannot be forgotten by England,' father claimed. He expected abrogation of the 'White Book' limiting Jewish immigration into Palestine and a massive Jewish immigration after the war.

Despite all that was happening around us, we could not have imagined the extent of the Holocaust. We did not expect that the Germans had behaved the same way in the West. 'The West is not Poland, the people will not stand for it,' Father said. We expected some form of intervention by the Allies soon. Mother was elated that Ukraine was liberated and that Lolya, Tamara and Grandmother could go back home. 'Where are they now? Was Lolya drafted? Did he survive?' She dreamt of joining them after the liberation. She had always considered Poland a foreign land and longed for Russia. Her nature, somewhat bohemian and passionate, was not quite at home in Poland, with its middle-class bourgeois mentality. She did not understand, nor did she care for, politics. Zionism to her was not a convincing idea. I think that if she had had her way she would have preferred to leave for America, like one of her relatives called *dyadya* [uncle] Andryusha. But, of course, we had to survive first.

22 *Spring 1944*

Winter was relinquishing its iron grip. The fields were again resonating with the voices of peasants sowing their crops. Leszko Staniewski was again singing his loud 'I prefer, I prefer, the sun, the forest and the field.' For Easter, *Gosposia* decided to slaughter the calf that was now five weeks old. After she had taken the calf away from Krasula, the poor cow kept mooing and bellowing for days on end. It was heart-wrenching to listen to her complaining and we were all dismayed by the intensity of her grieving. We had never heard such sad and strange sounds, unrelenting for days and nights. We wanted to return the calf to its mother rather than sacrifice it for meat. Ignorant city dwellers, we did not realize that animals could have such deep feelings.

At any rate, we did not have the money to buy the meat from *Gosposia*. She sold some meat on the black market and Misha bought some, but only for himself and Rozia. As we were completely 'dry', absolutely penniless, he had no choice but to pay for our dried peas, cabbage, black bread, onions and frozen potatoes, but he refused to provide for any 'luxuries'. He always claimed that, if we survived, Father would have food and shelter at once, but he would not. Father offered to pay him back after liberation when they had managed to earn some money, but Misha would not hear of it. My parents had too much pride to ask again, though I suspected that they wanted to secure some meat for me and Tolo.

The atmosphere at Easter 1944 was tense. Edward was very sick and did not leave his bed. His back was covered with bed sores. *Gosposia* was constantly in a very foul mood. She had eight Jews in her hut, without money, and an increasingly sick husband for whom Father could do very little. Where was the second front we spoke so much about? The Russians were still

450 kilometres away and apparently in no hurry to come. She dreaded the time of harvest with its back-breaking work and dangers lurking from all sides. The harmony that had existed between us all a year ago had gone completely. We were on a starvation diet provided reluctantly by Misha who, if he could have, would gladly have got rid of us altogether. We felt dependent on him and humiliated, and he did not shy away from telling us that we ate only because of his benevolence.

Under these wretched circumstances, something new occurred that caused us intense worry. Frania was crying more then usual. At first I did not pay much attention because she often cried about Ilana, but then I started to wonder: 'Why is she crying that much?' She often whispered with Mother, her voice interrupted by sobs. I thought that we should watch her constantly lest she do something to herself. Hillel, who was in love with her, tried to soothe her but to no avail. It was strange: Frania cried and everybody whispered. I observed that Father would not talk to Frania or Hillel. Mother and Father also whispered together often and Father would become all red in the face. What was making him so angry? Nobody whispered anything to me. What was going on? Finally, I understood from piecing together snatches of overheard conversations: Frania was pregnant and she wanted an abortion. After examining her, Father refused. Firstly, it was not his department, though in our tragic situation he would have considered doing it if he had had some sterile conditions and instruments. But with things as they were, Frania would probably not survive the procedure and neither would we. If *Gosposia* and Edward found out about her pregnancy and abortion, they would throw us all out or make sure the villagers 'took care' of us.

What could we do? Frania's pregnancy could remain hidden until June or July at most, by which time we could expect Aniela to throw us out. We now had a time-bomb ticking away and ready to explode. We started to plan our escape to the front for early July and tried to keep everything secret from *Gosposia*. Misha obviously had plans of his own. Without money we were only a burden to him and, although he said nothing, I knew he was planning an escape without us. Frania cried and cried, she did not want to live.

Spring 1944

The front at Orsha was not moving an inch. Were the Russians, after expelling the Germans from the Ukraine, too exhausted for a spring or summer offensive? Would the Germans surprise us with a new summer offensive and beat the overextended Russians? Our gloom was increased even more by the lamentations of Krasula, who day and night continued plaintively to call her calf. I could now see our last moments very clearly.

Someone was running through the fields towards our farmstead – an ominous sign indicating bad news from the village. It was Antek, a middle-aged man who knew the Staniewskis well. In no time we were engulfed by the darkness of our hideout. We heard agitated voices in the entrance and a few minutes later the voice of *Gosposia*.

'You must make room for Hela. The Germans are combing Yarmolitche, looking for young people for forced labour in Germany. They are searching the villages with dogs. They are turning everything upside down! They will be in Staniewicze in no time!' Petrified, Hela squeezed into the hide-out. We pushed and pushed one another, but fitting nine people in a hole planned for seven was nearly impossible. Hela had to stretch on top of our legs as *Gosposia* closed us in. We heard the rumble of potatoes falling on the lid. Complete darkness and fear invaded the shelter. Maybe the Germans knew that a 17-year-old girl qualifying for forced labour (or worse) lived here. If so, they would search the house with their damned dogs! Agonizing minutes were like hours. Our fears for the future were forgotten. We imagined the Germans approaching our farmstead with their dogs, as they had so many times before. Until now, miraculously, they had not stopped at the crossroads. The poor, lonely farmstead of Edward and Aniela did not arouse their suspicion. Would our luck still hold? Today reminded me of June 1941, the cellar, the darkness, the ever-closer explosions. Today there was silence, but the smell of death was in the air. My lips trembled out a prayer. 'Oh dear God, let us live, let them pass by!' We could hear *Gosposia* just above our heads shuffling cartons and trunks, making some last-minute changes. And then it came: a gentle tap on our ceiling to warn us, 'Stop all noise, the Germans are at the crossroads.' Some dirt fell on my head. We stopped breathing and my heart pounded like a sledgehammer. Hela's weight on my legs was unbearable. The air became thick and heavy; there was nothing to breathe. Father coughed and gasped. After what appeared an eternity, *Gosposia* opened the lid of the shelter and whispered: *'Niemcy proyekhali, nie zatrymalisya. Niech bedzie pochvalony Jezus Chrystus!'* [The Germans have passed by, they have passed by, they did not stop. Glory be to Jesus Christ!]. We remained in the hide-out for two long hours, waiting for the Germans to clear the village. They arrested several young people.

We could hardly get out of our shelter – our legs had turned to stone and our heads were spinning. Father was pale, he breathed heavily. Eventually we all crawled out, except Frania. Suddenly Mother called, 'Motek, Motek come here, Frania has passed out!' We took Frania out, laid her on my parents' bed and rubbed her gently with *samogon*. A few minutes later, Father fell on the ground after entering the vestibule to attend to his needs. He fell on his knees and passed out. When he came round, he was paper white and his forehead was covered with tiny pearls of cold sweat, just as he had been when he came back from the Gestapo. He had trouble breathing. 'It is my heart playing dirty tricks. It will be all right,' he said after resting a while on his bed.

We were all in a state of shock. I was very fearful for my father. His heart condition had worsened recently and he often breathed as if gasping for air. His eyes had sunk even more and new wrinkles had appeared, cutting deep into his cheeks; his jaw had sagged, his massive nose had become more prominent, and his remaining hair and stubble was snow-white. A terrible thought occurred to me: 'Even if we make it to freedom, he may not live long enough to see me grow into a man!' My heart ached at this thought and I kissed and kissed my dear father. I cried inside; only now had I suddenly realized how much he meant to me, how desperately I needed him.

We later speculated that when the Germans had seen the miserable farmstead with its crumbling hut from the road, they had decided not to bother. It was difficult to believe, but a miracle had happened again!

The most beautiful season was upon us once more. In the

evening, we could open the window and breathe in the air fragrant with the blossoms of lilacs, bird-cherry and honeysuckle. Sometimes Mother would hum an old Russian romance by Tchaikovsky:

Otvoril ya okno, stalo dushno nye v motch	I opened the window, it was unbearably hot.
I upal pered nim na koleni	I fell on my knees and the
A v litzo mne pakhnula vesenniaya notch	Scent of the spring night
Volshebnym zapakhom sireni	Overpowered me with lilac blossoms.
A v sadu gde to tomno zapyel solovyei...	Somewhere in the orchard the nightingale sang languorously...

The newspapers which *Gosposia* brought from Indura were dull, the central front dead. The Allies in Italy continued their turtle-like advance, covering less than 100 miles in eight months. Rome was still in German hands. 'At this rate they will reach the French border in exactly five years,' Father lamented.

Gosposia was sometimes absent from the hut and Edward became agitated, mumbling *'Zydowskaya Korowa'*, but the poor man was too weak to hop around the yard to spy on her. His friend Adolfik, whom we cursed for his long visits, came to keep him company. We could usually spot him on the road from far away and had time to prepare for the visit, but once in May he came from behind the barn, after cutting through the field, and only the explosive barking of Tsatsus saved us. Adolfik entered the front room just as Hillel was reaching the shelter – the rest of us were already inside. As we sat wondering if Adolfik had seen him, we heard *Gosposia*'s voice in the front room.

'*A golovu zavoratchivaiesh! Prisnilosya Tebye*' [You are talking nonsense! You are dreaming!].

'I swear to you by everything holy, I saw... I saw with my own eyes, I saw a big *muzhik* with a beard. He disappeared into the ground! The earth opened up and he was swallowed. A miracle! Unbelievable! I swear I saw it with my own eyes!

Maybe it was the devil!' Adolfik's voice trembled as he spoke. 'Eh, you stupid man,' *Gosposia* continued. 'You are dreaming! Did you have one too many? Go and take a good nap.'

But Adolfik would not give up and repeated, his voice still trembling, 'I swear I saw him, there is nothing wrong with me! A big *muzhik* with a beard, a red beard. The ground opened and he disappeared. It could not be the devil, could it, with a red beard?'

'You disgust me Adolfik,' jeered *Gosposia*. 'Maybe it was Saint Adolph or something?' she joked. As serious as our situation was, the scene was frankly comical and Frania, famous for her easy laughter in spite of her troubles, had to bite her handkerchief.

Adolfik, of course, had caught sight of Hillel jumping into the hide-out. We had been discovered! *Gosposia*, keeping her cool, casually came into our room and imperceptibly lowered the potatoes on to the lid. A few minutes later she asked Adolfik to come into the room to describe where and what he saw. He did not remember exactly but still insisted he had seen a bearded man enter the ground.

'Maybe you have some devil living here with you. I tell you Anielka, bring a priest and sprinkle the whole house with holy water!'

'Ah, you good for nothing,' retorted Aniela angrily, 'you think there are devils around me? Maybe you brought one with you. Eh? When was your last confession? What have you been doing lately? With whose wife have you been fooling around? Eh?'

Adolfik protested meekly, 'Anielka, I am a good Catholic. It's just I don't go to church and I like a drink or two. So what?'

'Sort yourself out, Adolfik. I tell you, go to confession quick and your hallucinations won't come back!' With these words, *Gosposia* packed Adolfik back into the front room. We had been holding our breath for nearly five minutes. Next to me, Frania was going through the double torture of stifling her laughter and controlling her bladder. It was 'laughter through tears'.

Adolfik was not as stupid as he appeared. 'He may very well come back from behind the barn once more and spy at us,' *Gosposia* said. Would he denounce us to the police for money or give us to the *soltys* – the village elder – or simply blab in the village? Our life in the hut was becoming evermore precarious.

We heightened our vigilance once again. Our infrequent ten-minute evening sorties 'behind the barn' were terminated. Only Hillel would occasionally go with *Gosposia* to 'help cut the hay' in the evening. We kept completely silent within the confines of the back room, with the curtains tightly drawn. Our faithful friend Tsatsus was attached to the front door day and night. And yet we knew that, despite all our precautions, a band of villagers might easily murder us at night whenever they wished.

Four of us were again sleeping in the hide-out. Tolo even stopped his nightly forays to the stove. *Gosposia* was at her wits' end and lashed out at us all constantly.

In the beginning of June we had direct confirmation that we were being watched. At dusk, Aniela as usual inspected around the hut and signalled to Hillel to proceed to the barn. As Hillel stepped out of the hut to cross the 30 yards to the barn, a shot rang out from a nearby patch of rye. A bullet whizzed by his head. He immediately fell to the ground and crawled towards the stable to take cover. It meant that somebody malevolent in the village knew about us. We now lived in a state of terror. At night, the slightest noise sent us hurtling into the shelter, although we knew full well the peasants would know where to find us, and how to deal with us.

A week later, Ziutek Kulikowski came running through the fields. 'Good news! good news!' he shouted. 'The Allies have landed in France! The second front is here!' We all embraced, the women cried. Was it possible that soon Germany would capitulate and we would be free? We all cheered; *Gosposia* brought in some *samogon* and sausage. We drank to the Allies and their successful landing; we passed around the AK bulletin with the wonderful sentence: 'The Allies have landed in France!' That night, sweet dreams of freedom came to us.

But the days passed, and nothing seemed to change. Some nearby villages were still being searched for meat by the German police. With the rye almost four feet high and the fields swarming with peasants, we had to sit in the hide-out for hours on end.

295

Then, one night we heard the muffled sounds of distant booming and in the eastern sky we saw a weak light, not unlike a faraway lightning storm. The horizon was faintly aglow with the purple of distant fires. Misha estimated the distance to be less than 60 kilometres. Was it possible that the front had moved that close without us knowing anything? We could not sleep; we listened for the next few days to these distant thuds of artillery – they were like the sweetest celestial melody. But then the sounds subsided and the glow on the horizon faded away. We pressed our ears to the shelter walls for hours, but in vain. *Gosposia* learned from frightened peasants that the Germans had brought several SS divisions to fight the partisans, who apparently controlled the forests east and north-east of Grodno. The battle moved east towards Lida, Novogrodek and Wilno as the embattled partisans retreated deeper and deeper into the forests before the overwhelming fire-power of the SS.

We were already three weeks into the second front yet the German newspaper scraps brought by *Gosposia* claimed complete containment of the Allied beachheads in Normandy and gigantic losses suffered by the Allies. We were afraid that the landing in France might end as tragically as Dunkirk, Dieppe or Narwik. The third anniversary of the German attack on the Soviet Union, 22 June, was upon us. The eastern front was still on the Orsha–Vitebsk line, more than 400 kilometres away after almost a year, and it was still not moving. We knew that the day of liberation was approaching, but we also knew that we were more vulnerable than ever, increasingly at the mercy of a denouncer or a mob of villagers. Frania was entering the fourth month of her secret pregnancy and Edward was dying. We had no money to buy ourselves out of even the slightest danger. The time-bombs were ticking.

23   The Red Army

It was the last week of June. For three years we had been
under German rule, three years ago Nadia was killed, I was
wounded and our house destroyed. While preparing for sleep,
Misha picked up a faint sound in the hide-out. We all pressed
our ears to the ground; it was like the muffled rumble of a
very, very distant train, or the distant stampede of herds of
large animals. It was so faint, and kept coming and going,
coming and going. Was this the long-awaited Red Army offensive on our front? We wanted it so much! We had prayed for
it so hard! Or was it a figment of our overexcited imagination?
We listened deep into the night. We pressed our ears to the
clay ground, observed the dark eastern sky. The sounds were
audible only in the shelter, persisting for hours until dawn.

In the morning we opened our eyes to the drone of motors.
Formations of German Junkers transport planes were flying
east, low over the village, filling the air with their rumbling.
Planes with red crosses painted across the fuselage were also
flying low in the same direction. We wanted so fervently to
believe that the long-awaited Russian offensive had finally
started. Father and Misha theorized that last-night's sound
could have been an artillery barrage of unprecedented power,
which we had picked up in the hide-out, some four hundred
kilometres away. They were right.[1]

For the next two days and nights we could not hear
anything, but the days were filled with intense air activity:
German planes in neat formations were heading eastward.
Where were the Russian planes? Why weren't they bombing
Grodno with its railroad bridge and military depots? We

---

[1] Ten thousand Russian guns and mortars, packed to 320 guns per mile,
were raining thousands of shells a minute for many hours at a stretch at
the central sector of the front.

297

feared deep inside that it was not a Soviet but a new German offensive. According to *Gosposia*, all kinds of wild rumours were circulating: a Russian offensive had put the Germans to flight, a German offensive was in the making. Instinctively feeling the long-awaited front approaching, our hopes swelled with every passing day.

At the same time, we feared the front might stop short of us. Our situation was rapidly becoming desperate: we were running out of food. We only had two slices of black bread, an onion and some frozen potatoes. We cooked them unpeeled to preserve the nutrients. *Gosposia* kept every bit of lard and scrap of meat for the rapidly approaching harvest season – the wheat and rye were almost man-high. Krasula was not well, not giving any milk, and *Gosposia* was thinking of slaughtering her for meat. Edward was very sick, he had a constant fever. There was no medicine anywhere. Frania's pregnancy would soon be visible. Where would the front line be when we would have to abandon ship?

In the first week of July, *Gosposia* went to Indura. We could hardly wait for the 'wrapping' papers. The war news was from the last week of June. We could not believe our eyes: Mogilev had been captured, Bobrouisk surrounded, heavy fighting had raged around Minsk. The Red Army had reached the pre-1939 Polish–Russian border. *Gosposia* claimed that people who had come from Grodno were saying that the city was swarming with German troops, the military hospitals were full to overflowing and trains with wounded German soldiers were now heading west into East Prussia. It was plain that in barely one week's time the Red Army had advanced some 200 kilometres and the central front – our front! – was crumbling. 'God,' we prayed, 'don't let this sweep stop short of us.' We feared the Germans would make a stand on the eastern side of the Niemen, and we were on its western bank!

In the west, the Allies were bogged down around Caen in Normandy; the beachhead was making little progress. But our eyes looked to the east. I had a lump in my throat and tears in my eyes imagining the grey lines of our liberators: simple peasants from Russia's plains or from the steppes of central Asia pursuing the Aryan 'supermen' in their flight. These were now my heroes, my liberators, the creators of a new world in which everybody would be entitled to live and grow. I saw Danyousha's finely chiselled face, I could still hear him addressing Mother, 'Tatyana Pavlovna, you'll see, our boys will not surrender. They'll beat the fascist swine, they will liberate us!' Maybe Danya's father was among those grey lines fighting the *Uebermenschen*, maybe he wanted to reach Grodno to rescue his son. Did he know that Danya had been murdered along with all the Jews of Grodno? How would we feel going back to our city, to Grodno, where every stone would remind us of a disappeared beloved relative or friend?

In the evening we sat again with our ears to the ground or straining our eyes to catch a glimmer of faraway artillery flashes or distant fires on the eastern horizon. In vain, but as the days passed the air activity increased: in addition to big Junkers transport planes, tight formations of Heinkels bombers were bound eastward. The Germans still had control of the air.

And then one day there was a distant rumble of heavy guns. *Gosposia* came from the village with great news: all the roads were blocked by the fleeing Germans, ambulances, trucks, self-propelled artillery, military vehicles of all sorts. Unshaven soldiers in ragged uniforms, with bloody dressings around their heads or limbs, filled the roads, in vehicles, on horse-drawn carts or on foot, in an unending procession. They were streaming west, faster, faster, terrified of falling into the hands of the advancing Russians or, worse still, the partisans. They all knew what they had done during their three years in Russia and they knew retribution was at hand. The peasants were laughing: 'Look at these "supermen", they flee with their underpants barely on!'

As dusk approached Mania came running: Ziutek had been ordered to join his AK unit to attack the fleeing Germans; he had no military training, he would be killed! We tried to calm her down. She told us that the Russians had already taken Wilno. In the evening we ventured cautiously outside, behind the barn, to hear the distant rumbling of artillery and to observe the eastern sky. It was a typical July night with all its head-turning scents. A slight breeze cooling off the heat of the day rustled in the trees and gently swayed the tall stalks of rye. And though the evening sky was perfectly clear, one could now and then hear dull noises like distant thunder. With our ears pressed to the ground in the hide-out we could distinctly feel the earth quiver. The eastern horizon had a weak glow and now and then we could see flares far beyond the Niemen, where the almost imperceptible grey line of forests met the sky. Our hearts were elated: where the flares went up to the sky, not that far away, there our freedom lay.

The retreating Germans, however, would kill us if they found us. Wouldn't it be a supreme irony to die when our liberation was so near? But we were now a happy bunch. Frania had stopped crying, Father ceaselessly repeated *'Dozhdalis! Dozhdalis!'* [At long last! At long last!], and Mother was crying, from happiness I supposed. Only Edward, weak and in pain, was made gloomy by the sight of those 'Antichrists', as he called the Soviets, arriving, even as liberators. He had hoped to see all of Poland liberated by the Western Allies, who were still bogged down in Normandy over 1,500 kilometres away.

After two days of hearing the roll of artillery and the thunder of distant explosions, *Gosposia* returned from the village claiming that the Russians had already reached the eastern bank of the Niemen. We now dreaded the Soviet offensive stalling there. However, in the evening, strong artillery fire came from the south and later from the south-west. Father argued accurately that the Russians had again seized the initiative and probably crossed the Niemen at the bridge at Lunna some 25 kilometres south of us. The night sky was lit up by red and yellow flares shooting upwards. The sound of artillery was now joined by a distinct staccato of machine-gun and even rifle fire. At times, a hollow-sounding crash tore the air of the night. Misha, the Polish Army reserve officer, claimed that mortar shells with their deadly shrapnel were exploding only a short distance away. At long last the front was here! The rumble of planes was overhead. To whom they belonged and where they were heading for was difficult to see at night, but the red glow of distant fires extended now to the northern and north-eastern sky. Grodno was being bombed by waves of Russian planes. We were spellbound, entranced, huddled behind the barn, watching and listening, listening to this 'sweetest sound'. The scent of freedom turned our heads and made us forget the ever-present danger: the Germans were still here.

After a sleepless night full of the rumblings of battle, the morning was unusually quiet. *Gosposia* sent Hela to the village for news. Hela returned running through the fields and emerged from a patch of rye out of breath. 'The Bolsheviks are in the village,' she shouted, 'Russians on horses! I saw them, they are definitely not Germans! They were wearing *roubakhas* and green caps. The ones on horses had round Cossack hats and black capes. I am sure they are Russians!'

We nearly ran through the field to greet our liberators, but explosions began to shake the farmstead. 'Oh-o, that one landed close!' Misha exclaimed. 'Stay put! What if the Germans counter-attack? We will be caught and executed! We must stay here, it would be a pity to die now.' We decided to stay hidden until the front line was solidly a few kilometres to the west. It was Sunday, 16 July 1944.

Some time later we saw brown-green torsos with heads and military hats floating above the tall growth lining the road. They must be the Russians advancing on horses! We took cover in the hide-out, but to sit in the shelter was emotionally impossible. Father repeated as if in a daze, *'dozhdalis, dozhdalis!'*, the women sobbed and my heart was racing with excitement in anticipation of freedom. I could not believe it: I had survived! I had survived with Father, Mother and Tolo. All four of us! My prayers had been heard and the miracle had happened – the Russians were in the village.

The Germans were still very close and the sound of battle was now unrelenting. Then *Gosposia* spoke urgently: 'They are coming here, they are coming here! Helka go into the hide-out!' Hela joined us in the shelter as we sat listening intently. The Russians were attracted by our isolated location. We soon heard the sound of hooves, the neighing of horses and then a loud voice in Russian, 'Tell us little mother, how many people live with you on this farmstead? We want to billet our detachment here for a few days.' We could not remain cooped up in the stinking dark hole of the shelter. We burst out like a cork from a bottle of champagne. We crawled out one by one. *'Tovarishchi osvoboditeli, milyie moi, my vas zhdali stolko let, stolko let!'* [Comrades, our saviours, our dear liberators, we have waited for you so many years, so many years!] Mother was crying. 'So much blood, so much blood!' she sobbed.

In the door stood a very tall man in a muddy brown-green uniform. He was young, maybe Tolo's age, with blond hair falling over his eyes, his face was sunburned and dusty. A bundle of maps was tucked into a leather haversack dangling from his hip and there was an open holster attached to his belt. He looked at us with utter, undisguised amazement: people crawling out from beneath the earth. He took a step back but already two other Russians were in the door, both shorter than the blond giant. One of them wore a German belt with the *Gott mit Uns* buckle. The older of the two had on his shoulders a blue-grey leather cape, such as worn by high-ranking German officers. First taken aback, I was reassured by the sight of his Soviet army cap with a visor and a red star. Mother, Frania and Rozia were scrambling to kiss the dusty boots of the soldiers, whose bewildered faces betrayed their emotion. Father, Tolo, Hillel and myself, after the first moments of stupor, also kissed and hugged our liberators.

'Comrade liberators, we have waited for you for so many years, Oh, how long we have waited for you!' We were now all sobbing out of control – even Father. It seemed to me that tears glistened in the eyes of these battle-hardened men. The shorter one, probably the commander, asked 'How have you survived here in this hole for so long? How?'

We did not mind a few explosions rocking the hut and outside the noise of battle intensifying. The day was beautiful, not a cloud in the sky, and a breeze cooled the heat of midday. I hesitated at the door: Should I go out? My heart pounded. A voice spoke to me: 'Alik, you are free, nobody will pay any attention to you, you have made it! Made it!' I stepped into the sunshine. So much light, so much brightness! It hit me in the eyes and I squinted. Another voice said: 'Don't go out in full sunshine, Alik, are you crazy?' Fear clutched me by the throat and I recoiled into the darkness of the vestibule. Tsatsus was barking furiously at the soldiers in the yard. Slowly, uncertainly, like a drunk, I stumbled out onto the path towards the road. I stopped behind the barn, afraid to go any further, at the very place I used to crawl to for cover at nightfall to watch the road. Soldiers in dusty, shabby uniforms were busy bivouacking. Some were tethering their horses, a few were already cranking water at the well. Others were looking for fodder and trying to open the stable. It was a motley crowd. I saw Prussian officers' hats, some German riding boots, a German tunic and many German belts with the credo *Gott mit Uns* proudly displayed around the soldiers' waists. Most wore the tall, round red-topped *papakha* hats and black capes of the Cossacks.

I did not pay much attention to them and started to run with outstretched arms into the nearest patch of rye. The whole world swirled around me. The ears pregnant with grain whipped my face. I fell to the ground and kissed the earth, so generous and so gentle. I wanted to shout my joy to the world: 'I have survived! I am free!' I still could not comprehend that I was in the open, in full daylight, stretched out in this patch of rye, looking at the blue of the sky and the swaying stalks filtering the warm sunshine. I am free! Free! I had to pinch my hand to convince myself that I was not dreaming.

I do not know how long I spent in this trance-like state, but I was awakened by frenzied screaming coming from the hut. Hela jumped out of the back-room window and ran for cover in the rye. A few moments later, a Russian with a drawn revolver jumped after her. Suddenly, two planes with black crosses on their wings swooped low above the horizon and passed over, almost touching the thatched roofs of the barn. They filled the air with their drone. The soldiers took cover. The officer who was chasing Hela did the same. This gave her a break and she disappeared into the rye.

I returned to the hut; where Mother, petrified, was looking for me. Everybody was on edge, *Gosposia* was crying, upset about Hela. The Russian, a second lieutenant, had apparently dragged Hela to the attic to rape her. Hela had kicked him in the crotch so hard that he had let go of her, only to run after her with his gun drawn. The man was drunk. The commander of the detachment, the officer who met us in the back room, apologized, embarrassed. The Russians were under strict orders to behave decently to the Polish population, which was considered friendly.

In the meantime the bombardment of the village intensi-fied, shrapnel was exploding all over Staniewicze. Scared peasants were running out of their huts and some were crossing through the field towards the farmstead. A man approaching our hut was yelling, 'We have wounded people in the village, children are wounded, we need a doctor! Doctor Blumstein please come out!' How did he know that Doctor Blumstein was hiding in Aniela's hut? Father immediately walked out to meet the man. Though helpless – he had no gauze or antiseptic, no medicine and no instruments – Father left with the peasant. As they set out, an artillery barrage exploded in the direction of Zaniewicze. First a few bursts and then a continuous barrage of explosions shook the earth. The barrage was some four kilometres away but, flattened on the ground, we could hear the howling of shells flying over our heads. We were right on the battle-line which ran somewhere along the Swislocz River. On its northern bank were the Germans, Indura still in their hands. It was awful to think the Germans could counter-attack and come back to kill us.

The Russians were going quietly about their business. The blond giant seeing our frightened faces, said to us, 'Don't be scared, this is our artillery.' And pointing his chin to the sky where a renewed howling of shells tore the air, he added with a grin, 'It's time for the Fritzes to get a good afternoon snack.' The barrage lasted half an hour and was followed by a furious crackle of machine-gun and rifle fire in the direction of Zukiewicze. We tried in vain to make out who was pursuing whom and where, all the while praying the Germans would not come back. The Russians appeared unconcerned; a few were eating their lunch of black bread and some heavenly smelling canned pork from the USA, called in Russian *Svinaia Toushonka*. They were drinking from canteens and I could smell vodka.

All these emotions – fear, joy of freedom and happiness – had made me forget about food and my constant hunger pangs, but now I was ravenous. In the hut Edward, overcoming his pain, was hopping on his crutches, afraid the 'Bolsheviks' would rob him of all his belongings. A big sack with potatoes harvested before last-year's early frosts stood in the room. Frania and Rozia were peeling them. Kostik, the blond giant, was opening a can of American pork with a bayonet and greasing a big frying pan while Mitya, the commander, was lighting a fire in the stove. Soon a delicious smell of fried potatoes spread around the house and made my mouth water. Dead drunk on my parents bed, stretched out like a corpse, snored the second lieutenant who a short while ago had set out to rape Hela. Misha, Hillel and Mother were talking with our two warriors-turned-cooks. It was reassuring with all this din of battle to see their lack of concern.

The sky suddenly turned dark and sprinkles of rain fell. The *isba* was hot, but cosy with a crackling fire, the wonderful smell of fried lard and potatoes and those friendly uniforms. I still could not believe that I was free and not dreaming. While *Starshina* [Sergeant] Kostik handled the frying pan, First Lieutenant Mitya put on the table two loaves of German pumpernickel bread neatly wrapped in silver foil, such as I had seen at the *pastorat* many years ago, the open tin of American canned pork, a bottle of French champagne and a bar of German chocolate!

Mitya explained that his detachment always operated behind German lines. Their task, in addition to scouting, was to interrupt German supplies and spread panic in the rear of the enemy. That very morning they had ambushed a car with German officers near Indura.

'They were some important Fritzes,' said Mitya, showing us three pairs of silver epaulets, 'one major and two lieutenants. And these are our trophies,' he exclaimed, pointing to the victuals and opening a multicoloured box of silver-wrapped German cigarettes. 'For every day behind German lines, we get a day of rest,' Kostik intervened. 'Now we are at rest.'

This was a funny rest, I thought, under enemy fire, but what was frightening to us was 'rest' for these daredevils. Kostya was barely 22 and Mitya 25 at most. They had been on the front lines for over two years. Kostya had been wounded seven times, several times severely, and he had spent a total of six months in various military hospitals. Mitya had also been wounded several times, he showed us a big scar on the right side of his torso. 'I got this at Stalingrad,' he said, 'I did not think I would pull through, they had left me for dead, but after two months at the hospital I recovered. Here is another bad one,' he pointed to a scar on his left shoulder. 'I still can't move my left arm very well.'

The giant Kostik removed the frying pan from the stove

and, using a big spoon, carefully piled the deliciously fragrant lard and crisped potatoes into a deep wooden bowl supplied by *Gosposia*. He now in turn removed his shirt displaying several scars on his torso. 'Not too bad, mainly splinters and ricochets from artillery fire. This, for example, is not much – *tchepoukha*,' he said, showing us two small scars on either side of his left bicep. 'It went in here and came out here, a clean rifle shot by a sniper, didn't touch the bone. It could have killed me on the spot if the Fritz had aimed more carefully. But this one was bad,' he showed an ugly scar on his right calf, 'a bayonet wound from a dying Fritz. It touched the bone and was badly infected. I spent many weeks at the hospital before I could walk again.'

For these men facing death every day, such moments behind friendly lines were compensation for a difficult and dangerous job. They had been on the heels of the retreating Germans for over two weeks. 'It is good to have horses,' joked Mitya, 'those bastards run so fast we could never catch up with them on foot!'

We all sat around the table, even Edward somehow managed to sit, helping himself with the crutch. We ate the marvellous crisp potatoes with lard, black bread and German pumpernickel, and drank *samogon* and French champagne, which I found unpalatable. The *samogon* sent me spluttering and coughing out of the room. When I came back, still red in the face, Lieutenant Mitya jokingly asked, 'What kind of a man are you, Sasha? In Russia this stuff is fed to babies and you, a big boy, are making such a show!' I took an instant liking to Mitya; there was something very warm and very human about him. I munched with delight on slices of black bread thickly spread with the famous capitalist American canned pork. I savoured the rich, creamy, fragrant spread with the delicious meat in it. It was absolutely heavenly! Heavenly also was the silver-wrapped German chocolate, a taste I had almost forgotten. After the feast we all sat next to the fire, on which a large cast-iron basin full of water had been placed. Kostik and Mitya were very mellow, they showed us photographs of their families. Mitya was an engineer, he had graduated from a VTUZ (Technical University) in 1941 and had only recently married. He had no children. Kostik proudly took out a photograph of his sweetheart, a typical Soviet beauty, blond hair, beret and all. He then produced a harmonica and struck up a sad Russian melody. He played well and soon Lieutenant Mitya joined him, singing a song about a girl whose black eyes were full of tears as she sent off her beloved on a long journey, to the front. It was unreal; only this morning we had been hidden in our 'grave' and now we were free and singing.

Dievoushka stoyala moltcha na vogzale,	The girl stood silent at the station,
Na glazakh navisla kroupnaia slyeza.	Big tears glistened in her eyes.
Vidno v pout dalekii drouga provozhali,	On a faraway journey they were seeing off her beloved,
Tchernyie ryesnitsy, tchernyie glaza.	These beautiful black eyes.

Some soldiers bivouacking near the window joined in and the sad melody was soon carried by a multitude of young voices. It flew over the thatched roof of our hut towards the German lines.

The water in the basin was hot and filling the room with steam. Kostik took off his military *roubakha* and added some cold water from a bucket nearby. Mitya sat on my parents' bed where, still drunk to oblivion, insensitive to all commotion, snored the would-be rapist. We could hear soldiers pulling some heavy object and installing it in position not far from the back window. The object, which turned out to be a mortar, produced a crashing sound every few minutes. With the approaching evening, the cannonade slowly died down.

Lieutenant Mitya signalled me to sit next to him; his face became very serious. 'Sasha,' he said, 'you have been through a dreadful time, you have seen far too much in your short life. This should never have happened.' He sighed. 'In my two years at the front I saw nothing but *smyert da slyezy* [death and tears]. We are fighting the biggest scourge mankind ever produced, we are fighting to liberate the world once and for all from Fascism. I do not hate the Germans,' he continued, 'there are also decent people among the Fritzes, but they are trapped. I know what you have been through, but you should not hate blindly. It is now over for you: you will resume your school, you will become a good *Komsomol* and a useful Soviet citizen.' He patted my hair. Looking at his hardened face and at his understanding eyes, the officer's cap pushed back on his head, brown curls under the visor, I felt gratitude and admiration towards this man who came here all the way from Stalingrad to reclaim my life for me and to tell me these few simple words. A generous heart was beating under his battered uniform. Suddenly a dreadful thought took hold of me: he could be killed any time; the road to Berlin was still long. I wanted to express to him all that I felt for those simple Soviet soldiers who were giving their lives so that I might live, and I kissed him on both cheeks like a brother.

The door opened and Father appeared. With him was a tall officer, undoubtedly of higher rank, since Lieutenant Mitya saluted him first. The officer shook hands with all of us.

'Major Khaikin,' he introduced himself and, not hiding his emotion, asked us, 'Show me, *grazhdane* [citizens], how you survived.' Khaikin, with a very Jewish-sounding name, was at least in his early forties, with salt-and-pepper hair. He inspected our hide-out on the outside, then crawled in and out. 'You have lived here, the eight of you, for a year and a half, in this grave?' He shook his head in disbelief. 'Are you the only survivors of the Jews of Grodno? What are they doing to our people, these beasts?'

Mother and Frania started to cry and, for a moment, it seemed to me that Major Khaikin was fighting back the tears when Mother spoke to him in Yiddish, sobbing, 'Where is our Eili, how did He let it happen?'

'Yes,' he said, 'it happened, it happened . . . I know only too well. This is the first time since our advance that I have heard *mame loshen* [Mother 'speak' in Yiddish].' The major tried in vain to hide his emotion. His lips suddenly twitched and he wept, covering his face. We learned later from Father that the Germans had killed his parents in a mass execution of Jews in Gomel. My father then showed him his notes, 'Unprecedented Crimes Against the Jewish Population of Grodno'. I will soon be on leave in Moscow,' he said. 'If it's alright with you, I can give this to the Jewish Anti-fascist Committee, which will certainly make good use of it.' Father agreed.

Khaikin warned us that German resistance in the north-western direction of Byalystok had stiffened. 'We are now very close to East Prussia and the Germans have got considerable reinforcements. The Vorstadt of Grodno is still German and the west bank of the Niemen north of Swislocz is still in German hands. The Germans have retrenched only six kilometres from here.' He pulled out a map of the area from a leather case. 'Look here. They are retrenched at Prokopowicze and Kopciowka and on a strategically located hill. Our supply lines are stretched, our heavy artillery, *Katioushas* and armour have not yet arrived. We might have to wait several days for heavy equipment before we can throw them out of their hilltop positions. You are exposed here to a German counterattack. I advise you to evacuate at least 20 kilometres from the front, behind the Niemen if possible. The Germans will shoot you on the spot if you are denounced. The Wehrmacht and the SS work hand-in-hand as far as Jews and Communists are concerned. I will help you evacuate as soon as I am deployed at Laniewicze. I always have many empty trucks leaving the front line, it won't be a problem. Give me 24 hours before you come.'

Lieutenant Mitya intervened. '*Tovarishtch* major, don't worry. Our mounted detachment is bivouacking here until new orders arrive. Should something happen, we shall take all of them with us on our horses. We will not abandon them to the Fritzes! You have my word on it!' I could have hugged Mitya again for these reassuring words, but I almost laughed imagining Mother on a Cossack's horse. Khaikin left visibly shaken. We all saw him out. He stepped into an American jeep and soon disappeared in a cloud of dust.

Father had met Major Khaikin in the village while trying to take care of the wounded peasants. Khaikin, who commanded a front supply unit passing through the village, was to take position further south, in Laniewicze. He supplied Father with first-aid materials. Father was very tired, after caring for the wounded in the village. At least ten people had been injured mainly by shrapnel, most not seriously. They were lucky that Khaikin's front supply unit had been moving through Staniewicze at the time. Hearing Father's name,

Khaikin had become very interested and drove Father back to the farmstead in his jeep so he could visit the first surviving Jews he had met since the start of the offensive.

We all walked slowly towards the main road. It was the first time I had ventured that far. Beyond the barn, I instinctively wanted to turn back, but I told myself, 'Alik, you are free. You can walk into Staniewicze if you want to and nobody will dare harm you. You are free!'

We turned back at the crossroads. The sky had cleared after the rain and the horizon was all purple in the west, promising another hot and sunny day. Fires were blazing in Zaniewicze, and further north and north-west in the direction of Grodno the evening sky was faintly aglow. Grodno must be burning, concluded Father. Back at the farmstead, Lieutenant Mitya was busy giving orders. Horses were being tethered, sentries were posted and trenches dug. Some distance from the barn a heavy machine gun was being installed in a trench by two soldiers, with its muzzle pointing towards the main road. Men were scattering into the barn and stable to get some sleep.

'Do you expect the Germans to come back?' Mother asked fearfully.

'No,' answered Mitya, 'but we are taking no chances.' The mood in the *isba* was gloomy. Hela was still hiding, probably at her mother's in the village. *Gosposia* was very upset about having 25 men sleeping and roaming around the property. Edward was edgy and in pain; he groaned on his bed as Father prepared to give him an injection.

I was a free human being, guarded by a detachment of battle-hardened Cossacks who had promised to take us out of any German encirclement. I slept well despite the sporadic noise of battle. It must have been music to my ears – I must have smiled in my sleep.

I woke up early, at dawn. The noise was intense, the guns deployed around the village firing furiously. My eyes still glued by sleep, I remembered the happy events of the previous day. I still did not believe that I was free, that I was not going to die. The crushing sound of the mortar installed close to the window got us up in panic. It now fired at frequent intervals. Guns from all sides rained fire on the entrenched Germans. During the night, the Soviets had deployed quite a number of field guns around the village. We all dressed hastily, not knowing where to hide now. Should we go back into the hide-out or remain flattened on the floor?

The cannonade slackened eventually and I peeked outside with Father. The sentries were in their foxholes. Behind the barn stood Lieutenant Mitya, training his binoculars in the direction of the Swislocz River and beyond it to the villages where the retrenched Germans had just got a thorough peppering. Indeed, we could see with the naked eye a cloud of haze covering the horizon in this direction. *'Zdravstvuitye,'* Mitya greeted us. 'This is the Fritzes' breakfast,' he said, pointing to the cloud. I was fascinated and intensely happy to see all this hail of fire raining on the heads of the hated enemy. All the field guns firing around the village made me nervous, but I was surprised at how 'calm' I was now, compared with the terror I had felt during the dreadful bombardment on the 22 June 1941. True, I was only 11 then and on the receiving end, while now it was mainly the Russian guns that were firing; yet I was discovering joy, pure joy, to think that at that very moment some German *Übermenschen* were dying on that hill beyond the Swislocz.

The guns fell silent some time later and a relative quiet descended, interrupted only by a distant thunder of artillery and a faint staccato of machine-gun fire. We guessed what that relative quiet meant. It meant that at that very moment, waves of brown-grey coated soldiers – men from Russia, central Asia and Siberia – were advancing with fixed bayonets on the entrenched Germans. I knew from Father that there was no armour support and that yesterday such an attack had been unsuccessful, resulting in heavy casualties. I looked at the face of Lieutenant Mitya who peered intensely through his binoculars. He was distressed.

'Madness, sheer madness,' he exploded.

'What has happened?' Father asked.

'Nothing,' Mitya answered gruffly, putting the binoculars back into their case. He went quickly away.

We hastily ate our breakfast of black bread and *bavarka* to the sound of reappearing German planes. Bombs were dropped on neighbouring villages. The earth shook and we stayed flattened on the floor. The soldiers, scattered about the farmstead, were taking pot shots at the planes. No Russian planes were in sight. We had hardly had time to swallow our breakfast when the guns around Staniewicze and other neighbouring villages opened up again with fury. A new concentric barrage on the Swislocz position was in the making. Mitya was now swearing. *'Sumashetstviye!'* [madness!], he shouted. He could not contain his anger at continuing attacks on the strongly entrenched German position without armour and support from heavy artillery or aviation. The whole morning passed this way. Three times the Russians tried to dislodge the Germans, three times they were left reeling with considerable casualties. The villages were full of wounded soldiers. There was a field hospital in Laniewicze, where Khaikin had installed his field supply base. He sent a jeep for Father whom he had 'drafted' to help with the wounded soldiers. They were arriving in droves and the military medics were overwhelmed. The major was irritated: the attack on Swislocz had been a failure, an unnecessary slaughter. They should have waited for tanks, heavy artillery and *Katiousha* cannons before trying to make further progress. It was clear that the Germans were determined to hold back the Soviet advance on East Prussia.

The guns fell completely silent as the sun stood at its zenith. The soldiers were now dispersed around the hut, some clustered in the shade of trees for a measure of relief from the midday heat. Then suddenly I heard *Gosposia*'s voice raised to its highest pitch and saw her waving her fist at some soldiers, shouting furiously in Polish and Byelorussian. *'Zlodzieje! Vory, Vory!'* [Thieves, thieves!] First you try to rape my girl, and now you kill our livestock and steal our food! What kind of liberators are you? What kind of friends are you? Plunderers and swine, that's what you are!' She was red in the face, yelling and cursing boldly.

I feared that such insults might spell trouble for her. Lieutenant Mitya listened in silence. He ordered the three soldiers, whom *Gosposia* pointed out with her finger, to step forward and said, '*Matushka*, you are very fresh, you call my soldiers thieves and swine. They brought you life. I am sure you are wrong, but I forgive you for your foul mouth.'

He ordered the three men to empty their haversacks. The soldiers protested, but upon the lieutenant's insistence obeyed the order. One of them had a dead chicken and a number of dry sausages. The other two had nothing. Lieutenant Mitya went red in the face.

'Is this your sausage and your chicken?' he asked Aniela.

'Yes,' she replied. 'He killed the chicken and he broke into my larder!'

Mitya ordered the soldier to be disarmed and arrested. He ordered him to be taken behind the barn and barked, 'For plunder it's the death sentence; shoot him!'

I could not believe my ears. He was ordering a man's execution for a piece of sausage! The lieutenant ordered two soldiers to dig a grave for the prisoner. He repeated angrily: 'In the Red Army there is only one punishment for pillaging and plundering: *rasstryel* [to be shot.]' The soldier was trembling, he tried to say something but was led behind the barn by two other soldiers with fixed bayonets, where in the sweltering heat of the afternoon two more soldiers had started digging his grave. We were appalled. In a few minutes a man would be executed for no good reason. Mother begged Lieutenant Mitya: '*Tovarishtch starshyi leitenant, milenkii* [Dear comrade lieutenant], please pardon him. He might have been hungry, he is not a robber. For God's sake, don't take his life!'

Now that Aniela had also realized what was going on, she changed her mind and pleaded with the lieutenant to pardon the soldier, but Mitya was unswerving. When the hole was of sufficient size, Mitya ordered the unfortunate to approach his grave and get on his knees. He pulled out his *Nagan* pistol from his holster. The man was on his knees, sobbing and begging for mercy, as the lieutenant brought the pistol to his temple. The soldiers watched in stony silence. Mitya, my hero, was a murderer! I almost hated him as I ran back into the hut, plugging my ears, afraid to witness this awful execution. Mother, and all the women with the exception of *Gosposia*, were in the hut. Then I heard Hillel's voice from outside, 'He has not been shot, he is free!' At the last moment, instead of pulling the trigger, Mitya had grabbed the man by his collar, shouting that the next time he would be mercilessly shot and so would any soldier engaging in plunder.

Shaken by this unpleasant experience, we stayed inside the

hut all afternoon. The drone of oncoming bombers returned. They were coming low and we just had time to flatten ourselves on the floor when the bombs fell on Staniewicze. The earth shook but our open windows were spared. The Germans from behind the Swislocz now opened fire on the Russian positions. It was mostly mortar fire. The shells exploded with a frightening sound, peppering the thatched roofs and the walls of *isbas* with shrapnel.

'It looks like a German counter-attack,' Misha said. 'We had better be ready to leave with our Cossacks.' Encouraged by their morning successes, the Germans had indeed attempted a counter-attack. They succeeded in throwing the Russians back behind the Swislocz River, but were unable to cross it. And as the disc of the July sun moved towards the west, the situation was tense.

Father came back around 5 p.m., saying that he had arranged with Major Khaikin for our evacuation 25 kilometres from the front, to Lunna. He said we might stay there with our former cook Liuba and her husband, Alexander, who lived in a village a few kilometres from Lunna on the eastern side of the Niemen. Father said we should all leave immediately on foot for the *Polyevaya Basa* (field base) at Laniewicze. If we got there early enough, Major Khaikin could arrange to send us in an empty truck to Lunna before evening. Lieutenant Mitya agreed; it was safer for us to leave. As a farewell present, he gave us a *pepesha* sub-machine gun with a disc charger. 'Take it, you may need it to protect yourselves from marauding Fascists. Farewell and good luck,' he said, handing the weapon to Hillel. We rapidly kissed Aniela and Edward good-bye, packed a few necessities and set out for Laniewicze.

We walked in single file at least 20 feet apart, trying to keep our heads low and hiding behind the rye. The sun was low, its oblique rays making the crops appear pure gold. It was still very hot. When I reached the main road, I turned my head to see the three thatched roofs of the little farmstead where I had been captive for over a year and a half. I saw the bivouacking soldiers and horses scattered around the yard, and Aniela waving her hand in farewell. I turned on to the road to the village of Staniewicze and the farmstead disappeared behind the swaying rye.

The Red Army

We walked, Hillel in front with his *pepesha* and Misha last in line. It was still hard for me to believe that I was marching along the very road that we had scrutinized with such fear for so long. I still had the impression of dreaming. We reached Staniewicze and turned a sharp right eastward towards Laniewicze, where the *Polyevaya Basa* was located. We still had to cover some four kilometres, almost an hour of brisk walking. We walked along a gully bordering the dirt road. Even though the stretches of rye and wheat along the road were interrupted by fields of potatoes, where we had to bend even more to remain unseen, the gully protected us to some extent. Mortar shells were landing to the right and left of us. It was very frightening, but they were actually exploding quite far away and we were not in danger. As we approached Laniewicze, we were already out of the range of German mortars.

We were now in the village, running along the main street. Military trucks were moving towards the field base which was located in a pine forest at some distance from the village. A great many trucks were camouflaged in the forest. Tents put up under camouflage canvases were also dispersed among the pines. At the entrance to the base Father told the sentry we were to see Major Khaikin. The sentry looked with suspicion at Hillel with his *pepesha* hanging from his shoulder, but let us inside. Khaikin told us that an empty truck would be going to Lunna in an hour. In the meantime, we stretched out in a meadow near the entrance to the base. Big boxes were being unloaded from the trucks and camouflaged in the forest under large canvasses. Misha pointed out that the trucks were all American, big Studebakers and GMCs. From time to time a German shell landed in the vicinity. German planes flew quite high overhead in an easterly direction and soon afterwards we heard the dull rumble of explosions. The anti-aircraft guns around the base opened up. The air was filled with crashing noises and acrid smells, but no bombs fell on the *basa*. Where were the Russian planes? Why did we only see German planes? We became increasingly weary of waiting for the empty truck and our fear of a German counter-attack returned.

An empty truck finally approached, an open Studebaker with a canvas top. The driver, a burly, red-faced fellow, was

315

leaning out from his cab, screaming *'Anuka zadavay!'* [Move it!]. He was obviously inebriated, his eyes were bloodshot and he stank of alcohol.

'How are we going to get anywhere with such a chauffeur? He needs to have a good nap before driving anywhere,' said Father to us in Polish, while asking the driver in Russian, 'Where are you going?'

'Lunna,' said the driver, and we could smell the alcohol ten feet away.

'Do you know how to get there?' asked Father.

'Of course I know! Move it!' answered the driver angrily and stepped on the accelerator. A strong jerk, a jolt and the truck lurched forward. Father and Misha had to jump to get into the back and we helped them scramble inside. The truck shook on the bumpy dirt road, the engine raced and the brakes squealed. We were underway, but it was obvious that the truck was leading the driver. We reached some crossroads and turned north towards the village of Balicze and the Swislocz, instead of turning south towards Kaleniki and Lunna. We were going straight for the German lines! To our left we could see the sun low on the horizon beyond the Swislocz river and we could again hear distinctly the crackling and sputter of machine-gun and rifle fire.

'Lord, this idiot is driving us directly into the German positions!' screamed Misha. We tried to shout a warning to the driver, but he was unconcerned. Now we were all banging with our fists against the roof of the cab, while Misha and Hillel were pounding on the rear window. There was no reaction. In the meantime it looked as if we had been spotted by the Germans as more and more shells began exploding closer and closer to us. Our chauffeur, maybe continuing to doze off in his alcoholic stupor, drove the truck over bumps and stones without altering his speed. At one point the vehicle leaned dangerously to one side and we narrowly escaped falling into a ditch, desperately hanging on as best we could. Hillel was about to fire the *pepesha* into the air to attract the drunk's attention when a shell exploded some 20 yards in front of the truck, raining debris on us. We all became hysterical and Hillel was about to break the rear window and force the driver to make a U-turn when the truck came to a sudden halt; our chauffeur had been sobered by the German shell. He looked through the rear window; we were all shaking our fists at him.

'Don't get so excited, *y... vashu mat* he swore rudely in Russian. 'OK, OK, I will turn around, I don't want to end up with the Fritzes either.' He yawned, got out of the cab, spat and looked around, trying to understand where he had gone wrong. We shouted that he had made the wrong turn a few kilometres back! He crawled back into his cab and tried to start the engine. It wouldn't start. Another shell whined above our heads and exploded not far from the road.

Mother cried, 'We are lost! We are finished! Was it worth surviving so long just to fall into German hands because of this idiot?'

The drunk tried again to start the truck, the accelerator screeched, the engine coughed and spluttered but petered out again and again. The driver crawled back out of the cab and opened the bonnet swearing, *'Tchert vazmi, motor piz... nakrylsya!'* [May the devil take it, the motor is covered with muck!]. He wiggled something under the bonnet then crawled back. Nothing. He wiggled under the bonnet again and again.

The engine finally started, but now the driver had to make a U-turn in the narrow road. At one point, he went too far back and got one of the wheels stuck in a gully. We all helped to push the truck. Luckily for us, the German fire was sporadic and inaccurate. Every few minutes a shell would land near us, but no one was hurt. At last we were moving in the right direction away from the German lines. We passed the cross-roads and drove in the direction of Kaleniki and Lunna.

We were out of range of the German mortars and field guns as we entered the village of Kaleniki. The sun was casting its last rays on the horizon but we had at least another hour of daylight to get to Lunna. Kaleniki was full of troops and trucks heading towards the front, the Studebakers and GMCs filled with soldiers and supplies. The main street of the village was completely jammed and traffic slowed to a crawl. Our inebriated driver could hardly make headway, trying to avoid the stream of vehicles moving in the opposite direction. At this slow speed, the engine was constantly stalling. Then without warning, our chauffeur decided to take a break right in the middle of the stream of vehicles. He simply stopped on the right side of the road. We were soon blocking the passage of a column of artillery while our driver slept off his alcohol. Hillel and Misha tried get him to move out of the way but only received a torrent of swearing in return. He told them to get lost! The long column came to a halt, a whole brigade on its way to the front stopped by a sleeping drunk. Soldiers knocked at our driver's window. 'What the hell is going on? Why are you blocking the road? Move your truck out of here at once!' The driver had only one answer, 'Can't you see that I'm sleeping, get lost! Y... *tvoiu mat!'*, he rudely swore.

We got out of the truck. We were scared of being accused of sabotage. Some soldiers looked at us with suspicion, especially at Hillel with his sub-machine gun. A group of officers from the artillery column came towards us. One of them, a lieutenant colonel of aristocratic appearance, with grey hair, approached our truck and commanded the driver to park on a side street. Our driver continued to slumber, slouching with his boots on the seat and his cap over his eyes. The officer, repeating his order, tried to force the driver out of his seat. I was amazed when our driver suddenly pushed the officer out of the cabin and locked the door, yelling, 'Get out of here, don't raise your hand at me! I, am a party member, five times decorated, decorated at Stalingrad!' This was followed by a torrent of obscene swearing.

I was convinced that the officer would shoot him on the spot, but nothing happened. It was a tragicomical situation. The colonel clearly had no stomach for a confrontation. I could not even imagine such insubordination in the German Army, yet here nobody knew what to do as the truck was surrounded by soldiers knocking at the door of the cabin and shouting insults at the driver who, unmoved, continued his slumber.

Then, something unexpected happened. A group of soldiers approached the truck, one of them a short man with a leather jacket. He wore boots and a round military hat with a peak. He jumped on the foot-plate, yelling '*SMYERSH!* [Military Counterintelligence] Move the truck immediately!' The driver sobered up as if by magic; in a few seconds the truck was off the road, in the yard of a burned-out house. Soon the long column resumed its crawl towards the front. Our truck was surrounded by soldiers; the officer in the leather jacket examined the driver's papers while two soldiers held their *pepeshas* at the ready. The driver was incoherent and I could only hear words like 'Hero...Communist...Medal of the Red Star...'

'*Vy aryestovany*' [You are under arrest], said the officer. 'Take him away.' The driver was led away. Then the officer from *SMYERSH* turned to us. He was visibly disturbed by the sight of Hillel with his sub-machine gun, and ordered him to be disarmed, arrested and taken away. Father tried to plead Hillel's case, explaining our story, but the man from *SMYERSH* was not in the mood for discussion. After briefly interrogating Father and Tolo, he dismissed us in the middle of the street, taking Hillel with him to be interrogated at divisional headquarters.

We walked along the main street of Kaleniki wondering where we could find a place to spend the night. Some peasants passed by, others were staring at the unending columns of trucks, artillery and armour creeping towards the front. Then, I couldn't believe my eyes; in the crowd was Vanya Karputch, a Byelorussian boy who used to be one of my classmates at the Russian middle school. 'Sasha Blumstein!' he shouted in disbelief. 'You here? How did you survive?' His face radiated amazement and elation.

To avoid the siege of Grodno, Vanya had been sent by his parents to spend some time with his relatives in Kaleniki. What a coincidence! Vanya looked at us with sympathy. We were all in a pitiful state. Patched and repatched by Mother, Father's trousers were all worn out and torn in places. His old jacket was full of holes and the drawn features of his white-stubbled face gave him the appearance of a very poor and exhausted old man. We were all dressed in old torn clothes, frail-looking and tired. Vanya knew us from better days when he used to come to play or do his homework with me. He was from a Byelorussian family of modest means, not very keen on Polish rule and rather sympathetic to the Soviets. He was a quiet and studious boy two years my senior, who had helped me with Russian when in 1939 we were both admitted to the third grade of the Russian middle school. It was extraordinary to see him here 15 kilometres from the front.

Vanya took us to his uncle's house, where we were invited to sleep in the barn. Father, Tolo and Frania left for the local field headquarters to look for Hillel and our chauffeur, whom we still expected to drive us to Lunna early the next day, after having slept off his alcohol. We were so exhausted that we did not even feel hungry. As soon as we entered the barn, I fell on the straw and was asleep immediately.

Somebody was gently shaking my shoulder. 'Sasha,' I heard Vanya whispering, 'I brought you some bread and sausage.' I was still half asleep and did not realize where I was and what was happening to me. I followed Vanya out of the barn, shaking the straw out of my hair. The night was not yet completely dark, the sky was cloudless and a warm breeze rustled the branches of an old oak that dominated the courtyard of the house. From time to time a yellow flare climbed into the sky only to explode into a myriad of shining fragments. The uninterrupted thud of artillery reminded us of the proximity of the front. The main street of the village resounded with the steady noise of engines and the clatter of heavy tanks. I was touched by Vanya's attention and we sat down under the oak as I ate my food. Mother, Rozia and Misha were with us. Father, Tolo and Frania were still not back from headquarters and Mother was very concerned. It was ten o'clock – I had slept almost two hours!

Finally, Father, Tolo and Frania returned with Hillel, who had been released after a thorough interrogation. The truck driver had also been released and was sleeping off his vodka in a barn somewhere. Tomorrow at 5 a.m. we were to resume our journey to Lunna. Most of us wanted to go to Grodno as fast as possible: Frania to recover Ilana, Hillel to learn what had happened to the remainder of his family, Father to find out about Aunt Ada. Everybody wanted to recover some belongings. Misha, visibly unwilling to return to Grodno, said that as long as the western suburb of Grodno was still in German hands it would be foolish to go there. This reasoning made sense but Father was adamant as usual; rain or shine he would go. Mother said, 'No way! First we go to Liuba's village on the eastern bank of the Niemen.' It was time to catch a few hours sleep. I said goodbye to Vanya and we promised to get together as soon as we had returned to Grodno.

24 Return to Grodno

Our ways parted the next morning in the small town of Lunna. Frania and Hillel decided to go to Grodno at once, while Misha said he was going to return to his native Wilno. As for us, we were going to the village where our former cook Liuba was living with her husband Alexander. We split between us the few roubles that Major Khaikin had given Father and kissed goodbye.

Liuba and Alexander were Byelorussians. Liuba had come to work for us as a live-in cook when Tolo was still a toddler and continued to work during the summer season after marrying Alexander. As with all her staff, Mother had been generous to Liuba and Liuba in turn was devoted to our family. She happened to live 15 kilometres east of Lunna on the other side of the Niemen. There in the peaceful surroundings of a Byelorussian village we hoped to rest, appease our hunger and wait until Grodno was entirely liberated.

We found a peasant willing to drive us to Liuba's village. We waited a long time to cross the Niemen bridge, which the Germans in their hasty retreat had forgotten to destroy and through which poured an uninterrupted stream of military vehicles in the opposite direction, towards the west bank of the river. A girl-soldier directing the traffic finally allowed us to cross. It was a long trip to Liuba's village, first on a narrow sandy road along the east bank of the Niemen, then along a long dirt road passing through fields of heather and clover. Liuba's hut was a short distance outside the village. She was working in the field with some other village women when we arrived. Seeing a cart full of people approaching her farm, she stopped her work. We waved our arms. She did not recognize us at first but then, thunderstruck, she cried, 'Pan doktor, Pani doktorowa, Tolya, Aliczek, Yesos Khristos, you are alive!' She ran towards us with open arms and kissed us all. Huge tears flowed down her wide Slavic cheeks and Mother burst into sobs. Both women were holding on to one another and crying.

'Come on, get them to our house!' she shouted to the peasant who drove the cart. 'I must tell Alexander!' She ran towards their hut, calling out in Byelorussian, *'Alexander, Alexander, idi sioudy, batch kto do nas priechal!'* [Alexander, Alexander, come here, look who has come to visit us!]. Their hut was larger than Aniela and Edward's but otherwise very much the same. Alexander was working in the barn. He was a huge man with a thick black moustache hanging down *à la* Taras Bulba. On his visits to Druskieniki to see Liuba, he had often played with me, taking me on his powerful shoulders and running around the garden. Alexander was shaken by our appearance. *'Batiushka radimyi!'* [Father Almighty!], he kept repeating while helping us out of the cart. 'I cannot believe my eyes. You are alive!' Alexander and Liuba had two daughters, Valya, who was 15, and Nyura, who was ten. Valya had dark hair worn in a long plait, a well-developed and pretty girl. Nyura was a child with blond bunches. Both girls looked at us with wide eyes. These were the wealthy Jews about whom their parents had talked so often? They looked like they had come straight from the other world!

Liuba gave us a room with two beds. On the table she put everything she had: potatoes, black bread, sour milk, cottage cheese, salt pork and even – Oh wonder! – a small jar of real, authentic honey! Alexander brought out some *samogon*. I drank plenty of milk and ate as I could not remember eating for a long, long time. After the meal Mother told our story, wiping her tears every few minutes. Alexander listened quietly and Liuba cried. Alexander told us about rumours of a huge camp near Malkinia, west of Bialystok, where trains had discharged thousands of people and returned empty; about an awful smell that hung over that area. That was how we learned about Treblinka.

That night I slept for the first time in ages in a bed with clean sheets. Even though I shared it with Tolo, I slept like a king. I felt secure and finally began to really believe that I was not dreaming. I stayed at Liuba's for an unforgettable five weeks, during which I came back to life. Father and Tolo left after a few days, as soon as Grodno was completely liberated.

The front advanced west towards Bialystok but was still very close. I went to bed early and got up early too. I feasted on fresh vegetables, milk, honey, sunshine and freedom. I ran along paths in the fields and forests. I bathed in a river, a small tributary of the Niemen, and basked in the warm July sun. War was now far away for me, though occasionally recalled by the wind bringing from the west a dull, distant pounding of heavy guns. Stretched out in meadows and forest clearings, looking at the majestic pines above me, I listened to the buzzing of bees and dragonflies. Magnificent butterflies by the hundreds hopped from one wild flower to the next. I looked with awe at their beautiful colours and listened to the rustle of their wings. I had read that these bewitching creatures lived only for a single day...just like my young friends, gone for ever. Maybe, just maybe – the thought came to my mind – the butterflies would carry their souls...Shura, Danya, Lutek, Mirek, Mareczek...right into the blue yonder...

The whisperings of nature were often interrupted by the roar of Soviet combat aircraft formations, *Ilyushins* flying low. The planes hugged the tree tops and sometimes I could even spot the pilots' glasses reflecting the sunlight in a myriad of shining spots. I prayed for them until they disappeared, so many dots in the western sky. It usually did not take long for the planes to return. I counted one, two, three...six. Thank God, today they had all come back! But often a few were missing, some flew with an uneven stutter, some trailed smoke. At the end of July, one *Ilyushin* crashed two kilometres from the village. We ran towards a column of black smoke in the middle of a field of wheat. The plane had disintegrated on impact. Smouldering pieces of wreckage were scattered all over the field. I did not see the bodies of the pilots, I turned around and ran home. I did not want to watch my heroes being killed.

Slowly I made some friends in the village. They were all a few years older. One of them, Danilko, was 17, a rather simple country boy who looked at me with some sort of admiration that made me uneasy. I could not understand what he admired in me since he was so much better at swimming, running, riding a horse, swinging a scythe and many other things. Then there was Valya, Liuba's dark-haired, dark-eyed daughter. She at 15 was a full year older than me. She did not pay much attention to me, but I liked her. Once, as she was feeding the animals in the barn and I was just loafing about in the hay, I offered to help. She accepted, gently laughing at my clumsiness. I was indeed clumsy and troubled by the proximity of this healthy girl; and then it happened: I grabbed her, pressed myself against her body and kissed her on the neck. She pushed me away. Confused and laughing, she ran out of the barn. I was so ashamed of myself. Why did I do it? She would tell her friends and I would become the laughing stock of the village. Alexander and Liuba would take a dim view of my behaviour.

We tried to be useful to our hosts and repay them in help for at least a part of our food. I helped with the harvest, at first clumsy in using the sickle, then becoming better at it. We were all engaged in harvesting, Liuba, Valya, Mother, myself, and even little Nyura. We worked with sickles and tied the harvested wheat into neat sheaves. Only Alexander used a scythe, making deep inroads into the sea of wheat and rye.

In the evening, after work, I loved to stroll along the field paths with Valya, Danilko and other teenagers, while the sun was setting behind the forest. It was a delight to breathe the warm August air of the countryside. I enjoyed listening to the jokes and carefree laughter of my companions but I could not participate in them. I was far removed, too earnest for my age, always on alert. I did not know how to let go. I did not know how to laugh. At night I savoured the warm breeze full of the scents of harvested fields, the croaking of frogs and the incessant chirping of crickets through the wide open window.

A peasant from the village brought us a letter from Father. Father wrote that he had found an apartment on Piaskowa Street and was already working at the hospital. Tolo was working at the railway station. Only a handful of Jews had survived in Grodno, but maybe more would come back. A miracle had happened and Aunt Ada, Izak and Aviva had survived in the forests. Father had managed to recover a few things and some family photographs from *Pani* Marta, but otherwise all our possessions and furniture had been lost. The front had moved behind Bialystok and was already not far from Warsaw. Lublin and Brest-Litowsk had been liberated. In the north-west, the front was in the lake district of Augustowo on the former East Prussian border, still only 50 kilometres away from Grodno; the Germans were stubbornly resisting the Soviet advance there. Father urged us to come to Grodno by the third week of August at the latest, because the schools were slowly being organized in the city and I had to think about my future after an interruption of three years in my education.

On the day we left Liuba, many people from the village came to say farewell. Danilko was there, very sad: he had received his mobilization order on the same day. His mother was crying. (Six weeks later, Danilko was killed in East Prussia.)

When we climbed on the wooden cart for the five-hour trip to Grodno I felt regret for my five marvellous, carefree weeks at Liuba's and I was fearful of returning to the city. I had lost years of schooling; I had lived a life of idleness and daily fear for three years, and dreaded returning to class to face the duties of a student. I was apprehensive of Grodno, of all the places that would remind me of Shurik, Lutek, Mirek, Danya, Basia, Rita, and all the others. Yet I still had a glimmer of hope that they might come back.

I did not recognize the city, the destruction wreaked on it during a week of ferocious fighting was immense. Burned-out houses stood in silence, with black holes instead of windows. The whole centre of town, including Batory Square and Dominikanska and Brigitzka streets, was in ruins. The houses were just heaps of rubble with only a few walls still standing. In the streets people went grimly about their business. There were many soldiers and one could sense the proximity of the front. Our cart was stopped at the crossing of former Rydza Smiglego and Listowskiego streets. A long column of Red Army soldiers was marching along Listowskiego. The soldiers were singing in the best tradition of Russian choruses. The powerful voices of one or two lead singers – the *zapyevala* – singing a few verses was followed by the refrain taken up by the whole column. It was a beautiful song calling the country to the life-and-death struggle with the dark forces of Fascism. The second *zapyevala* intoned with a mighty voice:

Arise our huge country, arise to a life-and-death struggle
With the dark forces of Fascism, with the odious horde.
The black wings of the enemy should never fly over our county,
Its vast and resplendent fields should never be trampled by his
boots.

Another one continued forcefully:

We shall resist the slaughterers of all lofty ideas,
The rapists, suffocators, tormentors of people.

Then the whole column responded, hundreds of young voices
singing:

Let our noble fury swell like a mighty wave.
A war is being fought, a holy war!

It was powerful and rousing. I felt for a moment like jumping
from the cart and following them into battle. How I hated the
Germans!

We soon reached Father and Tolo's quarters at 21 Piaskowa
Street. The dwelling almost faced our old bombed-out apartment on 10 Rydza Smiglego. It was a big, brick, three-storey
house, and had been left untouched by the fighting. The apartments were well furnished, as the house had been occupied
previously by German officers and their families, who had
fled in haste. We took over an entire six-room apartment on
the ground floor.

The house was the focal point for the handful of Jews who
had survived. We all felt more comfortable and secure being
together among survivors. Also in the house lived Aba
Tarlowski with his pretty 17-year-old daughter Hela, who
later became Tolo's wife. Aba had lost his wife and son but he
and Hela had both survived, like us, hiding in the country.
There was also his brother-in-law Niankowski and another
relative, Mr Yelin with his seven-year-old daughter Bella.
They too were the only survivors of their families. Two young
girls lived in the house as well: Fania and Helenka, 19 and 20;
like us they had been saved by Dr Antoni Docha. Both girls
had lost their entire families. Another Jewish doctor, Dr

Gershon Woroszylski, had miraculously survived in hiding with his wife, his 17-year-old son Witek, and two daughters, Rita and Cesia, aged 20 and 7.

Felix Zandman stayed there for a short time. I remembered him from my violin lessons with our common music teacher, Mr Wigderowitch. Felix, who was 17, had lost his parents and his sister. He and his uncle, Sender Freidovitch, were the only survivors in their family. Above all, we were happy to learn that Aunt Ada, Izak and Aviva had survived. Izak had fought in the Partisan Brigade of General Davydov and had been decorated for bravery.

Our reunions with Polish acquaintances and friends brought mixed reactions. Some were moved, a few even cried when they saw us alive, but many looked at us with suspicion or outright hostility. We were greeted with a false smile. 'You are still alive? How lucky. How did you make it?' Some tried to get out of giving back the goods left with them for safekeeping. Maria, our laundress, who owed a lot to Mother's generosity and was supposed to have kept some furniture, silverware and clothes for us, now came up with various explanations for the 'disappearance' of all but a few large pieces of furniture. Everything else, she said, had been lost or stolen. I was particularly sad about losing my magnificent stamp collection. The other surviving Jews had similar experiences with their former Aryan friends, many of whom were unwilling to give back property that had been entrusted to them.

The survivors were pathetic – pale, emaciated and haggard. We could be identified at once by anyone, not only because of our bedraggled appearance, but because fear was stamped all over us, it was burning in our eyes. We were a mere handful, only 100 out of Grodno's 25,000 Jews. Most of us had lost their nearest and dearest. We still did not have a full picture of the German atrocities, but the death camp of Majdanek was liberated in the last week of July and the ghastly stories of nearly a million Jews, men, women and children, gassed in a most horrible way were all over the Soviet press. In spite of all this, as the Red Army advanced deeper into Poland, some glimmer of impossible hope twinkled in survivors' minds. 'Maybe there is still a chance of my loved ones returning. Maybe there is still a chance,' their weary eyes were saying.

I could not fathom the extent of my luck. The probability of any one of us surviving was less then one in 200, and all four of us had survived! My prayers had been heard. But for a long time after my liberation, at night I continued to see the image of an unending procession of people with bundles. Among them were Rita and Lutek, Shurik and Shula, Mirek, and always Danya. The delicate Danyousha with his big, green, hungry eyes. I could see the frail silhouette of my teacher Sala dragging a big suitcase. They were all marching somewhere, I knew not where. I wanted to speak to them, I shouted, but they could not hear me. In one of my recurring nightmares the Germans were after me and I was trying to escape, but I was caught and stood against a precipice to be shot... I was falling into a black pit... This nightmare clung to me for many years and I would wake up in a cold sweat, screaming.

It was painful to walk in the streets. Every corner, every house was linked to some memory. Here on Listowskiego was Shurik's house; here in his yard we used to play football, there we fought the *shkotzim*, the Polish boys; here on Horodniczanska was Mirek's house, where we used to play in the yard now inhabited by a Pole, and here lived the Birgers. On Hoovera, the Gitisses' house brought memories of warm Seders where I asked the *kashot* and Dr Gitis, with his kind and clever face, answered. Here, behind this window, I had sat trying to overcome the pain of Roza's dental drill. The voice of Shula laying out her cards on that dark afternoon in January 1943, when Rita, Shurik and I sat around the table, still rang in my ears. 'You, Alik, shall be the only one to survive.' I sometimes thought that everything was unreal – that if I only waited long enough, somebody would appear and I would see my friends coming out of their apartments. But in vain, the town was inhabited by strangers.

Although the city centre was in ruins, the houses in both ghettos had somehow survived and so had the Great Synagogue / *Umschlagplatz*. I tried to avoid this part of town, it was just too painful. My only wish now was to leave Grodno with all the memories of the past and its present dreariness, to leave its inhabitants, strangers fattened up by our misfortune, housemaids with their Jewish fur coats, street sweepers in their Jewish suits and high hats, children with their Jewish toys. I retreated into myself, turning to the books I had been deprived of for over three years. Father wanted me to join the eighth grade as if nothing had happened to my schooling!

In the evenings I could hear through my open window the distant thunder of heavy guns near Augustowo; the war was not over. Columns of German prisoners were often led through the streets. Once, I ran into a long column of German prisoners on Orzeszkowa Street going towards the railway station. It was escorted every 20 yards by a Russian soldier. The street was lined with onlookers, Poles and Byelorussians shaking their fists and shouting insults. Some tried to break through the guards and come close to the unshaven, bedraggled representatives of the 'master race' to kick them or spit in their faces; some threw stones. The guards did their best to protect the prisoners but were not always successful. Looking at those filthy, miserable green-clad creatures shuffling along the road it was difficult to imagine that three years earlier they had been marching along the very same street, singing defiantly 'Germany is ours today and tomorrow the whole world!' I could hardly believe that these broken figures, with their sunken eyes gazing at the ground, with their heads pressed into their shoulders, were the sadistic murderers of yesterday. Looking at them, I almost felt compassion and then I felt ashamed of pitying the Germans. I promised myself not to look at German prisoners ever again.

What a joy it was to see Aunt Ada again. Ada had survived against all the odds. They had survived because Izak did not harbour any illusions. His terrible experience in the summer of 1941 at Fort Number Seven in Kaunas had opened his eyes. 'I am not going to extend my throat to the German knife,' he said to Father, and he hadn't.

25 Aunt Ada's Story

On 3 November 1942, a day after the ghettos were sealed by the Gestapo, Izak woke up Ada and nine-year-old Aviva, who slept on the table in their minuscule room in Sidranski's apartment on Peretza Street in Ghetto I. They took Grandmother to the *Judenrat* and left her in the custody of a friend who promised to bring her over to us in Ghetto II. With the help of a Jewish policeman who was their friend, they passed to the Aryan side through a secret passage in the ghetto wall. Ada was reluctant to leave Grandmother and was very distressed, tears were blinding her. 'Well,' said Izak, 'I do not want a step-mother for my child, so you'd better hurry and leave this mouse-trap with me!'

It was a beautiful November morning and people on the Aryan side were on their way to work. Izak, Ada and Aviva walked away from the centre towards Grandzicka Street, where Izak had contact with a friendly Pole. Izak had a lot of friends among the Poles, dating back to his work at the trucking depot under the Soviets. He had warned many of impending arrests. The risk to Izak had been high; if caught he would have been executed by the NKVD as an 'enemy of the people', or, if he was lucky, sent to the gulag. He had persisted, sometimes from generosity, sometimes because of romantic entanglements with pretty wives of Polish officers, and many Poles had remained grateful.

As they went through the centre of town, Aunt Ada was recognized by a number of passersby, who had known her before her marriage as the sister of Dr Blumstein, or just simply *Panienka* [Miss]. Some crossed themselves, some whispered '*szczesc Boze*' [may God help you]. Nobody denounced them. The Pole who accepted them into his apartment did not want them to stay for more than 24 hours. They left the following day for the home of another Polish friend who lived three miles outside the city. It was a sunny autumn morning. On Grandzicka Street, a handsome German officer in full regalia was riding a stately white horse. It was a postcard scene that would stay for ever in Ada's memory.

The people in the village were good to them and Aviva was able to play outside. The lady of the house, however, was very afraid; her hand shook pouring hot milk into the cups at breakfast. When our former house-cook Mitroshova, who happened to live in the same village, recognized Aviva, their situation became too dangerous and they moved at night to another nearby village where two poor peasants, Stakh and Halka, agreed to hide them for money.

Ada desperately wanted to find out what had happened to Grandmother after she had left her at the *Judenrat*. She decided to go to Grodno with Halka, who sold milk from her farm on the market. They approached the ghetto gate on Zamkowa Street, which was divided in half by the barbed wire, and joined the small crowd of Aryan onlookers gawking at the 'cage' and the Jews inside. Ada was waiting for a propitious moment to approach the barbed wire and a Jewish policeman who was standing near the ghetto wall to ask about Grandmother. A Pole approached and as he came closer Ada recognized him. Petrified, she thought, 'How stupid of me to have come here, he will now shout "Jews!", the Germans will scurry from the police station at the gate and I will be shot!' Instead, the Pole whispered, 'How lucky that you have succeeded!' and quickly went away. Ada walked up to the barbed wire and addressed the Jewish *Ordnugsdienst*, whom she happened to know personally. When he saw her, he desperately signalled to her not to get close to the barbed wire.

'Let me know what happened to my mother. Ask Sidranski,' she asked him. It took about ten minutes for the policeman to reappear.

'Ghetto II,' he shouted. That was all that Ada wanted to know.

All this took about 15 minutes during which Ada could easily have been spotted or denounced. But the danger was not over yet. They still had to go to the market on Skidelski Square in Slobotka. In Batory Square, they ran into our former laundress, Mania. Stupefied, she stopped, crossed herself, and asked, 'Miss, what are you doing here? How have you got out of the ghetto?' 'Shhh, shhh!' Ada admonished her, and quickly went towards Brigicka Street. On Brigicka, they walked by a German truck filled with Jewish workers. One or two recognized her and foolishly waved, freezing the blood in her veins. On the way back from the market, Halka stopped several times to gossip with various women about Germans and Jews. The women looked at Aunt Ada with suspicion, each time frightening her to death.

Stakh was a good-hearted man, good to Aviva and Ada, but his wife Halka was very stupid. She prattled and blabbed to the neighbours about 'these Jews' she was hiding and the money she was getting and the things she could now buy. They decided to leave before it was too late. Izak wanted to move away from the city towards the forests of Lithuania and his native village of Marcinkance, where he was well known from his former mushroom trade with the locals. It was over 60 kilometres away on muddy roads, a long way to walk with little Aviva and Ada, whose legs were always swollen and painful. Stakh accompanied them far out of the village on the side road to Pozecze. He gave them food and milk for Aviva. They were sorry to leave this warm-hearted man, but they were running from his stupid wife who sooner or later would have brought disaster on them all. Along the road, peasants who knew Itchke greeted them with, *'Kobrowski kholera na tebye, ty yeshtcho zhivyesh?'* [Kobrowski, the devil take you, are you still alive?].

After spending the night in the forest, they arrived at the small town of Pozecze. Izak left Ada and Aviva in the forest and went off to visit some peasants he knew in the area. One of them directed them to a tiny house located at the very edge of a village called Piesciuki. The house, Ada told us, looked just like the 'house on chicken feet' from a Russian fairy tale. Everybody in the village was named Piesciuk.

'There are only a few Germans in the district here,' said Izak's friend. 'You will be able to get shelter here for some time.' It was high time: the freezing rains of November started and frost appeared at night. Soon the first snow covered the ground.

The household consisted of an elderly peasant named Michal, his wife Bozena, their older son Michal and his wife

Zosia, a younger son Lolek and his young wife Halina, who came from Warsaw, with their two small children, Joleczka and Wiesio – and a dog called Urs. They were incredibly poor: they had a few acres of questionably fertile land, one horse, one emaciated cow which never gave any milk, and a few chickens. Their trade was mushrooms, in which the forests abounded. Old Michal, a decent man with a gentle disposition, was sick and could hardly move. He was illiterate and so was his wife, but he had a deep understanding of people. The sons Michal and Lolek both had a high-school education and Lolek worked as a country teacher in a nearby village. Their daughter was a medical doctor in Warsaw. Both sons were good people, especially Lolek who was a very sensitive man. How this couple of illiterate, poor peasants had succeeded in giving an education to their children was a mystery. Father and son were sceptics and, most unusual among Polish Catholic peasantry, anti-clerical. They felt the clergy were misguiding the peasant, sucking his blood and perverting the very gospel of love and brotherhood they were supposed to serve. Considered as oddballs, they were rarely visited by other villagers, which for the Kobrowskis was a blessing.

They remained in this house through the winter, hiding during the day behind a big cupboard and sleeping on straw on the floor. Dirt, bedbugs, lice and fleas abounded. Izak helped with heavy work in the forest, Ada washed floors and did household chores and odd jobs she had never done in her life before. She took plenty of abuse from Michal's wife Bozena who called her 'a good-for-nothing city dweller'.

They were paying for their stay in gold roubles; when they began to run out of money and were forced to slow down their payments to save some money for an emergency, the family never reminded them of it. They shared their meagre fare of black bread, dried peas and onions with the Kobrowskis without complaining.

However, they received violent anti-Semitic messages in letters from Jadwiga, their educated daughter, the doctor from Warsaw. Jadwiga's letters were especially full of hatred during the winter and into the early spring of 1943, when the Warsaw ghetto agonized, and the Jews there were preparing their last and desperate stand. 'When', she lamented, 'will Warsaw be free of Jews at last? These Jews are still 25 per cent of our city's population, they are the scourge of our country. I am grateful to the Germans for trying to get rid of them.'

The letters from Jadwiga were read aloud to his illiterate parents by Lolek. He was very embarrassed to read the passages his sister wrote about the Jews in the presence of Izak, Ada and Aviva. Michal did not approve of his daughter's opinions, saying that life with all those 'fancy people' in Warsaw had turned the girl's head. In the beginning of May a letter came in which Jadwiga wrote: 'I feel joy because there are no more Jews left in our city as the last of them are chased like rats through the sewers.' This is how Ada learned of the end of the Warsaw ghetto and, in it, of her brother – my uncle Eliasz, with his wife Sonya and my cousin Lenka. That night, she could not stop crying.

In May, a girl from the village herding cows to pasture came for Michal's cow. Bozena always tried to meet the girl outside to give her her lunch, a hunk of black bread and dried cheese, but this time the girl stepped into the hut, surprising Ada and Aviva. Soon the whole village knew that Michal was keeping Jews. There was nothing they could do but leave.

It was a beautiful spring morning when Lolek and his mother accompanied Izak, Aviva and Ada along small side roads into the thick of the forest. Bozena hung a medallion of the Virgin around Aviva's neck for protection and gave them food for the road. Ada was grateful to these decent and good-hearted people for having taken care of them during the dangerous winter months.

Izak decided to push further east into the dense Lithuanian forests near his native Marcinkance. This was his country, where he knew every village and every path in the forest. He felt they had a chance to last through the summer and, God willing, reach the end of the war. They were several miles into the dense forest of Sobolany, moving along a sandy path. The forest was full of the hum and chatter of birds and the excitement of all creatures large and small celebrating the arrival of spring. At midday Izak decided to knock on the door of a cabin by the roadside to buy something to eat for the evening. He left Ada and Aviva hiding in the thicket some distance from the road. The woman who opened the door recognized in Izak a wandering Jew and suddenly yelled: '*Zydy!* – kikes!'

Izak at once ran back to the thicket where they all remained for some time. When they ventured on to the road again, they were hungry and thirsty, Ada's legs were like lead and Izak carried Aviva on his back. They proceeded cautiously, ready at any moment to run back into the dense forest. Some peasants driving by in their carts jeered. '*Vas shukaiout. Ot smyerty nye utetchete!*' [The police are looking for you. You will not escape from death!].

'*Poprobouiem!*' [We shall try!], replied Izak in a strong voice. The peasants laughed as they looked at Izak carrying Aviva, and at Ada with her thick glasses, limping along.

They walked and walked for half the night until they finally reached a village where Izak knew a number of peasants. It was a large village with a mixed population of Poles and Lithuanians – an explosive mixture. The peasant who gave them shelter was Polish and very poor. They were hidden in the stye, on planks in the straw, above the pigs and the cow. Once again the wife of the peasant boasted to her friends that she could now buy whatever she wanted and they were forced to leave their shelter. They decided not to go far. The dense forest, where Germans rarely ventured, offered protection. Another Jewish family from Druskieniki joined them and together they built their camp some three to four miles from the village. The villagers were glad to sell them potatoes, onions and peas.

In mid-July, a forest guard came to warn them of an impending combing of their part of the forest by the Lithuanian police and German units. He also told them that Izak's younger brother, Leiba, was looking for them and led Izak to Leiba's place. Leiba insisted they should all move from their current location to the forest near Marcinkance, where a sizeable group of Jews from Druskieniki, Marcinkance and Pozecze had gathered, including two of Izak's brothers. They would be safer there, since the forest was much denser and access was more difficult. They left the next day, walking through pine forests, then leafy thickets dominated by maples and oaks. The road wound through ponds and long stretches of swamps with swarms of mosquitoes which devoured them alive. They walked through a burned-out forest, a depressing sight: everything black and dead, just like their lives and their mood. Ada's legs were on fire, then the frame of her thick glasses broke and although she mended it with a string, they were constantly falling off. She was slowing down everybody. Izak and Leiba alternated in carrying Aviva, Izak had to drag Ada through streams, around swamps and often carry her on his back over difficult passages. They walked for five days before emerging into a little clearing in the midst of a swampy, steamy thicket at least ten miles from the nearest village. The encampment was a shallow dug-out covered with planks and branches and lined inside with dry leaves. Nearby, a big fire was burning. Some women were cooking soup and baking flat bread on a large pan placed just above the fire. There were now more than ten people: the four Kobrowski brothers, Leiba, Chaim, Yankel and Izak, and some of their families; Mr Kaplan with his wife from Druskieniki; and three young men from Marcinkance, Fishel, Itzyk and Abram, all in their early thirties.

Every ten days, the men walked some 20 kilometres to Lithuanian villages to buy yellow peas, bread, flour and onions. They carried the food on their shoulders. Once, they were ambushed in a field by some Lithuanians who robbed them of their money and reported them to the Lithuanian police. The police arrived on motorcycles just as the men reached the forest, opened fire, killed Itzyk and nearly killed Leiba.

This episode was a watershed in their existence. Izak came to the conclusion that they had to have weapons: their money was running out and the only way to survive was to take food by force. A decision had to be made – were they to buy weapons or use the rest of that money to buy food and hope that the war would soon be over? Izak, who unlike most Jewish men had served his time in the Polish Army and knew how to handle a weapon, argued for the purchase of guns.

'Weapons are better than money!' he shouted. 'We'll be able to defend ourselves, and get food from the peasants.' But some of the men were not convinced, their mentality instinctively repelled them from weapons. They were afraid of holding a gun and even more of using it. Weapons were very expensive, even though the peasants had hidden entire arsenals, obtained from retreating armies. The peasants knew the value of weapons to those who wanted to survive in the forest. Izak's money was almost at an end, but some of the people had enough money to arm everyone but argued passionately against it. It was, for a *shtetl* Jew who had never served in the army, a dangerous, uncharted territory. Izak used persuasion and pressure, threatening to leave, and finally prevailed. A young Polish peasant, Longin, a friend of Izak, sold them two rifles, one sub-machine gun, grenades and some ammunition. Izak had to teach the men how to use and clean a weapon. They cursed Izak, and they cursed Leiba for having brought Izak.

The going was rough, but Izak kept repeating, 'If one can teach a bear to dance one should be able to teach a *shtetl* Jew to handle a weapon.' He was sure that, in the case of a serious encounter with the Germans or the Lithuanian police, they would drop their weapons and try to flee, yet he was glad that they had weapons for protection during food forays. The four brothers were still grieving over the death of their brother Moyshe who several months before had been killed in a 'food operation'.

The 'food operations' now dominated their life. The men would pick a faraway village, as far as 40 or 50 kilometres from their camp in the forest. After arriving at their destination they would observe the activity in the village and around the target house before going in, preferably on a dark night. They surrounded the house with four men, though two of them were unarmed, and Izak, with the sub-machine gun, was the one who demanded food. They usually took flour and dried peas; potatoes were too heavy. They sometimes took a calf or a pig which they slaughtered and cut into chunks on the spot. The round trip took about four to five days.

Fishel was particularly clumsy. He could not keep quiet in an ambush, could not learn to fire a rifle, and above all panicked easily. A danger to the group, he soon was left with the women and children in the camp. The others performed more or less well, but cursed Izak for maintaining discipline in the camp, including sentry duty, and the tempo of their 'food operations'.

November arrived, and the first snow, bringing a reprieve from mosquitoes. They kept warm by making bonfires, their feet close to the glowing logs, with one man always on sentry duty. One warm November day, Ada was sitting in the dug-out, mending some socks. Fishel was on guard. Suddenly Fishel yelled in Yiddish, *'Daytshe gehen! Daytshe gehen!* – Germans! Germans!' Everybody ran for the dug-out. Izak grabbed his sub-machine gun and pointed it at two Germans and a peasant who were approaching. The group was marking trees with chalk for cutting. Seeing people in the forest and a man coming at them pointing a sub-machine gun, the Germans yelled *'Partisanen!'* and started to run, followed closely by their guide.

Once again they had been discovered and once again they had to escape. They moved deeper and deeper into the thick of the nearly virgin forest, the trees so tall and so dense that the sun scarcely filtered through and it was difficult to distinguish day from night. They marched for five days, carrying whatever food they had and their few belongings on their backs. They avoided swamps and built fires around the camp at night to keep at bay packs of hungry wolves, whose howling could be heard all around them. It was only in December that the first snowstorm penetrated the thicket and covered them and the fire around which they slept with a foot of snow. They lived like trapped animals, moving their campsite every two weeks. They cut the awesome trees with an axe and a hand saw. They carefully collected stones and made them into a fireplace that was kept alight around the clock. The stillness of the forest was impressive; sound did not travel beyond a few yards.

No German ever ventured into these remote places. The danger came with their regular forays into the Lithuanian villages, always at least 40 kilometres away. Their prime target were peasants who were either informing on Jews or cooperating with the Germans. Snowstorms provided the best time to go on 'food operations': the Germans and the Lithuanian police were inside drinking schnapps, footprints were quickly covered by falling snow, and police dogs lost their sense of smell.

With the return of spring, swarms of hungry mosquitoes

devoured them alive yet again and a dense mist hung over the swamps. Their group now comprised over 30 people. Several young Jews from Druskieniki had joined them during the winter, after a daring escape. Spring also brought hope: they heard more and more low-flying aircraft – maybe the front was near.

At the same time, the forest became alive with all sorts of bands. One day during a 'food operation' they stumbled upon a detail of the AK who wanted them to disclose the location of their camp in the forest. However, Izak knew that giving this information could cost all of them their lives. He knew from peasant friends that some AK units, instead of fighting the Germans, were combing the forests and killing Jews, especially isolated families. The right wing of the AK intended to have a post-war Poland without Jews. It was rumoured that they were acting on secret verbal orders from the Polish Government-in-Exile in London, and a great number of Jews were to die in the forests and villages at the hands of the AK. The Poles, who were armed with rifles and pistols, respected the sub-machine-gun and grenades ostentatiously displayed by Izak and Leiba, and left them alone.

They returned to the camp by a tortuous route, which took them almost a day longer. Not far from their camp, they encountered a detachment of regular Red Army partisans. Well dressed in warm *foufaikas* (parkas stuffed with cotton and wool), well fed and well armed, they were supplied through air-drops. The site of the family camp was attractive to them because it was well camouflaged. The partisans gave an ultimatum: 'We are here to fight the Germans. If you want to help us in this task, you are welcome to stay. If you don't, get out of here, because you will endanger us all!'

The unit was composed of some 25 men and five women, all volunteers. The commander, comrade Finkel, was in his early thirties, a Jew from Moscow, a graduate of a teachers' college. The deputy commander was a woman. They had all recently parachuted into the forest in a major effort by the Red Army to disorganize the thinly stretched Wehrmacht supply lines before a major attack that was to begin in the summer. Devoted body and soul to the Soviet regime, they were from very poor families that, under the Tsar's rule, could not possibly have afforded an education and a decent future for their children. They often said that everything they had, especially their education, they owed to the Soviets. 'We shall fight to the death to get these Fascist devils out of our country! We serve the Soviet Union.'

The *shtetl* Jews viewed this encounter as a mixed blessing. They were already used to their former life of 'survival'. There was, of course, some risk involved in taking food by force from angry peasants, but there was much more danger in attacking German military convoys. There was much arguing about whether to join or to go away. Izak argued that there was no alternative; on their own they would be murdered by an AK unit or one of the other bands now roaming the forest, or by German or Lithuanian police action. With their few weapons, and no training, they stood no chance. Finally, after much haggling, Izak prevailed and Commander Finkel made him *Natchalnik Spetsyalnovo Semyeynovo Partisanskovo Otryada* [Commander of the Special Family Partisan Detachment]. So started their new life as partisans, dug in and camouflaged.

Given their combat inexperience, the Jews were assigned to the job of placing high explosive charges on railways rather than ambushing German convoys. Every week they were ordered to dynamite a German military train on different points of the Grodno–Wilno and Grodno–Kaunas railways. Izak's superb knowledge of the area became a great asset. The missions were dangerous, because it was easy to be spotted by German track-clearing vehicles with their mounted machine guns, as the Germans cut a wide swath on either side of the railway line to keep the partisans at bay. They had to transport dynamite immediately before the train was to appear and detonate it electrically from a distance of 50 to 100 metres. They destroyed five military supply trains during April and May. Once they narrowly escaped death when they were spotted by the Germans before they could lay the explosives. One of them was wounded and they had to carry him back to the camp, a distance of over 30 kilometres. Ada was petrified waiting for Itchke to come back each time but they were very lucky: in two months, only one man was wounded.

In June, a huge anti-partisan operation with the participation of a German SS police division was organized in their forest. They were on the move day and night, changing their campsite constantly. Ada suffered the most with her swollen legs and impaired vision; she slowed everybody down. They somehow made it through the month of June and were liberated by the advancing Red Army in the beginning of July. They waited in Marcinkance for Grodno to be liberated completely and finally proceeded along roads strewn with the bodies of retreating Germans and the blackened wreckage of trucks and *panzers*. They passed burned-out villages and approached the still-smoking ruins of our city with death in their hearts. Ada was convinced that we were all dead. And then she learned that her brother and his family were alive! Father and Ada fell into each other's arms and sobbed. Their thoughts were with Grandmother and the tragic way she had died.

26 My New Life in Grodno

My new life was dominated by the stark reality of the huge gap in my schooling. I had left the Russian middle school in June 1941, after completing the fourth grade of the *diesiatiletka* (Russian ten-year middle-school curriculum) and would have now been entering, were it not for the war, into the eighth grade. Since 1941 I had not seriously touched a book and I had forgotten almost everything I had learned. The only subjects I felt even a bit confident about were algebra and geometry which had been taught to me sporadically by Sala in the ghetto, and by Father.

I was eager to start my preparation, but where to begin? Everything was in a complete shambles: all the Jewish teachers, with the exception of Moishe Byalodvorski, had been killed; many Polish and Byelorussian teachers had been murdered by the Germans in their insane drive to eradicate any trace of Slavic culture and establish the supremacy of the Germanic master race over the Slavic *Untermensch*. There was no paper to write on and a complete lack of textbooks. Nevertheless, schools were supposed to open at the end of September. Some teachers were coming out of hiding and some were coming back from Russia.

In view of the chaotic situation prevailing in the liberated territories, it was decided by the Soviet authorities that students would be admitted into whichever grade their parents deemed appropriate, following a very lenient examination. Father wanted me to leap into the eighth grade of the *diesiatiletka*, the class I would have been in had it not been for the war. 'Work,' he said, 'and you will make it.' All this was to me unreal, I was so empty. Having forgotten even my third- and fourth-grade subjects I could not so much as imagine being a successful student in the eighth grade. And yet I knew that I had to catch up and not allow Hitler to take an immediate toll on my future life. I somehow got hold of a few old books and started to work like mad, day and night. My main emphasis was on mathematics and science. Father helped me for over an hour every evening.

With the end of August came a string of Allied victories: we cheered the liberation of Paris and the victorious march of the Anglo–Americans through France. The Red Army was on the Vistula, deep into Poland, advancing into Hungary and Romania, as Romania now turned around and declared war on Germany and Bulgaria capitulated. Praga, the Warsaw suburb on the eastern side of the Vistula, was liberated and we were anxious to learn what had happened to Uncle Eliasz, Lenka and Rysio. Our own front, however, was still near Augustowo, on the East Prussian border, 60 kilometres from Grodno. Every evening we listened to the deep, electrifying voice of Levitan, the famous Jewish broadcaster of Radio Moscow, announcing which cities had been taken by the Red Army in its drive westward.

It went like this: 'Attention, attention, Radio Moscow speaking. Today, the 30th of August, the armies of the Third Ukrainian Front under the command of Marshall of the Soviet Union Malinovskii took by assault Bucharest, the capital city of Romania.' Then came the listing of the various participating divisions and brigades, as well as their commanders, followed by: 'Today, Moscow, the capital of our motherland, salutes the valiant armies of the Third Ukrainian Front with 24 salvos from 220 guns.' The voice continued, extraordinarily solemn and deep: 'Eternal glory to the heroes fallen for the freedom and independence of our country!' At the end of the broadcast, the voice boomed: 'Death to the German invaders! Supreme Commander, Marshall of the Soviet Union, Stalin.'

It was always an extraordinary performance, giving goose-pimples to all who listened. I imagined Levitan as a tall, handsome and powerful man. Incredibly, this magnificent and mighty voice, which galvanized millions of people, was the voice of a hunchbacked midget.

The Soviet Army advanced through Poland. We heard for the first time the dreadful name of Treblinka, a death camp near the town of Malkinia on the Bialystok–Warsaw line, which had recently been overrun by the Soviet Army. Unlike the death camp of Maidanek, which the Wehrmacht in their hasty retreat from Lublin had no time to destroy, Treblinka had been completely eradicated. We read accounts of German death camps in the Soviet press, we saw the emaciated bodies of dead prisoners and the living skeletons of liberated inmates for whom it was too late to do anything except to say a prayer. We cried, looking with horror and disbelief at the mountains of human ashes from the crematoria; at the toys, glasses and shoes lying in heaps in the warehouses of Maidanek. We read about mounds of hair, which it seemed the Nazis used to stuff their mattresses, lampshades made of human skin and soap made of human flesh. We read about the gold fillings extracted by special commandos from the teeth of gassed victims and then melted into ingots which were dispatched to Berlin.

We sub-let a room of our apartment to a wing commander of a bomber squadron, Major Mikhail Tchernitzkii, whom we all called simply 'Misha'. Misha, who was only 26, missed the warmth of a family and liked the atmosphere of our home. When not on bombing missions into East Prussia he ate with us and spent time with Father discussing and playing chess. Misha liked me and we struck up a strong friendship in spite of, or maybe because of, our differences. Misha, who was Jewish, was also a devoted Communist and a militant anti-religious crusader. I was lukewarm about becoming a *Komsomol* and I believed in God. He teased me, saying, 'You know, Sasha, I fly very high. If God exists, how come I have never met him or any of his angels?'

Father and the young Byelorussian doctor Nitchiporuk were the only surgeons left in Grodno. They had plenty of work, but father was physically and emotionally exhausted: he was gaunt, his eyes sunken and his complexion sallow, he looked sick to me and I prayed for his health. Things were tough. There was little to eat. Even the peasants had little food – the Germans had taken all they could and most of the crops had been destroyed.

In the beginning of September Father sent me to the Vorstadt to pick up a jar of real honey from a grateful patient. Honey! The stuff we ate sometimes was a sweet glue called *Kunsthonig*, German *ersatz* honey. My mouth watered as I thought of the delicious honey cake Mother would bake. On my way back, I carried the heavy jar in a net shopping bag. Daydreaming as usual – or maybe doing some mental arithmetic – I ran up the stairs two steps at a time, swinging the bag with the jar. I heard a slight 'tack', and realized to my horror that I had struck a step with the bottom of my honey jar. The precious golden fluid was now all the way down to the ground floor. When he saw the disaster, Father became so enraged that he struck me repeatedly, for the first time in my life...his hand was very heavy. I locked myself in my room and cried and cried. I cried for myself and for Father and for all my friends whom I was missing so much.

It was the only time that Father ever beat me, leaving me feeling sick inside for many weeks. Mother was quick to anger, she would shout and scream, even slap me, but her fiery temper was always short-lived; a few moments later she would come back, ready to forgive: 'Aliczku, come child, why don't you eat something?' she would plead. I was never very impressed by Mother's anger and beatings, but with Father it was different.

Edward died at the end of August, barely six weeks after our liberation. *Gosposia* – with our financial assistance – hired two farm hands to finish the harvest and often came to visit us. The villagers of Staniewicze had ostracized her for saving Jews and endangering the safety of the village; she was now an outcast. Hela also came to visit us. She was still in love with my brother. Tolo worked at the railway station, which was in dire need of literate employees, and often remained there overnight when traffic was heavy. His work ensured him a *bronirovka* – a reprieve from the draft. I was happy, because I did not want Tolo to be killed. The Red Army casualties in East Prussia were incredible. Liuba, who came to visit us at the end of September, told us that poor Danilko had been killed in East Prussia only six weeks after being drafted. The life of a Soviet foot soldier was a brief one.

The big house on Piaskowa Street was inhabited by the remaining handful of Jews, and Jews passing through town would stop to visit the survivors. As our material condition slowly improved, our house opened, like it had in 1939, to the many Jews who came out of hiding. Everybody had a fascinating story of survival. At Rosh Hashanah a captain of the newly formed Polish Army of General Berling was staying with us. A native of Warsaw, he was a sturdy man in his early thirties. He had blond curly hair, a blond moustache and piercing blue eyes, and his face was hard and tanned. He had a perfectly 'Aryan' appearance, although he was a Jew by both his parents. As we all sat around the table for a modestly festive meal, he told us an extraordinary, incredible story. Not remembering his name, I will call him Alex.

Alex had been a student of mechanical engineering at the Warsaw Polytechnic Institute, one of the few within the Jewish quota. A Communist sympathizer, he joined the crowd of refugees fleeing Warsaw in September 1939 into the Soviet zone. In June 1940, he graduated with the highest honours from the Lvov Polytechnic Institute and was sent to Moscow for further engineering studies. With the outbreak of the war, Alex volunteered for service in the Red Army and became a tank commander. He was sent into battle in the spring of 1942, south-west of Moscow.

Fate decided that two of his men in the tank crew were Volga Germans.[1] They were all taken prisoner by a Waffen SS unit. Alex said he was a Volga German and the others, knowing the destiny of Jewish prisoners, confirmed his claim. The SS *Sturmfuehrer* interrogating the crew was jubilant. 'A real anthropological discovery!' he shouted. 'Perfect Aryan types of German blood preserved for centuries in this country of Asiatic barbarians.' He showed his findings to his superiors, who called the SS headquarters in Berlin, and orders were given to take these 'rare specimens' under the protection and care of the Waffen SS. An exciting life started for Alex who was driven to Berlin and from there to the Waffen SS school in Munich. He knew German from school and was fluent in it. He was terror-stricken when his circumcision was noted and he had a hard time explaining his 'operation' following an 'infection' at the age of 18 near his 'birth place in Saratov'. At the school in Munich he was an object of particular attention: his skull was carefully measured, his features were evaluated

---

[1] 'Volga Germans' were farmers originally brought to Russia from Germany by Catherine the Great to improve Russian farming. These Germans settled around the Saratov area on the Volga. They formed a well-respected ethnic minority for generations.

time and again, and he was finally proclaimed 'one of the most truly Aryan types east of the River Bug'. Alex travelled across Germany as a 'living proof of Germanic survival and Aryan ascendency in the East'. There was no suspicion in anybody's mind that *Sturmfuehrer* Alex could be Jewish. During the autumn of 1942 and the winter of 1943, when the Sixth Army agonized at Stalingrad, Alex had a great time with the prettiest girls of Munich and other cities where he was displayed to the public as the 'truly Germanic Aryan of the Russian steppes'.

In the summer of 1943, he was sent to the Eastern Front as a tank commander in an SS Panzer unit. Taken prisoner near Orel, he startled everybody by speaking to the interrogating officer in perfect Russian. 'I am a former lieutenant of the Red Army,' he screamed. 'I am a Polish Jew and I was forced by the Germans to join the SS. I am a Communist and I hate the Nazis more than you do!' He received a beating for lying but his life was spared and he was sent to a prisoner-of-war camp near Moscow for further interrogation and 'political action'. He astounded the Soviets by his knowledge of Marxism and Leninism, forced on him three years previously at the Polytechnic Institute in Lvov, but they still kept a watchful eye on him. Sheer luck had it that after two months in the camp he met an officer of the Berling army, a Polish Jew whom he knew vaguely from Lvov. The Berling army was in the process of being organized by the Soviets for the liberation of Poland. It lacked everything, including genuine Poles. And here he was, a real find, a competent tank commander who spoke perfect Polish and was born in Warsaw. Alex seized his chance and offered to enrol, while his friend vouched for him at the highest level, with General Berling himself. He was now passing through Grodno, a captain in Berling's army on his way to his unit near Warsaw.

On Erev Yom Kippur of 1944, the Grodno survivors assembled at the Great Synagogue. There was no rabbi, no cantor, no congregation. Out of the 25,000 Jews of Grodno fewer than 100 remained. Only a few knew Hebrew and even fewer the ritual. Mr Aba Tarlowski, father of the pretty Helen, was to conduct the service. The sun was setting on Zamkowa Street as we approached the former Ghetto I and the temple. We walked with heavy hearts, with memories still so fresh and so painful. It was the first time that I had ventured into the former ghetto, but today was Yom Kippur when we were supposed to cry out our pain. We entered the streets of the ghetto so cruelly familiar to us, the narrow streets and passages of the historical Jewish quarter where in better times little shops dispensed all sorts of goods – spices, dried vegetables, Jewish specialities from halvah to bagels and byalys. These streets had been filled with a colourful crowd of street vendors, bearded orthodox Jews and children from the *heder*, loud voices in Yiddish had once been heard and the smell of garlic permeated the air. Now they stood silent, their empty houses staring at us, the handful of survivors, through the sockets of broken windows.

'*Rebonai Shel Oilem!'* [Master of the Universe!]: this tragic, piercing cry filled the silence of the empty streets. On Ciasna we passed the very house of the *Judenrat* where we had lived just before our escape. Now some Poles lived on the ground floor, but the upper floors were empty. In a flash I recalled my life there, Grandmother with her eternal book, my working at the 'ladder to heaven' which was supposed to lead us to the 'Aryan' side. Here they had marched in rags, frozen in minus-30-degree weather, dragging their pitiful belongings: the crowd from the *shtetls* and Kielbasin, emaciated children with their big, black, hungry eyes...*Rebonai Shel Oilem! Rebonai Shel Oilem!*

Here, by the Great Synagogue, the *Umschlagplatz*, were the same narrow streets through which columns of haggard people had been driven with whips at four a.m. towards the transport...*Rebonai Shel Oilem!* As we entered the big *schul* and its yard, it was like an electric shock running through our bodies. The temple, witness to a vibrant old Jewish community, stood empty and abandoned. From here over 20,000 Jews went to their death. Here, among the thousands of ghosts, we pondered the miracle of our survival. We moved into the prayer hall in deathly silence, men and women side by side. There was no torah; all holy objects had been desecrated and destroyed. We moved forward into the big emptiness of the hall towards the *bimah*. There we stood, a miserable handful huddled together, keeping away from the walls and pillars that had witnessed the agony of thousands, splattered with blood and pock-marked by bullets from Wiese's and Streblow's *maschinpistolen*. Obscenities written in German and in Polish were scribbled on the walls.

The pale light of a swiftly falling evening filtered through the high windows as Aba Tarlowski began the prayers. He had a powerful voice but when he sang the *Kol Nidrei*, he choked, sobbing – *Rebonai Shel Oilem*. I had rarely gone to the synagogue, I had forgotten whatever I learned of Hebrew and I could not make much sense of the prayers, but I was overwhelmed by emotion. Tears streamed down my cheeks. Everybody here had lost loved ones, everybody cried. Sobbing and wailing provided the background for Aba's crying and praying. There were among us a few soldiers in uniform and they also cried with us. With the mourner's Kaddish Aba broke down altogether, cried with every single word in Hebrew: '*Yitgadal vyitkadash shemei raba...*' We all sobbed uncontrollably, there were no coherent words or prayers, there was only lament. Aba asked Mother to come forward to sing. Mother did not know Hebrew, but she knew Yiddish and she sang in her beautiful soprano. Her passionate *Eili, Eili* resounded through the temple:

Eili Eili lama azavtoni? O Eili, Eili lama azavtoni?	O Lord why did you forsake us?
In Feier und in Flammen hot men uns gebrennt.	In fire and in flames we were burned.
Iberal hat man uns gemacht tzu Schand un shpott,	We were shamed, jeered and derided,
Doch obtzuvenden hot uns keiner nit gekent	Yet none among us turned away
Fun dir mein Gott, mit Dein Heiliger Toire	From You, my God, with your Holy Torah
Und mit dein Gebott.	And Your Law.

And as she continued, her voice broke into sobs:

Tag und Nacht nur Ich tracht, und Ich bet:	Day and night I pray:
Schitz mit moire unsere Toire, und Ich bet:	Protect our Torah and I pray:

Rete uns, rete uns wie a mol...	Save us, save us as before...
Her zu mein gebet und zu mein gewein	Listen to my prayer and to my lament
Weil helfn kenst Du, nor Du allein!	Because You can help us, only You!
Shma Isroel Adonai Elokheinu! Adonai Ekhad!	Hear O! Israel, the Lord is our God, the Lord is one.

We all left exhausted, drained. We felt as if we had been to a funeral service for the 25,000 Jews of Grodno. *Eili, Eili* why did you forsake us?

By the beginning of October, after an interruption of three years, the schools in Grodno started to function again. It was unbelievably hard to follow subjects of which I did not have the slightest idea, despite working day and night for several weeks. In maths we were well into algebra and trigonometry. I had never had a formal course in algebra, trigonometry or physics, while a proper student of the eighth grade was supposed to have had at least two years of physics and to know algebra and trigonometry quite well. In Russian, I was lost completely. I had never learned any of the grammar and parsing taught in the fifth and sixth grades, nor had I read any of the required classics. Most of the students in my class were either children of recently arrived Russian army personnel from inside Russia, who had not interrupted their schooling, or local Byelorussians, who like myself had had no schooling for three years under German occupation, but they had more knowledge than I did. They were several years older and most had already graduated into the eighth grade at the outbreak of the war. They could refresh their memory: not one had been made to leap from the fourth to the eighth grade. Going to school was draining, but it was also fun and I made new friends, mostly among the Russians. I was again the only Jew in my class, although in the ninth grade there were three survivors, Witek Woroszylski, Lowka Trachtenberg and Felix Zandman, all three 17 years old.[2]

---

[2] Witek Woroszylski stayed in Warsaw to become one of the better-known poets in post-war Poland.

In spite of all my difficulties I liked the Russian Middle School. Some of my Byelorussian classmates showed their hostility towards the only *Yevrey* (Jew in Russian) in the class by making anti-Semitic jokes. I especially resented jokes about Jews fighting on the 'fifth Ukrainian front' – there were only four Ukrainian fronts, the 'fifth' was shielded by the Caspian Sea. This was a crude reference to Jews trading in goods in Tashkent instead of fighting in the 'Great Patriotic War'. It was, of course, an anti-Semitic untruth since, as I read with pride in the *Pravda*, Jews ranked third among the Soviet nationality groups, just after the Russians and the Ukrainians, in numbers of medals awarded for bravery in combat – notwithstanding their small numbers in the general population. But there is no arguing with anti-Semites, their minds are made up once and for all.

All in all, however, I did not feel derided or deprived of my humanity as a Jew in the way I had felt among the Poles. I even flirted with Tanya Roditeleva, a pretty, rather chubby blonde with big green eyes. My fellow Jews in the upper class were popular with the Russian girls. Felix Zandman was going out with Clara, a rather pretty, delicate blonde with big blue eyes, while the well-built Valya Kulikova was going out with Witek Woroszylski. We all went to the cinema together. In town there were three cinemas and they usually ran Russian patriotic films such as *She Was Defending the Fatherland*. There was a film called *Dva Boitsa* [*The Two Fighters*] with some beautiful, romantic war songs like *'Temnaya notch'* [Black is the night]. A song which I particularly liked was called *'Zhdi Menya'* [Wait for Me]. It went like this:

Zhdi menya i ya vyernus,
  tolko otchen zhdi
Zhdi kogda navodyat grust
  zholtye dozhdi
Zhdi kogda snyega myetut,
  zhdi kogda zhara
	Wait for me and I'll be back, but
	  wait with all your strength
	Wait when gloomy autumn rains
	  make you very sad
	Wait when snows will fiercely
	  blow, wait through summer's
	  blaze

Zhdi kogda drugikh nye
  zhdut, pozabyv vtchera
	Wait when others are given up
	  for dead and forgotten

| Zhdi menya i ya vyernus,
    vsyem smyertyam na zlo
Kto nye zhdal myenya to
    pust skazhet povyezlo!
Nye ponyat nye zhdavshim
    im, kak sredi ognya
Ozhidanyem svoim, ty spasla
    myenya.
Kak ya vyzhil budyem znat,
    tolko my s toboi:
Prosto ty umyela zhdat kak
    nikto drugoi. | Wait for me and I'll come back
    foiling all the deaths
Those who would not wait
    would say: fortunate is he!
They'll never understand how
    through battle's hell
By your steadfast waiting you
    have saved me.
How I have survived will be our
    great secret:
Simply you knew how to wait
    like nobody else. |

There were even some innocent films from before the war and American musicals with pleasant melodies. As hard as I worked, I still found time to go to the cinema with my friends.

A Polish Jew from Wilno joined our class at the end of October. Helped by Polish friends, he too had miraculously survived with his mother and father in a cellar. Mietek Piasecki was two years older than me, but had also forgotten most of his previous schooling. We became close friends and worked together. Mietek lived in the direction of Grandzicka Street, behind the city park and the Lutheran church. On my way home from doing homework at Mietek's house I usually took a shortcut through the dimly lit park where drunken soldiers often staggered about in the evening. One rainy day in November, I stayed a bit longer with Mietek. When I left it was pitch dark. I was already well into the park when I heard someone calling out to me in Russian, '*Stoi!*' [Freeze!], and the sound of boots running. My heart started to pound. What should I do? This drunk might kill me and nobody would know until tomorrow! A few weeks ago some drunken Soviet soldiers had killed a young Polish woman and wounded two of her friends not far from here – Father had operated on them at the hospital. I decided to make a run for it towards the gate.

'*Ty sukin syn stoi, ili ya tyebye shpyona oubyou!*' [You s.o.b., freeze, or I'll kill you, you spy!].

I ran as fast as I could but my pursuer was catching up with me. I could hear the heavy breathing of the Russian as the distance between us decreased. 'You spy, you s.o.b., I'll kill you!' he yelled again. Some 20 yards from the gate, he grabbed me by the arm. I dropped my briefcase and with all my strength yanked my arm out of his clutch. Gasping for air I made a dash for the gate. I was in the street when he grabbed me by my hair; my hat fell into the mud. He stank of vodka and garlic. I tried to break loose but he had me in an iron grip. He hit me in the face and we both fell into the gutter. As we rolled in the mud, he tried to open his holster and pull out his revolver, still shouting 'Spy, I'll kill you!' but I managed to escape and began running again, zig-zagging along the street as he shot at me.

'*Stoi a to stryelyat budu!*' [Freeze or I'll shoot!]. I stopped at once. Two Red Army soldiers with fixed bayonets ordered me to raise my arms and follow them. The drunk was on the pavement, leaning on the lamppost with one arm and pointing his gun at me with the other, repeating '*On shpyon* – He is a spy.' One of the soldiers asked me for my papers; I did not have any. He searched my pockets and motioned me to follow him to the *Kommendantura*, which was only a few streets away. I was led between the two soldiers with fixed bayonets. The drunk with his gun still out of its holster, followed us, none too steadily on his feet, but did not enter the *Kommendantura*. I was left to wait for a long time, interrogated, and released. When I finally reached home everybody was frantic with worry, but when they saw my battered face and heard my story, it was too much. Major Misha became incandescent with fury. 'That s.o.b. will have to be court-martialled, I will see to it,' he thundered. Misha insisted we go back to the *Kommendantura*. The officer on duty sprang up and saluted the major, but nobody knew where my assailant was. Misha went purple in the face and screamed at the officer: 'You are not only stupid but derelict in your duty, letting a dangerous drunk on the loose to attack children in the streets! I demand a court martial for the assailant and your apologies!' The officer saluted again and said the assailant, a lieutenant of the guards on leave from the front, was probably sleeping off his alcohol. If we wished, we could lodge a formal complaint against him, which in due course would trigger a court-martial procedure. We went back home. I was tired and emotionally drained. The lieutenant of the guards was on leave from the hell of the front and would soon go back to fight the Germans. We decided to drop any charges. It was a wise decision.

A few days after this incident, a letter came addressed to me in Russian. It was from the District Court requesting me to be a witness at the upcoming trial of Frania Broide against Tadeusz and Marta Kowalewski. I had not seen Frania – now married to Hillel – since our farewell in Lunna almost four months ago. Frania was in a difficult situation: heavily pregnant, she could not work, while Hillel like all young men, lived with the prospect of being drafted and sent into battle. He had no job and the couple were having difficulty making ends meet. Father still held a grudge against Frania and Hillel for their levity in endangering our lives, but Mother had wholeheartedly forgiven them for the all-too human weakness of love. She liked Frania, and kept in touch with her, helping her out with whatever she could. Frania had tried all possible ways of getting her child back from the Kowalewskis, who in the meantime had been blessed with their own baby, but the Kowalewskis stubbornly refused. They loved Halinka (Ilana) and could not part with her. They allowed Frania to visit the child to see that Halinka was loved and did not lack for anything. It was obvious that she loved her 'parents', calling them 'Mummy' and 'Daddy', and she treated Frania as a friendly stranger. After a while the Kowalewskis decided that they no longer wished Frania to disturb what they now considered their child and their family life, and Frania had no choice other than to file a lawsuit against the Kowalewskis.

For Frania – whose first husband had been shot by the Germans, and who had lost a baby boy before Ilana was born – the war was still on and her ordeal far from over. The trial was scheduled for the second week in November and I was to be the key witness as the person who took the baby from the mother and slipped her on to the landing outside the Kowalewskis' apartment. This made me very, very excited and proud. In my excitement I did not comprehend the dimension of the tragedy that the judge's ruling would visit on everyone concerned, above all the child, no matter in whose favour it would be cast. For me there was no grey area: Frania had to get her child back and that was that.

It was a sunny November morning when I entered the District Courthouse on Orzeszkowa Street. As a witness, I was not allowed into the courtroom and was led into a lounge. A number of witnesses were already seated there, including Maria Siewko who I assumed was a witness for the Kowalewskis. As the trial got underway, we could hear through the closed door pitched voices, frequent sobbing and the hammer of the judge bringing people to order. When my turn came, I was so excited that I trembled all over. The court-room with its high Venetian windows was filled with sunshine. It was packed with people, among them many survivors. The Kowalewskis were seated on one side in the front row with the child and Frania and Hillel were on the other side. The district judge and two other officials sat on a platform opposite me. On the wall behind them hung two pictures, one of Lenin and one of Stalin. A huge picture of Stalin in a Red Army uniform adorned the wall on the left. Neither the plaintiff nor the defendant was represented by counsel. Only now, a few yards from the pulpit, did I realize that the judge was a woman. I was ordered to stand before her and solemnly swear to tell the truth. I was really shaking all over my body. The judge told me in Russian, 'Do not panic, there is nothing for you to get nervous about, young man.' As I raised my eyes, I met the blue eyes of the judge; she was a blonde, in her mid-thirties, and pretty. Her voice was soothing and I became more relaxed. I recited my name, age, address and school affiliation. I spoke with some difficulty because my Russian was still far from fluent.

First I had to identify little Ilana as the child I took from Frania on 6 February 1943. Then I was asked to tell the whole story. As I stuttered and stalled the judge addressed me again.

'Sasha,' she said, 'try to remember, there is nothing to be afraid of. I know that you've passed through painful moments, but try to think about the importance of your testi-mony to the life of this child and these two families.' Her tone of voice had a calming effect and I began again. I spoke about our meeting with Frania in the wake of our flight from the ghetto, about our escape from the ghetto on 4 February 1943 and my taking Ilana from Frania and leaving her on the landing outside the Kowalewskis' apartment, with the cross, the medallion of the Virgin and the message to the prospective mother. I talked and talked. I heard sobs in the room. Of course, Frania was crying.

'Thank you Sasha,' intoned the soft voice of the judge, 'thank you.' I raised my eyes and I saw emotion on her face. I was asked to keep myself ready for any additional questions. There were other witnesses. Some praised the parental virtues of the Kowalewskis, some stressed the dangers they had had to face to keep a Jewish child during the occupation, some even tried to smear Frania. There were shouts and repeated calls to order by the judge. The climax came when Marta Kowalewski took the stand: she burst into tears, saying how much she loved the child whom she always considered as her own. She repeated how she had risked the lives of her entire family, including her recently born baby, to keep Ilana during the occupation.

'The child is properly christened and this Jewess wants to take her from me. I gave her a home, but what does she have to offer? I'll never give her away!' And before anybody could object, she asked the child who was on the lap of her husband to come up to her.

'Tell us, Helcia,' Marta asked the child, 'do you want to go to this woman?'

'No, Mummy,' the child answered, 'I don't want to go to that Jewess!'

An anguished cry came from Frania's bench. 'God,' she cried, 'you have spared me nothing! My child, my baby! You were taught to call your mother "that Jewess"!'

Then Frania was up on her feet, red in the face, defiant, clenching her fists. 'I accuse you of racism, you Nazi bitch,' she shouted at Marta. The voice of the judge and her desperate attempts at restoring order were lost in the uproar. People were now at each other's throats: the Poles on one side, the Jews on the other. Insults were flying and were it not for a forceful intervention by the police, who suddenly appeared in the room, a fight would have erupted. After order was restored, the court retired for deliberation. The verdict came back swiftly: the child must be returned to Frania. However, a period of six weeks of adaptation was granted during which both families were to cooperate, with the welfare of the child in mind.

When I left the court it was already afternoon; the bright

sun of the morning was hidden in a steely wintry sky and a cold wind swirled swarms of dead leaves from the large chestnut trees lining Orzeszkowa Street. I was chilled to the bone and emotionally drained, as were my parents.

In December we got a new tenant. Misha, the pilot, was transferred west, inside Poland, and his room was taken over by a Polish Jew from Lodz, Ludwik Brysz, whom we called *Pan* Ludwik in Polish or Ludwik Davidovitch in Russian. Brysz was a strong, healthy man with a very Jewish face. Like most, he had a very sad story to tell. Ludwik had fled his native Lodz in September 1939 with his wife and teenage son and crossed the Soviet border into Bialystok, where he had taken a job as the book-keeper for the Byelorussian Ensemble of Song and Dance. The war caught him on a tour deep within Russia and, since Bialystok was occupied by the Wehrmacht within hours, there was no way that he could rejoin his family. It was only in September, 1944 – after Bialystok had been liberated and after his resignation from the ballet – that Ludwik was able to travel to Bialystok in search of his family. There was no trace of them among the few survivors of the Bialystok ghetto. He nurtured some illusions about his son joining the partisans, getting through the lines and being somewhere in the Red Army, but recently he had met a survivor of the Bialystok ghetto who brutally told him that his son and his wife had died during the liquidation of the ghetto. Ludwik was consumed by grief. He had become a shadow of his former self, but living with an intact Jewish family of survivors made him slowly come back to life. Ludwik ate with us, played chess with Father or bridge with Tolo and some friends (he was an excellent bridge player) and integrated into our family life. We handled him with utmost care so as not to open his festering wounds and he slowly began to heal. I even saw him smile every now and then and tell the odd joke.

The snow fell, the first snow of freedom. Walking on the pavement without the yellow patch, in my new leather boots Mother had got me, holding my head high, breathing in the cold air, such small, insignificant activities were a source of joy to me. I was free!

But I had little time to enjoy my freedom, I was so hopelessly behind the average student in my class. I was desperately struggling with maths, physics, chemistry, Russian and other subjects. I was used to being a good student and now I was trailing behind in spite of all my efforts. Even in military preparation and gymnastics I was poor. With years of physical inactivity, my body had become lazy and stiff. My eyesight was also weak: I could not clearly distinguish the features of people and things even a few yards away. I had to sit in the first row to see the blackboard, exposing myself to frequent questioning, especially by our maths teacher Rodion Nikolayevitch, whom I suspected of being a closet anti-Semite. There were, of course, a few students whose performance was even worse than mine; my friend Rostik, the director's son, was not that great himself, but 'Blumshtieyn' was expected to perform well. Another *Yevrei* (Jew), Felix Zandman, almost three years my senior and one grade ahead of me, performed brilliantly in maths and was always cited as the example to follow. Felix, who had survived with his uncle in a hide-out in Pyszki, spent a year and a half solving maths problems dreamt up for him by his Uncle Sender, who was an engineer. Now whenever Rodion Nikolayevitch could not get an answer to his question out of me, he would shake his head and comment with a malicious smile: 'How come, "Blumshtieyn", that you are so much weaker than Zandman?'

I resisted pressure to enrol into the *Komsomol*, just as I had resisted becoming a Young Pioneer at my school before the German invasion. I was one of the few 'spoilsports' holding back my class from being 100 per cent *Komsomol*. Being a *zapadnik* [a Westerner] I was not unduly bothered by my teachers, with the exception of our history teacher, Vera Fyodorovna. I was grateful to the Red Army for saving my life, I was sympathetic to Communist ideas of equality and non-exploitation, but I could never accept their idea of 'dictatorship of the proletariat', a euphemism for the tyranny of the Communist Party and the terror of the NKVD. Besides, I believed in God and I was always convinced that only a Jewish State could solve the Jewish problem. I was a Zionist by conviction, and therefore an 'enemy of the people'.

I had to be careful because the authorities, after a period of relative quiet, began again seeking 'spies and enemies of the

Soviet power'. People were arrested and never heard from again: prominent Poles who had expressed some reservations about the proposed new border between Poland and the Soviet Union, based on the famous Lord Curzon line;[3] Jews arrested for 'Zionism' and 'economic sabotage'. Rumours spread that a blacklist was being drawn up by the NKVD. The atmosphere became even heavier when one of our good acquaintances, a police officer from Moghilev, a convinced and devoted Communist, was arrested. We recalled the spring of 1941 when we all awaited with dread 'the knock on the door' at night which would take us to Siberia. We recalled Nadia's sister Mania and her husband disappearing for ever in Stalin's concentration camps. Fear, our dreaded companion, was back.

It was at the end of 1944 that we learned about an agreement between the Soviets and the Polish government in Lublin authorizing Polish citizens residing in the territory of the Soviet Union to choose to emigrate to Poland. We registered with the ZPP (the Union of Polish Patriots representing the Polish authorities in Lublin) and expressed the wish to keep our Polish citizenship and emigrate to Poland.

The only one who had some second thoughts about moving west was Mother. She did not want to abandon her family now that she had found out through our former tenant, Major Misha, that her brother was alive and working as the chief surgeon at Semashko Hospital in Ryazan, where he and his family had been evacuated in 1941 before the Germans occupied the Don-Bass region. How Misha found out about their new whereabouts in a country where private addresses and phone books were not available to the public at large remained a mystery to me.

Mother and Uncle Lolya corresponded through Major Misha. Lolya wrote his letter in a code referring to us as *'Tanya, Matvyei i deti'* [Tanya, Matthew and the children], that is acquaintances rather than relatives. Lolya emphasized that Mother should not write to him directly but only through

---

[3] The eastern border of Poland as drawn by the Allies at Versailles in 1919 is known as the 'Curzon Line'. It was subsequently shifted approximately 200 kilometres to the east as a result of the Soviet–Polish war and the 1921 treaty of Riga.

A Little House on Mount Carmel

Major Tchernitzki. 'Misha can explain things much better to Mother than you can; otherwise,' he wrote, 'Mother could get very, very upset.'

It was quite clear what he meant. Obviously, nothing had changed under Stalin. Yet again I saw Mother crying while writing letters to Lolya and Grandmother in which each sentence had to be couched so as not to betray their close relationship and the pain she felt at being so far away. At least we knew of each others' existence. 'I am not happy to leave for Poland, but there is no future for us here,' Mother acknowledged as the atmosphere in Grodno became more and more suffocating. After Misha moved away from Grodno with his squadron our 'postman' became another military man: Sergeant Gregorii Abramovitch Lyoubitch, through whom Mother now sent her letters to Lolya and Grandmother.

Gregorii Abramovitch, Grisha, was a big, broad-shouldered man in his mid-forties, with some grey hair peppering his otherwise dark mane. A large scar, the trace of a German bullet, ran from his temple to the back of his head. He had been wounded in the chest near Moscow during the winter of 1942, then again a year later near Rzhev during an attack on a German position: three fingers of his right hand had been destroyed by machine-gun fire. Missing his 'trigger finger' he was removed from the front infantry and placed in a transport unit. He made frequent trips from Grodno to the front lines in East Prussia. The Red Army kept slowly advancing into this most easterly territory of the Third Reich, in spite of ferocious German resistance, and Grisha often came back to Grodno with trucks full of German 'goodies' – chocolate, pumper-nickel, Tilsit cheese, sugar, sewing machines and much more. For our New Year's dinner he brought all sorts of delicacies, including a bottle of French champagne. I wondered how it was that Grisha, a mere sergeant, not even a Party member, had so much more than Major Misha, a wing commander, a devoted Communist and a Party member, whose 'goodies' from 'special rations' were the standard American canned pork and corned beef and some powdery Soviet chocolate. It was clear that Grisha was a *Preidokha* [a resourceful wheeler-dealer], the archetypal Soviet survivor.

One day in January we were galvanized by the deep, electrifying voice of Levitan announcing that the armies of the
First Byelorussian Front under the command of Marshall
Zhoukov had taken Warsaw, the capital of 'fraternal Poland'.
We were all moved to tears. Soon we might know what had
happened to Eliasz, Sonya, Lenka and Rysio. We had so many
friends in Warsaw. Had anyone survived? We feared that our
family and friends had perished in Treblinka, but we still had
some hope. Eliasz and Lenka with their blond hair and blue
eyes looked so Aryan!

Shortly afterwards, the whole German front on the
Vistula crumbled and Poland was liberated in a blitz that
resembled in reverse the 1939 German thrust into Poland.
We saw photographs of liberated Warsaw, a sea of ruins,
destroyed street by street by the Germans during the AK
uprising. A quarter of a million Poles had perished, the
remainder had been herded to labour camps in Germany
and the city had been systematically blasted. Cracow was
liberated. The Red Army entered some concentration and
death camps; the most notorious were Auschwitz and
Birkenau near Cracow, where well over a million people,
predominantly Jews, had been murdered. The retreating
Germans were in such a hurry that the camp had been only
partially destroyed. Some crematoria were left untouched.
Mountains of toys, spectacles, tooth-brushes, baby shoes
and clothes, and human hair were on display in their naked
horror.

I had already seen such pictures in the Soviet press after the
liberation of Maidanek in July; in Auschwitz, the papers
claimed, as in Maidanek, special factories produced
lampshades from human skin and soap from human fat,
which were sent to Germany along with gold teeth extracted
by special squads of prisoners. German perversity reached
another peak when some liberated prisoners told about
grizzly 'medical experiments' performed on inmates by SS
doctors under a certain Joseph Mengele.

In the beginning of February the front rapidly moved deep
into East Prussia, away from Grodno. At the same time one of
the most brilliant Soviet commanders, General Tcherniakhovskii, the commander of the Baltic front, fell in the bitter

battle for Koenigsberg. I took considerable pride in the fact that Tcherniakhovskii was Jewish.

The pincers tightened around the Third Reich, the Allies were approaching the Rhine and the Red Army was advancing towards the Oder and beyond. The war was clearly coming to an end and we, as Polish citizens, were preparing to leave Grodno and move to Poland. Our papers were ready. We had decided to move to a big city. The city of Lodz had hardly been touched by the fleeing Wehrmacht and Ludwik Brysz, himself from Lodz, had convinced us to settle there. I was elated by the prospect of moving. The West was somehow synonymous with freedom. A number of survivors had already left Grodno for Poland. Among them were Izak, Aunt Ada and Aviva, Frania and Hillel, with Ilana and their newborn son Moshe. Felix Zandman and his uncle also left and so did Dr Gershon Woroszylski and his family. With every Jewish survivor who left Grodno the urge to follow got stronger. Tolo, who worked at the railway station, arranged for a goods wagon for our family with the help of a fat bribe.

I bade farewell to my classmates of the Russian Middle School. We had a long and moving goodbye with *Gosposia*; we tried to convince her to leave for Poland. Many Poles, especially the young, were now preparing to move west into the 'recovered lands', former German territories promised to Poland by the 'Big Three' at the very recent Yalta Conference. *Gosposia* was adamant: she would never leave. She had seen in her life Russians of the Tsar, Germans of the Kaiser, Soviets of Stalin and Germans of Hitler – they all came and went, but the Polish farmer stayed. She had nothing, nothing to look forward to in some faraway land. Here was where her father, grandfather and great-grandfather had lived. It was where she had been born, where she had married Edward, where they had both struggled to survive, but had been happy. This was the earth that had nourished them and had now taken Edward. She wanted to be buried beside him. She could not and would not leave her country. She was like a tree with deep roots in the soil of Staniewicze. I understood now the almost mystical attachment of the peasant to the soil, intermingling Poles, Byelorussians and Lithuanians on this land. No conqueror could tear them away. The young people were nevertheless seriously considering leaving. Within a year, they were leaving the Soviet Union in droves for the 'recovered lands' and the opportunities promised by the new Polish government.

We left Grodno on 9 March. We loaded our belongings into our wagon which the station master promised to hitch to the first available train for Bialystok, Poland. In the middle of the wagon we installed a *pyetchka*, an iron stove in which we burned coal and wood. Plenty of straw was spread on the floor. Counting Ludwik Brysz – always extolling the virtues of his native Lodz, our destination – we were five people. We had plenty of room to sleep and move around. We sat from early morning until the afternoon on an auxiliary track waiting to be hitched to a civilian train to Bialystok. And then we were off! I peeked through a small opening in the sliding door of the wagon at the rapidly disappearing houses, church steeples, chimneys and burned-out buildings of the city of my childhood. We were crossing the Niemen bridge and were winding our way westward. A new chapter in my life was about to begin.

27   Lodz

The 80-kilometre journey to Bialystok across the new Polish border took hours, with frequent stops in the open country and a long halt at the border. The warmth of our cast-iron stove was quickly dissipated by the cold drafts blowing through cracks in the walls of the goods wagon. Stretched out on the straw next to Mother and Tolo I was cold, but the thought of moving 'west' towards freedom, the four of us together, comforted me. At the border our papers were checked by Red Army border troops in their green-rimmed caps and officials of the new Polish government, some in leather jackets.

Our papers did not allow us to travel beyond Bialystok and we had to get a permit from the Polish authorities for our journey to Lodz. Most refugees were seeking similar permits because Lodz was one of the few major Polish cities left intact by the retreating Germans. Warsaw was in ruins and Cracow still dangerously close to the front. It took Father two days of running from one office to the next to validate our papers for travel to Lodz. Considering the prevailing chaos and the notorious Polish red tape, this was lightning speed. Tolo impressed the authorities with his new leather jacket, such as worn by the Polish secret police, the *Bezpieka* which was modelled on the NKVD. Tolo paraded about with the nonchalant body language of a '*Bezpieka* man', and made a fearful impression on the bureaucrats: doors opened, queues gave way and he was treated with a politeness bordering on obsequiousness. After 48 hours of hanging about on sidetrack in Bialystok, we were given our papers and hooked up to a train to Warsaw.

As the train moved away from Bialystok I could hardly contain my excitement. I recalled my trip to Warsaw in 1937 and the everlasting impression it had left on a seven-year-old boy from provincial Grodno. Macius Cukier, a friend who had been a faithful guest at the 'sanatorium' and had always brought me my favourite chocolate waffles, had told me 'in great secret' that before the train arrived at the station an old man with a very prickly beard kissed every child coming to Warsaw. So, back then, I had been in a frightened state all the way, asking Tolo, my very reluctant travel companion, 'when will this old geezer stop the train and kiss me?' And then came Warsaw: the hustle and bustle of a big city, the taxis, trams and trolley buses, the crowds rushing along Marshalkowska Street, the tall buildings, the night illuminated by neon signs and glowing advertisements, the glittering asphalt; the beautiful park of Lazienki and the Belweder castle; the fascinating zoo and the Vistula River. Everything was so much bigger, wider and more exciting than in Grodno, and I took it all in with wide eyes. We stayed on Krolewska Street with our dear friends Nika and Herman Alapin, and their daughter Lusia showed me around the city. Everything was so enchanting and fascinating. Where were they now? Where was uncle Eliasz, where was Lenka, where was Rysio?

Bialystok disappeared and soon we were rolling through forests. It was warm and caps of heavy snow lay in patches on the pine trees. My thoughts wandered. I thought of Shurik, Lutek, Danyousha and all my friends: they must have travelled on these tracks, maybe looked at the same woods. What had they thought about? Was that their last journey? A few hours later we approached Malkinia, the marshalling yard where, according to reports, hundreds of thousands from east and west were diverted towards the slaughterhouse of Treblinka. I shivered; some put the number of those murdered here at over a million. No trace was left of this death factory – it must have been somewhere behind the woods. Here they may have all died: Lenka, Eliasz, Sonya, Rysio, Herman and Nika and Lusia, no trace, no grave, their ashes scattered to the four winds. How had they felt approaching this place, what had they thought about before they died?

I again felt my helplessness as a Jew. How could we have escaped this cruel fate? Who had wanted to help us? The British barred our way to Palestine; the Americans bolted their doors. Europe was overrun and many had shamefully cooperated with the Germans. We were rejected by our fellow citizens, we were cursed by the Pope who did not condemn the horror of Nazi death factories. Was this the moral conscience of Christian Europe? To me Israel was our only hope, the only way to hold our heads high, to recover some measure of dignity after so much humiliation.

Father told me that he would strive to go to Palestine – 'a little house on Mount Carmel' was his dream. 'But you should finish high school first and Tolo, oh Tolo...' Father said, sounding dejected, 'he must finish his medical studies. There is a university forming in Lodz and Tolo will have to enrol and study very hard to make up for lost time. Let's bring some order into our lives before going to Palestine.'

After a very long stop at the marshalling yard of Malkinia, we arrived late at night in Praga, a suburb of Warsaw on the eastern bank of the Vistula. I slept through all of it and woke up in the morning as we crossed a makeshift bridge into Warsaw. I was appalled by the desert of rubble which stretched as far as my eye could see. There was no Warsaw! We were shunted to a sidetrack and left there. Father and Tolo tried to argue with the station master to get us hitched to a train to Lodz. Under normal circumstances a little bribe would have gone a long way, but with the preparation for the final Russian offensive all civilian traffic had been halted. Military transports were passing westward day and night. I looked at these long trains pulled by several steam engines. Some were exclusively composed of flat freight wagons, their platforms filled with tanks and self-propelled artillery. On many gun barrels one could read splash-painted with big Russian letters, 'For a Just Cause', on others 'Onward to Victory'. Some wagons were full of munition crates marked 'For Berlin'. I was fascinated by this mighty war machine on its way to smashing the hated Germans in their own lair. For two days and nights we were stranded looking at these transports. On the first day, Father and Tolo went out to see Warsaw. Father came back appalled. 'This is unbelievable,' he exclaimed, 'there is no Warsaw, it has been flattened – there are not even ruins left! People are living in cellars and holes in the wall, like rats. Thousands of bodies are still buried under the rubble. They say as many as 200,000 people may have died in the August–September uprising.'

It was difficult for me to commiserate with the Poles after having listened to stories of Jews who had been in Warsaw on the Aryan side during the April 1943 ghetto uprising. There had been little help for us from the openly anti-Semitic Polish underground Home Army, the AK. Many Poles had been happy to see the ghetto going up in flames. On Easter Sunday, dressed in their holiday clothes, they had taken their families to watch the Jews jumping from their burning buildings beyond the ghetto wall. I could never forgive the picture I saw in one of our 'wrapping papers' in Staniewicze, showing the joy of the Polish population in a Warsaw made *Judenrein* at long last. To me there was a certain measure of justice in what happened to the Warsaw Poles. Father was visibly shaken; he, who grew up in this area, who as a young surgeon had lived and practised in Warsaw, could not fathom the extent of devastation visited on the city of his youth.

After two days of waiting for a civilian train, we left Warsaw well past midnight, and as we pulled out I was woken by the knocks, jolts and creaks. Soon the dull bouncing and the rhythmic talk of wheels with the rails sent me back to sleep. When I awoke early in the morning, we were approaching Lodz. The morning was bright, the air warmer than in Grodno. We were some 500 kilometres to the south and this was apparent as the roofs and treetops had hardly any snow left on them. I tried to get a view of the approaching city. Lodz was the 'Manchester of Poland', with its smokestack-studded suburbs, tall houses and green squares, animated pavements, overcrowded, noisy blue trams. I could see some civilians with red and white armbands, carrying rifles. This was, Father explained, the civilian militia which had replaced the 'navy-blue' Polish police, so compromised by their cooperation with the Germans. In contrast to all the other cities we had visited, Lodz appeared intact.

We were again manoeuvred to a sidetrack at a big railway station located in the heart of the city while Father, Tolo and Ludwik went to find a place to live. By evening, Tolo was back in a state of great excitement. 'We have found a fantastic apartment vacated by Germans! It is not far from here on Narutowicza Street. We can move in at once.' Apartments vacated by Germans were easily 'requisitioned' by anyone with some authority: the military, the police and, of course, people of the *Bezpieka*. Our apartment had been requisitioned by some officer of the Polish Army. Lubricated by a bribe and duly impressed by Tolo's leather coat, the officer 'temporarily' gave the apartment to our family. At the city hall where all new arrivals had to register, nobody in his right mind would argue with 'a man in a leather coat' and thus the apartment was approved as ours.

Lodz had been taken by the Russians almost without a shot being fired barely six weeks before our arrival. It still gave the impression of a city stunned by its liberation and had not yet been invaded by refugees from the east, Jews and Poles alike. The 'requisitioned' apartment was on one of the main streets, on the second floor of 47 Narutowicza Street. It consisted of seven rooms, a master bedroom, a dining room, a bathroom and, at the end of the corridor, a large kitchen. The windows of the master bedroom looked out on Narutowicza and faced a large bowling green with benches. We moved in the same evening. The move was easy, considering the few possessions we had.

Tolo and Ludwik set out to 'organize' some furniture, a fairly simple task as many German apartments had been abandoned and the huge ghetto of Lodz, second only to the Warsaw ghetto with its population of 200,000, stood empty. Many thousands had survived in the Lodz ghetto until August 1944 only to be 'evacuated' to Auschwitz and murdered there six months before the liberation.

Father installed his office and a waiting room with a sofa in two of the rooms. However, very few patients knocked at our door. While looking for work Father stumbled again and again on officials who were not impressed by his name: Chaim Blumstein. Although Lodz lacked physicians, and particularly surgeons, he was assigned to a job in an outpatient dispensary, *Kasa Chorych*, and not in a city hospital. Father was very depressed by this turn of events. He, who used to work as chief surgeon in a major hospital in Grodno, now held a small job taking care of boils and callouses. It was apparent that, Communist rhetoric about 'equality of races and creeds' notwithstanding, a strong anti-Semitism prevailed everywhere, even in Lodz which unlike most Polish cities was 'pink' because of its large proletariat.

This realization came to us forcefully a few weeks later when one evening Father was summoned by an emergency call to an apartment a few streets away. It turned out that the call was from one of the local high officials of the PPR, (Communist Party) who had been shot and wounded by his mistress. He was bleeding profusely. Father extracted the bullet and went to visit the man regularly. The high official, who wanted his affair kept secret, was grateful and tried hard to place Father in a city hospital, but without success. He finally told him, 'I cannot do anything for you as long as your name is Chaim Blumstein. Don't be foolish, Polonize your name, for example to Mateusz Kwiatkowski [a free translation of his name into 'Aryan' Polish] and I will be able to place you at once in a responsible position in a large city hospital.'

Father was appalled: 'You are asking me to change my name after all I have been through? My name was Chaim Mordechai Blumstein through thick and thin, and it will continue to be just that, Chaim Mordechai, the son of Nussen Mendel Blumstein from Plock!' This was the end of Father's quest for a better position.

Among the Jews who survived 'on the Aryan side', most kept their new Aryan names and some of those who were returning from Russia also Polonized their names. Many survivors never really came out of hiding. People joked that a typical conversation between survivors ran like this:

'Do you know that very Catholic Kazimierz Wykszewski?'

'Isn't he the man whose maiden name was Zilberstein?'

Some doctors resorted to advertisements such as: 'Dr A. Wrobelski, Paediatrician, Christian Patients Welcome' – a not so subtle way of saying 'I am not Jewish.' It was good business practice, since now in the post-Holocaust era, the overwhelming majority of clients were Poles, but it was painful for us to accept the extent of anti-Semitism even here in the workers' city of Lodz.

I soon enrolled at a school called The Accelerated High School of Magister Duczyminski. It was accelerated all right: It covered the curriculum of two years in one. Such schools were badly needed because under the German occupation, Poles had been forbidden to attend high schools and universities, and many students needed to make up for lost time.

Father insisted that I should take advantage of this opportunity to get my *matura* (high-school diploma) that much faster. I was reluctant; I was barely 15 and did not need an accelerated curriculum. Even in a normal high school I would still have been the youngest student. But Father insisted, saying that if we were to emigrate to Palestine I had to have my diploma as soon as possible. And so I enrolled in this school into the junior grade. If I worked hard I could pass my *matura* examinations before the year was over, at the age of 16. The students in my class were, on average five years older than me and I felt a little out of place. Although Felix Zandman, Witek Woroszylski and Lowa Trachtenberg were in the senior grade, I was once again the only open Jew in a class of 30. Some of my classmates harassed me by intentionally misspelling my name or speaking to me with a mock Yiddish drawl. Such incidents bought me near to breaking point. My sensitivity was stretched very thin; it became almost pathological.

The teachers at the Duczyminski high school were a motley crowd. Our physics teacher, for example, was an engineer, our chemistry teacher a former chemistry student and our Russian teacher somebody who just happened to know some Russian.

More and more people were coming to Lodz, among them many Jews. Jews spotting other Jews in the street approached them and asked in Hebrew, '*Amchu?*' [Are you one of our people?] When the stranger knew the meaning of the word, one would share stories of survival. Polish Jews who had fled in 1939 to the Soviet-occupied part of Poland and subsequently had been deported east started to trickle back. The conditions in Russia during the war had been appalling for everyone, Russians and deportees alike, and millions died from starvation and disease. Mr Ludwik Brysz's brother-in-law, Max Lifszyc, came back from Tashkent with his 13-year-old daughter Lenka. Lenka's mother, Ludwik's sister, had died there from hunger and disease. Our friends Stefa and Mila Chorazycki came back from Kazakhstan. Unfortunately, Stefa's husband Nitek and my youthful friend from 1940, their brother Marek, had both died there.

In April more Jews from Grodno and Bialystok came to Lodz. Our apartment was 'open house' to many of them. We took in two orphaned teenagers from Grodno to live with us.

One was 19-year-old Yona Zarecki. Yona's entire family, mother, father and sister, had been killed by the Germans. Yona escaped from the transport by jumping into a cesspool, and subsequently survived in hiding. He was very thin, with big glasses that kept sliding off his nose; his small face betrayed fatigue and deep sadness. He desperately needed a home, the warmth of a family and, above all, food and shelter to finish high school. Another teenager we 'adopted' was Lusia Epstein, a tall, pretty, 18-year-old, curly-haired brunette. Her parents had died in a death camp while she had managed to escape and survived in hiding on the 'Aryan side'. She was also finishing high school. We took them in with open arms. Lusia was a responsible and mature person whom Father often pointed out to us as an example, citing her *menschlichkeit*. She was, I suspected, in love with Tolo who, parading in his leather coat, was going out with many girls, especially with *shikses*.

To supplement our meagre income we sub-let an additional room of the apartment. Father's pay from the *Kasa Chorych* amounted to a pittance and because of his unwillingness to Polonize his name, he had practically no private practice and could not find a better job. Few Poles would come privately to an unknown Jewish doctor when there were Polish or would-be Polish doctors around. Tolo had a temporary job and now was all for the Communist party, the PPR. Mother was trying, together with four Jews from Grodno and Bialystok, to start a small business, a shop with textile wares and fabrics which materialized only some time later. Mr Brysz, who was also a lodger, revived some connections from before the war and was partly back in his pre-war business of recycling fabric scraps at the mills of Aleksandrow and Lodz. Everybody worked hard to make ends meet.

I was very distressed to see my father withering away. Very dissatisfied with his work, he was disappointed in post-war Poland, Poland for which he fought in 1905, about which he dreamt in 1918. Poland, which disillusioned him so much in the 1920s and 1930s was now again a source of bitter frustration. 'After all we have been through,' he repeated, 'I have to hear that to make an honest living I have to Polonize my name.' His gloom deepened as we learned from Mr

Meilachowicz, a Grodno Jew who had survived on the Aryan side in Warsaw and who knew Uncle Eliasz and Lenka, that the Blumsteins had been taken to Treblinka in the early autumn of 1942. Lenka had escaped to the Aryan side but was denounced shortly thereafter by a Pole who recognized her in the street. She was tortured and murdered at the Gestapo headquarters on Aleja Shoucha. Rysio Gherman, Lenka's husband, perished in the Warsaw ghetto uprising in April 1943. Mr Meilachowicz's own son Ziunia fell as a Pole in the AK Warsaw uprising in August 1944.

28 Victory

The days of the Thousand Year Reich were drawing to an end. The Red Army captured Vienna and, after crossing the Oder and the Neisse rivers, opened a powerful two-prong drive on Berlin from the east and from the south. The Western Allies were swiftly occupying western Germany and racing towards the Elbe. Newspapers had pictures of liberated camps, of skeletons and dying inmates. The horror and stench of the opened Nazi sewer was choking Europe. It was in this climate that we learned about the death of Franklin Delano Roosevelt. He was mourned by millions who associated his name with humanitarian causes, help to the needy and resistance to oppression. We were grateful to him for the food we ate – from the powdered eggs nicknamed 'Roosevelt's eggs' in Poland, to Spam, corned beef and Hershey bars. We were grateful for the hope of freedom dawning over Europe. We associated all this with Franklin Delano Roosevelt, and the day of his death was a bleak day for all of us. Good news, however, followed the bad: the fall of Berlin and Hitler's suicide.

One sunny Sunday in May, full of the scent of lilacs and lilies-of-the-valley, the silence of the early afternoon was shattered by a powerful sound of sirens from all sections of the city and all factories. Church bells were ringing. It sounded like the end of the war! I stood on Piotrkowska, stunned. Strangers were kissing each other and crying. People were running and gesticulating. The sound grew mightier and something squeezed my heart, tightened my chest. My God, I am here and I have survived! I felt elation and gratitude: we had survived, all of us, our whole family together; my prayers had been heard!

Tears welled up in my eyes. I remembered the far-off day of 1 September 1939 in Druskieniki when Mother had cried listening to the radio announcing a state of war between

Poland and Germany. I did not understand her tears then. Now I stood and tears streamed down my cheeks, tears of gratitude, tears of happiness, tears of sorrow, tears for Danyousha and Shura and Lutek and Rita, tears for Dr Klinger and Rosa Gitis and little Mareczek and all my dearest friends who did not make it, tears for all those who gave their lives to smash the Nazi beast, so that I could live. They are all holy... all of them holy!

Julian Tuwim, the great Polish poet, was coming back from New York, where he had spent the war. He was an assimilated Jew who had not always identified with the aspirations of his people, but now he wrote an open letter from New York, published in the Polish press, that touched me deeply. The letter was called 'We Polish Jews'. It was a cry from the heart of the poet returning to his people. It was also very idealistic and naive, with passages like these:

On the armbands which you were forced to wear was the Star of David. I believe in a future Poland in which this star from your armband will become one of the most honored medals given to the most heroic Polish officers and soldiers. They will wear it with pride next to the former Virtuti Militari. There will be the symbolic Ghetto Cross. There will also be the medal of the Yellow Patch, more honored than many a medal of today. And there will be, in Warsaw and in every other Polish city, a fragment of the ghetto preserved for future generations in its original state of desolation and ruin. We will surround this remnant of shame for our enemies and glory for our martyrs with chains cast from Hitler's conquered guns and every day we shall plait fresh flowers into their links, so that for generations the memory of the massacred nation be fresh and alive and that alive and fresh will remain our pain...

We Polish Jews, we truth of graves and illusion of existence, we millions of corpses and a few thousand of maybe not-corpses. We limitless brotherly graves. We a stump history has never seen and will never see again. We, suffocated in gas chambers and made into soap which could never wash off the stains of our blood or the sins of the world toward us. We whose brains were spattered on the walls of our poor tenements and walls of mass execution – only because we were Jews.

We, a Golgotha on which stands an impenetrable forest of crosses. We, who two thousand years ago gave to humankind one innocent Son of Man murdered by Imperium Romanum – and this was enough to make Him God. What religion will grow out of millions of deaths, tortures, humiliations and arms outstretched in desperation?

We Shloymes, Srules and Moyshes, derided, despised and downtrodden, we whose names will surpass in dignity the names of Achilles, Boleslav the Brave or Richard the Lionheart.

We in the sewers of Warsaw, shuffling in the stench of their discharge to the astonishment of our companions the rats.

We with rifles on barricades amongst the ruins of our bombed out houses. We soldiers of freedom and dignity.

We, who made a fortress from each house collapsing on our head.

We Polish Jews, wild in the forests, feeding our bewildered children roots and grass.

We, crawling, creeping, afraid, in our hand – obtained by miracle or bought for a fortune – an old, rusted weapon…

We, bottomless pits of broken, squashed bones and deeply scarred twisted bodies.

We, a long scream of pain. A scream that will be heard for centuries to come. We, a sob and a lament. We, a funeral chorus wailing on our grave 'El Mole Rachamim' which one century will transmit to the next.

We, the bloody mound of compost fertilizing Poland, so that those who survive us may eat a tastier bread of freedom.

We, the Last Mohicans, the biggest sensation in the world! Polish Jews – alive and natural! We the cabinet of horrors, the *Schreckenskammer*, the *Chambre de tortures* – 'Nervous people should leave the room!'

We, who will never find the graves of our children and mothers.

We, the tears of Jeremiah. We Polish Jews, we a legend of tears and blood.

Such a deluge of martyred blood was unknown in history and the blood of Jews was flowing in widest and deepest streams. These blackened torrents form a stormy roiling river – and in this new Jordan I take a baptism over all others: a bloody, martyred and passionate brotherhood with the Jews.

Take me in, brothers, to this honored commonwealth of innocent blood spilled, to this community, to this church I want to belong.

This degree – the degree of a Jew Doloris Causa – please, bestow it on a Polish poet, the nation who gave him life...

A giant, ghastly and ever-rising human skeleton stands over Europe. In his empty eye sockets burns a fire of dangerous anger, his fingers are clenched into a bony fist. He, our Leader and Commander will decree our wishes and dictate our rights!

Tuwim's letter reminded me of Dr Klinger's conviction that after the war we would witness a tremendous upsurge of pride for being Jewish under the Nazis. We would be respected by our non-Jewish fellow citizens and, like Tuwim, I remember him saying, 'We would proudly wear the "medal of the ghetto".' The book about us, the survivors, which he intended to write under the title 'I Wore the Yellow Patch', would have been a best-seller. Had he lived, I thought, he would be surprised to see that many among the pitiful remnants of his city's Jews were still hiding their names, their origins and religion; that having saved Jews was considered as an unpatriotic act by a large segment of the Polish popula-tion; that to express sympathy towards Jews was not popular.

As a Jew I was often a subject of derision in my school on the part of students and teachers alike. One day my Polish litera-ture teacher assigned me to read aloud to the class excerpts from Krasinski's anti-Semitic poem 'Not So Divine a Comedy', portraying Jewish converts [*maranos*] in a secret gathering. Unaware at first of the contents, I read aloud to the class:

Let us suck and suck and suck the pages of the Talmud Like the milk from a mother's breast...

Realizing the meaning of this offensive poem, I went red in the face and stopped abruptly. The teacher, enjoying my anger and confusion, asked me, 'What has happened to you, Blumstein? What bit you so hard?' The class laughed and I gritted my teeth.

There were some students at the school whom I suspected of being Jews. Behind me sat a pretty redhead with freckles whom I thought of as being Jewish in spite of the cross dangling on her neck and a super-Polish name: Maria Krystyna Krajecka. She never made fun of me and looked at me with a softness in her brown eyes that for me was unmistakably Jewish. I was convinced that she was one of those Jews who were still in hiding. Shortly after my unfortunate incident with the Polonist, while walking home in the evening (our classes were held in the late afternoon and early evenings since most students worked during the day), I caught up with her, and kissed her. She let herself be kissed. I asked her outright, 'Are you Jewish?' She became terribly agitated, pushed me back and cried, 'No! I am not Jewish! I do not like Jews!' She ran away from me. This episode convinced me that she was Jewish indeed. But the most painful thing for me was the sense of being isolated. I did not have any friends in my class and felt terribly lonely.

It was hard because the school became increasingly the centre of my life as I got better at maths, sciences, and even Polish. Was it because my intensive work was finally paying off or because of the ignorance of my classmates? Whatever the reason, at the end of the school year I was one of the better students in my class and was grateful to Father for having pushed me into it. The other few declared Jews were also doing very well: Witek Woroszylski was first in the Senior Class, Felix Zandman was a close second. Witek, a devoted Communist, a Stalinist even, became more and more known because his poems were sometimes published in the *Trybuna Ludu*, the official newspaper of the Communist Party, the PPR. A militant atheist, he made very little of his Jewish origin, in fact he rejected it as being of no significance. He rejected Zionism as the manifestation of a Jewish nationalism sometimes tinged with fascist overtones. I argued endlessly with Witek but his arguments, however unconvincing to me, were always based on impeccable Marxist dialectic logic for which I was totally unprepared. Neither of us convinced the other in the end, and it was remarkable that after so much arguing we continued to be good friends. That Witek was Jewish was known to all anti-Semites in the school. Otherwise, it would have been impossible to guess: he was a tall, blond, blue-eyed exemplary 'Aryan' type, straight out of a Nazi textbook, putting the racial theories of Hitler and Rosenberg to shame. His name also had an all-Polish ring to it and the family did not exactly advertise their Jewishness.

One day in June Witek came running in, out of breath, looking for Father. His father had suffered a heart attack. Father rushed to his bedside but it was too late. Dr Gershon Woroszylski was buried the next day at the Jewish cemetery of Lodz. It was my first opportunity to see this vast cemetery, the largest in Europe, with its hundreds of thousands of graves. It had been vandalized during the occupation, expensive tombstones had been stolen and others had been desecrated with obscene anti-Semitic graffiti and swastikas. Now that a Jewish community had appeared again in Lodz, some restoration work was going on.

The Woroszylski family stood weeping at the graveside. There was Witek, his stepmother and his two sisters – his nine-year-old half-sister Cesia and his older sister Rita. It was such a sad occasion. Gershon Woroszylski had died at the age of 59, after all he had been through, a belated victim of Hitler, when at last the family could have enjoyed some happiness in their new life. We went home with sadness in our hearts, with the sense that for us the war was still far from over – or rather for our parents, for whom the strain of adapting, of starting from scratch after such a long struggle was just too much. I was worried about my father. He was the same age as Gershon, approaching 60. He looked very tired and depressed, and lately his heart had begun to trouble him again. I did not even want to think that he might die.

In the evening after supper, we listened intently to the BBC and sometimes to the news from Palestine where Jewish resistance to British rule was growing. We learned with pride about the Jewish underground army, the *Haganah*, and the Jewish Brigade composed mostly of volunteers from the Palestinian *Yishuv* who had fought the Germans in Italy alongside other brigades of the British Army. But we also learned with dismay about the unbelievable perfidy of the British who, even as millions of Jews were dying in Hitler's death camps, had kept a tight blockade on Palestine, sending back shiploads of Jewish refugees from Hitler's Europe to certain death. The fate of the *Struma*, a ship sent back to Europe only to be sunk by a submarine, with 700 Jewish refugees and 70 children on board, was just one tragedy out of many. At such times I hated the British and applauded whenever a violent act was committed against them by freedom fighters in their over-extended and shaky empire. I was now very nationalistic and dreamt of leaving this land soaked with Jewish blood, and the inhospitable people among whom I happened to have been born, as soon as possible. I dreamt of Palestine, at long last a land of our own.

Father said that we could only leave when I had completed high school, Tolo his medical school, and we as a family had 'a little something' to start a new life in Palestine. Under Father's pressure Tolo very reluctantly registered with the newly forming Medical School in Lodz. Tolo did not want to study; he wanted to make money, and his enthusiasm for medical school was nil. But Father insisted and, after long argument, made him register into the fourth year – almost as if the war had not happened.

In the meantime Tolo was preoccupied with other things, among them a new fad, the *Drang nach Western* [the rush to the West], meaning former Germany. News was filtering through from the occupied German territories that millions of Germans were going to be expelled as soon as the western borders of Poland were confirmed along the Oder and Neisse rivers, leaving a vast booty of German belongings to be 'recovered' by adventurous Poles. In the context of the time, such 'recovery' was considered morally justifiable and even a 'duty'. People formed expeditions into Soviet-occupied Germany; these activities even introduced a new word into the Polish vocabulary: *shaber*. To *shaber* meant going to Germany to 'recover' goods.

Tolo and many other men were swept by this irresistible urge. The stories of *shaber* were very enticing; the roads of Germany were paved with gold! We were very concerned about Tolo going to Soviet-occupied Germany, it was a dangerous place, teeming with drunken soldiers, refugees, deserters and common criminals from recently opened prisons. But, as the saying goes, 'where there is no risk there is no fun'. Tolo left in June with five other men from Grodno, including Izak's brother Leiba. He came back after two weeks on the road, bearded, bedraggled and far from having struck gold.

We all had a good laugh when he told us of their adventures. They had left Lodz and had never got further west than Lignica, a town in upper Silesia. There they had met some half-drunk Russian soldiers in a jeep who, in exchange for a case of vodka, had given them a German DKW car and 18 scrawny horses. Our lads had decided to use the car to transport themselves and the fodder for the exhausted animals. They had counted on bringing the horses to Lodz and selling them to peasants in the local market. The deal had looked good, as horses were worth a lot, but unfortunately the Russians had sobered up, turned around and swiftly caught up with the cavalcade. They had thrown Tolo, Leiba and another fellow out of the car, repossessed it, and left the young men with the exhausted horses. In the skirmish, Leiba had been beaten over the head with a rifle butt and had to be taken to a local doctor. It must have been a great sight: five Jews who, with the exception of Leiba, had never been on a horse in their life, riding bareback and leading two or three horses each. They had dallied in the hot sun along the dusty roads filled with army vehicles, soldiers and refugees. It was no wonder that their horses had started to die before they reached the city of Breslau (Wroclaw). They had lost about ten horses before they reached the Polish city of Wielun and then had no choice but to travel on foot alongside the remaining animals, cursing the very moment they had left Lodz. Some horses had died on the road from Wielun to Piotrkow and some had collapsed with exhaustion just before they entered Lodz, and had had to be shot. The two remaining animals had survived by some miracle and had been sold to local peasants. After dividing the spoils they were left with less money than they had had when they left Lodz. Thus ended the dream of wealth. The *shaber* fever was over.

29   My 1945 Holiday

In the middle of July, I passed easily into the senior class of the Accelerated High School of Magister Duczyminski and was planning my first holiday as a free young man. There was very little money in our house and I decided, with Yona, Felix and other young people, to go to Gdansk on the Baltic shore because Tolo was already there and I thus had my room and board assured. Gdansk – Danzig in German – had been a free port before the war; the war began when Germany annexed it on 1 September 1939. It was a beautiful baroque city, mostly German. Although severely damaged by the recent fighting it was a big port and an important commercial centre for the new Poland. Many refugees from the east were coming to Gdansk, looking for luck. Tolo and his partners had gone to Gdansk for a rest after their failed *shaber* expedition and had already been there for over three weeks.

One early August afternoon, I went to the railway station to board the train for Gdansk with Yona and Felix. Felix was exploring the possibility of enrolling as a student at the Polytechnic Institute of Gdansk and his Uncle Sender was already there. Most of the rolling stock was still used by the army and the few available passenger cars were packed to over-flowing with a human multitude: soldiers, civilians, adventurers – mostly men – were all cramming into the cars, pressing, pushing and shoving, standing in the corridors, or sitting almost on top of each other on the hard wooden seats. By some miracle we managed to get one seat for the three of us, and alternated standing and sitting. Mother equipped us well with sandwiches, cold meat and lemonade; enough food and drink for a whole day. When the train began to move off, some people left on the platform tried to squeeze into the carriage and 'bunches of human grapes' hung from the steps and windows of the moving train. Some even climbed on to the roof.

It was a nightmarish 24 hours in a crawling and frequently stopping train. We halted for many hours in the middle of nowhere when the engine broke down and had to be repaired. Between stops, the train advanced in the best tradition of a *Schlepp-Zug*, with top speeds of some 40 kilometres an hour. It was impossible to push through to the overflowing lavatory. The early August sun was merciless and the night did not provide much relief from the heat and the stench of human sweat and urine. People were restless, hungry, thirsty, dirty and clammy. Tempers were short and fist fights erupted over 'stolen' seats. We managed to keep ours, while trying to avoid the hostile looks from those standing around us. It seemed that the journey would never end. Exhausted, and looking like chimney sweeps, we finally made it into the station of Gdansk.

My first impression of Gdansk was of a sea of ruins, another Warsaw, but soon I noticed the difference. The city had not been systematically blasted, not all the buildings along the broad streets and avenues had been destroyed. Some were only half-burned, half-caved in; many were even still intact, revealing their former beauty. Some lamp posts had been twisted like wires, and some had been left untouched, as if an angry giant had hit the city at random. Danzig must once have been charming with its broad avenues, green squares and parks. Even the rubble from the desperate German resistance with its house-to-house fighting had not erased the beauty. To my surprise I saw entire blocks of comfortable houses that had been left untouched. Trams were on time and the crowds more orderly than in Lodz.

Tolo and his friends were rooming with German families. It was a sort of symbiosis: they protected the family from marauding soldiers and greedy civilians who went about seizing German apartments, sometimes assaulting or even throwing the owners out into the street. 'Protectors' were also useful because they brought in badly needed food; the German family, in return, provided its 'protectors' with the comforts of home and took care of all their wishes. 'Protectors' were given most of the space in the apartment, the family cooked for them, cleaned up after them and turned a blind eye to the relationships that developed with the young German women of the household.

Tolo lived in the roomy, cosy apartment of Herr and Frau
Weimert, an elderly German couple. Their daughter Ruth, and
her three-year-old son Hans, lived with them. I was surprised
to find Tolo ensconced like a pasha in this German household.
I was scandalized and shocked to hear *Hochdeutsch* spoken
again; it made my skin crawl. I almost shouted, 'How can you
stand to live with Germans, people who were murdering us
only a year ago?' But soon my dismay gave way to amazement: Ruth was tall, she had blue eyes and long flaxen hair –
one of those lanky, gorgeous mermaids that populate the
shores of the Baltic sea, a truly 'super-Aryan' female, she was
in love with Tolo, the brown-eyed Jew with his black curly
hair. She cooked for him, cleaned up after him and took care
of all his needs while her parents were happy, after the many
tribulations they had lately endured (when the Russians
entered Danzig, Ruth was raped like most German women
and much of their belongings were plundered), to have found
'protection' from rampaging soldiers and civilians in search of
loot and revenge. When I entered the apartment, Herr and
Frau Weimert greeted me with a deep bow of false respect; I
was the brother of Herr Tolo, the 'Protector'. Yona was a friend
of Herr Tolo, and was also fawned upon and pandered to. I
was first taken aback and disgusted by the servility of Herr
and Frau Weimert, angered by the German spoken around
me. To top it all, I learned with revulsion that Ruth's husband,
the father of her little blond Haenschen, was an SS soldier lost
in Russia. The Weimerts quickly freed a room for the two of
us, made up beds with their best linen and prepared a hot
bath, which we so badly needed. We were given a hot meal
with food that Tolo had helped to provide. I soon felt like a
prince surrounded by obedient servants who came running at
my slightest whim. It was not a bad feeling.

After a good nap we went to the beach to see the Baltic sea.
The shore was barely a mile from the Weimerts' house. We
crossed the dunes and there in all its splendour for my eyes to
behold for the first time in my life was the dark blue expanse
of the sea!

The three weeks with Tolo in Gdansk turned out to be a
most pleasant holiday for Yona and myself. We were waited
upon and pampered. The subservience and kowtowing of the

old Weimerts was somewhat annoying as I was convinced that in their heart of hearts they hated us. Ruth was different. I soon got to know her well and did not sense any covert hatred or contempt for the Jews in her. How could she have been married to an SS?

Our days were spent mostly sunbathing at the beach and swimming in the cold waters of the Baltic. We were especially fond of sunbathing on a surf board. Yona, who could not swim more than a few yards without being submerged by waves, always kept close to the shore. But one morning, as I dozed off in the sun, Yona fell asleep on his surf board and drifted out towards the open sea. When I realized what was happening it was already too late; he had drifted almost a kilometre from the shore; I could only see from afar his huge sunglasses covering half of his face. Yona's scream for help was muffled by an off-shore wind and was hardly audible. There were no people on the beach and I was unable to help him, he was simply too faraway for my swimming skills. I ran like mad to the house. Ruth and Tolo were just preparing to leave for the beach. She dropped everything and ran with me. By the time we arrived, Yona had drifted even further out. Being short-sighted I was unable to see him at all, but Ruth said he was almost two kilometres from the shore. She threw herself in to the water. Born on the Baltic, swimming was second nature to Ruth. With increasing tension, I observed her getting further and further away until I lost her from my myopic sight and had to rely on Tolo for information. Yona's surf board was now a dot in a silver shimmering sea. 'She's got him,' Tolo shouted. Ruth was dragging Yona on her back. The rescue took well over an hour, and Yona was all blue from chill and fright; he had lost his huge sunglasses but had kept his spectacles, which were attached by an elastic round his head. From then on, my attitude towards Ruth changed. I started to like her and I forgot that she was German.

Some of our friends told us about their experiences. Yosha Weiss lived with a woman who visited his bed at night while her husband, aware of the relationship, closed his eyes for the sake of keeping a 'protector' happy. All our friends in Danzig had similar tales about the Germans debasing themselves for 'protection' and food. They all grovelled to their new

My 1945 Holiday

'masters'. How could those people who only yesterday had been so convinced of their innate superiority that they were ready to enslave half of Europe, who were so cruel in their victory, now crawl so low in their defeat? I recalled in a flashback the many Soviet civilians trapped behind German lines; left without means. Their fate was much worse, but they retained their pride. Even the Jews in the ghetto – downtrodden and condemned to die – had miles of pride. We wore our Jewish armbands and yellow patches with dignity and if we bowed to Germans it was only because we were beaten and shot for not obeying. Everything we did was under extreme coercion, but in victory we were all accessible to compassion and even ready to forgive. Even though the Germans were now being maltreated, it was a very far cry from what we had suffered from them. They were not being killed. They were not starving. They still had their living quarters and their belongings. They were free to move, if temporarily limited in their travel. Their human dignity was not in question. How could one explain such a wave of grovelling and debasement?

The summer finally came to an end. In September I entered the last grade of the Accelerated High School of Magister Duczyminski. I promised myself to work hard for the *matura*, the high school diploma, which I intended to get before I turned 16 in January. Mother, as usual full of energy, started a wholesale business of textiles, woollens and ready-made clothing with three associates, investing our last penny in the venture. They named their store *Jednosc* ['Unity' in Polish], which was rather funny given that the associates did not totally trust each other.

The climate in Poland was never good for us Jews but now it was even worse than before the war. The Poles accused the Jews of causing all the misfortunes that came to Poland, and the fact that relatively many Jews held responsible positions in the government and in the army did not help. Poland was still a democracy of sorts. The Government of National Unity was multi-party, but dominated by the Communists (PPR) and the Socialists (PPS). The National Council was also multi-party but the referendum of June 1945, which amended the Polish constitution of 1921, paved the way for a Communist takeover. Nationalization of large private property, planned by the Communists and the Socialists, was slowly carried out. The opposition parties had practically no power. The Poles, resentful of the outcome of the Yalta Conference, considered themselves betrayed by the West and were very bitter about their future in a Soviet-dominated Poland – hatred of Russians was deeply anchored in Polish history.

This was the atmosphere in which the traditional anti-Semitism of the Poles exploded into violence. Units of the former Polish underground, the AK, and its extreme right-wing faction, the NSZ, murdered Jews while ostensibly leading partisan warfare against Russian army units and Polish security forces. Even during the German occupation, right-wing elements of the AK, especially in the Galicia and Kresy regions of Poland, killed Jews who had escaped from ghettos and camps. Izak Kobrowski claimed the Polish government in London had given secret orders to exploit the German genocide of the Jews to make sure that Poland would be free of its Jewish minority after the war. This campaign now intensified.

The Jews were an easy target: haggard, exhausted, mentally anguished, trickling in from occupied Germany, from Allied hospitals, survivors of Nazi labour and death camps, mere shadows of humans. Some Jewish refugees were returning from Russia. They came to their *shtetl*, to their village or town only to find locked doors, closed shutters and heartless words. Even cemeteries were desecrated. NSZ snipers often murdered Jews who had the audacity to come back to reclaim their belongings, to ask for justice, sometimes just to enquire about the fate of their loved ones. Trains and buses were stopped in the countryside, passengers were ordered out and Jews – men, women and children – separated from the rest, together with Red Army soldiers and Communist officials, and executed. Travel became dangerous for Jews. In the cities, NSZ execution squads broke into Jewish apartments at night, murdering entire families. The aim was, as they themselves proclaimed, 'to rid Poland of Jews'. This indiscriminate terror was theoretically opposed by the official authorities but at the grass-roots level the local police often turned a blind eye when Jews were singled out for punishment. The Polish government mobilized special security forces who, under Soviet supervision, were engaged in tracking down and battling against the nationalistic underground and the NSZ, 'the boys from the forest', as they were so endearingly nick-named by a sympathetic population.

Poland slowly became a ground for partisan warfare, with the pitiful remnants of Polish Jews paying the price. The area of and around the historic city of Cracow was the most affected, since Cracow was traditionally a hotbed of Polish nationalism. Lodz, an industrial city populated by factory workers who were much more socialist in their outlook, was less implicated in this violent anti-Semitic wave sweeping the country. Nevertheless it became unsafe for a Jew to venture alone into the outskirts of the city, even by day, and we installed safety locks and chains on the massive front door and on the back door of our apartment. Father brought home a German Luger with 20 bullets. I carefully cleaned and greased the heavy pistol and we kept it loaded on top of my parents' large wardrobe in their bedroom. We certainly intended to fight it out if ever NSZ terrorists ventured into our apartment.

These were difficult, dark times for me. Father's health was rapidly declining. One day he collapsed while trying to catch a tram to work; it was a heart attack. He was brought home in an ambulance and had to stay in bed for a week without moving at all, with severe chest pains. He recovered temporarily. Mother was very busy working at the store. She often battled with her partners in *Jednosc*, whom she consid-ered only marginally honest. I worked very hard at school to prepare for my *matura* examinations, scheduled for the begin-ning of January. I knew how happy Father would be to see me as a high-school graduate.

At this time I also became deeply disturbed by a romance that was developing between Mother and Ludwik Brysz. Ludwik was coming back to life in the warm atmosphere of our now extended family. At mealtimes we were seven people seated around the table: Mother, Father, Ludwik, Yona, Lusia, Tolo and myself. Ludwik became one of us, devoted to our family, sharing our joys and sorrows; shedding his depression, he became almost cheerful. It had been obvious to me for some time that he liked my mother. This did not bother me, but what I had seen lately disturbed me profoundly: Mother was beginning to reciprocate. While Father and I went to bed early, both of them stayed up quite late, completing jigsaw puzzles together. They also went out shopping and took long walks together. Mr Brysz was now a boss, having partially recovered his textile plant, where he employed a whole crowd of young German girls. Once I paid him a visit. Girls, some of them pretty, were sorting out mountains of rags. They were speaking German and laughing. The girls were quite ready to flirt with me; I was, however, not ready to flirt with them. Ludwik teased me. He was not a bad fellow but, as time went by, I started to see him in my imagination as a messenger of Father's death, wanting to take his place and wishing him ill. I felt repulsion and, as Father's condition worsened, outright hostility. My admiration and love for Father knew no bounds; I saw in him our saviour, my guide and moral reference, my pride. I prayed every day for Father's health and his life. But I knew instinctively what I rejected with all my soul, that time was running out.

Autumn in Lodz is drizzly and the winter foggy, much more unpleasant than in Grodno, where biting frost was softened by bright sunshine. I was now preparing for the final exams, working day and night. I wanted to succeed for Father. With Tolo, Father had problems. Tolo, who was now enrolled into the fourth year of medical school, was reluctant to study. He preferred to be out with girls, and rumour had it that he was going out with the young and pretty Hela Tarlowska from Grodno. Instead of studying, he often went out at night to shows and cabarets. He often hummed the latest songs of the famous comic Sempolinski. At home, father subjected Tolo to 'inspections' of his books to make sure he was reading enough medical literature. But Tolo would usually have two books on the go, some pot-boiler and a medical manual. When Father was about, he would hide the novel and read the medical book, but as soon as Father left the room the manual was swapped for the pot-boiler. It was so easy to take Father in, but I had no illusions of Tolo ever becoming a medical doctor. For my part I decided to pass my *matura* at all costs in January. Yona and

Lusia were hoping to do the same in May. We all celebrated New Year's Eve, the first year of peace, with vodka and an excellent dinner.

30   1946

I passed the *matura* examinations with reasonably good grades, not a bad performance for someone who had skipped so many years of school. But my best reward was to see Father's happiness about his *funfurek*, not yet 16 and already a high-school graduate. This made my birthday a very joyful event. I was finally free from having to work every evening and every weekend for hours on end, and I now looked for friends of my own age – but not many were left, mostly some survivors from Russia. I joined the General Zionist Organization, the *Ichud*, that had recently formed in Lodz. A warm atmosphere prevailed there and I found young people who thought like I did. We sang Hebrew songs (which I did not understand, but that did not matter), recited Hebrew and Polish-Jewish poems, looked at slides and films about the *Yishuv*, commented and discussed the problems of Zionism and the Jewish State. It gave me a feeling of pride and belonging.

Also, around this time, I finally stood up to Tolo, who was still in the habit of hitting me whenever he decided that I was irritating. It was a sort of tradition. One day as Tolo hit me I decided that I had had enough; I threw myself on him with fury and almost knocked him to the ground. He was surprised: I was becoming dangerous! Mother and Father tried in vain to separate us, but we were too strong for them. Finally, exhausted and shaken, we gave up and soon we were embracing. It was the last time that Tolo ever hit me.

During the first few months after my graduation from high school I felt free like a bird. I went often to the *Ichud*, participated in the activities of the Zionist Organization, played football and volleyball, and tried to make up for the time lost cooped-up studying. I had the wonderful feeling of being carefree. I also acquired more self-confidence; I had, after all, succeeded in covering six years of school in barely 18 months. I was proud of myself.

In April, I was placed on the list of the next year's prospective students at the Department of Chemical Engineering at the Polytechnic of Lodz, but actual admission was contingent upon my satisfactory performance at the entrance examinations. It was time to start preparing for the September entrance examinations, but I had fallen in love with a pretty girl whom I had met at the *Ichud*. Ruth was a tall blonde with magnificent, almond-shaped blue eyes. She had a baby face with a few freckles on her cheeks, a little snub nose and full, red, slightly sulky lips. Ruth was from Wilno and she had survived the war with her family in Russia. Like me she was 16. It was a time of sighing and vowing eternal love under blooming lilacs, picnics at the swimming pool and Sundays at the football games. By June, Ruth had left for Germany with her parents, on her way to joining her uncle in Capetown. We swore fidelity and promised to meet again after my studies were completed.

We were becoming a community of future exiles; everybody was planning to leave for somewhere and, although we sang the *Hatikvah* and the *Tekhezaknah*, read Herzl, Jabotinsky and Pinskier, and dreamt of the future Jewish State, we all knew that many were heading elsewhere: South Africa, America, Australia. I even struck up a warm friendship with a boy of my age, Julek Feldman, whose family had also survived in Russia and who eventually headed for… Finland. He had an uncle there and told me how great the Finns were, how civilized, and there was no anti-Semitism whatsoever. I was deeply moved by the story of the brave Danes who, led by their king, all donned armbands with the Star of David when the Nazis ordered Danish Jews to wear them – the badge of shame became the badge of pride for an entire people. I was fascinated to learn how they saved their Jewish citizens by smuggling them into neutral Sweden.

Why is it that peoples are so different? Here, in Poland, we lived in fear of an NSZ bullet. Father's dream of 'a little house on Mount Carmel' was in my mind all the time, but first Tolo had to graduate from the medical school and we all hoped the Unity store would bring us something to leave with. Mother worked very hard and Lusia helped too, but private initiative was very uncertain under the government of National Unity and the future of the store was doubtful at best; more and more private businesses were being expropriated and nationalized. Rumours about a possible ban on travel to the West circulated as relations between the former allies deteriorated.

It was at that time that Father became angry with me during one of our 'BBC evenings'. I listened first to some comments from the Arab world citing the Grand Mufti of Jerusalem, the Nazi collaborator and now the spiritual and political leader of the Palestinians. The Arab leaders were promising to push the Jews into the sea at the first opportunity. A recently published US plan to admit 100,000 Jewish refugees from European Displaced Persons camps and abolish the British prohibition on Jews buying land in Palestine was also heatedly discussed. One of the parties expressed vehement opposition to this plan because 'the Jews will chase the Palestinian Arabs from their land'. I could hardly take it any more.

'To hell with them!' I exploded. 'Instead of them pushing us into the sea, we should chase them out of Palestine, once and for all! They can go to hell and live with their Arab brothers and their accursed Mufti! Let injustice befall our enemies for once in history!'

Father became very upset. 'Alik,' he said, 'you disappoint me very much. How can you, after all we have been through, insist on chasing people from their homes and the land where they have lived for centuries? We the Jews, of all people, should not replace one injustice by another. Otherwise our state will lose its moral justification. I envision,' he continued, 'eventually, a bi-national state on both sides of the River Jordan, where Palestinian Arabs and Jews will live in peace side by side – a sort of Switzerland of the Middle East. It will not be easy, but we should not jeopardize this future.'

It was one of the last discussions I had with Father on Palestine. It revealed to me the complexity and humanity of this man, who did not harbour any illusions about the necessity of armed struggle against the perfidy of the British empire and against the feudal Arab world. But his wish to be just and magnanimous after achieving our ultimate objective, a state for both Arab and Jew on both sides of the River Jordan, will stay with me for ever.

In the last week of May Father's health suddenly took a turn for the worse. He collapsed with chest pains at work and was brought home in an ambulance. The cardiologist, our friend Dr Libo who came to his bedside, told Mother that it looked very serious, probably a blood clot. Father should remain immobile in bed for at least a week and then take it very easy.

Saddened as I had been by the departure of Ruth, I suddenly realized that I could lose my father, and everything else became insignificant. I realized how much he represented, how much I loved him and how much I needed him. He was the guide leading us to safe harbour through the worst of hurricanes. With him nothing seemed difficult; he was my reference. I spent hours at his bedside talking and listening to him, and at night I prayed for him. Father's chest pains were crushing and returned with increasing frequency. He suffered in silence and only pearls of sweat on his forehead indicated the pain. Dr Libo came regularly to take his pulse, measure his blood pressure, listen to his heart and give him an injection to ease the pain. There were new drugs in America that could have helped my father, but unfortunately there was no way to get them – they were very expensive and hard to obtain. Father knew exactly the difficulty of his condition and yet he remained the most cheerful of us all. His illness hung like a cloud over me, while everything in nature cried out for life – apple trees and linden were blooming, the scent of honeysuckle hung in the air and girls were wearing their summer attire. I could not allow myself to go out while Father was so sick. I started to prepare for the admission tests to the Polytechnic of Lodz. Every evening I listened to his shallow, painful breathing and I prayed.

By the middle of June Father felt better and was able to get up and walk about for a few hours a day. Friends came to visit him. Aunt Ada and Izak came by too. They were preparing to leave for Austria quite soon. Izak desperately wanted to go to America but first he had to get on a long waiting list in a refugee camp in Austria. Felix Zandman also came to see Father. He had just passed into the second year of the

Polytechnic Institute in Gdansk. Father liked Felix, '*Z niego beda ludzie* – He will become somebody,' he would say.[1]

Happy that Father felt better, I started to go out again. Playing volleyball at the *Ichud* with friends, going to football matches, I almost forgot about Father's illness. The reminder came soon enough, suddenly, like an avalanche. One day, just back from a game of volleyball, I learned that Father had had yet another heart attack.

'I thought he was not going to pull through,' Mother sobbed. 'Dr Libo gave him an injection, he left a few minutes ago.' I ran to father's bedside.

'Shhh...,' warned Lusia, 'he is resting. Do not disturb him.'

Father was ghostly white, his eyes were half-closed. I could read on his face the agony he was going through and the trouble he was having breathing. What a fool I had been to think that by some miracle he was over his illness. He saw me entering the room and made a weak sign to come closer and sit at his bedside. I sat and took his hand, fighting the tears that filled my eyes. I sat there still, caressing his hand. 'Oh God, how I love him! It just cannot be that these are our last moments together, the last time I can see this dear face and hold his hand. No! I will stay here day and night until he gets better!'

It was getting very hot. It was the end of June and I worked on my maths problems with my window open. A radio from the neighbour's apartment across the yard constantly blared out songs. A new languorous melody, *Warsaw, My Warsaw*, written by the Jewish composer Harris who had survived the war in Russia and had just returned to Poland, was played on the radio every day. A man's voice sang:

Jak usmiech dziewczyny kochanej,	Like a smile of my beloved girl,
Jak wiosny budzacej sie spiew,	Like the song of the awaking spring,

---

[1] Felix Zandman eventually moved to the United States to become a captain of industry. His '*Fortune* 500' company, Vishay Intertechnologies was named after his grandmother's *shtetl* near Grodno. He also played an important role in the economic and military life of the State of Israel and acquired, among others, the famous German Telefunken radio company.

1946

Jak swiergot jaskolek nad ranem,	Like the chatter of swallows in the morning,
Mlodziencze uczucia nieznane,	Like the stirrings of youth,
Jak rosa blyszczaca na trawie,	Like the glitter of dew on petals,
Milosci rodzacaj sie zew –	Like the call of a nascent love –
Tak serce raduje piosenki mej spiew –	I sing with joy in my heart –
Piosenki o mojej Warszawie.	A song about my Warsaw.

It was a long, sad song about the Warsaw of yesterday and today, and it constantly distracted me from algebra, calculus and analytical geometry, the main topics of the entrance exams, and from running to Father's room to check on how he was feeling.

July came. Father had been better for a week, and I went out for the first time in two weeks to a meeting at the *Ichud* where we discussed the recent attacks by the Haganah and Irgun on British airfields, the arrest of many *Yishuv* leaders and the death sentences meted out by the British to some of the Irgun prisoners. I stayed later to play volleyball in the gym and came home at around ten o'clock. As I was going up the backstairs leading to the kitchen, I heard Mother's desperate voice.

'Alik, Alik, go quickly and get Dr Libo! Run! Run! Father is dying! Quick! Oh God, quick!' Dr Libo lived quite a distance from us, on Przejazd Street. My ears rang with Mother's desperate cry: 'Run! Run! Father is dying!'

I had to run a long way on Narutowicza, turn left on Piotrkowska, run along Piotrkowska until its intersection with the Przejazd, turn left and run a few blocks before I reached Dr Libo's house. I was out of breath, my heart was beating like a wild caged bird but I kept running, 'Faster, faster, faster!' A voice in me resonated: 'No matter how fast you run, it is too late.'

I was sobbing, everything was a blur, the whole world swirled and danced as I continued to run, praying that Father could be saved and knowing that he was dying. Without realizing yet what it would mean to my life, I knew how poor I would be without him. He had brought us to a safe haven and now he was leaving us for ever. I ran and sobbed, tears streaming down my cheeks. Another few hundred metres:

Przejazd and the staircase of Dr Libo's house. First floor! Black and white spots flashed before my eyes. I rang the bell and Mrs Libo opened the door. She understood in a flash; she sat me in a chair and gave me a glass of water, which I could hardly swallow, while Dr Libo went to get his coachman with the carriage he used for emergencies. It started to rain. The hooves of horses resonated endlessly on the asphalt: 'Father is dying! Father is dying! Faster, faster!' We stopped and Dr Libo leapt out and ran up the staircase. I went slowly... far behind... afraid... I heard Mother's sobbing and instantly I knew... Father had died. I stopped and grabbed the banister; everything swirled around me and it felt like a black chasm had opened up and was engulfing me. I did not know what to do, where to turn. I had no will to go up the stairs. I had no will to live.

Dr Libo left soon; there was nothing he could do. Father had passed away, victim of a final heart attack. Before dying he had suffered massive pain. His last words to Mother were: 'Tell the children that I want them to be honest and harm no one, as I have tried all my life not to harm anyone... Poor Esterka, how will you manage?'

Tolo came home past midnight. He cried. Lusia consoled Mother. In deep shock I wrote a few lines dedicated to Father which I keep with me to this day as one of my most precious mementos. I spent the rest of the night sitting in my room, staring blankly at the wall. I had no tears left.

The morning of 5 July 1946 started with preparations for the funeral. Aunt Ada came with Izak; they were just about to leave for Austria. The day was bright and beautiful, one of those summer days with a deep blue sky and warm sunshine, contrasting with the darkness that invaded my soul.

Ludwik Brysz came from town bringing bad news: a bloody pogrom had taken place in Kielce, a city some 100 miles from us. A mob, excited by rumours about 'Jews who kidnapped a Christian child and took his blood to make matzoth' – that old anti-Semitic canard spread by the Catholic clergy in medieval times – had broken into a Zionist transit centre preparing young Holocaust survivors to leave for Palestine. Nearly 50 Jews, men, women and children, had been murdered. Pregnant women were killed with knives and pitchforks. The police had stood by without intervening. The local police chief was placed under arrest by the Communist authorities. Troops were dispatched to Kielce. Throughout Poland, Jewish communities were placed on alert for possible other pogroms. What a country! What a people! What a homeland!

Bewildered, I walked behind Father's coffin, which was placed on a horse-drawn hearse, all the long way to the Jewish cemetery. With my left hand I held my mother's arm; she was supported on her other side by Tolo. My right hand was in my pocket, clutching the handle of our loaded Luger. The feel of the cold steel calmed my fever. I was tormented by everything that had happened and was ready to shoot to kill any Pole who dared interfere with the Jewish funeral of my father. It was a long way to the Jewish cemetery. We had to move along Narutowicza Street and then Piotrkowska, cross through the former ghetto and proceed for a long while out of the city. I walked as if in a bad dream, thinking about the future without Father, in a country which I increasingly hated. I was certain that Father's demise had been hastened by the persecution of his Jewish name. He had been demoted and stripped of responsibilities because he was a proud Jew. But these small individual persecutions were not enough. The NSZ, with the help of mobs and even local authorities, was savagely killing whatever remained of us here in this Godforsaken land.

That was the end of your journey, Father. You were spared nothing. You fought for a just Poland against the Tsar, you were arrested and banned from schools in Russia, only to see an anti-Semitic Poland emerge and persecute your people. You went to study in Germany, where a German student, an anti-Semite, insulted you in Leipzig. You challenged him to a duel and you chose pistols: but the German did not show up for the duel, he lost his nerve. As a young lieutenant surgeon of the Russian Imperial Army in the First World War you saw the misery of defeat and slaughter at the killing fields of Tannenberg. You spent two years in a German prisoner-of-war camp, escaped to England and then made your way back to St Petersburg in 1916. You were decorated with one of the highest honours that could be bestowed on a Jew in tsarist Russia: personal knighthood. You got this distinction only to see the empire disintegrate in 1917 while you were fighting

the Turks at Erzerum in Armenia. There you were overcome
by typhoid fever and almost died. You saw the revolution,
misery and pogroms in the Ukraine and you found your own
father assaulted by the Ukrainian hoodlums of Petlyura. You
were spared nothing.

You went back to the country you were convinced was
yours by right of birth and heart only to realize the depth of
hatred and intolerance pervading the new Poland. If you were
not wanted you would not stay. You became a Zionist and a
partisan of armed struggle with all the enemies of our people.
You dreamt of 'a little house on Mount Carmel'. You were
trapped by the Germans in the Grodno ghetto and displayed
inordinate courage, standing tall even at the Gestapo. *'Der
Jude war frech!'* [The Jew was arrogant!], this phrase spoken by
the SD killer Wiese gave one measure of the man you were.
You led us out of the ghetto and you saved us, but at such a
cost to yourself when you were forced to abandon your old
and helpless mother. You were spared nothing. You were
ready to cut your veins when your friend and saviour Dr
Docha insisted on us converting to Catholicism. You were
spared nothing. In the aftermath of the Holocaust it was not a
'Medal of the Ghetto' that awaited you but the new humiliations of a menial job in a small dispensary, because you
refused to 'catholicize' your name to Mateusz Kwiatkowski.
You always proudly bore the name of Chaim Mordechai
Blumstein and would never dream of changing it for
expediency or profit. You were spared nothing. When illness
struck, you knew that the end was near, yet you never lost
your composure and never let us know what you alone knew
so well. Your thoughts were for your family; your wife – who
you knew could not remain alone – and your sons whom you
wanted more than anything to set on their way in life. You
looked beyond the surface into the future. You were spared
nothing.

I stood next to the dark deep hole into which Father's body
was lowered, wrapped in a traditional Jewish shroud and his
tales. I felt all my world was disappearing into it. I was blinded
by the tears that streamed uncontrollably down my cheeks,
falling on the freshly excavated earth. *'Iskadal, v'iskadash, shnei
raba...'* The Kaddish...The choking voice of Tolo, his eyes full

of tears. Then came my turn. With a supreme effort to stifle the sobs tearing at my soul, I read the Kaddish. And then came the most difficult and the most painful moment of my life: I threw a handful of earth down into the grave, a handful of cold, unfriendly Polish earth. Why not Palestine? Why not 'a little house on Mount Carmel'? The dream was dead. You were spared nothing. The world danced before my eyes, people, people, everyone from the tiny community of survivors from Grodno, some Christians too. People shook my hand, stopping to say a few words of commiseration, but I was in a dream, incapable of distinguishing one face from another. Suddenly I felt a slight touch and a whisper. It was my new friend from the *Ichud*, Julek Feldman. He cried, he pressed my hand and I pressed his; we both sobbed and hugged each other. I was deeply touched by this mark of friendship coming straight from the heart. I knew that he was leaving in a few days for Helsinki, but he had come to comfort his new friend. Julek was a sensitive boy who had seen a lot of misery in Russia. He was fortunate to have his family but he did not take his luck for granted. He felt my pain and shared it with me from the depth of his heart. It is strange that this moment of shared pain, these tears coming from a friendly heart gave me more strength and comfort than all the other condolences put together. That moment will stay with me for ever and, if somebody asked me today, 'How many friends did you have?' Julek – whom I knew only for a fleeting moment in my life – would be the first among them.

I was no longer the teenage youngster I had been. In all those years full of anguish, uncertainty, mortal danger and deprivation, nothing touched me deeper and made a stronger mark than the loss of my beloved father. I had seen death at close range many times and felt her cold breath on my face, yet only now did I realize her ultimate message. In my pain I withdrew from the world into myself. I ceased to laugh, to see my friends from the *Ichud*. I even didn't pay attention to the blowing up of Jerusalem's King David hotel, which filled the news. I devoted my time to mourning and work. Every Saturday I spent the morning at the grave of my father. I felt then he was with me: I could still hear his dear voice and feel his presence. After my visits the pain receded and I felt better.

Tolo and Hela Tarlowska had decided to get married and leave Poland for France. Hela had a maternal uncle in Paris, Monsieur Zablocki, whose family had been saved from the Germans in the south of France. He had owned a pharmacy near the Place de la République. He had invited the young couple to go to France. A great opportunity presented itself: an international meeting of Jewish students, the first after the war, was to be held by the *Union des Etudiants Juifs de France* in Uriage-les-Bains in September. Felix Zandman, who was a student at the Polytechnic Institute of Gdansk, was one of the organizers of the Polish delegation. Tolo applied for a place as a student from the Medical School in Lodz. I was also persuaded to apply as a prospective student of the Chemical Engineering Department of the Polytechnic in Lodz. We were all on the list of official delegates.

Mother was supposed to join us later with a normal emigration visa. To my distress and pain, she was spending more and more time with Ludwik. I wanted to get away: out of Poland and away from a home that now, after Father's death, I considered broken. I was slightly unhappy with Tolo's plans to be married only six weeks after Father's death, within the full period of mourning. But we were on the list of departure and it was a golden opportunity for the young couple to travel together to France as man and wife.

At the beginning of August, Ludwik Brysz was arrested for some illegal dealings and sentenced to 18 months in prison. I was not entirely displeased with this turn of events. I resented Ludwik very much for his courtship of my mother and I resented her reciprocating. Ludwik had tried hard to please me. He had told me that Father, who had been well aware of his heart condition and had given himself less than a year to live, had asked him in January to take care of his family. He said that he had promised Father to look after us and that he was grateful for this second chance in his life to have a home and a family. Whatever the truth, I was not ready to listen to such talk.

Tolo and his fiancée had decided to go for a short holiday to Sopot, a spa on the Baltic Sea. Mother insisted I go with them, thinking it might bring me out of my emotional withdrawal. I protested at first, not even willing to consider missing my

Saturdays at Father's grave. But I also wanted to get away from home and I let myself be convinced. We flew to Gdansk in an old Douglas, my first flight ever. It was a lively trip;the plane vibrated and sparks flew out of the motor housings. The noise of both propellers was deafening. Strong head winds made the old bi-motor shake and squeak, now suddenly climbing, now suddenly sinking into an air pocket. Hela became air-sick and I felt my stomach floating. We stayed at a hotel next to the beach. Mother joined us a few days later, too depressed to stay alone in Lodz. Hela's father and her uncle, Mr Niankowski, came as well. The weather was hot and very sunny. I admired the beautiful sunsets on the sea from the bench by the pedestrian crossing below my room.

Hela turned out to be a very fine girl and I took a liking to her. I later called her 'my sister'. She was soft-spoken and good-hearted. She saw my pain and tried her best to help, but I hurt so deeply that it was difficult for me to escape. I exhausted myself swimming in the morning for more than four miles along the Sopot pier, but the thought of Father came back to me painfully again and again. I refused to go to theatres, cinemas or dances; it was just unthinkable for me to interrupt my mourning.

Yet the week in Sopot was a blessing; I swam and hiked along the beautiful beaches of the Baltic, in the pine forest of Orlovo and along the Hel peninsula with its sandy banks. My slow healing began. We came back by train. The trains were now functioning relatively well; it took only seven hours, a far cry from my adventurous trip to Gdansk a year before.

Tolo and Hela were married after our return but there was little joy at the wedding. Hela and her father cried, thinking of their entire family who had been murdered by the Germans. We cried for Father. It was a swift wedding: the *huppah* [wedding canopy], the broken glass...kisses...and a lot of tears.

The recent series of events made me change my decision to leave for the International Jewish Students' Congress at Uriage-les-Bains. Mother was going through a very difficult period of her life: she had lost her husband, her older son had married and was leaving, the person she loved, who was courting her, had been imprisoned. She was irritable and took it out on Hela, who now lived with us. Tensions at home made life unbearable. Mother often burst into tears, crying that she did not want to stay in Poland or go to France or, for that matter, to any other foreign country. She wanted to join Lolya and her mother in Ryazan. She sobbed, calling out to her brother, *'Lyola moi Lyoletchka ya takaia nistchastnaia!'* [Lolya, my little Lolya, I am so unhappy!] Adding to her despair, the trickle of letters between Mother and her family in Ryazan was interrupted in April by the departure of Major Syrkin, the Soviet go-between whom we had befriended soon after our arrival in Lodz. Mother could not write to Lolya directly lest he be arrested and all his family destroyed by corresponding with the 'West'. As had happened previously in Grodno, the correspondence passed through the field mail of the major. NKVD terror in the Soviet Union was now reaching its pre-war intensity. We were delighted to have left in time, escaping this collective madness, but this did not make Mother any happier. I could not bear watching Hela suffer, Tolo suffer and Mother suffer, and I realized that I could not leave Mother alone.

One other event confirmed in me the belief that I should not leave my mother at this time. Mother was irritable and quarrelled with and was insulted by one of her business partners at their Unity clothing store. Some of her partners were crude, thick-skinned and unsentimental. They were out to make a fast buck and leave Poland as soon as possible. Mother told us that she caught one of them falsifying some receipts and embezzling money from the store. In her usual way, she confronted him directly. In the verbal exchange the man insulted her deeply and even raised his hand to her. My anger swelled as I listened to Mother sobbing as she recounted this ugly incident. Finally I lost my self-control and, determined to teach him a lesson, I grabbed the Luger and ran out. The store was located on our street some 500 yards from the house. I intended to hit the man and produce the Luger to frighten him into behaving properly. I would shoot only in self-defence. As I burst into the store, I saw only one of the partners; the man I was after was not there. My voice trembling from excitement and anger, totally oblivious to the customers whom the partner was serving, I screamed: 'Where is the son of a bitch who insults and attacks defenceless women? I'll shoot his ears off!'

Scared to death, abandoning the customers, the partner disappeared behind the door of the storage room in the back of the shop. As I burst into the storage room, I saw the man I was after climbing on the table and stepping on to the windowsill. Seeing him panic, I wanted to make him even more scared.

'Stop!' I yelled. 'Come down and fight, you scum, or I will shoot you like a dog!' I drew my Luger. But the partner was already out of the open window and running. I tried for several days to find this man and humiliate him publicly but he could not be found anywhere. He was sure that I was insane and that I would shoot him.

This sad episode convinced me that I should not leave Mother alone. The organizers of the trip, furious at me for wasting a valuable spot on the list of delegates, gave another young man the opportunity of taking my place and using the name of Alexandre Blumstein.[2]

Tolo and Hela went to Warsaw, where the Polish delegates to the International Jewish Student Congress in Uriage-les-Bains assembled before boarding the train for Paris. Everybody was supposed to return after the meeting in October, but none did. They all were allowed to remain in France.

I was now busy preparing for my admission tests for the *Polytechnika*. My social background was such that I had to perform very well indeed to be admitted. Students of worker and peasant background were given special consideration as the Communist party, the PPR, slowly assumed total control over social and educational life in Poland. Political parties other than Communist and Socialist, such as the Polish People's Party of Mikolajczyk, still struggled for influence but, with the end of the nationalization drive that expropriated all but the smallest of private businesses and with the defeat of the AK and the NSZ, the balance of power had decisively shifted in favour of the Communists. Elections to the

---

[2] Two years later in Paris, while extending my residency permit, the police were puzzled by the existence of two Alexandre Blumsteins, both born in Grodno on the same date but with completely different faces. I had trouble explaining to the police sergeant at the *Préfecture* what had happened in September 1946. Fortunately, the other 'Alexandre Blumstein' soon left France, thus returning to me the sole ownership of my identity.

Narodowa Rada [National Council] were scheduled for January 1947 and everyone knew that in Communist hands the elections would be a farce confirming the dictatorship of the Communist party. But frankly for us, so intent on leaving Poland, this was the least of our worries.

In October I passed the entrance examinations to the *Polytechnika* and was admitted as a full-time student into the first year of the Department of Chemistry. I continued to work hard to maintain myself among the best students, feeling that it would have made Father happy. I wore the distinctive headgear of the *Polytechnika* with pride: a crimson cap with a visor and the emblem of the school.

I was still in full mourning, going every Saturday to visit my beloved father's grave and gathering strength for the week to come. Mother, having somehow patched up her quarrel with her partners, worked hard at the store. She was the breadwinner. Ludwik Brysz was still in prison. His lawyer promised to get him out by spring and I was not looking forward to his return.

The dreadful autumn of Lodz had arrived with its mist, smog and cold drizzle hanging over the monotonous rows of ugly houses and heavy textile mills. The early dusk descending upon the dark streets, the few huddled passersby fleeing the cold dampness, the occasional ear-splitting screech of trams driving to their depots on the outskirts – those are my recollections of Lodz. There is hardly any city in my life with which I associate so much gloom. It may well be that these memories were reflections of my inner feelings, as in the words of Prevert: '*Il pleut sur la ville comme il pleut dans mon coeur*' [It rains on the city as it rains in my heart]. I will always look back on the 1946–47 winter in Lodz as one of the darkest periods of my life. Even the execution of the 11 Nazi chief criminals in Nuremberg and, a month later, the joyful news about the UN Commission's recommendation to divide Palestine into a Jewish and an Arab state did not lift me out of my gloom.

At the *Polytechnika*, calculus and physics occupied most of my time, but I also learned chemistry, especially analytical chemistry from the textbook by Treadwell which we followed rather faithfully. My nemesis was industrial drawing, in which I had negative skills. We were about three Jews in a class of 40. From time to time, I had to assert myself to keep the open anti-Semites at bay, but most of them left me alone. Since my early days at the grammar school in Grodno I somehow instinctively understood that anti-Semitic thugs were in reality a bunch of posturing cowards who were covering up a lack of confidence in themselves by cultivating racial hatred and violence. Nothing excited them more than those who gave in to their threats and aggression. One of my fellow Jews in my class at the *Polytechnika*, Michal Malkes, was a case in point. He had survived in the Soviet Union with his family, finished high-school in Russia and had just returned to Lodz. He was an excellent and very capable student, first in most subjects, but he passively submitted to anti-Semitic abuse. I was often disgusted by those big oafs, with their jeers and innuendoes, surrounding Michal and taunting him, imitating derisively his slightly Jewish accent and his Jewish-sounding name, 'Malkees, Malkees...' But they refrained from violence, perhaps afraid of the secret police, the *Bezpieka*, which included quite a few Jews in their ranks.

In January, 1947, there was an election to the National Council of Poland. As everyone had expected, it was a giant farce. The elections were held under the watchful eye of the *Bezpieka*. Voting was done by city blocks deciding to vote collectively for the Workers Party, the PPR. Every inhabitant of voting age from our house at 47 Narutowicza was summoned several times to meetings by the Citizen Voting Committee of our block, usually chaired by someone from the PPR or the PPS.

At such meetings, speeches praising the past and future accomplishments of 'People's Poland' under the leadership of the 'Socialist Parties' were delivered by party representatives. At the pre-election meeting, after a lengthy speech by the chairman of the Committee, it was 'proposed' as a sign of our 'admiration' for the accomplishments of the 'Socialist Coalition' to vote for it collectively as a block. 'Who is against this proposal?' asked the chairman while a few men in leather coats scrutinized the room. Of course, there was no opposition. 'Who has any questions?' There were none. The proposal was adopted unanimously. There was music and tea as the 'unanimous' resolution of our city block to vote for the 'Socialist Coalition' was read aloud.

In the national elections the 'Socialist Coalition' won 'by a landslide'. The PPL opposition 'lost' the elections and its leader Mikolajczyk had to flee to England. The victory of the PPR signified the end of the so-called multi-party system in Poland. By March the pressures on even small private businesses became unbearable. As a result, we could hardly make ends meet on Mother's earnings at the store. I worked very hard; my courses at the *Polytechnika* were difficult and my background very weak. My sadness combined with uninterrupted work were disquieting to Mother. She tried to drag me out to some of the few theatres in Lodz. The comic Sempolinski was frequently a guest on various shows, the Moyseev Ballets and the Alexandrov Red Army Chorus also appeared. But I adamantly refused to compromise my mourning.

Tolo and Hela sent cheerful letters full of admiration for France and Paris. They lived with Hela's relatives, the Zablockis. It was obvious that Tolo had once and for all abandoned the study of medicine, partly because it was just too difficult for a foreigner to practise medicine in France but mostly because he was more interested in making a living and laying the foundation for a family. He decided to join his father-in-law, Mr Tarlowski, and a few other refugees from Poland in a business venture.

By February we had started to think seriously about joining Tolo in France. We applied for emigration papers and began pushing our way through the swamps of Polish bureaucracy. This became possible despite the deteriorating international situation because the Polish government was eager to rid itself of the remnants of Jews in Poland, hoping their emigration would put an end to the country's endemic anti-Semitism and the bad publicity it brought to Poland. Consulates of South American republics such as Bolivia, Colombia and others were selling entry visas for as little as 50 dollars. Since the trip to any South American port of entry usually passed through Le Havre, the French consulate delivered a transit visa valid for three months to anyone whose passport was stamped with a South American entry visa. The French closed their eyes to the fact that many transit refugees were actually seeking permanent residency in France. Despite a difficult economic situation in the war-devastated country, France was willing to help tens of thousands of Jewish refugees from the East at a time when the doors to other Western democracies had been slammed shut. Recent anti-Jewish violence in Poland, including the Kielce pogrom, caused thousands of Jews to flee to the West, besieging South American consulates for entry visas. The US was still refusing to let in refugees, except for the trickle allowed under immigration quotas. Hundreds of thousands were cooped up like Izak and Aunt Ada in refugee camps in Germany and Austria, waiting for the UN decision on the Jewish State in Palestine or for an affidavit to the US, Canada or Australia, which was very difficult to obtain. In the meantime, a clandestine exodus directed by the Palestinian *Yishuv* wound its way through France and Italy into occupied Palestine in defiance of the British.

The rules and regulations of Polish bureaucracy were appallingly complicated, redundant and humiliating. It took anywhere from six months to two years, enduring innumerable hours in office waiting rooms and bureaucratic arrogance, to get an emigration passport. Translations and legalization were just as frustrating. The process of translation of my high-school diploma into French and its legalization stands out as a monument to Polish bureaucracy. The document had to be 'legalized' five times: First the translator's signature had to be certified by a notary, next the signature of the notary had to be certified by the President of Warsaw City District Court, whose signature had to be certified by the Director of the Personnel Office of the Minister of Justice, whose signature had to be certified by the Director of the Consular Office of the Ministry of Foreign Affairs, whose signature finally had to be certified by the French Consul in Warsaw.

I passed my examinations in June and graduated into the sophomore year of the *Polytechnika* at the age of 17. For me, with all the prodigious holes in my educational background, it was no mean achievement. I was looking forward to a well-deserved holiday and to our emigration to France. Everybody around me had left, or was leaving Poland. I was afraid, with the Communists now firmly in control, that the doors to emigration might be closed. My *Yurzeit* approached and I could not believe that it was already a year since my beloved father had died.

Tolo and Hela came to Poland in late June for the *Yurzeit*. They already had French residency papers allowing them to re-enter France. We planned to leave together in September. We went to the cemetery on 5 July and Tolo saw the tombstone which had been erected a few months earlier for the first time. It was a modest tomb with a heavy black marble plate and an engraved inscription in gold letters in Hebrew and in Polish: 'Dr Chaim Blumstein. Born January-1-1886, died July-4-1946. His wife, his sons and his sister.'[3]

I left in July for a Zionist student camp in Lower Silesia, near Wroclaw (Breslau). The area belonged to the 'recovered' German territories. Wroclaw had been devastated by bitter fighting during the winter of 1945. Most Germans had been thrown out of the city which was almost entirely populated by newcomers, most of them from the eastern part of Poland – like Grodno now annexed to The Soviet Union.

The camp was managed by the *Ichud* and prepared young people for the *aliyah*. The sky was an immaculate blue and the Riesengebirge mountains majestic and beautiful. We hiked, studied Hebrew and Zionism, and sang Hebrew and Russian songs around a campfire in the evenings. I was falling in love. Mania was 18 years old, small, with a little snub nose. She wasn't really pretty, but very attractive and cheerful. I devoured the joy of life that burst forth from her. My period of mourning was over and I could sing and even act cheerful despite the deep-seated melancholy that often separated me

---

[3] It is shameful that many years later this grave, along with many other Jewish graves throughout Poland, was vandalized by thieves who used the marble robbed from Jewish tombs as a building material. The marble plate of Father's tomb was lifted, broken into three pieces, and abandoned. Weeds overgrew the Lodz Jewish cemetery and with it Father's vandalized grave. It took me several years to have the grave restored but finally, with the help of a Polish friend, this was done, and I was happy to take my wife, my two daughters and my son-in-law to the grave in June 1996.

from many of my friends. Most of them came from Russia where they had survived often under terrible deprivations, but then everybody had suffered in Russia during the war. There were also a few Holocaust survivors, most of whom had lost either all or part of their families. Among them I was one of the lucky ones – and yet many seemed to me, on the surface at least, happier than me, but I did not know why. Take Mania, for example; she was from Warsaw, she had survived by escaping from the ghetto with her mother and managing on the 'Aryan' side. Her father and brother had been murdered in Treblinka. And yet she loved life so much! She was waiting for papers to Australia from her uncle. She told me that she had vowed, if she survived, to be happy and radiant, to never, ever be bothered by small things, small stupid things that poison everyday life. She could not understand why there was so much sadness in me, and neither could I. Nevertheless I enjoyed every day of my stay in the camp.

Soon came the time of departure, of the sighs, tears, sobs, pledges of fidelity and all the emotions that burst so forcefully from the heart of a teenager and make life such a painfully wonderful experience.

I returned to Lodz in time to leave for three weeks in Sopot with Tolo, Hela and Mother. I swam every day for hours along the pier. We went to Orlowo, Gdynia, Gdansk and the Hel peninsula.

Abandoning my mourning, I finally began to go out. We went to a theatre in Sopot to see a play by George Bernard Shaw and to a *Wald Opera* where the Warsaw Symphony played Brahms and Mozart. For the first time in my life I was stirred profoundly by classical music. I danced to American hits, English slow waltzes and tangos. Tolo as usual brought with him from Paris a pocketful of French songs and American hits by Gershwin and Berlin; one of them was *Swanny How I Love You, How I Love You, My Dear Old Swanny*, which I already knew from the radio of our Lodz neighbour.

Our exit papers were finally ready after 'only' eight months, which was not bad for Polish bureaucracy. Mother wanted to wait for Ludwik Brysz's release. He was still 'sitting', as we referred to people in Communist jails.

Although it was painful to leave her alone in Lodz, I did not insist she come with us; I understood her desire to rebuild her life while she still had a chance.

31   France

On 17 September 1947, on a hot, clear day, I said farewell to Narutowicza 47 and to Lodz, its smoking chimney stacks, grimy stone houses and noisy trams. We had a whole Pullman compartment to ourselves. Mother was crying and my heart was heavy leaving without her, but I did not want to jeopardize my studies in France, with schools and universities starting in a few weeks.

I had visited Father's grave the day before and had taken him some flowers. It hurt so much to leave without him. Then there were the last kisses and goodbyes, and slowly the train pulled out of the station. I saw Mother's small silhouette standing on the platform and waving a handkerchief. It became smaller and smaller, and tears pricked my eyes. The train accelerated, the last chimney stacks of the suburb of Pabianice disappeared. I sat next to the window, eyes transfixed on the running rails. Thousands of thoughts were crossing my mind. I never dreamt when I came to Lodz two and a half years ago that I would leave the city without Father. 'The little house on Mount Carmel', a dream that would never come true... To leave him in this Polish earth saturated with so much Jewish blood was so painful. This land on which we had lived for so many centuries, for nearly a thousand years, these forests, these fields now flashing before my eyes, were also our forests and our fields. And yet I did not want to live among such people, they did not want me. Tears, streams of tears, poured down my cheeks and I sobbed and sobbed as the train rolled, trailing smoke, whistling, now at full speed, through the plains of Radomskie towards Czestochowa and the Czechoslovak border.

The trip was smooth, the trans-European express Warsaw–Prague–Paris was on time and we were comfortably installed in our compartment. The only long stop was at night

411

at the Czechoslovak border, which separated the 'People's Democracy' of Poland from the genuine democracy of President Benes and Jan Masaryk, soon to be overthrown by a Communist *coup d'état*. We moved again in the morning and travelled swiftly towards Prague. We crossed into Germany in the late afternoon. Tall American military police entered the train and checked our papers. They were real giants, chewing gum with bored expressions on their faces. The scenery was bucolic: green pastures on rolling hills, cows grazing peacefully, small, neat, stone or brick houses with shingled roofs, so different from the straw-thatched, wooden huts of Poland. However, the deep scars of war were apparent in the cities. Interestingly, some towns had been literally obliterated while others remained hardly affected, illustrating the uneven German resistance to the Allies and contrasting with the almost total destruction prevailing in the east. Whenever the train slowed down at stations, I caught sight of people, of Germans who now looked so small, so tame, so innocent and poor. We approached Nuremberg and its marshalling yard as the sun was setting on the devastated city. Beyond the slowly moving engines, freight trains and commuter trains, beyond the collapsed buildings lining the tracks, extended the sea of ruins that had been Nuremberg, the cradle of Nazism. It was unreal. I remembered in a flashback the Russian newsreels showing the fanatical, ecstatic German crowds exploding in mass hysteria at the Nuremberg Nazi rallies. We stopped at the central station for some time. People climbed aboard, they all conversed in German. The guttural, harsh sound of spoken German made my skin crawl again. I shut the compartment door and clenched my teeth. Dusk fell and the train resumed its journey through Germany towards the French border. I was still asleep when we arrived in Strasbourg.

I woke up when French customs officers and border police entered our compartment. I caught the melodious sound of French. A dark-haired, dark-eyed Frenchman addressed Hela with a twinkle in his eyes: '*Madame ou Mademoiselle?*' He turned to me, looked at my passport, and gave it back.

These are different people, I thought, so different from the Germans and Poles. I liked them, I felt like singing the Marseillaise, the only words of French I knew. A morning mist hung over the fields of Alsace and Lorraine. On these fields some 30 years ago Germans and Frenchmen had been locked in the most murderous trench warfare of all time. I recalled for a brief moment my *Tante* Thea angrily muttering about *'Diese verfluchte Franzosen!'* [Those damned French!], remembering her nephew who fell on one of these fields. But I, from my earliest days, was on the side of the soldiers *bleu horizon*. As a boy in Grodno I had read Arnold Zweig, who described the horror of this war viewed from the German side – the battle of Verdun, the stronghold of Douaumont and the lines of soldiers *bleu horizon* advancing slowly in defence of their country against German machine guns. I suffered with every French defeat and rejoiced in French victory. My box of French infantry was among the most treasured from my collection of lead soldiers and they invariably were the 'good guys' in every game I imagined.

After a brief stop at Nancy, we moved on. The three of us went to the *wagon-restaurant* for breakfast: coffee, rolls, butter and jam were sold, but tickets had to be presented as food was being strictly rationed. The sun came out from the morning mist and the day was glorious. The country was flat like Poland, but so different. Here the harvested fields looked tame; they were designed, delineated and mastered. Even the forests and groves emerging on the horizon were planted in geometrical, pleasing patterns; scenic villages of stone houses with their tiled roofs clustered around the steeple of a church. Despite a few abandoned farms here and there, the French countryside was harmonious but, in comparison with Czechoslovakia and Germany, sparsely populated. Cities and towns were almost untouched by war and looked quite prosperous to me, used to so much ruin and misery. The train halted at Bar-le-Duc and then at Chateau-Thierry, the last stop before Paris. The people were noisier, friendlier and appeared altogether more relaxed than in other countries I knew. Tolo and Hela were now engaged in a lively conversation with a man and a woman in the corridor and I was full of admiration for their command of French, of which I understood not a word. We were approaching Paris, the number of rail tracks kept multiplying. The small-town stations were giving way to grimy buildings with walls covered in the graffiti of political slogans. The wheels screeched, changing tracks as we slowly advanced towards the centre of the huge city. We plunged now with a strident whistle into a long, dark tunnel. Acrid engine smoke entered the Pullman and we quickly shut the compartment windows. When we emerged into the daylight, we were entering the Gare de l'Est in the heart of Paris. The loudspeaker blared: *'Paris-Est, Paris-Est, tout le monde descend!'* [Paris-East, Paris-East, everybody off!]. We proceeded with the crowd along the platform. I dragged my two suitcases and looked around with wide eyes on this colourful, fast, noisy crowd. Mr Zablocki, Hela's uncle, was waiting at the station. The trunks full of books and household items were taken from the freight car to the customs office. We were to pick them up a few days later.

Emerging from the Gare de l'Est, I got my first sight of Paris. The day was splendid, the sun was bright in an immaculate blue sky. The *Grands Boulevards* running from the Gare de L'Est offered a wide perspective of the city. The tall chestnut trees on the boulevards were still green. The buildings were tall and the pavements wide, with busy outdoor cafés such as I had never seen in my life. There were flashing neon signs on hotels and advertisement billboards, cars blowing their horns, crowds of people rushing about their business and Parisian taxi cabs in red and black, mostly Citrôens and Renaults, pulling up in front of the station to pick up or discharge customers. The beat of life was here stronger than anything I had experienced, and I liked it.

We proceeded in Mr Zablocki's car to Tolo and Hela's apartment. Tolo and Hela, after living with the Zablockis for nine months had finally rented a small apartment in the thirteenth *arrondissement*, in a poor workers' district near the Place d'Italie, at the opposite end of the city. I looked in wonderment at those wide Parisian boulevards, so different from the gloomy streets of Lodz and the small, narrow streets of Grodno, at the green and white buses with their open entrance-platforms, at the orderly lines of people waiting at bus stops.I looked at the dense, rather chaotic, but altogether streamlined traffic. Above all, I looked at people, multicoloured people, laughing people, shouting people, free and easy people, so different from what I had known back in Poland.

Hela's uncle, who had come to France some time before the war, spoke only French and Yiddish. He owned a small pharmacy near the Place de la République and was quite satisfied with his life. Tolo and Hela helped me talk to him, as I was eager to ask him about his wartime experience. The Zablocki family had survived the war in a small town near Marseille, where almost everybody knew that they were Jewish yet nobody denounced them. Mr Zablocki had even worked as a pharmacist and his children went to school. A cousin of Mr Zablocki was in the resistance and fought the Germans. Many Jews were leaders in the resistance. How different, I thought, from Poland, where Jews had to hide their identity when joining the Polish Underground Home Army, for fear of being denounced or murdered. Seventy-five per cent of the Jews in France had survived, helped and sheltered by the local population in spite of an actively anti-Semitic minority and the anti-Jewish policies of the Vichy government.

I gazed at the city as we stopped in traffic jams along the Chatelet and the Boulevard Saint Michel. I looked at the Latin Quarter, at the lively, young, multiracial crowd relaxing in the pavement cafes. Paper boys were shouting: *'Demandez France-Soir! Demandez France-Soir!'* I had a glimpse of the Sorbonne and the Luxembourg Gardens. We finally emerged from the traffic jam and proceeded through the Boulevard des Gobelins to the thirteenth *arrondissement* and a small street off the Avenue d'Italie called Rue du Moulin-de-la-Pointe. This was a rather shabby district of Paris with old, small, stone houses, cramped pavements along winding, narrow streets paved with cobblestones. We stopped at number 9. On the pavement two small girls, undisturbed by our arrival, played hopscotch. We entered through a crumbling gate into a dark hallway and a narrow, winding, creaking staircase. The house was only two storeys high. The apartment was just one room and a tiny kitchenette. There was a sink with a cold water tap. There was no hot water, no bathroom, and the communal WC was very funny, Turkish style. I had never seen one like it before. It was so tiny that one could barely squeeze between the door and the toilet area. The light came on only after the door had been bolted from the inside, in total darkness. There was no toilet bowl, but a central hole with two marked positions for feet.

One had to squat after carefully positioning one's feet. After pulling the flush, one had to rush out to avoid a foot bath. The whole procedure was an exercise in agility and speed.

The front window of the apartment gave me the first glance at the roofs of Paris and its pastel-blue autumn sky. The neighbours' radio blared out the newest hits of Edith Piaf, and a song by Maurice Chevalier called *'Un petit bonjour de Paris'* [A little hello from Paris].

Un petit bonjour de Paris,	A little hello from Paris,
Un petit bonjour,	A little hello, folks
Messieurs-Dames	
Et tout Paris vous sourit	And the whole of Paris smiles at you
Un petit bonjour de Paris.	A little hello from Paris.

I found this song particularly welcoming. Two streets away was a big cinema which showed films continuously from 2 to 12 p.m. This was new to me, as in Poland films were shown only in the evening, or, exceptionally, in a matinée. I often went to the cinema with Tolo and Hela and saw some of the big hits starring Jean Gabin, Arletty, Raimu, Louis Jouvet, Jean-Louis Barrault, Gérard Philipe and many others. Everything was new and exciting in this marvellous city. I strolled on foot for miles and miles discovering Paris. I felt like a visitor from another planet who had come to a new and better world

While Tolo and Hela slept on a comfortable wide couch, I slept in an armchair that could be extended to accommodate a short person. It had a few broken springs, but I was too excited with Paris to complain. One calamity, however, was the loss of my war diaries.I was convinced that I had packed the large bundle of notebooks written in Staniewicze in a big packing box of books but when we opened the carton after it had cleared customs, we did not find any memoirs in it. I will always consider this loss, reflecting the haste in which I left Poland, as one of my biggest losses ever. A precious document written in hiding by a 13-year-old boy was irretrievably lost.

Tolo had to leave early in the morning for work. He was working as a weaver and also had a share in his father-in-law's business, a small textile mill producing scarves, socks and other items. It was located on Boulevard Diderot near the Place de la Nation. I had to go regularly to the Quartier Latin to take care of my student registration at the Sorbonne – classes were to begin shortly – but I also stayed at home, learning French and helping Hela. To my delight, I was admitted to the MPC (*Mathematiques, Physique, Chimie*) freshman programme at the Sorbonne on the strength of my impressive *matura* translation document, with all its seals and stamps. At least my suffering in the antechambers of Polish ministries and district courts had not been in vain. My freshman year with the Lodz *Polytechnika*, however, was not recognized by the French who gave me no credit for it. Classes at the university were free of charge and my student status gave me an automatic extension of my permit to stay in France. It also gave me access to the subsidized student restaurant network, where for less than 50 francs one could have a very decent three-course meal. It gave me free health insurance and substantial discounts on public transport and entertainment.

Felix Zandman came to visit us. He was studying mechanical engineering at the University of Nancy, but was spending his summer vacation living with his Uncle Sender in Paris. Felix's uncle lived in the very noisy district of Barbès. Two other friends and Holocaust survivors from Grodno, Yoshe Weiss and Kurash, shared the tiny abode. No woman lived in, and the apartment was a total mess. Felix, who was preparing for his autumn examinations for *Physique Générale* [General Physics], a difficult test by any standard, found it impossible to study there and decided to spend some time in the countryside nearby. He invited me to go with him. I had nothing very important to do in Paris and I liked Felix, so I accepted his offer.

The village we travelled to in a commuter train was Nogent l'Artaud, some 80 kilometres from Paris near the Marne River. We lived in an *auberge*, and we were treated like kings. In the morning we were served coffee with plenty of hot milk, delicious bread, butter and jam – luxuries by Polish standards. Food was plentiful and rationing not as strict as in the city. I took a liking to French cuisine. I loved *bifteck-frites*, but only when it was cooked to death, Polish style, *poulet roti, hachis Parmentier, cassoulet* and many other dishes which our innkeeper had great skill in preparing. She took pride and pleasure in watching these two young foreigners devour her French cooking. Although Felix was already used to red wine, my middle-European palate was not particularly impressed with its astringent taste. The meal usually ended with cheese. We loved the taste of Camembert, brie and other cheeses. One evening, the *aubergiste* served us a creamy cheese which we both found excellent and ate swiftly. We were almost done when suddenly Felix went pale, squinting at the remnants of the cheese left on his plate.

'Alik!,' he screamed, 'this cheese has legs! It is moving!' Looking closely, I discovered to my horror that small, squirmy white worms were crawling on the cheese. We both ran to the lavatory and threw up. When we came back, ashen and shaky, we reproachfully showed the plate to our innkeeper. She was offended.

'It is the best cheese I have, and you are complaining to me about its natural state?' The cheese was indeed tasty. A funny country!

Felix worked from morning until evening, immersed in the four thick volumes of Bruhat's *Physique Générale*. I studied French and enjoyed long walks in the well-groomed countryside of Champagne, with its gently rolling hills. I sensed from my few contacts with the people that here was a country of tolerance. Though *étranger* [foreigner] and *refugié d'origine polonaise* [refugee of Polish origin], I was not singled out for my creed, or the colour of my hair or skin. I felt the humanity of these people: nobody was condescending, patronizing or snooty.

I felt as a human being fully respected for my own human qualities. This came to me even more forcefully a few weeks later after I had started at university. I met a whole bunch of *refugiés d'origine polonaise* at the *Union des Etudiants Juifs de France*, at 6 rue Lalande near Place Denfert Rocherau and made some of my future friends: Valdemar Kobryner, Jozio Weissbrum, Maciek Gaschke, who had all survived in Russia, and there was Olek Kochanski, Alik Redner, Marta Arcos who were Holocaust survivors like myself. We had all been granted a temporary permit to stay in France. At the Sorbonne I struck up a friendship with some French fellow students:

Roland Boulanger, Jacqueline Penne and others. We worked together at *MPC*, preparing for quizzes and tests. Roland was also my 'labmate' in the physics and chemistry laboratories. The standards at the Sorbonne *MPC* were very high because in France, unlike in Poland, there had been no interruption of schooling during the war. Universities had functioned normally and few professors had been disturbed by the German occupation. Furthermore, requirements in Paris were by tradition higher than in the provinces. Many things that were assumed to be already known from the high-school mathematics and physics curriculum of the *lycée* were unknown to me. In addition to the inherent difficulty of the subject matter, for many months I was at a loss in understanding the spoken French of lectures. Here my French friends made a huge difference. We worked together and they taught me French while we all learned maths, physics and chemistry. I was pleasantly surprised when right from the start I was simply addressed by my first name, Alik. It was always music to my ears. As I was walking along Boulevard Saint Michel, discussing, arguing, I felt equal to others. This feeling of equality was so uplifting that even today I am grateful for it. It marked the beginning of my long recovery from the spell of the guilt projected on each Jew in Poland. And walking along the 'Boul Mich' with a bunch of French and Jewish friends, mingling with the multiracial and multi-coloured crowd, I was grateful to France for extending to me a helping and understanding hand at a crucial time of my life.

Afterword

As I look back now from a distance of many years, it is hard to believe the miracle of our survival as an intact nuclear family. Out of three million Jews on the territory of 1939 Poland (not counting the 250,000 refugees who were deported in 1940–41 to Russia), only some 30,000 survived the German occupation, less than one per cent of Polish Jewry.

We adapted to France rapidly. Mother married Ludwik Brysz upon his release from prison and joined us in Paris in January 1948. They lived in one room, like most refugees, in a hotel, on the rue Sommerard near the Sorbonne. Ludwik found a job in textiles, but the going was tough. After two years, they moved into a small but cosy apartment on rue Bénard in the fourteenth *arrondissement*.

I rented a room at 11 rue de La Tour in the Passy district from a nice older lady, Mrs Davids, the widow of a well-respected Jewish painter from Bordeaux. Mrs Davids treated me well. During the weekends, I visited Tolo and Hela at their rue du Moulin-de-la-Pointe apartment. As their financial situation improved, they soon moved with their baby son Michel to a more spacious apartment near the Place de la République, where their son Alain was born in 1950. Tolo stood by me. We travelled together to explore the opportunities at various engineering schools. My family continued to encourage me to study and helped me as much as they could.

The academic level of *MPC* was high for someone with my background. I worked hard, seven days a week, never going to bed before midnight. Having no financial resources, I needed to secure a scholarship if I wanted to continue studying. These scholarships were available only for those with an unblemished record of success. I could not afford to fail a single test – such were the rules. But not until March 1948 did I begin to understand the spoken French of lectures. My hard work paid off in June; lo and behold, I was the only foreigner to pass all the requirements of the *MPC* examinations! I was awarded a scholarship by the French Union of Jewish Students, then a year later by UNESCO through the French government.

I kept my scholarship, first as an undergraduate in sciences at the Sorbonne, then as a chemistry student at the University of Toulouse, from which I graduated as *Ingenieur Chimiste* in 1952. The rest of my studies I spent working at the CNRS and graduating from the University of Strasbourg in 1960 with a Ph.D. in the chemistry of polymers, after a two-and-a-half year interruption for military duties. While finishing my military service in Paris in 1959, I met my wife Rita, a survivor from Cracow. We were married the same year. After graduation, I was hired by an American company, in which Felix Zandman was one of the managers, and in November 1960 I sailed with my wife for the United States. We intended to stay in the US for a limited time only, but came to like the new country and decided to remain. Our daughters, Sylvie and Tanya, were born in the United States.

France was good to refugees from Eastern Europe. Everybody somehow scraped a living and managed. Some did very well. The important condition was to work hard. Most of my friends worked hard just like myself, and were given government scholarships which allowed us to acquire a profession and get a start in life.

I cannot forget that at a time when Europe was overflowing with refugees, when the pitiful, bedraggled remnants of the Holocaust were cooped up in UNRA camps in Germany and Austria or in British concentration camps on Cyprus, when the gates to the wealthy USA were locked shut, France extended to us all a helping hand. We shared with the French people equally the bad and the good: the scarcity and the rationing as well as the liberal social amenities of France. My psychological wounds were deep, but I healed quickly under the blue pastel of the French sky.

Aniela Staniewska would not leave her village and the grave of Edward. I visited her in her village in 1977. She died in 1982. Hela, her niece, married, had a family and moved soon after the end of the war to Olsztyn in Poland where she still lives. Dr Docha and his wife Janina moved to Sokolka on the Polish side of the border with the Soviet Union. After his retirement, the family moved to Warsaw. Dr Docha died in 1975. Dr Janina Docha died in 1994. They were all honoured in 1979 by *Yad Vashem*, the Holocaust Martyrs' and Heroes' Remembrance Authority in Jerusalem, with the medal of 'Righteous Among Nations'.

Frania and Hillel, with Ilana, Moshe and baby Yosie, were smuggled into Palestine in 1947 by the *Bricha*. They settled in a kibutz called Kfar Menachem. Hillel died in 1979, Ilana died after an illness in 1997, and Frania in 1999. Most of the family still lives in Kfar Menachem.

I never heard from Misha and Rozia Wystaniecki.

A few words about some perpetrators of the 'final solution' in Grodno mentioned in my memoirs:

Otto Streblow, the SD killer and *Kommandant* of Ghetto II, was shot by the partisans in 1944.

Most of the perpetrators of the 'final solution' in Grodno disappeared after the collapse of the Third Reich in 1945, The SD murderer and *Kommandant* of Ghetto I, SS *Oberscharfuehrer* Kurt Wiese, was caught while living under a false identity, thanks to the Nazi hunter Simon Wiesenthal. He was sentenced in 1967 by a German court (Cologne and Bielefeld Trials) to seven consecutive terms of life imprisonment. The *Kommandant* of the SD in Grodno, SS *Obersturmfuehrer* Heinz Errelis, Wiese's boss, was also caught but fared better. He was sentenced by a German tribunal to six years and six months in prison. The SD killer Schott, Errelis's deputy, committed suicide after being denounced to the police by his wife as a result of a domestic quarrel. The *Kommandant* of the camp of Kielbasin, the sadistic SD murderer Rinzler, escaped and was never brought to justice.